THE SEXUALITY OF HISTORY

THE SEXUALITY OF HISTORY

Modernity and the Sapphic, 1565–1830

SUSAN S. LANSER

THE UNIVERSITY OF CHICAGO PRESS

CHICAGO AND LONDON

SUSAN S. LANSER is professor of comparative literature, English, and women's and gender studies at Brandeis University. She is the author of *Fictions of Authority: Women Writers and Narrative Voice* and *The Narrative Act: Point of View in Prose Fiction.*

The University of Chicago Press, Chicago 60637
The University of Chicago Press, Ltd., London
© 2014 by The University of Chicago <!acquisitions: check contract to verify copyright holder!>
All rights reserved. Published 2014.
Printed in the United States of America

24 23 22 21 20 19 18 17 16 15   1 2 3 4 5

ISBN-13: 978-0-226-18756-3 (cloth)
ISBN-13: 978-0-226-18773-0 (paper)
ISBN-13: 978-0-226-18787-7 (e-book)
DOI: 10.7208/chicago/9780226187877.001.0001

Library of Congress Cataloging-in-Publication Data

Lanser, Susan Sniader, 1944– author.
  The sexuality of history : modernity and the sapphic, 1565–1830 / Susan S. Lanser.
      pages : illustrations ; cm
  Includes bibliographical references and index.
  ISBN 978-0-226-18756-3 (cloth : alk. paper) — ISBN 978-0-226-18773-0 (pbk. : alk. paper) — ISBN 978-0-226-18787-7 (e-book)   1. Lesbians in literature.   2. Lesbians' writings—History and criticism.   3. European literature—History and criticism.   4. Lesbianism—Europe—History.   5. Lesbian feminism—Europe—History.   I. Title.
  PN56.L45L36 2014
  809'.9335206643—dc23

2014017217

♾ This paper meets the requirements of ANSI/NISO Z39.48-1992 (Permanence of Paper).

FOR MICHAEL RAGUSSIS

FEBRUARY 19, 1945–AUGUST 26, 2010

BRILLIANT READER, BELOVED FRIEND

זכרונו לברכה   Να είναι η θύμηση του ευλογία

CONTENTS

ILLUSTRATIONS

CHAPTER ONE

How To Do the Sexuality of History

There is such an intimate relationship among the different parts of society that none of them could receive a blow without repercussions on the others.

—Jean-François Melon, *Essai politique sur le commerce* (1734)[1]

It is a truth almost universally acknowledged, that the seventeenth and eighteenth centuries gave the West a host of its modern arrangements, from the trivial (eating with forks) to the triumphant (the "rights of man") to the tragic (racial supremacy).[2] The tumultuous period bounded by Dutch revolts and French revolutions yielded governance by consent; a wildly inequitable global economy engineered by slaveholding empires; the stirrings of a self-conscious working class and the aspirations of a rising bourgeoisie; the incipience of secular nation-states supported by patriotic investments; the rising hegemony of print and the attendant force of public opinion; unprecedented population growth and geographic mobility; a new fealty to observable "nature" as the bedrock of truth; systemic challenges to hierarchies human and divine; a growing commitment to conjugal kinship along with an intensified interest in the distinctiveness of individual persons; and the formation of public subjects along lines of gender and color that enfranchised propertied white men *as* men while failing spectacularly to accord legal rights to women or full humanity to Africans.

For reasons that I will argue were intrinsic rather than incidental to these transformations, seventeenth- and eighteenth-century Europe also witnessed an intensified interest in lesbians. In genres from scientific treatises to orientalist travelogues, in the gossip of French royal courts and the records of Dutch legal courts, in bawdy poems, domestic fictions, and cross-dressed flirtations on the English and Spanish stage, poets, play-wrights, philosophers, and pundits were placing what I call sapphic sub-jects before the public eye.[3] Writings that ranged from passing comments to elaborate scenarios were already burgeoning by 1600 and flourished across the next two centuries in forms that connected erotically inflected desires, behaviors, and affiliations between women—and, more abstractly, female homoeroticism as idea and image—to the broad preoccupations of the times. The self-conscious reconfiguring of values and practices that marks emergent modernity induced not only the dramatic transforma-tions evoked in my opening paragraph but a complex attention to female same-sex relations perceived not simply as modern but as emblematically so.[4] Rather as gay marriage has become in recent years a charged site for concerns vaster than gays or marriage, intimacies between women became entangled with contests about authority and liberty, power and difference, desire and duty, mobility and change, order and governance. In short, the sapphic served the social imaginary as one way to confront challenges to the predictable workings of the universe.[5]

In *The Sexuality of History*, I will argue that the story of female same-sex affiliation that preoccupied emergent modernity can be read as a story of modernity *tout court*. Figuring as both agent and emblem, the sapphic became a flash-point for epistemic upheavals that threatened to disman-tle the order of things. The quality and quantity, variety and geography of sapphic representation across the long period of reform, revision, revolu-tion, and reaction from 1565 to 1830 point to investments far beyond sex between women. Imbuing female homoeroticism with powers and dangers exceeding any material challenge to the social order, the writings I ex-plore in this book illuminate the ways in which the (il)logic of "woman + woman" became a testing ground for modernity's limit points. Those writings provide us, in turn, with a testing ground for the relationship be-tween sexual representation and social change.

By asking when, where, how, and to what ends the sapphic took form in print culture, this project seeks to flip the scholarly coin from the history of sexuality to the sexuality of history. Taking its name from Foucault's paradigm-shifting volume,[6] the field known as the history of sexuality has deconstructed the assumption that sexuality is an unchanging natural phenomenon and focused attention on the ways in which sexual concepts, images, values, and practices—including the (gendered) question of what counts as "sex"—reflect and inflect their social and cultural contexts. As Martha Vicinus articulated early on, historians of sexuality retrieve "lost or submerged histories," study ideas and values about sex and sexual behavior in specific times and places, and analyze "structures of sexuality that are rooted in the social, economic, and political assumptions of the times."[7] The field of sexuality studies has investigated private lives and public opinions, historical facts and fictional fantasies, and it continues to illuminate the diversity of the world's sexualities and their discursive manifestations both present and past.

A shift from the history of sexuality to the sexuality of history retains these interests but reverses the emphasis. The reversal is already implicit in Foucault's contention that modern disciplinary regimes became newly preoccupied with "the manner in which each individual made use of his [sic] sex"[8] and thrives in scholarship that considers the more than sexual implications of sexual configurations.[9] In the spirit of that inquiry, though with a focus on the gender that Foucault almost wholly ignored, my approach reads history through, and as contingent on, sexuality rather than reading sexuality through, and as contingent on, history. Put more specifically if also sententiously, I am concerned less with asking how early modern Europe configured the sapphic than with asking how the sapphic configured early modern Europe. In contrast to the project of queer reading, whereby scholars expose embedded homoerotic content in "closeted" texts, I look for the breadth of concerns and interests that may be embedded in more obviously erotic surfaces. I am thus not quite looking for lesbians by whatever name, in beds or in books, but rather exploring the ways in which a historically specific interest in lesbians intersects with and stimulates systemic concerns that may (seem to) have little to do with sexuality *per se*.

In short, I hope to show not only that sexuality *has* a history but that sexuality *is* history: that just as the historical constructs the sexual, so too does the sexual construct the historical, shaping the social imaginary and providing a site for reading it. I am not, of course, claiming that discourses about female affiliations brought down regimes or altered Europe's course. But in the spirit of my epigraph from the economist Jean-François Melon, I do believe in the intricate and unpredictable but nonetheless multifarious overlaps among spheres of social and discursive practice. Not least among the implications of my inversion of terms is the possibility, largely ignored outside sexuality studies proper, that sexuality might be not only an effect but a stimulus and that sexual representations might thus have a kind of agency in organizing larger discursive frameworks and in fomenting or forestalling change. Indeed, I will argue that the sapphic constitutes a specific and even privileged site for studying culture writ large—that the insistent labeling of the sapphic as impossibility, in tandem with the production of that impossibility in text after text, underscores the ways in which "woman + woman" threatens to ravel the logic of an entire system. In making this claim, I underscore the dissonance between the apparently small material problem that female homoeroticism posed to Western Europe's social order and the larger space and excessive language accorded it in print. The sapphic may have derived its efficacy from that very gap between the imagined and the real, offering a defamiliarizing, distracting, or distancing displacement from more pressing material challenges of statecraft and slavery, colonialism and class. The entanglement of the sapphic with these larger challenges of early modernity enables it to occupy the position that Barbara Babcock identifies in another context when she observes that "what is socially marginal is often symbolically central."[10]

Supporting these large claims will be the challenge of the next six chapters of this book. My introductory chapter has a different goal: to outline the stakes and methods of the project in hope of contributing to a historiography that might "do" the sexuality of history, to turn a phrase of David Halperin.[11] Sexuality studies is already rich in approaches; it is not my intention to dislodge current practices but to augment them with what I hope will be a portable scholarly option. I do believe that a turn from the history of sexuality to the sexuality of history widens the avenues for intervention in several fields and thus enhances the relevance of sexuality to "mainstream" scholarship. Since I hope my methodological choices will carry a value independent of the persuasive power of any specific chapter or contention in this book, I have given those choices a fuller articulation on their own behalf.

In arguing for the significance of sapphic representations to history writ large, this project seeks to ameliorate both a heteronormativity in gender history and a gender imbalance in queer studies. In working comparatively across a wide (though Eurocentric) geographic, chronological, and generic terrain, it offers a counterpoint to tendencies within sexuality studies to address single cultures, private lives, and typological patterns. It articulates a strategy of confluence for positing interrelationships among texts that in turn supports a speculative approach to sexual history. And for the most part, it deploys a practice situated midway between close and distant reading to grapple with salient patterns in sets of texts. Through this aggregate of commitments, I hope as well to push against the supplementary status of lesbian studies by understanding the sapphic as a potentially paradigm-shifting phenomenon. I would go so far as to invert the conventional wisdom that modernity consolidates a heteronormative order to argue that modernity can also be read as the emergence of the sapphic as an epistemic plausibility.

LOCATING SAPPHIC SUBJECTS

In choosing the sapphic as the focus for a sexuality of history and in deferring gender to the subtitle of this book, I mean to signal the value of moving female homoeroticism to the center of sexuality studies as an unmarked case. The paradigms encouraged by Foucault's elision of women and gender from *The History of Sexuality* have long concerned feminist theorists, and it does not take much research to see that what Sheila Jeffreys has called "male gay cultural forms" still dominate queer studies in a "ghosting through assimilation" that Terry Castle was already exposing in 1993.[12] The problem is tautological: because projects using "queer," "homosexual," or "sexuality" as their banner often focus more heavily on men, masculine rubrics end up marking allegedly gender-inclusive or gender-neutral terms, perpetuating the androcentric cycle. Moreover, two decades after Eve Kosofsky Sedgwick's well-known axiom that the relationship between sexuality and gender cannot be determined in advance, queer theory still tends to constitute sexuality as a progressive and fluid "vanguard" that, as Biddy Martin argued, would relegate both feminism and femininity—and, I would add, the signifier "lesbian" itself—to anachronism while "the more radical work of queering the world proceeds."[13] That these problems have persisted despite a burgeoning scholarship on female homoeroticism suggests a tacit acceptance of the marginality of "lesbian" in distinction to the growing *cachet* of "queer."

By contrast, this project is guided by the conviction that gender must be theorized in tandem with sexuality in any project of queer history, whether focused on women or on men. What Joan Scott modestly called a "useful" category of analysis seems to me crucial so long as we are dealing with the human world as it has been rather than the world we might desire;[14] certainly in seventeenth- and eighteenth-century Europe the idea of a gender-free anywhere is literally utopian; even claims that the mind had no gender, precisely because they needed to be advanced only on behalf of women, are signs of gender's pervasive force. This recognition does not mean clinging to gender, to evoke a concern articulated by Robyn Wiegman among others; it means recognizing with Tom King that "gender is itself a social relation obtaining only through its materialization as practice."[15] Katherine Binhammer illustrates just this contingent relationship when she shows how a "mindful heterosexuality" grounds the gender identity forged in feminist writings of the 1790s.[16] Such a demonstration supports David Valentine's claim that the relationship between gender and sexuality is "ultimately ethnographic and historical rather than purely theoretical" and thus always a matter of "historically located social practice."[17] Even more than I had expected, the representations I examine in this book reveal imbrications of gender and sexuality, constituted in tandem with volatile vectors of class/rank and nation/race, at the heart of the ways in which the sapphic signifies in early modernity.

It is therefore plausible that the separate pursuit of "gay" and "lesbian" history is less "artificial," as Diane Watt describes it, than conditional, as Sedgwick suggests in *Epistemology of the Closet*.[18] Across significant theoretical differences, for example, Bernadette Brooten and David Halperin agree that male dominance and marital inequality have forged dramatic distinctions in the construction of male and female sexualities that in turn produce incommensurabilities between gay and lesbian history. In her pathbreaking *Love Between Women: Early Christian Responses to Female Homoeroticism*, Brooten reminds us that "historians who have conceptualized female homoeroticism as parallel to male homoeroticism have overlooked crucial historical evidence that could help us understand the history of female homoeroticism and periodize it properly."[19] Halperin argues that women "must submit to a system of compulsory heterosociality" and that "sexual relations among women" therefore "represent a perennial threat to male dominance, especially whenever such relations become exclusive and thereby take women out of circulation among men."[20] Brooten further suggests that continuities of patriarchal prerogative may explain what she sees as responses to erotic relations between women that are more static than responses to relations between men.

This recognition of persistent gender dominance might well qualify the claim of my epigraph that a "blow" to one sphere inevitably affects others; Judith Bennett may be right to argue that a "patriarchal equilibrium" kept European women in a kind of stasis "even in times of political, social, and economic change."[21] But I will propose that the copious representation of the sapphic in the seventeenth and eighteenth centuries already dislodges that equilibrium or at least recognizes that it might be dislodged, opening fissures in the relationship between woman's place and other social systems that intensify the potential agency of sapphic subjects. Thus, for example, although Alan Bray's *The Friend* echoes Halperin and Brooten in noting that "friendship has been no less asymmetrical than gender itself," when he reaches the seventeenth century Bray sees signs that women's friendship has now begun to inflect the public sphere.[22] Given the andro-centrism both of early modern cultures and of late modern queer studies, we may need a deeper understanding of how the sapphic operates in or-der to perform the full integration that sexuality studies ultimately needs; histories of sexuality that are fully gender-inclusive will be of immense value, but simply to "add women and stir" will not resolve the deeper and historically variant deviations between male and female erotic histories.

The challenge of studying gender and sexuality in tandem is not, how-ever, exclusive to queer studies, for lesbian history has fared little better under the rubric of "women" than under the rubric of "queer." Despite old quips that women's studies is a "lesbian plot," seventeenth- and eighteenth-century women's history, at least, remains quite heavily heteronorma-tive. While I have addressed this issue more extensively elsewhere,[23] a motivating purpose of this book is to demonstrate the historical signifi-cance of sapphic formations for understanding both the history of women and the European past.[24] It is of course true that most seventeenth- and eighteenth-century women participated, voluntarily or not, in a sexual and social economy that tied them to husbands, fathers, and brothers and to larger structures of patriarchal governance. But when we ignore the ways in which women evaded or exploited heteronormative economies or—just as importantly—were imagined to do so, we fail to understand the stakes and contours of those economies, and we learn nothing about the resistant practices that lie both within and outside the seemingly normative. What Judith Bennett wrote more than a decade ago still holds: that a "queering . . . of women's history" is "essential and long overdue."[25] While my own focus is not on lived lives, it remains a crucial aim of this book to under-score the significance of the sapphic for understanding the place of women within the multiple, contradictory, and shifting economies, both imagi-nary and material, of the seventeenth and eighteenth centuries. I will be suggesting, for example, that sapphic representations help to delineate the ways in which gender grounds large-scale systems rather than only familial arrangements. A queerer history of seventeenth- and eighteenth-century women would offer the opportunity not only to explore non-heteronormative relations but to use those relations as a lens for reading dominant practices. Sexuality, in short, is like gender a "useful category" that would "not only add new subject matter but would also force a critical reexamination of the premises and standards of existing scholarly work."[26]

That female homoeroticism has been sidelined in the scholarship on sexual difference has been particularly troubling, since in reifying hetero-normativity that scholarship ends up participating in the very process it aims to describe. Most historians of gender seem to agree that during the long period from the late sixteenth to the early nineteenth century, as traditional arguments for hierarchy lost their effective force, gender relations were reshaped or at least intensified along polarities of difference to reconfigure and thereby sustain male supremacy. Thomas Laqueur's contested but highly influential *Making Sex: Body and Gender from the Greeks to Freud* famously proclaimed that "sex as we know it" was "invented" at "some time in the eighteenth century," when a vertical, "one-sex" biology that regarded women as lesser copies of men yielded to a horizontal "two-sex" system stressing innate differences of body and mind, forging a literally sexual politics in which anatomies became "not the sign of but the foundation for civil society."[27] Although women are central to Laqueur's work as they were not to Foucault's, the sapphic gets no more attention in *Making Sex* than in *The History of Sexuality*. Geneviève Fraisse's *La muse de la raison: la démocratie exclusive et la différence des sexes* likewise overlooks the sapphic even where female affiliations beg to be discussed; Claudia Honegger's *Die Ordnung der Geschlechter* is similarly invested in the logic of difference that it is studying.[28] Moreover, this discourse often attributes historical significance to male but not to female homoeroticism; Todd Parker's *Sexing the Text*, for example, claims that the construction of sexual difference in England "is the result of a reformulation of male sexuality that takes place around the time of the Restoration and that is largely complete by the middle of the century."[29] Michael McKeon, as I have argued elsewhere, has similarly insisted on a crucial role for male homoeroticism in forming "modern patriarchy" while ignoring female analogues.[30] The paucity of attention to female homoeroticism—and sometimes even to male homoeroticism—persists in recent histories of sexuality such as Karen Harvey's *Reading Sex in the Eighteenth Century*, which grounds sexual difference in masculine heteroticism, and Faramerz Dabhoiwala's *The Origins of Sex* which, in its startlingly few pages devoted to same-sex relations, sets aside "the notion of sex between women" as an "obscure matter" that left only "vague" discussion and "very limited" evidence of "actual relationships."[31] Equally troubling is the symposium "Before Sex," appearing in a 2012 special issue of the feminist journal *Signs*, that minimizes the significance of the sapphic, correlates it to a (contested) male model, and repeats notions long ago challenged. None of these "mainstream" studies seems to have engaged with the past two decades of scholarship on female homoeroticism.

If we consider that the sapphic might constitute a cultural formation with historically contingent forms of agency, we can enlarge our understanding of its importance for modernity and thus for modern history. Lesbian scholarship on seventeenth- and eighteenth-century Europe is now rich and vital, at once theoretically sophisticated, archivally thick, and geographically varied; my own project owes an enormous debt to the archival discoveries, interpretive insights, and conceptual challenges offered by scholars who have brought the field to its current depth and scope. But sexuality studies as a whole—male, queer, and especially female—still remains largely hidden from history, to recall the title of an important early volume in the field,[32] vested in what Henry Abelove calls the "trope of marginalization" rather than the "trope of centrality."[33] Thus, as Laura Doan has observed, queer history is at once "thriving intellectually" and "languishing on the sidelines of so-called mainstream history"; sexuality has not yet "shake[n] the foundations of historical thinking" as the analysis of gender has done.[34] By reading representations of the sapphic within broad frameworks of social, cultural, and political history, I hope to show that scholars with diverse primary interests might find value in considering the ways in which sexuality is represented and deployed. This approach shifts the emphasis from studying lesbian history to studying "lesbian" and "history" as mutually constitutive.

My contribution to this large task relies for its core claims and findings on a comparative methodology, something Christopher Hill once described as "the nearest [the historian] can get to a laboratory test."[35] While I began simply with a comparatist's wish for inclusiveness, my claims about the cultural work performed by sapphic representations are now embedded in a geography with contours that I did not anticipate. My study has thus ended up mapping the sapphic imaginary across a broad swath of Western Europe in order to see which countries and cultures were most invested in sapphic representations at different times, to determine the distinctive forms these representations took, and to speculate about the etiology of national differences. As scholars have often noted, early modern representations of the homoerotic are themselves frequently "comparative" insofar as they figure same-sex relations as a foreign vice or a foreign import, whether from a catholicized Italy, a feminized France, or an orientalized East. Yet with a few exemplary exceptions, post-premodern scholarship on European sexualities is monocultural; tellingly, the first anthology with an explicitly different intention, *Comparatively Queer: Interrogating Identities Across Time and Cultures*, appeared only in 2010.[36]

Certainly comparative research on sexuality is especially tricky. Since the majority of archival, historiographic, and textual work is still being produced by scholars living in a few countries, writing about only a few more countries in even fewer languages, current scholarship, this project included, may tell us less about early modern Europe than about postmodern academia. That archives differ in terms of both access and preservation adds another layer of disequilibrium. We still don't know, for instance, whether any other country could match the 119 cases of female transvestism that Rudolf Dekker and Lotte van de Pol documented for the Dutch Republic, and thus we can't be sure whether that nation was an international magnet for would-be cross-dressers or just one location among several.[37] And although electronic databases are now publishing archival materials that a few years ago were inaccessible to the kind of needle-in-haystack work that sexual scholarship entails, it remains daunting to study historical periods in which allusions to the sapphic do not lend themselves to simple search terms. Moreover, the electronic archives also remain uneven and unevenly accessible, so that the very resources that enable comparative sexual history may also be skewing it. This book will not pretend to be comprehensive or even uniform across the genres, cultures, and periods I explore; while it draws on an extensive body of primary texts gleaned through my own research and the findings of other scholars, its geography is unquestionably tipped toward the languages in which I have the greatest comfort, the cultures about which I know the most, and the resources to which I have had fullest access.[38] More intentionally, different chapters of this project have lent themselves to differential attention to particular national cultures; I have yielded to this unevenness while hoping that other scholars will offer correctives in this as in other respects. In short, this "sexuality of history" must metaphorically be sketched in pencil rather than inscribed in ink.

The penciled version of my findings suggests, however, that the significant attention to sapphic subjects in particular countries at particular times, and the apparent inattention elsewhere, is crucial to understanding the cultural work that sapphic subjects may have performed. The sapphic seems to have mattered most when specific societies or social spheres were on the verge of certain kinds of change or engaged in certain kinds of struggle. I will not consider it accidental, for example, that the European countries most invested in sapphic representation at the turn of the seventeenth century were colonialist powers in which women were also accruing political and cultural capital. What appears to be a late entrance of German states into this conversation, and what appears to be a waning of sapphic representation in eighteenth-century Spain in contrast to a steady or burgeoning production in France and England, have demanded scrutiny and speculation. Such concerns underwrite my investment in what Valerie

Traub has called "cycles of salience" by which certain representational threads recur "intermittently and with a difference," not as perpetual essences but as sporadic strategies.[39] These temporal and spatial contours encourage a middle ground between cosmopolitanist approaches that see Europe as a coherent setting and particularist positions that emphasize cultural and social differences. The intersections between cultural production and sociopolitical practices that cross the pages of this book seem to be neither nationally bounded nor broadly cosmopolitan, a reminder that Europe's key intellectual and political movements—Reformation and Enlightenment, colonization and slave trade—involve major and minor participants, bystanders and opponents, in locations affected by unique circumstances and events. The case of sapphic subjects suggests that different cultural and social formations generate different national clusters upon the continental map, in effect portraying Europe as a shifting complex of "interest groups" that vary with the lens of inquiry.

The arc of discourse that I am tracing roughly from 1565 to 1830 marks what I see as a persistent if uneven investment in the sapphic that I believe to be continuous with certain aspects—though not with all aspects—of modern social formation. It became clear early in my research that encompassing only my own period of specialization, the "long eighteenth century," would mean starting *in medias res*. Sapphic representations seemed to me particularly plentiful in the decades around 1600 in ways that I could not attribute simply to a general increase in printed works, and they seemed likewise to taper off after the first decades of the nineteenth century; whether that perception is simply the misprision of the period specialist is still unclear. But the fact that this long period is arguably also the time during which the social, cultural, intellectual, and political systems of Western Europe sorted themselves into what are conventionally understood as modern forms is one reason why I believe I can make the larger arguments that constitute this particular "sexuality of history."

Such a focus confronts me, however, with the discomforts of relying for a conceptual anchor on that contested notion "modernity," a concept so vexed that it frequently goes undefined even in books that feature the word in their titles. My use of the term is at once conceptual and temporal, indeed founded on the conjunction of these elements to denote a perceived "break in the regular passage of time," as Bruno Latour marks it in his important critical essay.[40] I mean "modernity" to denote what Harvie Ferguson describes as "the unprecedented . . . consciousness of the human world as a self-generated and autonomous realm of meaningful experience" that took shape in Renaissance and Enlightenment Europe, a consciousness that rejected what it saw as the tyranny of tradition, that privileged experience as the signifier of the real, that valorized "human autonomy, novelty, and self-movement," and that fashioned itself against the putative non-modernity of (non-European or lower-class) others.[41] Ferguson rightly calls modernity a "promiscuous concept," and I know of no definition that could go unscathed. I take "modernity" here as a (consequential) field of perception, a belief that certain ways of thinking and doing *are* modern, together with a set of values and ideas meant to foster social, political, economic, and cultural practices that depart from those of a real or perceived past. Scholars disagree on the dating of this modernity, locating it as early as the fifteenth century and as late as the turn of the twentieth; I adopt here the narrower but still loose temporality of Anthony Giddens, who equates modernity with "modes of social life or organization which emerged in Europe from about the seventeenth century onwards and which subsequently became more or less worldwide in their influence."[42] For internal evidence, I point to the fact that early modern writers themselves designated the sapphic in terms of the modern, as will already be apparent at the beginning of chapter 2. Notwithstanding the play on Latour that titles my coda, I am by no means equating modernity with progress, as that coda itself should make clear.

Within the *longue durée* spanned by this project, I retain the more situated temporal objective of encouraging a scholarly shift from sexual typologies to positioned chronologies. My approach supports Valerie Traub's call to "investigat[e] the cultural conditions that render" particular types and tropes "salient at particular moments."[43] I have moved away from categorizing figures such as the "female husband" or "chaste friend," terms that I believe tend to reify representations that are often more hybrid and complex, in order to ask how different configurations of female intimacies in specific genres and settings took hold of the cultural imagination. I have embraced representations that vilify the sapphic and those that idealize it along with the vast range between; I have attempted to represent what my archive offers without investing in an ethic of either queer shame or queer pride. In principle, I agree fully with Melissa E. Sanchez that "to assume that relations between women naturally exclude tension and hierarchy is to impose a norm that may limit female affect and eroticism as much as the patriarchal prescriptions that queer feminist work seeks to challenge";[44] if the material gathered here renders female-female relations more harmonious than tendentious, that is the consequence not only of an unconscious readerly lens but of my hunch that these representations, perhaps because they resist their own deconstruction, are most invested with imaginative agency.

In seeking both temporal and textual specificity within the project's long arc, I consider sapphic representations at three different levels: textually, to ask how a particular discourse configures intersections of time and place along with the characters and events that can converge there; intertextually, to identify patterns and variants that converge in particular places at particular times; and contextually, to ask what circumstances characterize the material setting for a particular textual practice. While such a threefold process cannot be fleshed out in this large study for every textual instance or pattern, I do hope to have modeled a way to map practices within the texts in relation to practices that arguably produce or inform those texts to suggest the contours not only of those "cycles of salience" for which Traub calls but of the broader cultural investments that underwrite particular representational practices. Like most scholars of eighteenth-century sexualities, I read similarities between earlier and later social formations not as signs of a transcendent or continuous history but as invitations to identify the conditions under which those similarities appear. At the same time, I would not rule out continuities that the persistence of male dominance and of other large-scale systems might render plausible. In configuring my chapters, I have sought a balance between geographically contingent alterations over large periods and discrete dynamics within concentrated settings. I try to emphasize uneven developments and to avoid evaluative teleologies; clearly changes across this long period—and stases as well—are both progressive and regressive and, without recourse to hindsight, often literally immeasurable.

GOING PUBLIC

The aims and interventions I have been describing come with commensurate risks that have led to specific and sometimes unorthodox methodological decisions: a focus on public discourse in the form of print and thus the pursuit of lesbian representations through mostly man-made sources; the use of "sapphic" as an umbrella term; a reliance on what I call confluence rather than influence as an analytical rubric; and a strategy of "large" reading. To these one might add the uneasy relationship between the fields of "literature"and "history," and likewise between representation and material life, that typifies a good deal of work in sexuality studies including my own.

The most important decision I have made is to concentrate exclusively on written texts that circulated publicly, mostly in print and occasionally in manuscript. Although I have written about private texts elsewhere and occasionally evoke them in passing,[45] I do not include letters, diaries, or works that did not circulate until long after their date of composition. In the context of lesbian studies, which has often had evidentiary recourse to unpublished texts in conjunction with its keen interest in potentially queer persons, such a decision seems to me more consequential than it might appear. In focusing on public discourse, I emphasize the textual shapes and social implications, rather than the possible personal causes, of sapphic configurations in print. While I appreciate the importance of a queer history of persons and have contributed to that enterprise, I do not make strong connections here between individuals and texts or explore the private lives that may have underwritten the public pronouncements, except where those lives generated, and in effect served as, public texts. A majority of the writings I discuss in this book are attributable to men or deeply anonymous, and little can be traced back to "real" lesbians even by the loosest definition of the term. If this state of affairs appears as a limitation, it also suggests that public representations of the sapphic are less likely to come from desiring bodies than from imagining and inquiring minds even, as my fourth chapter will emphasize, when the writers are women. Here too I practice an inversion of the usual speculative linkage: if the history of sexuality typically infers desiring bodies as the impetus for erotic words, my sexuality of history infers erotic words as an impetus for desiring bodies—or, perhaps more aptly, for desiring bodies politic.

Also absent here is the considerable visual representation of the sapphic that appears during this same period. I do mention visual images on occasion, insofar as they appear either literally or referentially in verbal texts, but to have studied these would have strained both the limits of my disciplinary training and the scope of the project. Such a choice does risk reinforcing the problem Joan Landes rightly recognized when she charged scholars with perpetuating "the notion that culture amounts to the sum of so many printed words on a page," and certainly theorizing the visual and the verbal together would be a valuable comparative project.[46] In embracing print culture as my field of evidence, I include a multiplicity of genres from novels, plays, and poems to tracts, satires, and anecdotes, an eclecticism the rationale for which may become clearer through my discussion of "confluence" below. My interest lies in what circulated at a given moment, and although I attend to differences of genre and medium, locate different textual practices in time and place, and consider the ramifications of particular genres, I have not attempted to draw strict lines around discursive forms except where the texts seem bent on delineating their own generic specificity, as might be said of the eighteenth-century novel or of seventeenth-century anecdotes about women who "turn into" men. Where the sapphic functions distinctively in a discursive field or a generic genealogy, I have tried to distinguish its differential investment. And in unintended allegiance to my primary field of training, I have ended up giving greater attention to imaginative representations than, say, to philosophical or scientific genres.

Choosing public discourse, and discourse that brings sapphic subjects to textual surfaces, shifts this study rather far from the "uncloseting" that has been central to the project of lesbian as well as gay history.[47] Although it is of course crucial to recognize the coded strategies often adopted by erotic writings and indeed the tropological nature of all discourse, my work tacitly suggests that lesbian history may have more to gain from looking at public representations than from hunting down evidence of private desires. In *The Gentleman's Daughter*, Amanda Vickery observes that the two topics that even "proper" heterosexually married women did not "commit to paper" were "spirituality and sex."[48] Margaret Hunt further reminds us that "the evidence of real flesh-and-blood . . . lesbians is tantalizingly meager,"[49] especially if we are seeking self-authenticating evidence rather than documentation from legal trials or gossip sheets. Almost nowhere do we find analogues to the diaries of Anne Lister (1791–1840), with their encoded but frank tracings of her sexual relations with other women.[50] With respect to the seventeenth and eighteenth centuries, the shift from private lives to public investments seems to me to offer greater potential to turn the history of sexuality into the sexuality of history by opening links between sapphic subjects and a breadth of discursive domains, from law and science to poetics and politics.

It is in part to emphasize the difference between eighteenth- and twenty-first century textual formations, and in part to evoke a less identitarian canopy, that this book prefers "sapphic" to "lesbian" to designate discourses, representations, and social phenomena that inscribe preferential desires, behaviors, and affiliations—whether explicitly sexual or just implicitly erotic, whether frankly female or (less often) gender-queer—that wrest women from automatic inscription into a heteronormative regime.[51] As is already apparent, I do use the word "lesbian" on occasion to designate a broad intellectual field or the practices and identities that fall within its purview, and I agree with Bernadette Brooten that the term is no more historically discontinuous than "such other terms as 'slavery,' 'marriage,' or 'family'";[52] I concur likewise with Judith Bennett that at least since the tenth century, the adjective "lesbian" has "roughly signified what it roughly signifies today."[53] But I have settled on "sapphic," which I deploy as both an adjective and abstract noun, for its very vagueness, for its emergence but not overdetermination in the eighteenth century, and for its relative disappearance from contemporary use. Certainly no one term for female homoeroticism anchors this long period; seventeenth- and eighteenth-century European writers deployed a score of labels not only for homoerotic desires and behaviors but also for the women who were believed to practice them: tribade, hermaphrodite, sodomite, sodomitesse, *sodomita, bujarrona*, rubster, *donna con donna, ribaulde*, fricatrice, fricarelle, *lollepot* and, especially in the later eighteenth century, lesbian, sapphist, amazon, tommy, tribadist, and anandryne, to say nothing of euphemisms and circumlocutions including mannish, irregular, singular, unnatural, the "game of flats," and allusions to "matters not fit to be mentioned." All the more as innuendo was more prominent than outright naming, no one term adequately accommodates this diverse nomenclature of several countries and more than two centuries.

"Sapphic" as I use it is also meant to encompass "lesbian-like" discourses and representations like those sometimes signaled by "romantic friendship" that are plausibly if not provably sexual: desires and habits that give primacy to same-sex bonds through words amenable to an erotic rendering—which also means leaving it "permanently unclear," to follow Judith Butler, "what precisely that sign signifies."[54] I use the term "amenable"—a happy borrowing from Harriette Andreadis[55]—in order to work against a tendency in the reception of queer scholarship to demand incontrovertible evidence of homoerotic desires or acts. As Martha Vicinus has observed, sexuality studies has been burdened with a disproportionate mandate to "know-for-sure," to provide "evidence of sexual consummation, whereas heterosexuality is confirmed through a variety of diverse social formations."[56] Even if we were to know what people really did in bed, and surely in most cases we never shall, where marriage is a compulsory institution especially for women, and forcible sex all too commonplace, heterosexual consummation proves nothing about affective affiliation or sexual desire. Further, clear discursive lines often fail to demarcate the erotic from the "merely" affectional, particularly at a time when certain understandings of sexual behavior (for example, equating sex with penetration) may locate some behaviors below the sexual radar screen. If I err on the side of inclusion, I do so as a gesture toward rebalancing critical tendencies; when I term a constellation or representation "sapphic," I claim only its homoerotic potential.

As an illustrative example, I would certainly identify as sapphic—and will evoke in chapter 7—the most famous female couple of the eighteenth century, the Anglo-Irish pair Eleanor Butler and Sarah Ponsonby, dubbed the "Ladies of Llangollen," who in 1778 defied their families and eloped together to Wales. For the next forty-one years, Butler and Ponsonby shared bed, board, and belongings, performed themselves as a devoted couple, and were fetishized as such. Butler and Ponsonby would never have declared themselves sexual partners and indeed may not have been. If we look at the sapphic as a *social formation*, however, no logic could consider Butler and Ponsonby either heteronormative or undesiring; against the grain of familial, economic, and social injunctions, their life was structured entirely around a governing same-sex interest that left a legacy of representation. It is for this reason as well as for historical accuracy that I have eschewed the obfuscating term "romantic friendship" with its odd blend of discrediting (eighteenth-century) and desexualizing (twentieth-century) baggage.[57] In eighteenth-century fiction the term describes unwise and unstable friendships formed by naïve youth; in lesbian scholarship it designates emotionally intense nonsexual relationships. Ironically, the link between the sapphic and romantic friendship was forged in relation to Butler and Ponsonby themselves, when a relative wrote that their elopement was *merely* a "scheme of Romantic Friendship" devoid of "serious impropriety."[58] If romantic friendship does get queered in this instance, the term also obfuscates the erotic and marital quality of Butler and Ponsonby's lifelong partnership. In evicting "romantic friendship," I allow "sapphic" to include suggestive but indeterminate discursive formations like those evoked in representations of Butler and Ponsonby: without denying the importance of sex acts or their erotic implications, I consider it less the genital detail than the tapestry of relationship that ought to signify, just as it usually does when scholars approach heteronormative relations. It is the contextual sense of the sapphic toward which my project tilts, especially in studying a moment where, as Valerie Traub has noted, one of the most prominent characteristics of female sexual representation is the contest about whether something sexual is there at all.[59]

This apparitional character of lesbianism—to evoke an important argument advanced by Terry Castle—also operates in and as textual history.[60] One of the most frustrating problems for lesbian historiography is the degree to which sapphic texts and their travels get covered up: the in-

tense production of sapphic discourse over two centuries leaves startlingly
scant trace of *re*-production in the form of discussion, citation, review, or
even inclusion in catalogues, while the anonymity of many sapphic writings bars deep investigation at the site of origin. For example, the anonymous and baggy *Travels and Adventures of Mademoiselle de Richelieu*,
in which two women fall in love, tour Europe, and end up as lifelong partners, went through at least four editions between 1744 and 1758 but has
apparently left to posterity only one brief notice in a journal and not a single other comment or review, and efforts to identify the author have thus
far proved vain.[61] Sapphic subjects often seem to be written in sand, their
textual traces erased before and behind them, so that although we have
the physical evidence of their existence, the reasons why someone wrote
them, where they traveled, who read them, and whom they influenced still
remain locked secrets of the past. Yet insofar as we can understand textual
production itself as a kind of motive, and repetition—whether through
citation, reprinting, or imitation—as evidence of reception and response,
we can read the story of sapphic representations in the tropes and themes
that get reiterated or repudiated from text to text. The remainder of silence
makes it difficult to work at the level of the individual instance, however,
and particularly to figure out the "trade routes" by which any single text
might have influenced any another. Scholars have not (yet), for example,
been able to attribute to international influence the ubiquity of female
cross-dressing, with its homoerotic nuance, on the Elizabethan as well
as the Golden Age Spanish stage, let alone to find evidence that Shakespeare was familiar with, say, the French "female husbands" described by
Montaigne.

Making sense of similarity within this intertextual void argues, then,
for a logic not of influence but of confluence, a term the *Oxford English
Dictionary* equates with the convergence of "a numerous collection or as-
semblage, a large quantity gathered from various quarters." Rather than
implying causality across surface evidence, confluence suggests a convergence of relatively simultaneous phenomena from a deeper common
source, rather like symptoms of a systemic illness or surface waters from
an underground aquifer. The pursuit of confluence, a concept that I distinguish from the deservedly problematized *Zeitgeist*,[62] allows us to examine
what Claudio Guillén called "genetically independent" instances in order
to see whether a shared social, political, or cultural logic can explain their
aggregate.[63] Such a project, which necessarily recognizes a multiplicity of
discursive forces in play at any time, may be as daunting as the archaeolo-
gist's challenge to piece shards together in an effort to imagine the wholes

of which they are portions, to guess at the uses to which they may have been put, and to speculate about the world that made them. To evoke Foucault's understanding of archaeology, then, my project asks "within what space of order knowledge [about the sapphic] was constituted" and what created the "conditions of possibility" for different constellations of interest in sapphic subjects to burgeon, flourish, and often to "dissolve and vanish soon afterwards."[64]

While influence is the more common methodological approach within comparative textual studies, confluence has also been successfully practiced though rarely named as such. One of the most powerful confluence studies, in my view, is Walter Cohen's *Drama of a Nation*, which explores the "remarkable features of kinship" between the theatrical cultures of Golden Age Spain and Elizabethan England even though they emerged separately and in markedly different societies. Speculating that a "similar principle" must underlie their separate development, Cohen recognizes a "concurrence of social and political forces—most notable among them the early growth of capitalism" in an absolutist state, that fostered similitude between English and Spanish "theatrical institutions, dramatic genres, [and] individual plays."[65] In a different vein, Dror Wahrman's *The Making of the Modern Self* uses phenomena as disparate as fashion, representations of Amazons, and translations of Juvenal to show a fairly rapid movement in England during the 1770s and 1780s from "gender play to gender panic."[66] Wahrman's causal "common denominator" for this major change is Britain's traumatic loss of the American colonies, a controversial hypothesis suggesting the necessarily speculative nature of confluence study, which is especially vulnerable when it assigns a single cause to a cultural phenomenon, especially when the cause operates within a different sphere from the consequence, as is the case both for Wahrman and Cohen and arguably for my own practice as well.

The shift from influence to confluence carries several benefits. On the compensatory side, confluence helps to address the fact that for all the noble intentions of the newer historicisms to explore texts "within the actual means and conditions of their production," as Raymond Williams put it,[67] thick description at the level of the individual example may be impossible to achieve. As I have suggested, such is often the case for lesbian history; to take texts that I will pursue more fully in subsequent chapters, the motivations for both John Donne's elegy "Sapho to Philaenis" (c. 1601) and Álvaro Cubillo de Aragón's stage play *Añasco el de Talavera* (c. 1635) have so mystified scholars that in each case the work's authorship has been questioned against the material evidence. Moreover, while influence studies tend to emphasize like kinds and to seek out cohering representational surfaces, confluence recognizes that disparate phenomena may be related by virtue of their simultaneous occurrence. Finally, in shifting attention from textual surfaces to contextual depths, confluence almost inevitably anchors textual study to its larger social, political, economic, religious, and/or cultural environment. Where confluence and influence converge, we can shape even thicker understandings of the (sexual) past. In making a systemic argument that emphasizes confluence over influence, then, I am not discounting the role of the biographical, the intertextual, or the circumstantial; I am focusing on the broader forces that may stimulate the local, making particular tropes and postures available to "end users," in order to shed a more diffuse light on why individual representations may have occurred. As Peter Turchi reminds us in *Maps of the Imagination*, "the most detailed map is not necessarily the best map"; a full picture requires both close-up and distanced views calibrated to the span we are traversing. There are times when scholars, like mapmakers, must "choose our blanks," lest an excess of detail keep us from seeing the larger patterns in the plenitude.[68] To echo Italo Calvino's *If On a Winter's Night a Traveler*, "The world is so complicated, tangled, and overloaded that to see into it with any clarity you must prune and prune."[69]

In the end, then, what I am advancing is also a way of reading that knits individual writings both to discursive structures and, more speculatively, to social phenomena. In so doing, I raise a theoretical challenge for queer studies: the possibility that blatant representations of, say, lesbians may be harder for us to parse than their more closeted counterparts, given the strategies through which scholars trained in "close reading" have learned to read and especially to read queerly. Literary critics are taught, of course, to excavate hidden content and to prize what is least obvious about a text. This mandate has been particularly helpful for queer studies, which has succeeded precisely by exposing what is coded and covert. Thus the energies of queer literary studies, my own energies included, have focused on creating queer readings, on turning the "unrepresentable" into the represented, as it were, so that the scholarly reading in effect stands in for the text by speaking the text's silences. And necessarily so.

Yet this training has two potential and unintended drawbacks: to divert attention from more obviously queer texts and to screen out the "nonsexual" aspects that nestle with sexuality. That is, the mandate to uncover queer content may have limited the questions we ask by encouraging us to ferret out the words, tropes, and acts that embody the sexual rather than looking at how the sexual connects up to other discursive spheres and historical projects. To return to *The Travels and Adventures of Mademoiselle de Richelieu*, we might note that scholarship thus far, including an essay of my own, has been bent on extracting the lesbian plot from a more multifaceted surface of travelogues, commentaries, and inserted tales.[70] Attending to the language that connects that titillating lesbian plot to the text's religious, cultural, and political interests might show us more than titillating purposes. My aim in *The Sexuality of History* is to read across texts for tropes and practices that reveal potential connections to other historically salient concerns. Although I am working only with texts I consider "sapphic," if by a capacious and deliberately imprecise definition, it is thus not exactly sexual content that I am looking for, and so I am also less interested in what might be "closeted" than in what might be available to any reader, or at least to the knowing implied reader, on the surface of the text. At the same time, I am reading across texts for recurring themes and images, and most of all for language, tropes, and practices that are *not* exclusive to sexual representation. I am thus not looking *for* what is sapphic so much as looking *within* the sapphic for connections to other formations.

Necessarily, given the scope of the project, I read some texts more closely than others, often situating a key text within allusions to other texts in order to demonstrate a wider practice and attempting to provide some balance of representation among the different textual cultures the project encompasses. On the whole, I am neither engaged in the proverbial close reading that attempts to exhaust the meaning of a text nor extracting "data" from texts after the fashion of what Franco Moretti calls "distant reading" in ways that might wilfully overlook their complexities.[71] In addition to *largely* reading, then—by which I mean relying on texts for more than textual arguments—I am also engaged in *large* reading, poised between the close and the distant, in an effort to articulate what I think matters epistemically.

And that's a gamble. The choices I have made in pursuing this project—working with diverse genres of public writings about which little is known, encompassing several languages and cultures in uneven proportions within a swath of two-plus centuries, reading largely in both senses of the word—necessarily entail making leaps from texts to their potential significance, particularly where my claims of efficacy for sapphic subjects are at stake. I would argue, however, that despite the optimism of a book such as Martha Nussbaum's *Poetic Justice*, most studies of representation engage in similar guesswork insofar as the material effects of texts remain unmeasured and, in early contexts, probably unmeasurable. Apart from the case of sacred writings that get cited by adherents to justify acts both benevolent and mad, even when a work has been acclaimed as ground-shifting—for example, *Uncle Tom's Cabin*—it is almost impossible to establish firm lines from textual instance to social change. In this sense especially, *The Sexuality of History* is choosing the intellectually risky process of speculation. For worse or better, it is a practice I admire. I take as models the studies by Cohen and Wahrman that I have described above as well as a work like Henry Abelove's "Some Speculations on the History of Sexual Intercourse during the Long Eighteenth Century in England," which surmises that "cross-sex genital intercourse" increased during the later eighteenth century because pronatalist regimes of production encouraged reproductive sexual practices where formerly a range of erotic behaviors had been commonplace.[72] All three of these studies have faced the problem of cause-effect relations by hazarding some informed speculation that has certainly been challenged but that has opened new paths of inquiry. In the spirit of that boldness, I have ended up willing to be intriguingly wrong rather than timidly right.

Readerly judgment of this work may also rest on more basic matters of disciplinary or epistemological axis. My attempt at a sexuality of history, while grounded in the (inter)discipline of literary studies, also relies on an engagement with the subject matter and scholarship of a discipline in whose methods I have not been trained. A vast body of work in the history of sexuality has likewise been forged in the intellectual crucible signified by the conjugation "Hist & Lit." But I remain aware of gaps in approach and understanding and between these fields and also of my necessarily limited knowledge of both the material past and its scholarly lineage. On the other side, however, I am comfortable with a temporality that some literary scholars but fewer historians might disavow: this project is historicist in ways that scholars invested in the "queering of history" might well deem heteronormative. The analogical thinking that equates straight sexuality to "straight" historiography, and would thus eviscerate temporality in the name of a queer past, simply does not square either with my understanding or with my aims.[73] At the same time, and the unapologetic teleology of my opening paragraph notwithstanding, while I mark temporal difference where I see it, I do not argue here for a developmental history of the sapphic subjects I scrutinize. As I will suggest in my coda, different configurations ebb and flow within the long period embraced by this study, and my deferral of the largest temporal speculations to the end of the book should allow others to read the analyses advanced in my chapters against their own grain.

Two further points before I turn to the shape of the chapters. My project draws on a rich archive of textual materials though by no means a comprehensive one. Many of these texts I have unearthed myself in libraries in the U.S. and Europe and, more recently, in the primary-source databases that have become increasingly available during the course of my long engagement with this book. But this project remains very deeply in the debt of those whose archival labor, suggestive footnotes, or passing comments have pointed me to texts I would not otherwise have discovered: it *does* take a village to raise the history of sexuality or the sexuality of history. I owe a special gratitude to the pioneering scholars of lesbian history, many of them working in less congenial political and archival settings and with far less academic privilege, who have unearthed texts in their national literatures about which I, and so many other scholars and readers, might not otherwise have known.

I proceed too, of course, with the recognition that, as Luz Sanfeliú puts it, "our interpretations of other times are often nurtured by visions and conjectures imbued with our own reality and with the anachronistic projections of myths."[74] Anne Lister recognized this danger when, in a letter of 1822, she suspected a sexual relationship between Eleanor Butler and Sarah Ponsonby: "I cannot help thinking that surely it was not platonic. Heaven forgive me, but I look within myself and doubt. I feel the infirmity of our nature & hesitate to pronounce such attachments uncemented by something more tender still than friendship." Yet even Lister, hungry for the answer that would confirm her own sexuality, recognized the need for objective evidence: "But much, or all, depends upon the story of their former lives, the period passed before they lived together, that feverish dream called youth."[75] Lister asks the key question with which so many historians, and certainly historians of sexuality, have grappled: how, as Robert D. Hume puts it, to enter "a horizon of expectations other than one's own."[76] I take the risks of speculative exploration because I believe we still have too little in the way of lesbian history through which to stretch our sense of its possibilities. The sooner this book becomes superseded, the better for the field.

MODERNITY AND THE SAPPHIC, 1565–1830

This introductory chapter has sought to articulate my approach to material that subsequent chapters will analyze and interrogate. Each chapter explores a body of sapphic inscriptions in relation not only to their configurations of sexuality and gender but to the wider concerns that I believe they evoke. It is not only because I am a narrative theorist that I will emphasize narrativity as a broad feature of sapphic representations, and for at least two reasons. First, even sapphic writings that formally occupy other genres typically enact the temporal dynamics of narrative. Second, if any genre dominates the long period this book encompasses, it is the anecdote, that least and, as Andrea Loselle says, "least respected" of narrative forms: immensely detachable, insertable, and manipulable, on which so many truth claims have historically relied and which, as Mary Baine Campbell has eloquently argued is, in this same period, hard at work through its "miniaturized narrativity," to "package the newly emergent 'world' of America in small boxes."[77] The prevalence of the anecdote in sapphic representation suggests this same effort at reduction while also signaling the mobility of sapphic stories, their capacity to be drawn into a range of conversations, and their status as news—themes that will thread through this volume.

I will also attend across the book to three distinctive though sometimes intertwined configurations of sapphic discourse that I call, respectively, metamorphic, ethnographic, and horizontal or leveling. Metamorphic models, which dominate the early period but begin to wane toward the end of the seventeenth century, work through dynamics of absorption or conversion to turn same-sex into cross-sex relations by changing either physical identity or object of desire. Ethnographic models, which flourish especially from the late seventeenth to the mid-eighteenth century, present the sapphic as a site of discovery, a sphere of anthropological interest in either the physical or cultural meaning of that term, and often engage in interpretations with national contours. Horizontal models, which increase across the eighteenth century, accept same-sex relations as irreducible, see in them egalitarian or leveling possibilities whether for good or ill, and confront their conceptual and material implications. As I explore the shifting tendencies of these configurations, I find myself invested in the horizontal as the most radical site of what we might loosely call sapphic agency. I have organized each chapter along a different axis, focusing in turn on a specific historical moment, on changing patterns across a longer span of time, on a particular genre or discursive project, on a political or literary movement. Through this diversity of focus, I hope to create a set of differential lenses that form a prism of ways to read diverse and complex materials. At the same time, the (sometimes overlapping) chronologies of chapters move the study forward in time.

Chapter 2, "Mapping Sapphic Modernity, 1565–1630," explores the emergence of a sustained discourse of female homoeroticism toward the turn of the seventeenth century. I seek here to account for a vigorous print conversation about sapphic subjects in this period that can be mapped onto a specific geography. While the writings I study in this chapter offer conflicting and confusing messages for a history of sexuality, they present a more deeply coherent logic for the sexuality of history. Preoccupied more with potential habits than with specific acts, less with private desires than with their public accommodation, these late-sixteenth- and early-seventeenth-century texts point to underlying concerns about social mobility, personal alteration, and the unpredictable contours of change. Although metamorphic plots dominate this period, sapphic representations sometimes also advance a fascination with "leveling" that will persist in both dystopic and utopic forms across the next two centuries. In so doing, they test the logic of gender as the crux of a contest between dominant and emergent philosophical paradigms. Chapter 2 also attempts to account for the differential geographic distribution of sapphic representations by identifying potentially relevant features common to those countries where writings about the sapphic flourish. This geography, in turn, helps to interpret the cultural work in which sapphic writings are engaged in the decades around 1600.

The changing investments that attach to sapphic subjects across the next century, particularly those that implicate national agendas, form the focus of chapter 3. "Fearful Symmetries: The Sapphic and the State, 1630–1749" works with all three patterns of sapphic discourse to trace some of the shifting ways in which each deploys the sapphic to engage family and state politics. I argue that metamorphic plots attempting to resolve homoerotic relations through a logic of substitution are already becoming less tenable by the 1630s and that by the late seventeenth century the "leveling" potential of same-sex relations is being tapped for political purposes. A close look at two plays, Isaac de Benserade's *Iphis et Ianthe* and Álvaro Cubillo de Aragón's *Añasco el de Talavera*, shows how the impasse of the sapphic figures the collapse of predictable family and, by extension, state relations, while a briefer look at ethnographic representations shows how the sapphic gets connected to tropes of travel and empire and entangled with broader projects of classification and control; I look especially at the persistent association of the sapphic with the Ottoman Empire in ethnographies both physical and cultural. If the metamorphic texts can be read as efforts to erase the "same" in same-sex relations, the increasing plenitude of "horizontal" impulses insists on that similitude to produce polarized utopian and dystopian representations. By evoking fears and fantasies about "leveling," these representations tie the sapphic in surprisingly close ways to questions of governance, as my focal exploration of Jacobite-era English writings in the last section of this chapter demonstrates.

Not surprisingly, the importance of the sapphic in the social imaginary bears particular implications for the construction of women as subjects in an emergent public sphere. Chapter 4, "The Political Economy of Same-Sex Desire, 1630–1765," argues that erotic writings by women, especially in the form of what I call sapphic apostrophe, were able to advance class-specific protofeminist arguments in ways that reveal the seventeenth-century female subject to be something of a sapphic subject as well. I read these (mostly poetic) examples of erotic friendship, which became prominent in tandem with the entrance of elite women into print, as a cultural strategy too pervasive and too purposefully public to be explained by private desires—or, to push the argument further, I speculate that private desires may themselves be stimulated by public imperatives. Chapter 4 thus considers why women's interests might have been served by their constitution as subjects erotically bound to one another in representation. Class relations figure centrally in the cultural work both of the texts themselves and of this chapter, as I look at a practice that peaks in the late seventeenth and early eighteenth century and ebbs by the 1760s in the wake of reconfigurations of femininity that can be associated with such influential thinkers as Jean-Jacques Rousseau.

I noted earlier that narrative strategies are pervasive even in the seemingly non-narrative texts encompassed in this study, but narrative takes center stage in chapter 5. "Rereading the 'Rise' of the Novel: Sapphic Genealogies, 1680–1815" argues that the history of the European novel can be understood as—to put it most boldly—a sapphic plot. While such a claim may seem counterintuitive given the novel's legendary investment in consolidating a heteronormative order, my alternative history exposes the several and shifting strategies through which the sapphic marks the novel in both form and manifest content. I trace the arc of the sapphic through four stages in the novel's development, beginning with the erotic fictions of the late seventeenth century and moving through picaresque and domestic modes to the gothic interventions and revisionist representations of the *fin de siècle*. Recognizing the persistent practice of picaresque as a site of sapphic movement far into the eighteenth century in ways that challenge the novel's putative domestication, I also argue that seemingly heteronormative narratives often embed a version of the sapphic through the dynamics of intimate confidence and show how the repeated eruption of the sapphic into "mainstream" works evokes questions both about social relations and about the forms and functions of the novel itself. The multifaceted enactment of the sapphic over the long eighteenth century suggests that even as the novel is "rising," its domesticating project is sowing the seeds of discontent. Reading the novel through the sapphic also addresses the emergence of female narrators and narratees, protagonists and confidantes, often embedded in rites of rescue, in conjunction with the culture's increased interest in, but legal denial of, women's rights. The sapphic genealogy of the eighteenth-century novel that I outline here provides, then, a differential framework for considering the "realist" and more insistently heteronormative consolidation of the genre in the early nineteenth century.

The intellectual and social contests that intensified in an age of revolutionary turmoil and romantic subterfuge lead to the questions that organize my final chapters. Chapter 6, "Sapphic Sects and the Rites of Revolution, 1775–1800," asks how female intimacies became associated with fears and fantasies of power, exclusion, and secrecy in the era of the "rights of man." At a time when exclusive clubs and secret societies proliferate and reformist pressures escalate, the anecdotal spaces of print culture propel an unprecedented number of women into visibility through public claims about their affiliations with women. In particular, imaginary sapphic sects become imbricated with reformist and counter-reformist politics both in and beyond France as newspapers, pamphlets, scurrilous poems, and secret histories grapple with the broader threat of groups and their social powers in a world of political turmoil and potentially radical change. A discourse of similitude, attached to intensifying conversations about rights, puts the sapphic at the heart at once of class politics, fears of conspiracy, and hopes for collectivity. In the process, representations of female affiliation are invested with both utopian idealism and dystopian excess. Writings of the 1770s and 1780s often use female erotic association to work out both hopes and fears of a different future, but in the 1790s, the explicitly sapphic becomes so firmly aligned with counter-revolution that it loses traction as an exploratory site. Particularly but not only in France, sapphic subjects thus stand emblematically at the crux of late-eighteenth-century political crisis.

The vulnerability of both revolutionary agendas and sapphic representations sets the scene for chapter 7, "'Sisters in Love': Irregular Families, Romantic Elegies, 1788–1830." As a restabilizing brotherhood enfranchises the entrepreneurial classes of post-revolutionary Europe, we also see a dramatic drop-off in explicitly sapphic reference extending even to dictionary injunctions that seek to render female homoeroticism publicly illegible. At the same time, however, a domesticated version of the sapphic becomes a cultural site for reconfiguring the couple as a natural(ized) bridge between utopian intimacy and triumphant individuality. Representations of female couples offer a limit case for both family values and Romantic transgression as the sapphic gets memorialized through elegaic tropes. Here the heterosocial imperative of Romantic similitude, together with the gendered limits of Romantic ideology, converge to figure the idyllic harmony of the female couple as a kind of death knell. The explicit recourse to poetic "irregularity" in several of the texts I study suggests the unease with which the sapphic stands in for family in a gender-conservative age. Chapter 7 thus asks what we can learn from sapphic subjects about the Romantic imagination, and through it about early nineteenth-century configurations of domestic and poetic arrangements, at a time when explicitly homoerotic discourse is becoming less tenable. I focus in particular on the ways in which the female couple is conscripted into representational work that is paradoxically ennobling and self-annihilating.

Finally, my brief coda, "We Have Always Been Modern," looks back through the long period of my inquiry to assess the shifting stakes of the sapphic and to gather strands of discursive purpose that I attribute to sapphic subjects at different moments in this study. With particular recourse to issues of colonialism, class, family, gender, and governance, I speculate about the changing purposes of sapphic representation in relation to the challenges that comprise the opening litany of this book. I ask too whether any patterns of sapphic representation span the full period of this inquiry, and I gesture toward what I see as the implications for the cultural projects for which sapphic subjects have been engaged. As its title suggests, this short chapter also meditates further on the relationship between modernity and the sapphic and asks about both the gains and losses that might accrue in tandem with "sapphic modernity."

In emphasizing the sapphic as a modern emblem and in tracing its textual, thematic, and geographic movements, I am ultimately arguing for a reconception of the sexual order, and thus also of the social imaginary, that modernity constructs. Rather than seeing modernity as the instantiation of heterosexual difference, as scholars of sexuality have tended to do, I reverse the figure-ground relationship to understand emergent modernity as equally the instantiation of the sapphic within a logic of possibility. It is, to be sure, an instantiation uneven in movement and far from complete. But if modernity means compulsory heterosexuality as a normative practice, it also means the contrary or concomitant slippage of some women into alternatives variously construed as liberatory or limiting. If we may use Foucault's term *episteme* for the body of ideas that shapes knowledge at a particular historical moment, then I will go so far as to figure modernity in its boldest contours as a kind of *sapphic episteme*, a world view in which the *logic* of woman + woman is made available for good and ill. I do not mean that other logics are not also a part of what it means to be modern, but that the particular dynamics that female relations inscribe are able at once to tell us what modernity-in-the-making looks like and to act out a broad range of its perceived implications. In this sense, as I suggested at the outset, the early *il*-logic of woman + woman becomes a testing ground for modernity's limit points, revealing modernity itself to be essentially queer. Sapphic representations thus provide a potentially paradigm-shifting lens for reading the past.

CHAPTER TWO

Mapping Sapphic Modernity, 1565–1630

Men I say may live without women, but women cannot live without men.

—Joseph Swetnam, *The Araignment of Lewd, Idle, Inconstant, and Froward Women* (1615)[1]

I n 1566, the Geneva publishing scion Henri Estienne wrote a scathing attack on modern morals known as the *Apologie pour Hérodote*. To crown his chapter "On the Sin of Sodomy, and the Sin Against Nature in Our Time," Estienne offers a tale that he deems even more "amazingly strange" than his account of the woman from Toulouse who "prostituted herself" to a dog:

> A girl from Fontaines, which is between Blois and Romorantin, having disguised herself as a man, served as a stable groom for about seven years at an inn on the outskirts of Foye, then married a girl from there, with whom she lived for about two years while working as a wine-grower. At this point, the wickedness she used for simulating a husband's role was discovered, she was seized, and after confessing was burned alive. This is how our century can boast that beyond all the evils of the preceding ones, it has some that are specific and peculiar to itself. For this act has nothing in common with that of the sordid ones who were called *tribades* in ancient times.[2]

With this declaration, Estienne makes one ordinary woman's act of dressing as a man and marrying a woman the sexual crime of the century. In an explicit rupture of present from past, the *Apologie* sets up the transgressions not of powerful foreign men but of lowborn provincial women to signify the specific evils of the modern age. Indeed, Estienne insists that his female couple has "nothing in common" with the *tribades* of antiquity, a hefty claim for a scholar invested in a kinship more than linguistic between ancient Greece and modern France.

Estienne's separation of Greek *tribade* from French *paysanne* is all the more significant in that this text marks one of the first uses of "tribade," or of any noun alluding to erotic intimacy between women, in a European vernacular.[3] By negating the very word that he introduces, Estienne opens a conceptual vacuum for a modern malfeasance that has no name, and female homoeroticism gets demarcated from the history embodied in the only word by which it is evoked. Estienne also presents the marriage of two women not simply as a practice that must be condemned but as a story that must be told: with a disproportionate focus on details of time (thirty years, two, seven) place (Fontaines, Blois, Romorantin, Foye) occupation (stable groom, winegrower), and stages of prosecution (discovery, seizure, confession, death), he wraps material circumstance around sexual silence, rendering the "evil" as nameless as the "girls" themselves. In this way, the story inscribes an inability or refusal to define the very sin that it marks as a historic departure, and an unnameable practice enters French letters as a conundrum that stands for modernity but that modernity will have to figure out.

This deployment of female same-sex desire to herald a new age occurs likewise in one of early modernity's first and "most unabashedly homoerotic" printed love poems in which a woman addresses a woman,[4] the "Elegie pour une Dame enamourée d'une autre Dame" printed in the 1573 *Oeuvres poétiques* of the French bishop, poet, and philosopher Pontus de Tyard. Tyard's "Dame" identifies her desire as specifically modern—"never before seen"—and attributes it to a lack of male "honor" in "the age in which we live."[5] Once again sapphic desire is presented in epistemic terms, so that when the speaker's love for a specific woman goes unrequited, the loss is far more than personal. Indeed, the lady had hoped to elevate love between women above centuries of male-male and male-female bonds, so that "once in all French history / our love were lasting memory; / the love of women would prevail / beyond all loves denoted male."[6] The "dame énamourée" and her "aimée" would have taken their place in a lineage of such venerable pairings as Damon and Pythias, Aeneas and Achates, Hercules and Nestor, Chaerephon and Socrates, and male-female couples the speaker claims are too numerous to name. Here again, love between women is specifically French and specifically modern, a rupture with the past that also seeks the triumph of continuity through a gender-bent lineage. And like Estienne's anecdote, Tyard's poem underscores the need to tell a sapphic story, for nothing actually happens between the two women. The "Elégie" itself thus becomes the imaginary substitute for the speaker's fulfillment; her final wish is for her voice to wander the woods, repeating its tale of unrequited love. In both instances, then, a sixteenth-century French writer presents intimacy between women as the emblem of a modernity that is disavowed (Estienne) or disallowed (Tyard) but that insists on public articulation. And across differences of tone that make Estienne's a story of perversity and Tyard's of possibility, both texts sound something of an alarm over women's potential to displace men in social and sexual relations.

Why might a Protestant printer living in Geneva and a Catholic bishop connected to the French court concur in making erotic relations between women, relations in vastly different class settings, a sign of the times? While biographical probing might uncover individual motives,[7] my interest here lies in reading Estienne and Tyard themselves as a sign of the times. For what these writers proclaim to be modern about women is arguably modern about themselves, and what is new to late-sixteenth-century French discourse is not the sapphic as such but the recognition that the sapphic might intervene in history.[8] Both texts evoke antiquity, but only to herald a sea-change in sexual relations, marking a rupture between ancients and moderns that sits uneasily with these authors' investments in reviving a classical tradition in which the sapphic already figures. Also modern, of course, is this very distinction between ancient and modern that will eventually fuel a far-reaching philosophical and literary *querelle*. In the differences between Estienne's and Tyard's evocations, then, we can see the seeds of that quarrel sown on sapphic ground.

Estienne and Tyard are far from alone in imagining female-female relations as a defining feature of a new age: the late sixteenth century inaugurated an intensification of public attention to female homoeroticism *as* modern that was clearly more than personal whim or French fashion. Agnolo Firenzuola's *Dialogo delle bellezze delle donne* [*Of the Beauty of Women*] (1548) set the stage by emphasizing the antiquity of male-male desire while naming specific contemporary women, but not contemporary men, as practitioners of homoerotic intimacies and by focusing its concern on women who, for the love of women, "spurn marriage" or remain willingly in convents because they "love each other's beauty."[9] Jean Papon's legal commentary of 1563 foregoes the usual discussion of ancient tribades to focus on one modern couple, Françoise de l'Estage and Catherine de la Manière, to affirm the death penalty that they managed to escape. In the spirit of Estienne, the Democritus who leads the charge against women in Jean Tahureau's posthumously published *Dialogues* (1565) deems the lowest of today's women those so "virtuous" as to "comport themselves *à la tribadique*."[10] Pierre Ronsard celebrates the union of "Anne" and "Diane" that will "top all ancient loves [surmontera toute amour ancienne]," undoing even those once deemed perfect; though time might destroy "Murs & Chateaux" and "make everything crumble [tout fait plyer]," it cannot touch this union.[11] For the poet Pierre de L'Estoile likewise, love between women is "strange and new [estrange et nouvelle]."[12] This emphasis on newness is all the more significant given the fact that these men steeped in classical learning might have been expected to link female intimacies to the received intelligence of Juvenal, Martial, Lucian, Ovid, and Sappho rather than rupturing the sapphic from that past.[13] Indeed, this investment in the modernity of relations between women will persist through the eighteenth century. A 1691 dialogue laments the "new Crime" that Sappho is bringing to England that is again claimed as new in 1749. A 1775 journal describes sapphic practices as the only "ancient mysteries" that "our century seems tempted to renew." The 1777 *Laughing Philosopher* lambastes the age for its new tendency to the "Unnatural, unnatural, unnatural! Tommies, Tommies, Tommies!—Women kissing women; doating, languishing, dying, pining, crying, caterwauling, for each other ! . . . We beat all the ancients; nay, the very Jews."[14] And a 1784 secret memoir avers that while tribaderie has always been in fashion, it has never been displayed "with such show and scandal as it is today."[15] In short, the temporality of the sapphic, its tie to its moment for good or ill, is a repeated preoccupation.

The shape of that preoccupation around the turn of the seventeenth century will be the focus of this chapter. By reading in tandem a large body of texts that circulated during the decades around 1600, I will investigate a varied and vigorous discourse that manifests specific geographical contours. I argue that the very range of these representations makes the texts significant for, rather than despite, their confusing and conflicting messages. The specific tropes that cut across the apparent diversity help us understand the cultural work that the sapphic might have performed. Beneath large surface differences among sapphic representations, we can see how questions of habit, alteration, and mobility, and struggles with and against leveling, enable the sapphic to shape a sense of the times. The shared logic that structures these diverse imaginative projections, filtered through the differential modalities of metamorphic, ethnographic, and horizontal formations, also suggests that around 1600 what I have called the sexuality of history may be more coherent than the history of sexuality. I begin, however, with examples that give the flavor of the period's attention to sapphic subjects and that introduce the kinds of texts with which this chapter will be preoccupied.

AROUND 1600: THE QUEER TURN OF A CENTURY

"It was on St. Joseph's Eve, March 18, 1600," proclaims the eponymous narrator of the *Historia de la monja Alférez escrita por mi misma*, that a Basque convent girl allegedly let herself out of the cloister, took scissors to her habit, and turned herself into a boy. The *Historia* details Erauso's proudly patriotic career in Spanish America, soldiering and trading, brawling and gambling, dallying with young women and slipping out when pressed to marry them, until a near-fatal duel prompts Erauso to confess her sex, and then to journey to Rome for papal permission to live as a man.[16] The millennial dating has been proved as inaccurate as it appears precise, and the authenticity of the autobiography has been challenged, but by 1625 two embellished narratives of Erauso's colonial adventures had been published as pamphlets,[17] and in 1626 Juan Pérez de Montalbán's *La Monja Alférez* staged Erauso's story as the conundrum of a woman passing as a man but in love with another woman.

On 4 August 1600, the Chamberlain's Men officially registered *As You Like It*, the first of Shakespeare's comedies to play centrally with female same-sex attraction though not the first to flirt with it. The kind of passion that Rosalind/Ganymede stirs in both Celia and Phebe, doubling the "canonizing" love delineated in its source text, Thomas Lodge's *Rosalynde* (1590),[18] will take a still queerer turn with the twinning of Viola/Cesario and Sebastian in *Twelfth Night* (1602). Shakespeare thus intensifies a pattern of female homoeroticism on the Elizabethan stage that dates at least to Robert Wilson's allegory of sex and money *The Three Ladies of London* (1584) and that forms the core of John Lyly's Ovidian *Gallathea*, in which two cross-dressed young women fall in love, much to the consternation of their fathers, and are enabled to marry when Venus changes one of them into a man (1588).[19]

By 1600, the *mujer varonil* (manly woman) who attracts and sometimes pursues other women was also a pervasive figure on the Spanish stage despite legal and ecclesiastical efforts to prohibit it.[20] The pattern appeared in "concentrated clusters" that virtually every major Golden Age dramatist—Tirso de Molina, Ana Caro, Pérez de Montalbán, Guillén de Castro, Cubillo de Aragón, Calderón de la Barca, and especially Lope de Vega—would exploit. Typically in these plays a woman cross-dresses in order to pursue, avoid, or outsmart a man, making love to women or avoiding their pursuit along the way, but in the end settling down as a willing wife. The still more resistant *mujer esquiva*, sometimes but not always cross-dressed and often committed to the pursuit of learning, was also a prominent figure on the Spanish stage, declaring, as the protagonist of Agustín Moreto's somewhat later play, *El desdén, con el desdén* (1654), puts it epigrammatically, that "to marry and to die are the same [casarme y morir es uno]."[21] Attending public theater in England or Spain around 1600, then, almost surely meant seeing something sapphic on the stage, in the English case queered further since the women were played by men, in the Spanish case rendered perhaps more potent since they were not.

September 6, 1600 marks the death of Mary Barber of Suffolk, whose tombstone, as Alan Bray proposes, may be the first public inscription in modern Europe explicitly to proclaim an intimate female friendship as eternally significant.[22] After Barber's beloved friend the widow Ann Chitting died in 1606, followed soon thereafter by Mary's husband Roger, Ann's son Henry buried the three together in the church of St. James. Mary lies between Ann and Roger, the inscription declaring that the two women "whose soules in heave' imbrace" had "lived and loved like two most vertuous wights" and thus that "whose bodyes death would sever" the son "unites."[23] In so doing, Henry Chitting joins two politically connected families specifically through the heavenly "imbrace" of female friends.

On November 10, 1600, the children of Modesta Pozzo, the Venetian poet who wrote as Moderata Fonte, published the treatise their mother had completed just before her death eight years earlier. In a prefatory poem, Fonte's son Pietro hopes that *Il merito delle donne* will inaugurate a new age where women's "worth" and men's "misdeeds" "will be known from one end of the world to the other." An innovative intervention in the long philosophical debate about the capabilities and rights of women known as the "querelle des femmes," *Il merito delle donne* creates a dialogue among seven friends to show why women "are only ever really happy when we are alone with other women." Intimate professions of attachment among the women, and especially the "amor" between the ambivalent new bride Helena and the unmarried Virginia, underwrite the text's bold claim that "the best thing that can happen to any woman" is to live apart from "the company of men."[24]

In 1600, John Pory published the English translation that made the first European geography of Africa, the 1550 *Descrittione dell'Africa*, available in every major Western European language. Composed by the Grenadan scholar Al-Hassan Ibn-Muhammad al-Fazi known as Leo Africanus, the work describes a group of Moroccan "women-witches," with "a damnable custome to commit unlawfull Venerie among themselves." These "Fricatrices" who "burne in lust" for other women exact a sexual price for their services, but it turns out that some of those wives are "allured" with "delight" for the witches and feign illness so that they might return for a "cure."[25] The *Descrittione* was quickly followed by other works that conjoin the orientalist to the sapphic, most famously Nicolay's *Navigations*, Ogier Ghiselin de Busbecq's widely translated *Legationis turcicae epistolae quattuor* (1589), and Richard Hakluyt's *Principall nauigations, voiages and discoueries of the English nation to the remote and farthest distant quarters of the earth* (1589). Connections between female homoeroticism and witchcraft, already intimated in the widely used prosecutorial handbook *Malleus Maleficarum* (1486), become explicit in Jean Bodin's *De la démonomanie des sorciers* (1580), which claims that "when the devil is not available," witches "seek out young women and girls whom they exploit in the manner attributed to Sapho."[26]

Before 1600, anatomical science had begun producing a copious investigation of girls who could "turn into" boys, creating a dominant strand of sapphic etiology that would endure well into the eighteenth century. André Du Laurens's influential *Historia anatomica humani corporis* (1599), which quickly made its way across the European continent, offered a head-to-toe "anatomical history" of the sexual body that presaged such works as Rodrigo de Castro's *De universa mulierum morborum medicina* (1603), Jacques Duval's *Traité d'hermaphrodits* (1612), Jean Riolan's *Discours sur les hermaphrodits* (1614), and Helkiah Crooke's *Mikrokosmographia* (1615). Although Riolan disputed Duval on whether hermaphrodites existed,[27] both treatises follow the logic of Ambroise Paré's influential "Des monstres es prodiges" (1573) in linking female homoeroticism to an enlarged clitoris which, as Du Laurens opines, "grows so excessively in some women that it hangs out of the opening like a man's penis, and such women play with each other and are, for that reason, called tribades and fricatrices."[28] Juan Huarte de San Juan's 1575 *Examen de ingenios para las ciencias* argues, in a parallel Aristotelian vein, that excessive heat or cold during pregnancy creates feminine males and masculine females who are usually drawn to persons of their own sex. In a related project, Antonio de Torquemada's *Jardin de flores curiosas* (1570) furthered an incipient ethnography that catalogued the curiosities of "women who have been converted into men [conuertido en hombres]," citing both classical and modern instances in a compendium that would confront the world's diversities.[29]

By 1600, portions of Pierre de Bourdeille, seigneur de Brantôme's gossipy *Recueil des dames*, begun in 1582 though not printed until the 1660s, may have been circulating among his friends at court to provide a more local ethnography. While harking back to the rhetoric of Martial and Lucian, Brantôme emphasizes a modern moment in which "ladies and Lesbians" are sometimes synonymous and *"donna con donna"* an import from Italy by "a lady of rank" attached to the powerful queen regent Catherine de Médicis.[30] Piling example upon example, Brantôme provides a kind of sapphic census of court culture that implies a wide range of practices and an equally wide number of practitioners, some merely dabbling, others exclusively lesbian.

Between 1590 and 1600 the Spanish poet and scholar Fray Melchor de la Serna produced his elaborate narrative poem "El Sueño de la viuda," in which a widow who sleeps each night between her maidservants Teodora and Medulina finds herself directed in a dream to mount her husband, mistakes the "varonil" Teodora for the departed spouse, and begins making love to the sleeping maid who then miraculously sprouts a penis. After Teodora grows "weary and tired [laso y fatigado]" from night after sleepless night of mandatory performance, however, the two maids put an end to their mistress's sex life by substituting the "more delicate and feminine [mas delicada y femenina]" Medulina for Teodora, duping the widow to believe that the maidservant's penis has disappeared.[31] The triumphant maids—figures not unlike their contemporary *pícaros* in outwitting their employer—end up as a couple, Teodora having impregnated Medulina though she is still a woman. This sort of poetic ribaldry appears in other Golden Age writings such as Serna's 1792 "Hallándose dos damas," which burlesques women who try to have sex with one another without what the poet considers the right equipment.[32]

Soon after 1600, accounts of arrests for same-sex marriage began to appear in Dutch trial records. As Rudolf Dekker and Lotte van de Pol describe the initial instance, Maeijken Joosten, wife and mother of four, courted a young woman named Bertelmina Wale, convinced Bertelmina "that she was really a man," then "extracted a promise of marriage from her" and "got her into bed."[33] The couple married in Leiden on 8 March 1606, but in October Joosten was tried for sodomy and sent into exile in the first of several such prosecutions in the Netherlands. In a broader tendency, written injunctions against sex between women had been stepping up. Charles V explicitly amended the Holy Roman Empire's Constitution in 1532 to include in its sodomy laws "impurity" committed "by a woman," as did Augsburg in 1537 and the Spanish *Siete Partidas* revised by Gregorio López in 1555. In 1574 Treviso prescribed burning at the stake after a twenty-four-hour public exhibition for any girl or woman over twelve years of age who had sex with another woman; in 1602, the Portuguese colony of Brazil likewise made sodomy between women an explicit crime; and Gregorio García, writing in 1604, thought it worth mentioning that the Indians of New Spain punished women who "laid down" with women just as they punished men.[34]

Between 1597 and 1601 John Donne composed his startlingly frank "Sapho to Philaenis," a poem more graphic than Tyard's "Elégie" and similar poems by Ronsard, or such later works as Andrew Marvell's "Upon Appleton House." Donne's Sappho imagines love between women as founded on an idyllic similitude even as she mourns the unrequitedness of her desire. Donne is associated too with the first known use of "tribade" in written English: as Harriette Andreadis notes, a private poem sent to Donne by "T.W." [probably Thomas Woodward] in the early 1590s suggests the play of their muses as "chaste and mistique tribadree."[35]

In 1601 the word "tribade" entered English print not simply as an epithet but as a metaphor by way of Ben Jonson's elliptical usage. In a section of "The Forest," Jonson represents a poet in search of his "owne true Fire" as rejecting one muse after another including the three graces, whom he characterizes as a "Tribade *Trine*."[36] Similarly, in 1609 Jonson will accuse his intellectual rival Cecilia Bulstrode of "forcing a muse" with "tribade lust."[37] If the first printed French instance of "tribade" proclaimed the word inadequate to the modern moment, this first printed English instance suggests a logic quite specifically modern by which "tribade" is linked not to sex between women but to women's literary usurpation of men, suggesting that by 1601 the term has enough currency to carry complex figural significance.

What, beyond the happenstance of dating, might connect these disparate textual scenarios, variously alluring, accusing, analytic, and anxious, that I have gathered into a kind of centennial cornucopia? I do not bring them together to proclaim an originary moment that would deny either the rich "lesbian premodern," as an excellent collection names it,[38] or the Arabo-Muslim openness to "the tradition between women in the game of love" that Sahar Amer traces to the twelfth century.[39] Nor do I mean to imply connections from text to text even within a single culture or genre. Rather, by focusing on a period that seems to provide the most intense node of preoccupation with sapphic subjects in Christian Europe since the Roman Empire, I hope to understand why, during these decades, Europeans in several—but, importantly, not all—countries, writing in multiple discursive spheres, conjure female same-sex desire a feature of modern life that calls for consideration or comment, ending what Helmut Puff has called a discursive "politics of silence" imposed on female, even more than on male, homoerotic acts.[40] Reaching something of a "tipping point" by 1600, these writings place in ironic context the gauntlet Joseph Swetnam threw down when he tossed off his grammatically pointed comment that "men I say *may* live without women, but women *cannot* live without men" (my emphasis). Of course Swetnam's need to make such a proclamation, and in a widely reprinted treatise, already suggests the vulnerability of his claim.

I will suggest in this chapter that sapphic representations intensify around 1600 to become harbingers of social concerns about mobility, change, and incipient leveling. In imagining the possibility that women *could* effectively "live without men," actively in the world rather than behind the walls of a cloister, these representations unmoor deep cultural assumptions about social organization even when such accounts seem intended, like Swetnam's, to preserve the status quo. And while a profound challenge to gender hierarchy is its most obvious implication, the early modern preoccupation with sapphic subjects points to a wider disruption of the imaginary that exposes the sign *woman* as a critical social anchor. The resulting episteme suggests not only the radical autonomy of a subordinate caste but the potential demise of caste itself.[41] Analyzing the geographic distribution of these representations, as I will attempt at the end of this chapter, may also help us to understand the social, political, economic, and cultural factors that might explain the textual contours of this material.

There are strong scholarly precedents and evidentiary grounds for recognizing the period around 1600 as one of intensified preoccupation with gender transgressions in both discourse and material life. Claims supporting a "renaissance of lesbianism," to use Valerie Traub's resonant phrase, have been advanced by Marie-Jo Bonnet for France, Sherry Velasco and Adrienne Martín for Spain, and Harriette Andreadis, Denise Walen, and Traub herself for England.[42] Ruth Gilbert, Patrick Graille, Joseph Harris, and Lorraine Daston and Katharine Park all date to 1600 an intensified preoccupation with hermaphrodites,[43] while Dianne Dugaw and Kathryn Schwarz see a more intense flourishing of "warrior women" and "Amazons" respectively.[44] Alan Hunt identifies a transition around 1600 in the application of sumptuary laws from a focus on men's dressing across class to women's dressing across gender and argues that such laws were "enforced overwhelmingly against women,"[45] a claim that dovetails with

the discovery by Rudolf Dekker and Lotte van de Pol that in the Netherlands legal attention to female cross-dressing "appeared rather suddenly
at the end of the sixteenth century."[46] It may not be coincidental that the
querelle des femmes also intensifies around 1600 with a spate of French,
Italian, Spanish, Dutch, and English texts.[47] And of course Michel Foucault famously argued for 1600 as a watershed not only in European ways
of understanding hermaphrodites and other "anormaux" but in ways of
understanding understanding itself.[48] What Foucault does not acknowledge but the historical record strongly suggests is the extent to which the
weight of these discursive preoccupations falls on women, particularly in
cases where transgressions of gender and sexuality converge, even though
the weight of moral and legal sanction for sodomy falls with heavy dis-
proportion on men. The differential attention to women's gender transgressions seems readily explained, since the possibility that men might
become or displace women, a move that would entail a massive loss of
power and privilege, is so illogical within the early modern imaginary as
to be epistemically insignificant.[49] But reasons for the *increase* in that differential attention to women are less obvious.

The tacit scholarly consensus that around 1600 Europe paid intensified
attention to female transgressions including the sapphic dovetails with
the period's own perception of newness that I described at the beginning
of this chapter. Sex between women, once emphatically a *peccatum mu-
tum* with its details routinely expunged even from trial records, is now
getting a literally closer look as a more particularized discourse separates
sapphic relations from other "sins against nature."[50] This new specificity is borne out by the linguistic trail as words designating or implicating
sapphic behaviors enter European vernaculars,[51] sorting out sex between
women from "unnatural acts" in general and from the male-normative
category of sodomy. I have already documented early print appearances of
"tribade" in Italy in 1538, France in 1565 and 1566, and England in 1601.[52]
Both "buzerones" and "fregatores" have been noted in Italian usage by the
1570s, and "fricatrice" appears in al-Fazi's 1550 *Descrittione*; "bujarrona"
and "tribada" turn up in Spanish sources by 1603. "Frigarelle" can be seen
by 1583 in a French translation of Lucian's dialogues and appears in English by 1621, while the *Oxford English Dictionary* dates "sodomitesse" to
1611. That "tribade," "fricatrice," and "hermaphrodite" join "sodomite" to
count as epithets with metaphoric resonance for faults not literally sexual,
also augurs a new significance for the sapphic as an idea that means both
more and less than sexual practice.[53] The production of nouns also points
to a willingness within the cultural imaginary to attach subject names—

that is, words designating persons—to perceived behaviors in ways that give more than discursive resonance to the notion of "sapphic subjects" that I have been deploying here in a more restricted, topical sense.

It is also important to recognize that this varied representational project proceeds even as the law seems to have intensified its reach: the period when print representations of the sapphic increase in number, variety, and range seems also have been the peak period for legal prosecutions, if with a somewhat different geographical mapping. Women unprotected by rank who ran afoul of the law for alleged sexual congress with women fared badly and often fatally—particularly in the period between 1560 and 1630 for which I am claiming a more complex and often more benign *textual* interest in sapphic subjects.[54] This does not necessarily mean a dramatic opposition between material and textual practices, for we have almost no evidence of the extrajuridical social sanctions against women suspected of homoerotic alliances or, conversely, of instances when such women lived unharmed or even tacitly supported; as Dekker and van de Pol remind us, "toleration . . . tends to leave fewer traces in the archive than its opposite."[55] The legal picture has sometimes led scholars to explain away the mixed discursive one either by emphasizing negative representations, by claiming that what was not condemned must have been presumed "platonic," or by attributing a queer identity or agenda to the author of a "positive" text. Although I will admittedly be giving scant attention to legal accounts, they share with other representations some deep preoccupations, most notably with mobility and alteration, that sharpens our sense of the work that sapphic subjects are doing.

Despite the rich proliferation of research focused on specific texts and textual clusters that I have litanized in this chapter, no demonstrable chains of influence have yet accounted for the new plenitude. As I noted in chapter 1, there is no evidence that the female transvestite, with its sapphic nuance, crossed from the Spanish to the English stage or that Ronsard's and Tyard's love poems catalyzed John Donne's.[56] More significantly, there is almost no proof of relations across different discursive fields—no evidence, for example, as Stephen Greenblatt both acknowledges and arguably masks in his widely read "Fiction and Friction," that in imagining *Twelfth Night* Shakespeare drew on the story of Marie/Marin le Marcis or the execution of a "female husband" that Montaigne records in his journal.[57] And while many instances of sapphic representation stem from shared antecedents in Martial, Juvenal, and especially Ovid, the new popularity of these particular classical sources is not thereby explained. In short, the intensified production of sapphic representation that I have identified in the decades around 1600 is not plausibly attributed to intertextual influence; indeed influence, particularly across discursive domains, might have produced more coherent surfaces. Instead, there is so wide a diversity in the tenor of sapphic representations, sometimes even within a single text (Brantôme's *Recueil*, for example), that we clearly cannot explain the intensified interest in the sapphic through a logic of either universal opprobrium or pre-heteronormative fluidity. If on the whole, the texts are more curious than critical, more fascinated than shocked, on the surface more matter-of-fact than morally freighted, ideological questions hover at the edges of instances that range from the identification of individuals, whether gleeful (Brantôme) or spiteful (Jonson), to allegations about specific groups ("Turkish women," "gentlewomen of the court"), to burlesques about sex between women (Serna), to relatively neutral expositions (Torquemada and many of the anatomists), to idyllic revaluations (Donne, Fonte) and a smattering of indignant exposés (al-Fazi, Bodin). The aggregate suggests less a preoccupation with judgment than an insistent interest in what relations between women might signify.

The lack of surface coherence is counterbalanced, I argue, by the more unified deep logic of these texts. I turn now to ask how that logic reveals collective cultural investments and shared strategies of engagement. Scholars have richly demonstrated the ways in which many of these varied texts, genres, or national practices position the sapphic within an early modern history of sexuality rich in language and wide-ranging in contour. My inverted focus asks what these diverse representations say not so much about the sapphic itself as about the social impetus for making sapphic subjects so legible in this moment and about how that legibility gets articulated, deployed, and resolved through metamorphic, ethnographic and horizontal modalities.

CHANGING HABITS: THE DEEP LOGIC OF SAPPHIC MODERNITY

Diverse as they are, the representations I gather here undermine dichotomies even when they might seem bent on doing otherwise; they cannot be mapped easily along lines of criminal vs. ideal or sexual vs. chaste, let alone natural vs. unnatural or even feminine vs. masculine. In seeking their deeper logic, then, it is useful to remember that intimacies alleged innocent were often rewritten in sexual terms, as a corporeal lexicon of intimacy pulled the chaste toward the erotic even as an idealizing lexicon pulled the erotic toward the chaste. When, for example, the Barber/Chitting tombstone aims to unite those "whose bodyes death would sever" and "whose soules in heaven" now "imbrace," we face the kind of language that, as Alan Bray among others has argued, "can be read *both* as asserting . . . chastity . . . *and* as rejecting it."[58] Indeed, when texts take the trouble to use words such as "chaste" and "innocent" to describe intimate relations, we can infer at least an anxiety of interpretation if not a defensive or ironic stance. Moreover, what might count as chaste or lewd is itself inconsistent. With more or less the same knowledge, for example, Firenzuola's focus on mutual respect places Margaret of Austria and Laudomia Forteguerri among virtuous couples, while Brantôme's focus on physicality charges those same women with an "unholy" [*lascif*] love disguised by fine language.[59] Ronsard's Sappho describes her love emphatically as "chaste" and yet proclaims to her beloved that "you are the Mistress of my body [quand de mon corps vous estes la Maistresse"], and when that same Sappho vows that she and her beloved "have only one common body," so that "I am in you and you are in me with a knot so tightly tied you can never forget me without forgetting yourself,"[60] we might smile at the sleight-of-hand that evades the question of sexual congress by reducing two bodies to a singularity—and think too of Helena's "passionate" words to Hermia in *Midsummer Night's Dream* that figure the sisters as two berries "moulded on one stem" with "two seeming bodies, but one heart" (3.2.211–12).[61] In yet other instances of collapsed boundaries, Donne's "Sapho to Philaenis" renders blatantly sexual a relationship that the poem also renders idyllic; the womanizing Catalina de Erauso is lauded, like so many cross-dressed soldiers, for preserving her virginity as a woman among men; and the intimate friends of Fonte's *Il merito delle donne* are described as "virtuous" and "discreet" at precisely the moment when their "kissing and embracing" is reported. The erotic lurks likewise beneath innocent surfaces in Lyly's *Gallathea*, as Cupid implicates the (courtly) audience by vowing to "see whither faire faces be alwaies chast."[62] Conversely, the vociferous André Thevet, writing in 1584, defends (his constructed) Sappho by claiming that if she is "guilty of that horrid crime which is laid to her charge," then the same might be concluded about "all women in general who frequent company."[63] These texts seem to be recognizing that the relationship between sapphic sexuality and chastity is already queer and to be suggesting that the absence or presence of a sexual act is not necessarily the defining issue.

Indeed, when we begin to probe just what it is that draws attention, we discover that most of the texts show small interest in isolated sex acts—in some contradistinction, perhaps, to the treatment of male sodomy.

Certainly when Brantôme talks about *donna con donna* and *fricarelle* as
something women *do*, he exposes the centrality of performance in the
making—or rather the self-making—of the lesbian; in this sense, Valerie
Traub's view of the homoerotic in early modernity as "a position taken
up" operates quite literally.[64] And when Estienne proclaims the "girl from
Fontaines" to be modern, it is her behavior, not her "self," that he considers distinctive: "For this *act* has nothing in common with those of the
sordid ones who were called *tribades* in ancient times" (my emphasis). As
importantly, the act in question is quite clearly the young woman's way
of life rather than a single sexual instance. Likewise, in the aggregate of
these representations, the textual emphasis falls on repeated practice, and
practice, in turn, becomes the ground for applying subject names to particular women. Sapphic subjects are predicated, in other words, on a certain
consistency or continuity of behavior: the "tribade" by whatever name is
one who makes same-sex relations or interests a practice for which she is
known. Brantôme's ladies, Donne's Sapho, Lyly's Gallathea and Phyllida,
Serna's triad, Estienne's female husband, are all are engaged in repetitive
iterations of deed or desire, and what disturbs al-Fazi is the "damnable
custome" of his witches and the tendency of the wives to return to them
repeatedly. In an earlier moment, Fernando de Rojas's (in)famous and influential *Tragicomedia de Calisto y Melibea*, familiarly known as *La Celestina* (1499), makes the same point from the inverse angle when Celestina propositions the lovely Areusa on behalf of Pármeno, in a scene with
its own homoerotic layers, and assures Areusa that "a single act does not
make a habit [un solo acto no haze hábito]."[65]

It is thus useful to consider the resonant concept of habit proposed in
a different context by Mariana Valverde as a way to bridge the proverbial
distinction between acts and identities. Habit, Valverde emphasizes, "is
more than an act: it is a pattern, an indefinite series of acts. But it is less
than an identity."[66] More than mediating a scholarly bifurcation grounded,
as David Halperin has persuasively argued, in an oversimplification of
Foucault,[67] the notion of habit shifts the focus from the singulative to the
iterative and from isolated actions to ways of living in time and space,
whether in a material world or a represented one. It is perhaps not accidental that the *Oxford English Dictionary*'s denotation of habit as "a settled
disposition or tendency to act in a certain way, especially one acquired by
frequent repetition" emerges in just this period from its longstanding connection to dress, and of course where the sapphic is concerned, the sexual
habit may be accompanied by a sumptuary habit as well. At a historical
moment when both Aristotelian and Augustinian emphases on what John

Stephens calls "customary habit" are seen to form a cornerstone of character, the notion of the sapphic as habitual gives it a new *gravitas*.

The emphasis on repeated or continuing action in so many of the texts circulating around 1600 suggests that cultural interest in the sapphic is focused less on sexual behaviors than on their attendant social effects. Such a recognition might help to explain the tension in this body of writings between virulence and nonchalance, for the sapphic habit yields a particular configuration, and confusion, around fixity and change: on the one hand, as a repeated practice, it instantiates a disconcerting stability; on the other, as an unexpected outcome that usually depends on an unpredicted turn, it carries the anxieties of unanticipated and uncontrollable change. It is fair to say that in this period alteration is more often unwelcome than embraced: if late modern societies tend to "take continuing change for the better as axiomatic," Anthony Upton reminds us that "most Europeans in 1600 did not share this view"; to the contrary, "change, mutability, [and] interference with a traditional order of things which they believed had stood unchanged for centuries" were "evils to be avoided."[68] And certainly change might be especially confounding when it implicated members of the social order, not least women, on whose predictable positions the system relied. The world of 1600 might well have shared the consternation of Serna's altered maid Teodora: "I am so changed in shape / that I cannot recognize my own self. / Of what I am now, I know nothing."[69] If Mario DiGangi is right to suggest that "female-female sex *per se* did not have the potentially disorderly social consequences of male-female sex," he is right only when we emphasize that *per se* of the single act.[70]

It is the concern about change, I suggest, that leads so many of the sapphic texts produced around 1600 to raise questions of etiology that seem to have little direct parallel in early modern thinking about sodomy. Four relatively distinct explanatory frameworks emerge as ways to account for sudden or surprising instances of the sapphic; implicitly, these rubrics ask whether sapphic habits are a minority practice or a universal possibility and thus seem to be gauging how, and how far, the sapphic figures as an agent of change. The period's four dominant explanations—anatomy, circumstance, inclination, and contagion—extend confusions already evident in the classical sources from which many of these discourses, whatever their claims to being modern, take their cue. I rehearse them here not so much for their value in understanding the construction of sexuality as for their ability to illuminate the ways in which early modern writers might account for the epistemically unaccountable. It is worth noting that causality is often sought in retrospect, after sapphic behavior is perceived,

further underscoring the tenuousness of the etiological narratives. Sometimes, as in the anecdote from Estienne's *Apologie* with which I began
this chapter, causality is not even attempted, creating a silence that only
underscores the impossibility of prediction, understanding, or control. "El
sueño de la viuda," by contrast, posits several possible explanations for Teodora's sudden acquisition of a penis: fate or chance ("fortuna"), planetary
influence, the power of dream, the workings of the mind. But the sign of
that change, whatever its causes, is written on the body.[71]

While Teodora's altered body appears to be consequence rather than
cause, numerous other explanatory accounts give prominence to the body
as the source of female–far more than male—same-sex desire. As Helmut
Puff puts it, "In order to act like a sodomite, a man did not have to be different from other men,"[72] Yet medical discourse in particular, as Katharine
Park has observed, "reveals a persistent inclination to reduce what was
considered deviant female sexual behavior to deviant genital anatomy."[73]
Corporeal explanations vary in their particularities, but their obvious
underlying logic is that the homoerotically desiring woman is somehow
also—or really—in some sense a man. A paradigmatic instance is Torquemada's story, repeated or paralleled in nearly all the anatomical treatises,
of the Portuguese woman Marya Pacheco from whom there suddenly "is-
sued forth" at puberty, "a perfect and able member masculine, so that of
a woman she became a man." Here body determines habit: Pacheco goes
off to the East Indies, makes a fortune, and returns rich enough to marry
a "Gentlewoman of a very Noble house."[74] Such accounts, often shaped
by humoral theories of bodily heat, have the queer effect of normalizing
the aberrant woman by making her an ordinary, even exemplary (physical, social, legal) man—in this instance a colonial entrepreneur far better
behaved than Erauso. For all its specters of women usurping men's roles,
the anatomical argument has the benefit of restricting the sapphic habit to
a minority of masculine or intersex bodies who are simply following their
anatomical bent.[75] In one version of the pattern that I am calling metamorphic, such explanations also effectively nullify the sapphic by transforming same-sex into cross-sex relations, sometimes even against a text's own
internal logic. But often enough the temporality or circumstance of the
transformation undermines the causal argument: thus not only does Teodora's desire for Medulina precede her sex change rather than explain it,
but that change is attributed not to her own desires but to the widow's. In
such ways, anatomical causality is itself undermined by its own representation, and the power of the sapphic remains that of the unexpected, the
unsought, the inexplicable. At the same time, attributing or connecting

the sapphic to sex-change works to stabilize the unstable: almost never, once a woman has "turned into" a man, do imaginative representations enact a reversal, although sometimes legal cases demand a recanting as I suggested in the cases of le Marcis and Céspedes.

Almost equally frequent are texts that attribute sapphic desire to circumstance, foregrounding the unexpected yet again, though usually creating a situation readily resolved. If circumstantial explanations imply a universal polymorphous eroticism, they also suggest how easily that eroticism can be socially channeled. Serna's bawdy "Hallándose dos damas" sets the pattern: two girls try to have sex with each other, fail laughably, and are rescued when Amor turns up to insert his arrow.[76] All-female spaces such as the convent or the harem are of course common circumstantial settings, as are scenarios in which women passing as men for economic or social rather than erotic reasons (soldiering, for example, or fleeing an arranged marriage) allow themselves to become entangled romantically with women in order to sustain their subterfuge. More systemically challenging is the "circumstance" of male dominance itself, made vivid in Tyard's "Elégie" or Fonte's *Il merito delle donne*, where women come together because of what they see as the failings of men. In most cases, however, the circumstantially sapphic habit can be overcome by the simple expedient of introducing (the right kind of) male figure, who is usually assumed to be preferred. Later in this chapter I will explore the ubiquity, particularly on the stage, of this metamorphic strategy that embeds the sapphic even further in a dynamic of change. Circumstantial sapphic scenarios, indeed, have the benefit of suggesting the power of a reasserted social order: they provide the comforting possibility that a challenge—not least from women—can be contained or reversed. Both the anatomical and the circumstantial accounts of same-sex desire follow what I introduced in chapter 1, and will describe more fully below, as metamorphic modalities: they readily turn same-sex into cross-sex relations by changing either the sex of the desirer or the sex of the desired.

Two other causal models, respectively of inclination and contagion, are significantly less common around 1600 and, not incidentally, significantly more threatening because they foreground the resistance of same-sex desire to cross-sex amelioration and construct the sapphic as that which exceeds or evades control. Claims that some women simply have a sapphic inclination, infrequent at this time but soon to increase, are potentially more disturbing than bodily and circumstantial explanations because they render the sapphic an unaccountable predilection—what the physician Jacques Ferrand, writing in *Traicté de l'essence et guérison de l'amour ou mélancholie érotique* (1610), considered a change "rather of temperament and habit" than of sex.[77] Such representations leave unsettled the question of who might have homoerotic interests, when those interests might surface, and, most troublingly, whether or how they might be amenable to rechanneling. An inclination model also underlies Brantôme's efforts to distinguish women who are exclusively lesbian—his word—from those who dally with both women and men; his court features women who simply prefer "donna con donna," and who are also "braver and more courageous than others . . . as much in body as in soul."[78] We see inclination suggested in "El sueño de la viuda" insofar as Teodora and Medulina are attracted to one another well before Teodora's sex-change. Nearly all representations of Sappho as sapphic likewise adhere to inclination: as in Donne's poem, Sappho's own "fires" are what "draw" her toward Philaenis. Etiologies of inclination hover too over Ovidian works like Lyly's *Gallathea*, where the attachment between Phyllida and Gallathea is not detoured, as are the attachments of so many Shakespearean characters, by the revelation that both "boys" are actually women. Al-Fazi's witches are similarly drawn by inclination to sapphic "venerie."

Representations that attach the sapphic to cross-dressing, a practice with economic and social as well as sexual motivations, often render causal chains uncertain: is sapphic inclination a motive for or a byproduct of passing as male? Inclination ultimately seems paramount, for example, in the story of the convicted female husband put to death at Montier-en-Der that Montaigne records in his 1580 *Journal de voyage* and that Greenblatt takes up in relation to *Twelfth Night*. One of several girls from the town of Chaumont who "conspired to dress themselves as men and to live that way in the world," Mary—or *mari*—marries another woman but is then discovered and condemned to death. Montaigne underscores the inalterability of Mary's inclination when he reports that the accused said she would rather die "than go back to the condition of a girl."[79] While occasionally, and especially in orientalist accounts, inclination is seen as simply the sign of a fixed disposition—as in the case of the witches described by al-Fazi and Bodin—most texts follow Montaigne's agnostic view in suggesting that certain women simply tend toward a deviation that is never clearly identified as one primarily of sexuality or primarily of gender. The Dutch trial records of women like Joosten are likewise nonplussed: how to explain that one day, without warning, a wife named Maeke announces herself to be "Abraham" and looks for a wife of her own?

Clearly the fourth explanatory framework, that same-sex desire can be transmitted through influence or contagion, embodies the most fully universalizing threat. Thus al-Fazi's wives are not just inclined toward the witches but seem to have been transformed by them; that they keep returning to the witches, who have in a sense infected them, may be a particularly potent claim in an age of little-understood physical contagions, all the more as al-Fazi describes the wives as feigning illness so they can be "cured" by sapphic witchery. Sapphic contagion is often articulated as cross-national: Brantôme suggests that Italian women brought *donna con donna* to the French court and spread the practice like a disease, just as other texts locate cities and countries in and beyond Europe as carriers of sapphic (as sometimes also of sodomitical) sentiments; thus Nicolay sees the baths themselves as a circumstantial setting where women also, however, are drawn to linger and to return. This notion that sapphic desire is in effect both contagious and habit-forming dramatizes the possibility that any woman might fall prey to it. Especially given the extent to which the sapphic is displaced onto "other" societies, a contagion model emphasizes the sense of opportunity, whether benign or dangerous, that attends upon a real or perceived new global mobility. If this explanation is the least active of the four frameworks around 1600, theories of contagion and influence will increase over the next century along with models of inclination, especially in class-based configurations, while minoritizing anatomical explanations will decline and circumstantial explanations be challenged. In the episteme of 1600, however, the idea of a universal sapphic potential seems to have been the least imaginable of the alternatives.

Even across their crucial differences, the deeper logic of alteration and the challenge of control connect these four etiological models. Virtually all sapphic texts around 1600 rely on a dynamic of change, most of the time unpredicted and unpredictable, whether to the body, to circumstance, or to desire. Many of the representations figure that change through one specific, startling, quasi-magical moment: a wife puts on men's clothes and "becomes" a husband; a girl's genitals reveal themselves as boyish to an unsuspecting family; a lover taken for male turns out, in a moment of revelation, to be a biological woman. Some texts emphasize the alteration of desire itself: through some unexpected circumstance or logic, a woman cleaves to another woman instead of to a man. Thus alteration coalesces around surprise, emphasizing the unexpected character of the homoerotic, which readily becomes the figure of a social order beyond prediction or control. Moreover, the particular cultural anxiety embedded in the sapphic is not so much about change *tout court* as about the change that creates a temporal and epistemological fissure between what *seemed* or *was* and what *is*. It is a small step from this rupture between past and present to the notion of the sapphic as a break from tradition, tied to the new that is also the now.

We might further refine this focus on alteration by recognizing its tropes of mobility: repeatedly in these representations, and in ways that will intensify in the eighteenth-century novels I explore in chapter 5, the sapphic subject is a subject on the move. Like Estienne's female husband, the Joosten of the trial texts, the Catalina de Erauso of the pamphlets, even the women who gather in Fonte's garden, sapphic subjects travel and relocate, often ending up elsewhere from where they began, in a dynamic that links change of habit to change of place, often further distancing the transgressive woman from local control. Some texts evoke settings of pastoral wandering; many others, the self-reinvention enabled by urban anonymity, in plots often tied to the trauma of discovery by someone who knew the "man" when she was a woman; still others place the sapphic in an exotic elsewhere. As I have suggested, sapphic subjects are frequently located in settings already marked with cultural ambivalence, with particular countries and cities set up as carriers to (other) European sites: Brantôme's Italy, represented as both a site of (high) culture and a zone of promiscuity; Fonte's Venice as a commercial and cultural crossroads that is also teeming with every sort of foreigner; colonial outposts as a receiving ground for impersonators like Erauso; Nicolay's Turkey as an imperial rival and cultural elsewhere at Europe's edge that will take on a particular role in the construction of sapphic subjects vis-à-vis the state, as I will show in chapter 3. In a less literal sense, the sapphic imaginary around 1600 is itself a kind of foreign country peopled by strange creatures of uncertain anatomy, morality, or psychology, often therefore figured as foreign agents who invade the home space and reveal its unexpected underside. Sapphic representations are often preoccupied with rank, more fully at this historical juncture with the highest and lowest ends of the social spectrum than with the middle, and sometimes especially concerned with relations between upper- and lower-class women or with the implications of the sapphic as a mechanism of class mobility. We see rank at work both in Brantôme's court culture, where lesbianism is an aristocratic practice, and in the rural worlds of Foye and Montier-en-Der, where female husbands hide out; we see contests around class most obviously at work in "El sueño de la viuda," where female desire becomes the site for class struggle; and the authority claimed by Fonte's female friends is underwritten by their gentleclass standing. But if these early representations emphasize separation on the ground of class, representations over the next century will often foster a kind of mixity that challenges these neat divisions of station.

I have already suggested that the proliferation of generic forms, textual attitudes, and explanatory frameworks in these aggregated representations renders the sapphic far more a conundrum to be examined than simply a practice to be condemned. And where tropes of alteration, mobility, and uncertainty gather, it is not surprising to find the logic of narrative, indeed of what might sometimes seem to be narrative for its own sake. Virtually all the examples that I have mentioned in this chapter, even those that seem temporally static, embed a story, whether factual, fanciful, or counterfactual. We find narrative implications not only in Estienne's anecdote but in Pontus de Tyard's poem of unrequited desire. The medical accounts base their conclusions on tales about girls who become boys, and the legal documents construct life stories of deceptive marriage and its detection. Donne's elegiac "Sapho to Philaenis" embeds both an erotic fantasy and a kind of courtship plot; Serna's long poem is a narrative account of sexual triangulation; and Brantôme's chapter on *donna con donna* is a pastiche of anecdotes. Even Jonson's reference to the *"Tribade* Trine" embeds a narrative injunction to "go . . . invent new sports."

In this sense, it is fair to say that around 1600 sapphic discourse *is* story even when the discourse is also lyric poetry, medical treatise, or theatrical performance, and it is indeed the replication of particular narrative elements that creates the thread of continuity among these diverse texts. This claim does not, of course, deny the existence of pronouncements and dicta, whether legal, social, philosophical, or ecclesiastical. But the dominant impulse of these representations is an impulse to tell that enfolds imperatives of action and alteration, imperatives that may help to explain why, in an age when—at least in Spain and England—story finds its most pervasive and public outlet on the stage, the potential for intimacies between women is so much exploited there. And to the extent that the early modern sapphic subject is formed through habitual action and is thus effectively self-made, the sapphic arguably demands a certain narrative continuity for its representation. This conjunction between the sapphic and narrative thus suggests not only the necessity of story for constituting early modern sapphic subjects but also the potential significance of the sapphic in the development of modern narrative itself, a topic I will pursue more fully in chapter 5. Moreover, as I noted with respect to Estienne's anecdote, there is a strong realist imperative in these sapphic representations even beneath what is sometimes a recourse to the marvelous, as if pinpointing the axes of the sapphic in time and space will serve as a way to understand and perhaps control it. In this light, the attention to female homoeroticism in travel discourses and proto-anthropological writings suggests a need to provide the details that confer credibility on the "wonder" that female homoeroticism is so often seen to represent.

That the anecdote has a privileged place in the prose genres of sapphic representation, not only around 1600 but throughout the period encompassed by this book, also bears comment. It is fair to say that the anecdote renders the sapphic discursively portable, in a generic mirroring of the mobility of the sapphic figure herself: sapphic stories become detachable narrative, both insertable and extractable, relocatable to almost any discursive field in the company of almost any other subject, rendering the sapphic the ready agent of other political, social, and cultural projects. Generically speaking, then, there is no better emblem for the modern work of the sapphic than the ubiquity and flexible utility of the anecdote. It needs to be said, however, that the "packaging" work of the anecdote that Mary Baine Campbell underscores with respect to colonial representations is arguably enacted here too in the discursive violence of reduction.[80]

CONFRONTING THE SAME IN "SAME-SEX": THREE MODELS

That early modernity figures change through the mobile bodies of women is particularly significant as a sign of the times, for clearly the movement of women is troubling in a world in which women are (supposed to be) legally and socially anchored to the men who "own" them. By embodying the possibility that female same-sex relations might suddenly alter that expected order, representations of the sapphic abandon a (collective) regime of duty in favor of a (personal) regime of desire and, in the process, begin undercutting centuries of religious, social, and legal ideology that privileges the needs of polities—and of men—over those of individuals—and of women It may well be the relationship between these competing values that gives the sapphic such charge. Female homoeroticism intervenes in a religious tradition by which women's very existence is predicated on their relation to men; to evoke Thomas Aquinas, women "should have been made in the first production of things" precisely so that they might be helpmates to men and bearers of children. In this religious paradigm still taken for granted in the sixteenth century, and as the medieval scholastic Peter Abelard put it most openly, nature "created women's genitals for the use of men and conversely, and not so women could cohabit with women."[81] It intervenes likewise in a secular tradition by which coverture subsumes women as legal nonentities and in which, as Peter Stallybrass reminds us, woman is still a category of property, so that "wife, maid, ox, and ass" can be listed together "as a man's assets."[82] Both imaginatively and materially, then, female-female alliances and the attendant movements of women disrupt the most basic assumptions about why women exist and represent the ascendance of individual will over social prescription in a manner dramatic enough to force the reconception of a caste. What François Fourquet describes as the social conflict between the potency of desire—"the very mode of life"—and the repressive social forces bent on preserving equilibrium and productivity is writ large when women are dislocated from what is perceived not only as their proper place but as their singular *raison d'être*.[83]

In this way, the sapphic becomes a logical limit case for the promise heralded by Reformationist ideologies that do strive to wed individual will to social prescription by arguing for personal preference over consideration of status, property, and kinship in forming marital ties. In 1560, for example, the Reformed Church of Scotland, recognizing that "the attraction between young people was 'a work of God,'" officially declared that when two young people's "hearts" are "joined," parents should not resist their children's preferences.[84] Sapphic writings imply that the "hearts" of two women might also be so joined, and indeed a Scottish compilation known as the "Maitland Manuscript" that dates before 1586 includes an unsigned poem expressing the speaker's longing to seal her love for another woman with the "bond of Hymen."[85] But because the family was still recognized as "the oldest political society" out of which "emerged all subsequent government," it was also argued, as Keith Thomas notes, that "upon the good management of families" depended the "well-being" of the whole.[86] By implicitly wresting woman from the realm of property into that of subjectivity, then, the sapphic also unmoors the sign "woman" from the sign "man" that has held it in place for centuries. That is why, while I recognize the prominence of what Laurie Shannon calls "Renaissance homonormativity" and will explore in chapter 4 the ways in which women were able to draw upon the period's "almost philosophical preference for likeness,"[87] in terms of social relations and hierarchical systems, homonormativity is still gendered male. That is, it is fair enough to say that around 1600, the primary term linked to man is man. But the primary term linked to woman is also man.

Small wonder, then, that sapphic affinity would be epistemically challenging. The challenge helps to explain the repeated allusion to the sapphic as modern, since as Thomas Kuhn has famously argued, a phe-

nomenon categorically denied can in effect keep presenting itself as new
or even impossible.[88] When Swetnam says that "women cannot live without men," and says so in an England that has literally demolished its monastic spaces, he arguably refuses an independent existence as much to a
signifier as to a referent. It is thus not trivial that, in a textual project of
redirection, female intimacy enters early modern discourse in comments
like Swetnam's that seem to have no other purpose than to refuse a possibility that has not even been raised. In a similar vein, Alexander Niccholes's *Discourse of Marriage and Wiving* (1615), published in the same
year as Swetnam's *Araignment*, deploys a rhetorical question to dismiss—
but in so doing raises—the possibility of female relations, as the speaker
offers his sexual services to a wife while her husband is absent:

> And you, but with your Maide, left all alone.
> Where, least sad Care, or Melancholy, grieve you,
> My best endeavour's ready to relieve you.
> What Female Comfort can one woman finde,
> Within the bed with other woman-kinde?[89]

Women together, perhaps especially when one of them is a servant, are
"all alone," creating the illusion of absence into which the male speaker
discursively—and, he hopes, corporeally—inserts himself. Given the proliferation of sapphic subjects around 1600, Niccholes's question is arguably more than rhetorical; left unanswered, it invites readers to imagine
that "female comfort" could "relieve" the mistress and thus suggests the
potential for a categorical rupture both of gender and class. The mode of
rhetorical question gets repeated, if with less class inflection, in William
Goddard's *Satirycall Dialogue* (1616) when a maiden asks: "Alas, alas, what
pleasure and delight / Takes one mayde with an other in the night?" and
answers that "[F]or trulye (sisters) there is none that can / Give maydes delight in bedd, but a young man."[90] A rather different path toward the same
logic appears in *The Passionate Pilgrime* (1599), where manly advice en-
courages a suitor to use a "golden bullet" against a woman's "feeble force,"
while admitting the emotional benefits of female-female relations: "Were
kisses all the joyes in bed, / One woman would another wed."[91]

If the sapphic figures epistemically the disruptions wrought by mobility and change, then it is also not surprising that representations of
the sapphic often attempt to repair the problem they are producing by re-
anchoring woman to man. The poems I have just cited make that move
on the level of story, but other texts reinstate the excluded male term in

subtler ways, turning texts about women into texts about men so that, at least discursively, a man might enter the sapphic imaginary and alter its logic. These texts write same-sex relations through masculine figures of discourse that attempt to keep the signifier "woman" from floating free. When the female speaker of Pierre de L'Estoile's "La Frigarelle" (1581) insists at once on the femininity of her body and on the masculinity of her desires—"Know that I'm a woman, / No different from women like you / But I have absolutely the desires of a man"—it is man ("homme") that literally gets the last word, as it does again when Jeanne's partner Marie reports that "she tastes a pleasure without equal / And I embrace her too, just like a male."[92] Serna's Teodora likewise ends up with the anatomy to impregnate the woman she had already fancied before her unbidden sex-change. Most dramatically, Brantôme's *Recueil des dames*, even as it focuses emphatically on sex between women ("donna con donna"), reveals a startling incidence of male-centered language: lesbians "imitate men," "don't want to put up with men," approach women "as men do," copulate "like men," "use women more than men do," keep other women from "going to men," do "what men do," and so forth, so that textual practice reinstates what textual content supposedly eliminates.[93] Even Donne's "Sapho to Philaenis" can idealize female same-sex relationships only through contrast to the "rough tillage" of a man. The repeated effect on sapphic representations that circulate around 1600 is to make Swetnam's claim that "women cannot live without men" discursively true. Such textual practices remind us that while relations between men in this period raise questions about status, rank, and chains of (male) authority, relations between women, even when they too evoke issues of status, almost invariably also raise questions about men. The ways in which the early modern imaginary confronts this challenge, this rupture posed by the sapphic, can be mapped along the three modes—respectively metamorphic, ethnographic, and horizontal—that I introduced in the previous chapter; I turn now to those three modalities to assess the practices and potentialities of each, in this early moment, for configuring or containing sapphic agency.

Given the pressure I have been describing to relocate sapphic subjects into a masculine economy, it is not surprising that the most pervasive of all textual strategies for treating sapphic subjects around 1600 is the metamorphic. That is, as sapphic desire and social duty converge and conflict in representation, they do so most frequently, at this point, in an obsessively recurring plot with alteration and mobility as core principles. The metamorphic traces a double move: it instantiates an initial alteration by setting up the *possibility* of woman + woman, and then goes on to turn woman + woman into woman + man, modeling both a problem and its solution. Such a move effectively takes the "same" out of "same-sex," so that on the level of plot—or, failing that, on the level of discourse— sapphic subjects get rewritten in cross-sexed terms. As I have already suggested, the metamorphic plot takes two distinctive forms that operate in somewhat different generic contexts: one plot changes a woman's gender, while the other changes the object of her interest. In an epoch preoccupied with alteration, appearance, and movement, it seems to be necessary not simply to demand a change from same-sex to cross-sex affiliation but to show change as it is happening, even if—or because—that process is often covering a sleight-of-hand. For as many scholars have emphasized, these texts do not necessarily represent the change from same-sex to cross-sex desire as natural; rather, erotic transformation usually requires the kind of intervention and substitution that instantiates the social over the natural. In this sense, one could argue, the primary homonormativity of early modernity does obtain.

The first metamorphic pattern is emblematized in the Ovidian alteration, originally inscribed in the story of Iphis and Ianthe, that turns a woman literally into a man, usually through some means beyond individual control.[94] This scenario is present not only in obvious Ovidian borrowings such as *Gallathea*, in which the gods intervene to enact a sex-change, but also in the medical accounts that describe women who become men through the workings of some "natural" process as well as in the stories of women who cross-dress, change their names, and are socially reborn as men. As I have suggested, such resolutions often make sex-change the consequence rather than the cause of desire, though they may imply that the woman-turned-man is simply stepping into her "true" gender identity. This is the case even with the second, more tractable version of metamorphic plot in which change is wrought not upon the desiring woman but upon the object of her desire. Often a lookalike man—say, a twin brother—substitutes for the woman; or a character in drag is outed. But as scholars have amply noted, the substitution of a cross-gender object or the revelation of "true" sex does not always confirm or complete a concomitant alteration of desire. Thus in Ariosto's *Orlando Furioso* (1533), to take an early and generative example, Fiordispina persists in her passion for the cross-dressed Bradamant even when she knows Bradamant is a woman, so that Bradamant's brother Richardet must woo Fiordispina by pretending to be his own sister magically altered as if in answer to Fiordispina's prayers,[95] a scenario that gets repeated in Villalón's *El Crótalon de Christophoro Gnophoso* (1553) when at first Melisa needs heavy convincing that

the cross-dressed Julieta lacks the phallic equipment Melisa longs for—
and then needs convincing once again that Julieta's brother Julio, pretending to be a transformed version of his sister, is indeed male. Such instances
leave significant homoerotic residue as they emphasize not a change of
desire but a change of circumstance. Nowhere, perhaps, are the intricacies
of homoerotic desire and heterosocial necessity queerer than in *Gallathea*,
which effectively turns two boys into two women and then into man and
woman, "confounding loves" just as its prologue promises. Moreover, *Gallathea* emphasizes the arbitrary relationship between gender and desire by
refusing to say which of the two women will be transformed: the problem
it must resolve is not one of essential sex but of social gender. This comic
plot of sexual transformation, most prevalent in fictional and especially
stage representations, is thus not far in logic from the tragic plot, most
prevalent in legal stories, in which a "female husband" is punished with
imprisonment, exile, or death. In both contexts, it is less the body than
the subject position that is at stake: social arrangements should be cross-
gender even if they are not cross-sex.

One could argue, then, that it is social necessity that propels metamorphic plotting; what matters is not so much that same-sex *desire* be
altered but that cross-sex *affiliation* occur. The ubiquity of this alteration
plot suggests that it is not ultimately same-sex love but same-sex union
that must be circumvented; as Valerie Traub has put it, "the problem posed
by the *amor impossibilis* is less desire itself than the intractability of the
physical body and the body's social function as a legible marker of gender
within the patriarchal organization of reproduction."[96] I stress this point
because it reminds us of the crucial disjunction in the conceptualization
of early modern subjects between institution and desire, between the social and the bounded self. Reinforcing habit over act and form over feeling,
metamorphic texts suggest that the problem is not homoeroticism as such
but its public accommodation. This disjunction is intensified, indeed, by
the fact that so many of these texts display what David Robinson calls
"patriarchal tyranny," adding further onus to the metamorphic resolution
on which the texts nonetheless insist.[97]

It is worth emphasizing the recourse to the miraculous, the deployment of a literal or discursive deus ex machina that shapes so many of
these representations, as symptomatic of a wider *mentalité*. Although humoral theories sometimes lend natural explanations to sexual transformation, most of the metamorphic accounts I have been exploring suggest that
the social imaginary would rather inscribe implausibility than grapple
with the logically simpler but epistemically more challenging prospect

of permanent affiliation between two fully female persons. The appeal of
sex-change resolutions lies in their attempt to stabilize flux and restore
fixity: when girl becomes boy, same-sex eroticism is effectively erased and
the sapphic woman enters the social order as a man; and when girl meets
boy and transfers her affections, same-sex desire is effectively deprived
of social force. Whether the change is held to be the supernatural effect
of divine intervention or the natural effect of the body's own doings, the
sex change cannot simply be willed. To be sure, these metamorphic scenarios leave considerable residue, as I have been suggesting and as scholars who have studied them more closely have made amply clear, and in
later chapters I will turn to some of the more resistant seventeenth- and
eighteenth-century instances of Ovidian plotting and trace the weakening
of metamorphic scenarios. My point here is that the demand around 1600
lies emphatically in the direction of alteration—in effect, an alteration of
the prior alteration that created the unexpected sapphic scenario in the
first place.

The sapphic is more resistant to alteration in the less frequent texts
that I am calling ethnographic, which present the sapphic as a site of observation and discovery, a sphere of anthropological or scientific interest.
These often forego judgment for description, though they are as likely to
dwell, sometimes disapprovingly, on the queerer aspects of female relations or of those who practice them. Through them, we can most easily trace geographical patterns not so much in the sites of origin where
sapphic writings are produced, but in the sites of representation that get
associated with sapphic habits. Brantôme's *Recueil des dames* nicely illustrates an early form of sapphic ethnography, in this case of the French
court, and one that carries a surprising number of ethnography's persistent traits: historical background, expert opinion, reliance on informants,
diverse examples vividly described, eyewitness claims, generalizations
based on multiple cases, and something of a cultural-relativist mien. To
this example we might add other early ventures like Catalina Erauso's
Vida i Sucesos, geographies like al-Fazi's *Descrittione dell'Africa*, com-
pendia like Torquemada's *Jardin*, and fictions like Serna's "El sueño de la
viuda."

Like the travelers' tales that are also increasing in this period, ethnographic representations take something of a wide-eyed view of the "strange"
customs of certain women. And like metamorphic texts but without the
comfort of metamorphic resolution, they often confound gender by locating the sapphic simultaneously in both masculine and feminine subject
positions. Serna's Teodora is a useful emblem for this complication, since

the poem refuses to turn her into a man even after it gives her a penis capable of making Medulina pregnant; she is identified throughout the poem as "she." With similar queerness, the representations that give lesbians a kind of dual male-female status, as does Brantôme's panoply or many of the medical accounts that describe women with some masculine characteristics but set them short of sex-change, likewise suggest the fragility of any effort to stabilize the sapphic in conventional terms. Such texts foster "not just a category crisis of male and female," to evoke Marjorie Garber's well-known words about cross-dressing, "but the crisis of category itself."[98] Ethnographic representations are thus arguably the queerest of the three modes in configuring sapphic subjects as resistant to resolution, the most deconstructive. Where they cannot confine the sapphic to the exceptional instance, they also tend to wring their discursive hands rather than to point toward any sort of solution. Even more unsettlingly than the metamorphic texts, then, ethnographic representations unleash the possibility of pervasive and contagious deviation from norms and structures that will confound enlightenment fixities.

If we place metamorphic and ethnographic representations on a continuum, we can see that metamorphic texts attempt to reinstate the normative while ethnographic texts, in stopping short of resolution, emphasize the incompatibility of the sapphic with social norms. What I call horizontal representations take us in another direction: rather than transforming or confounding same-sex relations, they insist, in effect, on preserving the *same* in same-sex, loosing a pair or group of women upon the world with potentially epistemic implications. It is thus not unexpected that these "leveling" or "horizontal" representations are the least common textual practices around 1600, for they arguably carry the most powerful challenge to the body politic.

LEVELING: A SAPPHIC EPISTEME

The metamorphic slippage of same-sex into sex-change not only marks the textual triumph of duty and convention over disorder and desire that purports to settle the dynamic of alteration, but erases the possibility that the logic of woman + woman can stand alone: even where these texts retain what Valerie Traub calls a "contiguity" between homoerotic and heteroerotic desires, those desires cannot be loosed from a heterosocial matrix.[99] It is thus precisely in the insistence on similitude that I locate what seems to me the most dramatic epistemic challenge that sapphic subjects pose for early modernity: the potential to undermine hierarchical relations. It is a

commonplace that premodern Europe was shaped and governed by a strati-
fied order of "subordination and discipline," that expected its subjects "to
render unquestioning obedience to their divinely ordained superiors and
impose it on those entrusted to their charge."[100] Especially from the sixteenth century, however, it is just this system that the social imaginary
and, to a modest degree, the social order, challenges with horizontalizing
views. In a mercantile, colonizing, urban and reformationist Europe that
had some use for mobility and leveling of place both literal and figura-
tive, we can find horizontalist values in claims that priests do not need
to intercede for the faithful, that sons and daughters may choose their
own spouses, that governments should be consensual bodies rather than
divine-right impositions, that persons are equal by nature and should not
be enslaved, that enterprising commoners deserve a share of wealth and
power, that even "peasants" may revolt.[101] Moreover, print itself produced
and perpetuated a horizontal order by separating words from their authors,
providing literate persons of both sexes with some access to the cultural
authority of elite men, and thus fostering a heteroglossic public sphere beyond control of church or court. Significantly too, it is around 1600 that
we see the first uses of "level" as a figure for parity in human relations,
one that will turn political in mid-century England as "Levelers" attempt
to wrest control of government. It is also around 1600 that the English
words "woman" and "wife" split off from one another after being more
or less synonymous, a coupling that of course lingers in some European
languages even today; thus John Aylmer's *An Harborowe for Faithfull and
Trewe Subjects* (1559) argues that a wife is her husband's subject "in that
she is his wyfe, not in that she is a woman."[102] Leveling allowed Protestant
women to "abuse" "noble churchmen" as "godless men" and servants to
use the Bible against their masters, as Natalie Zemon Davis puts it, reversing hierarchies of class and sex in ways that many deemed monstrous.[103]

Even as horizontal notions began to permeate the social imaginary,
though, gender leveling remained at the political extreme, and the possibility that women might no longer occupy the bottom usually translated
to the specter of women on top. The extent to which gender grounds other
vertical systems is thus evident in the widespread imagery of sex-role reversal, where threats of leveling get rewritten into tropes of "symbolic
inversion"[104] as representations of a *monde renversée* get cast overwhelmingly in terms of gender. That is, even when threats to hierarchy concern
parents and children, masters and servants, or humans and animals, the
dominant trope, and one of "exceptional longevity and [wide] geographical
distribution," is the trope of gender, in which women "grow mankind"

and men turn "effeminate," as Humphrey Crouch put it in 1637.[105] Gender reversals thus end up embodying even "memories of the great medieval peasant revolts, and of nonhierarchical communities destroyed in the feudal and feudal-bourgeois eras."[106] And as Davis argues, although gender play can function as "explicit criticism of the social order," symbolic inversions "are ultimately sources of order and stability"; they "can renew the system, but they cannot change it."[107] Hierarchy thus sustains even most protofeminist discourse; hence, for example, Louise Labé's plea in 1555 that women not be "disdained as *companions*" to "those who govern and are obeyed" even though women themselves are "not made to command."[108] In the face of such views, it is radical enough to propose equality between men and women as marital partners, let alone to claim that women are able to thrive independent of men.

This early modern resistance underscores the radical potential of those few sapphic representations from the years around 1600 that, by insisting on the "same" in "same-sex," embody an irreducible leveling, allowing the subordinate to stand in the place of the dominant not by reverse domination but by deconstructing dominance itself. If we return to my two opening examples, we begin to guess how poorly horizontal dynamics fare in this period. Estienne's ire is directed at a girl who attempts her own metamorphosis, but what condemns her is the revelation that cross-sex is really same-sex. The "peculiar evil" of the age is thus arguably the girl's double move: beneath a hierarchical usurpation we find a horizontality through which a woman dares to take a man's place and thus to level his social position in raising hers. Conversely, it is the assertion of the same in Tyard's poem that opens a utopian imperative by which one woman hoped to create with another a superior form of love but whose desire for that woman is spurned. Both of these texts thus acknowledge the possibility of a horizontal female formation, but neither scenario is presented as materially viable.

This fragility of realization turns out to be true as well of other instances of leveling that present themselves in texts written around 1600. Two projects in particular, those of Moderata Fonte and John Donne, do open promisingly utopian fantasies of sapphic leveling—and, not incidentally, show vividly where biographical approaches to sapphic subjects fall short. Fonte's *Il merito delle donne* marks a dramatic shift from the androcentric and vertical modalities of the *querelle des femmes* launched by Christine de Pizan two centuries earlier. "Sapho to Philaenis" sets itself against androcentric representations of the poet of Lesbos to figure an idyllic intimacy that not only eschews hierarchical difference but creates through the sapphic a more pervasively horizontal world. Both of these texts, however, stop short once more of allowing a sapphic formation to flourish.

Pizan's *Livre de la cité des dames* and its sequel, the *Livre du trésor de la cité des dames* (both 1405) crystallize the distinction between a verticality, however protofeminist, and the sapphic horizontality I have in mind. Pizan claims to populate her "city of ladies" with "an infinite number of women," if not quite "of every background" as the text proclaims.[109] This city is indeed a city of text: its very mortar is mixed in Christine's ink bottle so that writing itself builds the utopian edifice. But Pizan creates this female paradise by cataloguing the heroic ministrations of women on men's behalf, building an atemporal discursive paradise through stories of individual women across time and place. While the text affirms the worth of women, it also decrees that women should remain "subject to your husbands, for sometimes it is not the best thing for a creature to be independent."[110] Those with abusive husbands are asked to be grateful that their husbands are not the worst, while those with husbands beyond reform are promised rewards in the afterlife. Pizan's conduct-book, the *Livre du trésor*, tells women to avoid envying one another or jostling for rank but offers no positive place for female relations; if women should avoid men and seek instead the company of women, that companionability is meant to preserve their virtue, not to foster female alliances.[111]

These strategies set the androcentric tenor of what will become, in Pizan's wake, the long-lasting *querelle des femmes*. Ironically, the vast body of *querelle* discourse necessarily takes men as both its starting and its endpoint; there is no way to measure a woman's worth outside her similarity to men. At best, the *querelle* can engage in symbolic reversal: Lucrezia Marinella's *La nobiltà et eccellenza delle donne co' diffetti et mancamenti de gli huomini* (1591) proposes, for example, that "the experiment of training a good-natured boy and girl of about the same age and intelligence in letters and arms" so as to prove "how much sooner the girl would become expert than the boy and how she would surpass him completely."[112] But Fonte's *Il merito delle donne* works through a different—and in my view sapphic—logic. If arguments for women's excellence worked by comparing women *to* men, arguments for women's independence had to separate women *from* men, a strategy I will explore further in chapter 4. *Il merito delle donne* enacts this shift from the vertical, atemporal, and androcentric configuration of the heavenly City of Ladies to a here-and-now alliance among Venetian women. Despite its conventional title, the worth of women is more or less taken for granted here; the organizing issue is the worth of men. The subjection of women is resoundingly rejected: "when it's said that women must be subject to men," the women joke, "the phrase should be understood in the same sense as when we say that we are subject to natural disasters."[113] Reversing the Aquinian logic, Fonte's women claim that "in themselves," men are "no good for anything" unless they are "united with a wife," except to be "handy around the house" (58). It is not women but men who need to change.

What enables this conversation about men is their absence, and in this sense *Il merito delle donne* creates a space that is both epistemically and, in a muted way, erotically sapphic. Leonora's garden is their "real paradise on earth" (53), a bequest from an aunt who lived "free and alone" and encouraged her niece to do likewise. In this private setting the women "are free to do just as we please;"[114] In an anticipatory reversal of Swetnam, the women claim that it is men who "cannot get by without women"[115] and that "the best thing that can happen to any woman is to be able to live alone, without the company of men" (47).[116] Cornelia calls upon women to "banish these men from our lives" and "claim back our freedom, and the honor and dignity they have usurped from us for so long" (237). None of the women stands up positively for men or marriage; at best, the newlywed Helena is ambivalent; at worst, Corinna will "serve no one; and belong to no one but myself" (49); she would "rather die than submit to a man!" (48).[117] The innovative textual structure of *Il merito delle donne* likewise models a horizontal mode in creating a dialogic community of seven women speakers who together create the culture that makes them full subjects. This culture rests explicitly on ties of affection: the women are "intimate and easy . . . with each other (194) [dimestichezza o convenienza che avemo (136)]", and although they are affirmed to be "chaste," and their friendships proclaimed "discreet" and "virtuous," there is considerable kissing and embracing. On the second morning of their two-day gathering, the women, including Helena the new bride—who arrived on the first morning, straight from her honeymoon, primarily for love of Virginia ["per amor di Verginia (15)]—turn up "almost in time to join [Leonora] in bed" and wish they had done so (119). In short, an erotic teasing underwrites the intimate relationships that, in turn, underwrite communal leveling. And "true friendship, true affinity, is the cause of all good. For it is friendship that keeps the world alive" (128).[118]

Moreover, in a utopian project of broader implications, the horizontal relationship among women is explicitly identified as a model for the just and harmonious society that will ensure that "cities can be built, kingdoms grow to greatness, and all creatures live in comfort" (128), a vision

without which "provinces and families [will be] exterminated, states overthrown, and whole peoples consumed" (129).[119] This is an elite order, to be
sure; all the women are from "the best-known and most respected families of the city and "united by breeding and taste" (45).[120] They see Venice itself as a potential utopia; the text opens with a paean to the noble
"Metropolis of the universe" that "harbors such a great diversity of races
and customs," yet where "an incredible peace and justice reign" (43–44).[121]
Yet present-day Venice is marked as flawed by its man-made government:
"What on earth do magistrates, law courts, and all this other nonsense
have to do with us women? Are not all these official functions exercised
by men, against our interests? . . . Do they not act in their own interests
and against ours? Do they not treat us as though we were aliens? Do they
not usurp our property?" (204).[122] The ultimate paradise lies in Leonora's
garden, at the edge of the Grand Canal, where the women create their own
consensual government—as necessary, they say, in a house as in a city.[123]
And no men may enter there.

  Nor may men enter the private world of John Donne's imagined Sapho. Despite dramatic differences of genre, setting, and apparent purpose,
"Sapho to Philaenis," like *Il merito delle donne*, also introduces a utopian
leveling, and one more explicitly sexual. First printed in 1633 but circulating earlier in at least nineteen manuscript versions, "Sapho to Philaenis"
is, as Janel Mueller observes, decidedly modern in "break[ing] with Ovid's
portrayal of an aging, desperate, suicidal Sappho who yearns for the sexual
attentions of a young man."[124] Not only is this Sapho sapphic, but Donne
uses her to imagine a love premised on resemblance that also figures an
earthly paradise. Representing women as "alike in all parts," the poem,
as I read it,[125] creates ideal intimacy through both the presence of internal likeness and the absence of external control. Sapho imagines herself
and Philaenis as a utopia unto themselves founded on the "naturall Paradise" of the body.[126] And as Mueller observes, the sexual economy of "Sapho to Philaenis" is an economy *tout court*: "all that Nature yields, or
Art can adde" is already present. Catherine Bates, reading the poem as an
"assault" on masculine *poesis*, likewise sees the poem as figuring an emphatic equality of person, an explicit refusal of the need for the male supplement, and a Sapho who embodies womanness and see(k)s the highest
good in its likeness ("thou art so faire / As Gods").[127] In this way, "Sapho to
Philaenis" imagines human harmony in sapphic symmetry, in a love that
is explicitly physical: "brest to brest" and "thighs to thighs." Moreover,
in separating Sapho fully from Phaon, and thus from most early modern
representations that render Sapho suicidal because Phaon has spurned her,

Donne creates a radically autonomous female subject, one who is "astonishingly anomalous within classical and Renaissance literature generally," as H. L. Meakin dramatically puts it, and arrests the ravages of time for a world where "daly change" cannot penetrate. While just what Donne himself meant to do with this pair of lovers remains open to critical contest, it is difficult not to read Sapho the character as projecting a lesbian utopia, a "private world which is manifestly superior to the world of 'dull sublunary lovers.'"[128]

It is worth a methodological digression to emphasize the fact that neither Fonte's nor Donne's "sapphic" writing can be explained by biography simply conceived. We can only conjecture why Fonte, allegedly an unusually happy wife in an unusually egalitarian marriage, wrote one of the most far-reaching feminist treatises of her time, one that without apparent irony urges women to "avoid the love of men," advances a justification for female separatism that sets up women's relationships as a social ideal and, if one reads beneath its nods to decorum, justifies same-sex affiliations.[129] Biographical distance is at least as apparent in the case of "Sapho to Philaenis," a poem far enough from the mainstream of the Donnean canon that its existence has confounded scholars from his generation to our own: some have questioned its authenticity despite the evidence wrought by textual history. At the time of its composition, Donne was probably courting Anne More, with whom he eloped in 1601; he had probably returned from a military expedition to Cadiz and he was moving from the Roman church to the Church of England, but whether any of these factors, or his descent from the ur-utopianist but hardly protofeminist Thomas More, played a role in his conception of "Sapho to Philaenis" remains unknown and probably unknowable.[130]

The chronological convergence of Fonte's *Il merito delle donne* and Donne's "Sapho to Philaenis" thus provides a fine example of confluence: two very different texts written in two very different settings by two very different authors for whom female-female relations, whether figured formally and "chastely" in dialogue, or tropologically and sexually in body parts, stand in for a new logic by which women can, *pace* Swetnam, "live without men." But only for a moment: in the end, each of these texts forestalls the sapphic order that it proposes. Fonte's leveled world lasts for a mere two days: at book's end, "the women all took their leave of one another and went off to their respective homes,"[131] a move that could allow the text to be taken "as a game" or the "idle chatter of women," as Janet Smarr notes, rather than as the "radical manifesto, written in full seriousness," that it appears otherwise to be.[132] Donne's Sapho remains achingly lonely; the union that the poem posits is realized only in the solitude of her mirror, and although I do not agree that its "nonhierarchical language unmediated by men" is ultimately "subordinated to a patriarchal scheme" as James Holstun argues,[133] the poem does end only with Sapho's begging Philaenis to "cure this lovinge madness and restore / Mee to mee, thee my halfe, my all my more"; it does not yet effect that restoration. As Paula Blank puts it, then, this love is "far more poignant than triumphant."[134] And in the end, not one text published around 1600 of which I am aware allows a sapphic utopia to stand. In this regard, Aemelia Lanyer's "Description of Cooke-ham" (1611) is also resonant: across differences of rank, the poetic speaker attempts to sustain an edenic egalitarian intimacy between women but ultimately laments the impossibility of bridging the hierarchical divide. Laurie Shannon rightly reads Shakespeare and Fletcher's *Two Noble Kinsmen* (1613) as an even more dramatic closing off of "female homoerotics"—a spatial closure, like that of *Il merito delle donne*, within the "zone of feminine autonomy" designated by the garden. In *Two Noble Kinsmen*, that space remains "positively coded as utopian," but its "apparent defeat by marriage is marked by funerals rather than celebration."[135]

Still, at a time when the horizontal is both frightening and attractive and sometimes both at once, sapphic representations are becoming a congenial space for trying out the anxieties and possibilities of leveling: they allow women to appropriate subject positions heretofore designed for men and in that process to rethink the logic of rulership. For by taking men out of the system, sapphic representations dislocate both men and women from their fixed places and posit the radical separateness and autonomy of a universally subordinated group. The idea of the sapphic, then, presents a place to think inside a horizontality marked by radical absence, enacting the imaginary displacement of real-world order on a grand scale. Such an absence might well be discomfiting: as Thomas Carlyle quipped in his history of the French Revolution, "leveling is comfortable," but "only down to oneself."[136]

During the seventeenth and early eighteenth centuries, as I will discuss in the next two chapters, cultural preoccupations with the horizontal will find fuller resonance in sapphic writings, and tropes of leveling will increase as metamorphic resolutions lose ground. The ridicule heaped upon what will later be called "the game of flats"—a horizontalizing term if there ever was one—suggests that "flat" may actually be the most disturbing of the disturbing possibilities that sapphic subjects raise. Sapphic representations reflect and perhaps foment a crisis of confidence that the hierarchy most basic to the social imaginary—individual men's

rule over individual women—will remain sustainable. It is not surprising, then, that what Ben Jonson called "tribade lust" could signify modernity in ways that point to other sorts of horizontal threats and explorations: for imagining the implications of human differences in a world
of class stratification and colonial practices and, conversely, for embodying emergent systems of governance. Because every man is legitimated in
early modernity to have power over at least one woman, and because it is
assumed that every female is ruled by at least one man, male-male relations, even in a society that stratifies those relations along lines of rank,
do not seem to carry the radical potential for leveling that female-female
relations bear.

It is in this context that I want to press on the aptness of the sapphic
not only to the horizontal but to the configurations of modernity that the
horizontal entails. It seems that the boundaries of thought around 1600
meet their limit point in a world that has been forced to imagine yet cannot sustain the logic of woman + woman. What I am calling a "sapphic
episteme," a worldview open to that logic, entails an epistemology within
which social relations are reimagined in paradigm-shifting horizontal
terms. In this sense, the sapphic subject poses not only the threat *of* modernity but a threat *to* modernity as it is being configured over this period.
Dror Wahrman argues that it is gender rather than rank that anchors the
new society and its modern subjectivities, and this position is consonant
with the views about emergent gender and gender differences of many
scholars including Carole Pateman, Thomas Laqueur, and Thomas A.
King. If so, then the sapphic disturbs and potentially deconstructs not
only the old regime but the new one: it challenges both the rule of men as
men and the heteronormative operations that femininity and masculinity
are coming to signify. As my discussion of the novel in chapter 5 may best
elaborate, the sapphic thus ends up positioned both as and against the modernity to which I have been arguing it owes its possibility.

GEOGRAPHY IN THE ARCHIVE

It is time to take a closer look at my geography as a way to understand
more deeply how and why the sapphic imaginary might have functioned
as I think it does. If we read for absence, it is clear from the texts I have
named that not every European country was producing sapphic representations around 1600; most of these are coming from England, France, and
Spain, with some representation from Italian states, Portugal, and the
Netherlands and little from anywhere else.[137] As I suggested in chapter 1,

the partiality of this mapping raises a larger question about the efficacy of studying Europe, even Western Europe, as a single entity. Certainly it is feasible to speak of specific qualities that characterize Western Europe around 1600: a fluid circulation of print and ideas; the continuing use of Latin and the emergence of French as *linguae francae*; intermarriage among Europe's monarchic families; the rise of universities; population shifts, food shortages, peasant revolts, and steep price increases; the growth of cities; and, almost endlessly, war. On the other hand, we can point to sharp religious divisions especially between Catholic south and Protestant north; the different states of public theater (Spain and England far ahead of other countries); differential conditions of effective print censorship (the Dutch provinces among the most stringent), and a wide range of governments from (oligarchic) republican Holland and Venice to absolutist France and Spain.

Certain pan-European conditions might help to explain the emergence of sapphic subjects at this point. Historians speak of a "general crisis" around 1600, of price rises throughout Europe, of increase in structural unemployment, and of a movement toward absolutism and broad state control even in the Dutch Republic. Above all, these were crises about order, a slide away from early-sixteenth-century optimism into uncertainty and anxiety as burgeoning ideas of rights and contract—indeed of political leveling—created "rapid and painful adjustment to previously unthinkable uncertainties and dilemmas."[138] These were crises, Anthony Upton argues, that left people "baffled, fearful and insecure."[139] As "old certainties" were "discarded, but not yet replaced,"[140] institutions and individuals scrambled to create new forms of coherence. At the same time, new enquiries into the workings of "nature," seeking "better explanations for observed phenomena," raised the new skepticism figured in Michel de Montaigne's famous query, "Que sais-je?" Concerns about mobility and change, especially arenas where phenomena might have appeared natural and therefore fixed, would not be surprising in such an environment.

Certainly the Europe of 1600 was "struggling to come to terms with a whole series of disturbing novelties," many of them wrought by its own rapacious colonial ambitions, but of which the underlying causes were not always evident. Fascination with and fear of "the other"—any "other"— was also palpable, as Christopher Black notes, "whether it was the Jew, the gypsy, the Anabaptist, or the threatening woman outside male control (and protection)."[141] Thus, for example, "virtually every jurisdiction in Europe passed laws against witchcraft in the later sixteenth century,"[142] with concern falling overwhelmingly on women unattached to or perceived as

independent of men. It may be no coincidence that an otherwise hetero-
dox thinker like Jean Bodin worried about witches—and sapphic ones—
and also wrote, as Charles Nauert notes, "two major works that justified
absolute monarchy."[143] Women were "numerically extremely prominent"
in many dissident religious sects and used religious autonomy to assert
authority in matters of church and even state, so much so that Ronald
Knox considers the history of religious "enthusiasm" to be "largely a history of female emancipation."[144] As Thomas Barnes and Natalie Zemon
Davis have shown, women also played major roles in many political actions, for example in the early seventeenth-century riots against enclosure
and for common rights.[145] The specter of a loosened tether on women—
or, worse, women in intimate association with one another—was thus
understandable.

If this generalized anxiety were the only factor, however, we should
expect a more uniform distribution of sapphic representations throughout Western Europe and more uniformly negative representations akin
to those directed at witchcraft or at women who take on husbands' roles.
And if the sapphic dovetailed predictably with interest in Reformation
and Enlightenment thinking, then the German states that were central
to these intellectual movements should also be producing sapphic texts.
Yet there seems to have been almost no published writing about female
homoeroticism of German origin before the later eighteenth century, and
this despite what Helmut Puff has recognized as the "highly significant
place" of attention to male sodomy in the pre-Reformation German imaginary.[146] Outside of the new and copious trial texts, there also is a lag in
Dutch representations that constitutes a tension with the influential role
of the Dutch Republic in the early Enlightenment and that is arguably
attributable to what may have been western Europe's most stringent and
successful censorship of sexual materials written in the vernacular; but it
is significant that pornographic materials from other European countries
circulated in Dutch provinces, and by the mid-seventeenth century Dutch
vernacular texts, if often of a more euphemistic sort, were already sur-
facing.[147] Neither the geographical nor the textual picture, then, supports
a simple link between sapphic representations and either a generalized
anxiety, a specific anxiety about women, or a close tie simply to modern
thought, though these elements are almost certainly in play.

While it is of course possible that countries producing sapphic representations do so for distinctive rather than shared reasons, it seems worth
asking what those polities have in common. I speculate that by 1600, England, France, and Spain, and to some extent also Portugal, certain Italian

states, and the Dutch Republic, shared a convergence of at least four
characteristics: a recent history of strong women rulers; the visible participation of women in vernacular print culture; a coastal and primarily
Atlantic geography that gives ready access to major European trade and
communication routes extending from highly cosmopolitan urban cen-
ters; and a heavy investment in colonial conquest. The geographic reversal is also true: except for Scandinavia, virtually all of Western Europe's
coastal countries show some preoccupation with sapphic representation
around 1600, while almost no inland countries do.

First, countries where sapphic discourse clusters show a striking visibility of women in positions of political power. From what had been a
stringently masculine monarchic economy, the sixteenth century saw the
intensified presence of powerful regents (Catherine de Médicis, Anne of
Austria, and Marie de Médicis in France), queens regnant (Mary I and Elizabeth I in England, Mary Stuart in Scotland as well as her mother Marie
de Guise, Spain's Juana of Castile and Aragón after the even more powerful Isabella, Margaret of Parma in the Netherlands), influential queen
wives and mothers (Catherine de Médicis, Marguerite de Navarre, Isabella

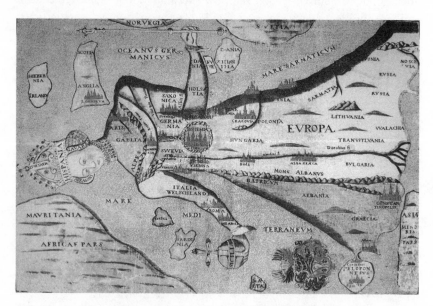

Fig. 1. *Europa Regina* (or *Europa Prima Pars Terrae in Forma Virginis*), one of numerous
sixteenth-century maps representing Europe as a queen. While the convention probably
originated in the imperial ambitions of the Holy Roman Emperor, it may have fostered,
or been fostered by, the concentration of women in positions of monarchical power. This
version is a 1581 engraving by Heinrich Bunting. Courtesy of Wikimedia Commons

d'Este), and influential heads of smaller Spanish, Italian, and French principalities (Jeanne d'Albret of Navarre, Marie-Josephine of Savoy).[148] Indeed, Gisela Bock notes that "in France, where the Salic law of succession excluded from the throne all females and those males who claim to rule was based on descent through a female . . . there was nonetheless an almost unbroken line of female regents" over two centuries.[149] Diatribes against the "monstrous regiment of women," as John Knox famously put it, never dissolved these concentrations of female power. If Jacques Barzun exaggerates when he argues that "the sixteenth century was full of women," including "women politicians" in multiple European courts and even in the Vatican, who "exerted their talents like men for all to see and judge,"[150] still the sea-change in women's public presence might well help to explain an increase in texts that represent, and often attempt to resolve, the conundrum of women arrogating the privileges of men. It may not be accidental that the medieval legend of a Pope Joan deviously subordinating Christendom to female rule also resurfaced so insistently around 1600 that Pope Clement VIII felt compelled to intervene. Certainly some of the examples I have given directly implicate particular courts—those of Catherine de Médicis and Elizabeth I most notably, and it is worth noting how many of the writers who inscribed the sapphic around 1600—from Tyard and Brantôme to Shakespeare and Lyly—had connections with court culture. The widely circulated image of Europe itself as "Europa Regina" (see fig. 1), especially popular in the late sixteenth century, may thus have a material etiology.[151]

A different form of female power that may be propelling sapphic representations is the one that Ben Jonson's reference to "tribade lust" underscores: the dramatic entrance of women into print. Women writers sustain a lively presence in the emerging book cultures of every country in which sapphic representation is strong—England, France, Spain, the Italian states and especially Venice, and the United Provinces. Like the rule of women but still more ubiquitous, the access of women to print culture erodes gender distinctions and provides a mechanism by which women could take independent authority. What Paola Malpezzi Price says of Italy was more widely true: "a favorable social, religious and moral climate and the wide acceptance of the vernacular as a literary language" made "women's visibility and participation in the domain of literature" one of the period's "most remarkable phenomena."[152] At the same time, a lively literature was being produced by both sexes that underscored women's access, indeed right, to deploy words as an unofficial channel of power; in Lope de Vega's famous play *Fuenteovejuna* (c. 1612–14), for example, the manly Laurencia forces her way into a town meeting and insists that even "if a woman has no vote, / She has a voice [que bien puede una mujer, / si no a dar voto a dar voces]."[153]

Unprecedented in number and power both as rulers and as writers, women thus participated actively in the two very different modes of authority—one hierarchical, formal, and traditional, the other quasi-horizontal, informal, and incipient—that arguably shaped social ideas and social practice in this period. Moreover, it is not simply the surge of women in positions of power and influence that seems significant, but also the tension between that surge and the contemporaneous reifying doctrines of female subordination. Paola Price has found that in Italy alone between 1471 and 1700, over 2,600 separate writings were published, almost half of these by 1600, aimed at regulating women's lives.[154] Between 1570 and 1600 too emerged the first spate of instruction books aimed solely at women, as if to reposition them through the very mechanism—print—that promised to release them. But the period also saw the emergence of writings by women themselves on a range of topics including the topic of women. Literacy was also, of course, a key to other new forms of power; as Federica Ambrosini notes, women who could write could also make wills and other legal documents, "punishing unworthy husbands" and others who had wronged them;[155] no wonder that Counter-Reformationists sometimes argued that women should not be taught to read on the grounds that women of letters, starting not incidentally with Sappho, were morally suspect and their books a potentially corrupting influence.[156] And it is a striking indication of the new potency of print that writing and rulership, as two mechanisms of female power around 1600, get linked through Sappho to one another. In John Lyly's *Sappho and Phao*, for example, the female figure so strongly associated with women writers becomes a female ruler clearly meant to evoke Elizabeth, and in a way that implicitly offers "an equation of female homosexuality with female political power."[157] Several critics, including Philippa Berry, Julie Crawford, and Valerie Traub, have proposed similar evidence of ties between Elizabeth and Sappho or the sapphic, just as Dorothy Stephens suggests that the last section of *The Faerie Queene* testifies to Spenser's growing dissatisfaction with the "female cult" around Elizabeth, who becomes, "finally, no one to whom any man can bond himself."[158]

It is therefore worth arguing that especially in France, England, and the Mediterranean, the "general crisis" of the seventeenth century was a crisis of gender as well. That is, among the destabilizing influences on the period, and thus among the issues that need to be reconfigured for a new age, gender looms heavily. The aggregate of my texts indeed suggests precisely what the individual examples attempt to contain, dissolve or diminish: that in the social imaginary if not in historical practice, this is not a time when a transgressive woman can simply be dismissed as aberrant. Although I am not suggesting that the crisis of horizontality was first and foremost a crisis about women, women figure both symbolically and literally in the imaginative reshuffling that early modernity entails.

But still other critical elements characterize the countries that are most actively producing sapphic subjects at the turn of the seventeenth century. It is not simply in Western but in westernmost, primarily Atlantic Europe that I have found the overwhelming preponderance of sapphic representations in the period around 1600. As Hermann Kellenbenz emphasizes, a coastal economy fostered greater social mobility and thus broader opportunities for contact with social, racial, and political "others,"[159] while an urban setting, as Fernand Braudel has suggested, was more likely to show a "deep-seated disequilibrium."[160] I speculate that sapphic representation would be encouraged by the ways in which early modern cities functioned as both powerful and dangerous crossroads of identity, places of cultural difference, leveling potential, and, relative to rural settings, rapid change. Those cities on or near waterways were better able, of course, to participate in a multinational cultural as well as economic network for the simple reason that travel by water was faster and extended farther than travel on roads; we might recall that even in 1789, news of the stormed Bastille reached London faster than it reached the French provinces.

But the coastal pattern may be less important in itself than in the colonial projects it fostered. Atlantic locations in particular facilitated colonial conquest and commerce, and it may not be accidental that the three major producers of sapphic discourse—England, France, and Spain—are also three of the most heavily expansionist European powers. I have found almost no representations of the sapphic outside countries involved in colonization; conversely, with the possible exception of the Scandinavian countries, nearly all of Europe's major colonial powers—England, Spain, France, Portugal, the Dutch Republic, and the Italian states including the Venetian Republic, with its own colonial history—show some preoccupation with sapphic subjects around 1600.[161] The German states, by contrast, had little involvement in colonialism except as auxiliaries to the major imperial powers, along with significantly smaller number of women in positions of either political authority or, at this point, participation in print

culture—and as far as I can tell there is also no sign of the intensified interest in sapphic subjects that I have been describing. I speculate, though I
cannot of course prove, that these are related absences.

It is a commonplace, of course, that imperial countries place their subjects in contact with "new" human differences real or perceived, with new
challenges to social order, and with new cultural formations. That an interest in the sapphic erupts in cosmopolitan, urban, colonialist, turbulent
settings suggests that it may be serving complex functions not limited to
sex-related ones—or that sex itself is serving complex functions not related to direct concerns about women. I speculate that sapphic subjects
may erupt into print when societies need to work out the possibilities—
variously dreaded and welcomed—that difference might be not just "out
there" but "in here." All the more within a social imaginary dominated,
as Foucault argued,[162] by analogical thinking and tropes of resemblance,
the vast change that colonialism represents finds an at-home correlative
in the notion of unfamiliar bodies and practices that stir fears that others
might rise up to claim autonomy and even rulership. Strikingly, (sexual)
disorder becomes associated in the European imaginary not only with the
colonized "others" but with the colonizers themselves, a sign of the inability to maintain lines of distinction between self and other under the
pressure and license of unequal encounter. The vast change wrought by
colonialism finds an at-home correlative in the notion that some others
might not be as they seemed, might in fact be "foreign" in the sense of being unfamiliar and unpredictable, and might rise up to claim their powers.
And though arguably no society is well prepared to understand its Other,
"it is hard," Euan Cameron insists, "to imagine a people worse prepared
intellectually, culturally, or morally for the role of colonial overlords over
the rest of the world than late medieval Europeans."[163] Actually, of course,
these Europeans were very well prepared to be overlords; what they were
not prepared to be were equals or peers. And it is ultimately the question
of equality or parity—a question at the heart of the very making of modernity that around 1600 takes a sapphic form—that, as I hope to show in
the next several chapters, sapphic subjects will more fully come to represent. It is small wonder, then, that "tribade lust," to repeat Jonson's terms,
might become a signifier of modernity itself, a rich site for horizontal explorations of all sorts: for imagining the implications of human differences
in a colonizing world, or perhaps even for imagining full equality between
males, as Donne is arguably attempting through the mask of his Sapho.

Clearly no single factor explains the intensified eruption of sapphic
representations or the emergence of what I am calling a sapphic episteme.

But the convergence around 1600 of particular constellations of power, difference, and social contact enable the sapphic to be a pliable trope, variously a safe and dangerous harbinger, and an attractive, even titillating site
for confronting the implications of a world that carries the promise and
danger of leveling. Fernand Braudel has argued that "whenever splits and
chasms begin to open up in a society, it is the ever-present culture which
fills them in, or covers them up, holding us to our tasks."[164] Sapphic subjects show us that the "ever-present culture" also exposes and even creates
the splits and chasms that it is also perhaps trying to fill in or cover up.
The sapphic subjects of 1600 reveal, and attempt to come to terms with,
the fissures in societies that are on the verge of an excess of change. Varied
and contradictory, blending moral opprobrium with erotic play, the aggregate of these representations forms an equivocal tapestry of fascination
and anxiety that takes hold of the cultural imaginary to provide representational dynamics that will lend themselves to still more pointed social
and political purposes. Chapter 4 will show how a significant number of
women writers of Italy, England, France, Spain, Portugal, and the Dutch
Republic were able to use a sapphic discourse to constitute collectivity. In
the next chapter, however, I explore the ways in which sapphic representations insinuate themselves directly or analogically into state concerns.
These texts confront the radical potential of female-female relations to
challenge or to solidify systems of power.

CHAPTER THREE

Fearful Symmetries:
The Sapphic and the State, 1630–1749

Not content with our Sex, [Sappho] begins *Amours* with her own, and teaches the Female World a new sort of Sin, call'd the *Flats*, that was follow'd not only in *Lucian*'s Time, but is practis'd frequently in *Turkey*, as well as at *Twickenham* at this Day.
—*Satan's Harvest Home* (1749)[1]

In 1678 the English cleric and poet Nathaniel Wanley published a voluminous history with a voluminous name: *The Wonders of the Little World: or, a General History of Man in Six Books. Wherein By many thousands of Examples is shewed what Man hath been from the First Ages of the World to these Times. In respect of his Body, Senses, Passions, Affections: His Virtues and Perfections, his Vices and Defects, his Quality, Vocation and Profession; and many other particulars not reducible to any of the former Heads.* In six sections comprising over two hundred anecdotal chapters, Wanley catalogues human phenomena near and far, from virtues to vices, from feasts to feats, from unusual birthmarks to unusual births. Extending the tropes of discovery to the "little world" in ways that show "the human person herself as a 'wonder,'" Wanley's book epitomizes what Mary Baine Campbell felicitously names the "age of the plethora."[2] Within Wanley's plethora appears a chapter that draws substantially from Torquemada's *Jardin de floras curiosas* to enumerate twenty-four instances "Of such Persons as have Changed their Sex,"[3] in twenty-two of which the alteration is from female to male and in several of which sexual desire is redirected as well. The effect is an ethnography that, through its accretion of examples from ancient Rome to modern Spain, makes sex-change both anomalous and commonplace.

During the next century, *The Wonders of the Little World* was popular enough to be reprinted in at least seven editions between 1704 and 1806, variously reordered or abridged. In a change I propose as emblematic, however, the chapter on sex-change did not reappear.[4] By the eighteenth century, especially as humoral theories declined in credit, claims about women suddenly turning into men were waning along with credence in magical proofs.[5] As Campbell reminds us, the "compartmentalized" Enlightenment world "of the intelligible, with its departments and dissociations" becomes "the cure for that unmanageable excess" of the plethora.[6] While strategies of wonder continue to shape some sapphic stories, the formations that I call metamorphic slide more frequently into the ethnographic and the horizontal as the "same" in same-sex becomes a site for either resistance or appropriation. In that process, I argue, sapphic subjects increase in political potency, particularly as their inscriptions also become preoccupied less with the anthropology of isolated bodies than with the anthropology of cultures or with the ties between the two, rendering the sapphic a matter of national interest that raises its imaginative capital.

As my first chapter explained, it is not the goal of this book to survey the extensive field of seventeenth- and eighteenth-century writings in which the sapphic figures within a history of sexuality. Particularly in England, France, and Spain, though waning early in Spain for reasons about which I will speculate at the end of this chapter, sapphic representations between 1630 and 1749 are hardly less wide-ranging than their 1600-era counterparts and at least as voluminous. Chapters 3, 4, and 5 take up distinctive aspects of this body of writings to ask how they foster a sexuality of history. In an overlapping chronology of chapters, the strand of representation through which women themselves forged a public presence as female subjects will be the focus of chapter 4, while chapter 5 will take up the challenges both to the novel and to its social projects in a revisionist history that begins with the last decades of the seventeenth century. The present chapter looks selectively at ways in which metamorphic, ethnographic, and especially horizontal tendencies get put into play to make the sapphic increasingly responsive to questions of family and state power and the possibilities of leveling for which the English slang of "flats" becomes an apt figure. As sapphic representations funnel toward a logic of sameness, and as the "same" in same-sex becomes increasingly difficult to dissolve or explain away, its utility as a figure for matters of governance intensifies for reasons on which I hope to shed some speculative light. The representations I gather in this chapter suggest that the logic of woman +

woman handily inscribes, even epitomizes, the fears and hopes of a polity deeply concerned—if from antithetical political positions—about the consequences of political and social leveling.

In making these claims, I am underscoring a potential agency for sapphic representations that I believe scholarship in the history of sexuality has minimized or overlooked. While early modern drama does tend, as Valerie Traub has long noted, to render female-female relations "simultaneously crucial and insignificant" to "romantic plots," the very pervasiveness of those plots suggests a social purport. Traub rightly argues that in the context of the individual drama, "female-female desire becomes an issue—becomes significant—only when the time comes for the patriarchal imperative of marital alliance."[7] Through the prism of a sexuality of history, I aim to underscore a different kind of significance that attends to these sapphic representations in relation to their potential to figure epistemic challenges. As Robert D. Hume has argued, and as Melissa Sanchez's *Erotic Subjects* demonstrates with respect to heterosexual conquest plots, seventeenth-century comedies "nominally concerned with marriage, sex, or gulling" may often "really exist for their political import."[8] While I agree with Michael McKeon that male homoeroticism carried significant agency to reconfigure sex in the early eighteenth-century, I argue that female homoeroticism carried an agency overlooked by McKeon that engages both with sex and with other major social concerns.[9] This chapter argues for such (shifting) purposes configured in alterations of metamorphic scenarios, in intensifications of ethnographic projects, and in the charged language of horizontal representations. In short, during the long period embraced by this chapter, all three modalities show female homoeroticism becoming entangled with national identities and the politics of power.

My primary purpose in this chapter, then, will be to explore some specific ways in which the sapphic, in these various configurations, sets itself up to serve the state. In so doing, I seek to explore the elusive logic by which a rather surprising number of seventeenth- and eighteenth-century texts open discursive connections between female same-sex relations to matters of governance. I begin in metamorphic mode with a reading of two little-known plays, Isaac de Benserade's *Iphis et Iante* (1634), and Álvaro Cubillo de Aragón's *Añasco el de Talavera* (c. 1635),[10] that complicate the (already complicated) standard plot of sex-change, in the first case from female to male body, and in the second from female to male partner. These texts show how, even in the decades after 1600 when metamorphic stage representations are still flourishing, some of these plays are resisting their own metamorphic dynamics to challenge configurations of power in the family and, by implication, in the state. In a briefer interlude, I take up the geography of the sapphic as it is produced in a range of ethnographic works to recognize that the most persistent settings are located within the Ottoman Empire and to chart the connections metonymized by the move "from Turkey to Twickenham" signaled in this chapter's epigraph. Finally, I focus on the striking number of writings produced in England during the turbulent decades between the Exclusion Crisis of 1678 and the years immediately following the last significant Jacobite uprising of 1745. I ask how the surprisingly prominent agency of sapphic representations during that long period of monarchic instability acts out tensions between Stuart and Hanoverian values and thus between autocratic rule and consensual parity. I suggest that the place the sapphic holds in this discourse might help us to understand both the cultural work that sapphic subjects can perform and the period of crisis that motivates this performance.

SINS OF THE DAUGHTERS

In chapter 2, I discussed the "displacement of the homoerotic by the heterosexual," as Valerie Traub describes it, that appears to dissolve the "tension between the two modes of desire" in the metamorphic scenario typical to sixteenth- and seventeenth-century drama.[11] If women seem to love women (or men, men), some form of sex change will occur either by revelation of the beloved's "true" gender, by a change of partner, or by supernatural intervention. Where same-sex affiliation persists in these settings, then, it persists as a corollary or supplement to what becomes a socially primary union. I do not mean to minimize the power of these conventionally metamorphic texts or the impact of their sapphic remainder: as I have already suggested, the very necessity of sex-change suggests that erotic difference must be created rather than assumed and is thus implicitly artificial. It is significant that these scenarios are so plentiful in the public theaters of the late sixteenth and early seventeenth century—all the more as theater becomes, in this period, arguably *the* crucial way in which early modern society "speaks to itself," to adopt a phrase of Philippe Sollers;[12] this plethora evinces a kind of repetition compulsion that in itself speaks to a socially preoccupying conundrum that is never quite settled. The recursion may be occurring because the metamorphic plot is so willing to sacrifice rational to epistemic plausibility: turning a girl into a boy or a same-sex relationship into a cross-sex one is epistemically more comfortable than enabling girl + girl, but it is logically vulnerable enough to warrant compulsive revisiting, a reminder of Foucault's suggestion that "literature is that which compensates for (and not that which confirms) the signifying function of language."[13] This tension between forms of plausibility is already exposed in one of the theater's earliest metamorphic productions, John Lyly's *Gallathea* (1588) which, as I have noted, makes the sex change as arbitrary for its female characters as it is crucial for the social fabric.

Benserade's *Iphis et Iante* and Cubillo's *Añasco el de Talavera* do not manage their metamorphoses so easily, and in that near-failure they expose the challenge that sapphic subjects pose for reconfiguring family politics and, synecdochically, the politics of state. Staged respectively in France, where a public theater was just emerging, and Spain, where the sapphic was routinely intimated in a flourishing stage culture but not usually confronted openly, these most explicit of seventeenth-century dramas make the sapphic a topic of "public" conversation among the characters. Moreover, both plays turn their emphases away from personal morality and forbidden desire toward questions of authority and social cohesion. While once again scholars do not (yet) know why either playwright chose this subject, the plays themselves imply the sapphic to be more means than end. Both texts enact a challenge to paternal power, and both use female desire to alter the represented world and the assumptions that have governed social relationships. Although *Iphis et Iante* carries out the Ovidian conclusion of turning girl into boy, and *Añasco* effects its metamorphosis through a superficially heterosexual ending, both plays leave a more than usual residue of unease that marks the fissures in a literally patriarchal system that has lost its way.

Because Benserade is working directly with a story that would be well known to his audience given the renewed popularity of Ovid's *Metamorphoses* in the seventeenth century,[14] the basic plot offers no surprise: Benserade's Iphis, like Ovid's, was raised as a boy because her father would have destroyed an infant daughter; she falls in love with Ianthe; a wedding looms; and the goddess Isis transforms Ianthe's sex in order to legitimate the union. But *Iphis et Iante* not only delays the sex change until after the marriage, giving the couple some version of a lesbian wedding night; it also shifts the discursive emphasis from the private preservation of a secret to the public resolution of an impasse. By revealing to all the characters the knowledge that in Ovid remains exclusive to mother, daughter, and nurse, Benserade's play can explore the nature of patriarchal power, mull the implications of difference, and dramatize the consequences of shattered trust. These elements, in turn, make the sapphic a space more for social than for moral struggle in a culture where the pressure of normative controls is already displacing a logic of external sanction.

As the play opens, the site of contest is the marriage itself, with Iphis (recklessly) and her father Lidge (unknowingly) pressing for the union that Iphis's mother Télétuze is trying desperately to prevent. The occasion exposes the tangle of early modern motivations for marriage, as Lidge proclaims that it is "up to [Iphis's] young heart to love whoever pleases him" while also insisting on the parents' responsibility to secure the child's "interest," which he considers obvious in this instance because "the beautiful Ianthe is good as she is rich." Télétuze's efforts to stop the marriage are vain since Lidge has the "absolute power [absolu pouvoir]" of approval, and maternal authority is quashed in full by the supervening authority of Iphis's own desire: "Ianthe has a complete power over my soul, and for you two I have only obedience."[15] Moreover, paternal power has been compromised from the outset by Lidge's decree that a girl born to him be put to death, and in defying her husband in complicity with other women, Télétuze has already created a subversive polity that further undermines the paternal order. So blind is the play's represented public, however, that when Ergaste, who is in love with Iphis and as desperate as Télétuze to prevent the marriage, proclaims the truth of Iphis's sex to Iante and her family, he is seen as having "lost his mind [perdu le sens]" (89): the elders are literally incredulous when Ergaste warns that "you're going to commit a crime instead of a marriage."[16] The "vieillards" who hold official power, as Ergaste contemptuously labels them, live under illusions born of a system closed upon itself that cannot see its own faultlines.

One of those generational faultlines, clearly, is same-sex desire, which is vested in more than one of the play's characters. For starters, it is not Lidge but Iphis herself who most strongly insists on this marriage. Here is none of the original Iphis's distress at experiencing a "monstrous" desire that Ovid's Iphis believes no girl has felt before. Nor does the French Iphis deem her feelings unnatural; to the contrary, as she tells Ianthe on their wedding night, she simply has "a heart that nature has made unlike others."[17] The wedding night does not fail to fulfill her; she "sometimes forgot I was a girl" and was "delighted [ravissait]" to "possess" Iante: "I touched, I kissed, my heart was happy."[18] Her wrong, as she sees it, lies not in loving Iante but in having deceived her.

In a moving soliloquy after the stunning revelation of her wedding night, Iante likewise acknowledges that the problem is not one of satisfaction: "This marriage is sweet; it attracts me quite enough,"[19] and "if a girl could marry a girl," her "heart would certainly not be upset." But the demand "that a girl make her vow to men, / And that none but a man may have her / Iphis not being one, / that's where I've gone wrong."[20] A textual plethora of "ifs" ("si") sets up the conditions under which this marriage could stand: "if no one would laugh"; "if one weren't profaning the marriage bond"; "if it would not trouble our parents"; "if a girl could marry a girl without offending heaven and natural law"; if "some people [would not] gloat over my sad fate"; if they "would not judge by outward appearances"; and even, in a sweetly metatextual moment, if "they would [not] talk about us in the theaters."[21] Shame ("honte") is a particularly thick logic here: the concern over same-sex marriage is not a lack of fulfillment but a departure from norms: while nodding to religious and moral logic, Benserade has made most vivid and poignant, in this rendering, the sapphic as a problem of social relations.

Iphis et Iante makes clear, moreover, that this social problem reaches beyond the individual or her parents: linked with the complications of paternal power, the sapphic threatens an order that implicates four different families: those of Iphis, of Iante, of Ergaste, and of Ergaste's intimate friend Nise, whose sister loves Ergaste. Rather than cementing families, as marriage in classical comedy is meant to do, this union implodes relations both within and between families in complications that its dea-ex-machina ending does not resolve. Iante's father Téleste is outraged at being deceived in what is effectively a breach of contract: "What, then: my son-in-law is a girl? . . . This is not how one deals with decent people."[22] Iphis, ready to die to free Iante, accuses her mother of having betrayed her but also implicates the father whose "criminal" misogyny set the problem in motion by "smother[ing] paternal love."[23] Télétuze is furious at Iphis for having ignored her warnings against the marriage; Lidge is furious at Télétuze not only for having deceived him but for having let Ergaste and his sister into the secret early on. And although Lidge blames Télétuze for protecting her daughter rather than accepting her husband's fatal decree, and Télétuze blames Iphis for insisting on the marriage, it is ultimately Lidge whom the play itself blames for behaving in what he himself now admits was "a revolting way [une horrible façon]" (117).[24] When Télétuze complains "My God! How little joy our children give us,"[25] we can see that the promise of new generation that opened the play has collapsed into vitriol, and that the sins of fathers are indeed visited on children. To these complications we could add the side drama of Ergaste, his sister, his friend Nise, and Nise's sister Mérinte, relations that carry hints of incest, on the one hand, and more than hints of male homoeroticism, on the other, placing further pressure on family dynamics. Indeed, the play creates an impasse in which hierarchies (father over mother, parent over child) falter but efforts at reversal or leveling likewise fail.

Faithful to its source text, Benserade's play will bring the goddess to intervene so that Iphis and Iante can stay married, forcing Ergaste to give up Iphis and settle for Mérinte. But even aside from this less than felicitous secondary ending, the demonstration of familial disintegration and interfamilial disharmony is powerfully rendered and the sex change a textually last-minute affair. Lest Isis's rescue of Iphis seem like a reward to the father, providing the desired son after all, the goddess makes it clear that Lidge is "inhumain" (121) and that she grants the sex-change only to satisfy the passion that is driving Iphis, in effect acknowledging the legitimacy of same-sex desire.[26] In effect, Isis is helping the social to conform to the sexual, rescuing Iphis and Iante from shame and ridicule and, as the play's literally last word emphasizes, enabling reproductive sexuality: the proof of sex change will ultimately lie not in Iphis's "mâle vigeur" (122) but in the promise that her fertility will prove itself in nine months ("prouvera dans neuf mois qu'Iphis est un garcon") (124). The quick resolution gestures toward resuming the orderly hierarchy of generations, but it also suggests that the collateral damage wrought upon the present may be irreparable, for the text does not undertake even a modicum of conventional reparation.

A less sanguine resolution and one similarly delayed until the final moment characterizes Cubillo's *Añasco el de Talavera*, also first performed in the mid-1630s and possibly one of only two, among the dozens of dramas of *mujeres varoniles* and *mujeres esquivas*, in which a woman, known *as* a woman rather than masquerading as a man, openly pursues her passion for another woman.[27] Dionisia, the play's (anti)heroine, is the extreme of the *mujer esquiva*; despite her feminine beauty, she has "broken the law of Nature [rompido la ley de Naturaleza]" and sees herself as entitled to a man's rights and desires.[28] Like Benserade's Iphis, she insists that she is *naturally* unlike other women: "although I was born female, I am different," a judgment echoed by her cousin Leonor ("although she was born a woman, she doesn't seem like one") and intensified by her own father ("your cousin is no woman").[29] Dionisia's transgressions range from rejecting female accoutrements such as cosmetics and needlework to violence with sword and pistol, from refusing even to look at her suitor Don Diego to making unwelcome advances to Leonor. Once again, same-sex desire is a public affair, discussed openly by friends, suitors, and servants, its eroticism undisguised. Dionisia openly woos Leonor, to the "horror" of her father, and openly envies Leonor's suitor Don Juan. Most egregiously, as the

play has it, Dionisia sins against the code of honor when, in her disdain for
men and her obsession with her cousin, she refuses hospitality to a visiting Count (El Conde) and thereby shames and insults her father. These
turns of plot have Dionisia, disguised as the man Añasco, wounding Don
Juan in a skirmish over Leonor, then getting herself arrested when, still in
disguise, she causes a fracas after she fails to win a place in Madrid's pres-
tigious literary academy for her erotic love poetry about Leonor.[30] That her
poetry is quoted at length in the text gives the knowing audience, if not
the unsuspecting characters, a particular vividness to same-sex desire.

But instead of a dea-ex-machina sex change in *Añasco*, we get an even
less motivated, dramatic, and illogical breach between the plot and its
resolution that also turns on the twin ruptures of dishonored fatherhood
and disallowed desire. When Dionisia first declares her love for Leonor,
she admits her jealousy of Don Juan in the same sentence. By the middle
of the third act, she has dressed as a man, wounded Don Juan, spent jail
time, and been pursued by a woman of questionable virtue named Juana.
Don Juan, for his part, has also dishonored Dionisia's father by breaking
the elder's walking stick when Marcelo questioned his intentions toward
Leonor. In the duel that follows between Marcelo's second and Don Juan,
it is the disguised Dionisia who takes a wound for Don Juan before learning that she is "defending the one who offended" her own father ["defiendo
a quien le ofende" (3.2044)].[31] If we go back through the chain of Dionisia's
actions, it is clear that in *Añasco el de Talavera* the passion of one woman
for another leads to the violation of virtually every social code on which
this society operates and especially to violations of paternal honor and patriarchal right.

If one were imagining for *Añasco* the full resolution of metamorphic
comedy, then, one would see the daughter finally submitting to the father's
rule, and by extension to the rule of law, by honoring his marital choice for
her and marrying Don Diego. Father and daughter are indeed reunited at
the end of the play, but Marcelo is by now a self-declared "viejo" (the same
word used for the fathers in Benserade's play) whose power his wayward
daughter simply appropriates. Even as she professes obedience, it is the
daughter rather than the father who takes charge of the play's resolution,
not only determining her own fate but orchestrating the fate of the other
characters and dictating who will marry whom. In a closure of murky
motivation that vividly demonstrates the daughter's arrogation of power,
Dionisia declares that Don Juan is to marry her, not Leonor. Whether motivated by some need of Dionisia's to marry the beloved of her beloved or
by some need of the author to punish the lesbian character, this startling

move wreaks vengeance at once on Leonor, on Don Diego, on Don Juan, and on Marcelo. And even though she has vowed on the battlefield that "if I am protecting Don Juan / it is to kill him and drink his blood,"[32] she also claims that "although I / have wounded him twice / I have put myself at his side / when the occasion was offered."[33] In a bizarrely belated reversal, Don Juan, having been saved by Dionisia/Añasco, professes himself likewise obliged to marry her. To Leonor Dionisia gives Don Diego, in what amounts to the most autocratic of arranged marriages, and in a startling exchange of power, the cousin who has warded off Dionisia's advances in the strongest language, and who has been meeting Don Juan in secret, simply capitulates, if with a negative phrasing: "I won't argue with what my cousin orders [No replico / a lo que mi prima ordena]" (3.2428–29). Thus, as Sherry Velasco notes, "unexpectedly, Dionisia orchestrates a conclusion that denies everyone in the play the true objects of their affections. . . . If Dionisia cannot have her love interest, then nobody else will either."[34] Instead, desire is thwarted at every turn of this supposed comedy, and who is punishing whom, and why, becomes the more salient question along with the question of Cubillo's own unknowable intentions: it is not clear whether such unexpected outcomes caricature Dionisia, Marcelo, the system, the play itself, or all of these.

Here again and still more dystopically, a sapphic plot, resolved through its own rupture, marks the disintegration of familial order. In place of the paternal, we have the rule of the sapphic character herself, effectively turned man of the house and head of the family even as she is becoming a wife. And since Dionisia's entire involvement with Don Juan has been as the man "Añasco," the text has arguably traded the marriage of two women for the marriage of two men, with a clear sense of which "man" will be the ruler. Certainly the entire dynamic of comedy is thwarted here: every narrative move that should have led to a union is turned aside. When, in the last lines, Don Juan begs the audience to forgive the comedy's own "faltas," the move may be not simply a nod to convention but a recognition of the fault-line in this play. *Añasco el de Talavera* has written itself into a corner in its attempt to confront explicit sapphic desire—or, conversely, confronted sapphic desire to write the system into a corner, and its way out is to render the father impotent and to abrogate the very relationships that the play itself sets up in the name of its *pater familias*. It is ironically apposite that when Dionisia loses the literary contest in act 2, the judges fault her for a lack of verisimilitude, a charge that could surely be brought against the play itself.

While Benserade's *Iphis et Iante* underscores the damage wrought by

paternal failure and effectively both validates and rewards same-sex desire, Cubillo underscores the arbitrary order that results when same-sex
desire can be neither accommodated nor metamorphically transferred. In
their display of same-sex desire and its problematic resolution, both plays
suggest that the metamorphic logic so pervasive on the stage around 1600
has started already to erode, and so it is fitting that it takes a literal thun-
derbolt to summon Isis and an equivalently shocking textual machinery
for Dionisia to get a vengeful version of her way. These plays also suggest
that the sapphic is not only a disruption that cannot wholly be righted,
but a disruption born of misbegotten hierarchies of power. Put differently,
through the sapphic these plays ask what gets exposed when a socially
unworkable desire enters a family and, by extension, a polity. That the
unworkable desire would place a daughter outside a patriarchal structure
begins to suggest why the sapphic story has such political resonance: it augurs in both of these plays the leveling of a traditional, hierarchical order
of power that is in some sense justified by the failings of the fathers; at the
same time, a sapphic solution is rejected as each play seeks an effective
middle ground against both absolutism and anarchy. These questions also
lay at the heart of Spanish domestic and military politics under Philip IV,
leading to a monarchical crisis in the 1630s that Cubillo may well be attempting to figure if not to work out. Benserade and Cubillo also, however,
augur the growing recognition that the sapphic could neither be erased
nor accommodated without changes in the status quo. It may not be insignificant that both *Iphis and Ianthe* and *Añasco el de Talavera* fell into the
discursive silence that I described in chapter 1 as not atypical for sapphic
texts: both were performed and subsequently published in book form, yet
neither play was included in subsequent collections of the author's works,
neither was reprinted before the late twentieth century, extant copies remain rare, and contemporary responses were almost nonexistent, as scholars of both works have noted.

A poem in the Abbé Antoine de Torche's *Toilette galante de l'amour* of
1670, "Le mariage de l'amitié entre deux Belles. Celle qui fait le personnage
du Marx parle à l'autre," produces a more playful and differently resistant
version of this dual recognition that the sapphic subject's metamorphic
days are numbered, but that there is also no imaginative place for *same*-
sex relations. Staging a bedroom monologue by the girl who is "playing the
husband" in a "marriage of friendship between two beauties," the speaker
admits that she is jealous of potential rivals whose anatomy can best her
own and laments her inability to provide more than an "imperfect joy."
In order to satisfy her partner, she tells her, she would have to "have what

you don't have."[35] Glad as she is for the two women's *rapports* "in mind, in attractions, in merit and in birth," it is precisely their "too-great resemblance" that "halts our designs, and our sweetest transports."[36] In the end, she says, Nature should have put some "inequality" between them in order to enable Hymen's "sweet pleasures." Instead, what will be "without equal" is their *torment*, and that is where the poem leaves off: "without a metamorphosis / In faith, I see no cure for this misery."[37] The cure is of course sexual difference, which in Torche's poem takes on a value that demands but also exceeds the physical, and it is telling that the horizontality or leveling potential that I have attributed to the "same" in "same-sex" is explicitly rejected here.

Unlike metamorphic stories in which the romance of the same must be relinquished for the reality of difference, then, Torche's poem laments resemblance, and with it the conceptually horizontal, while also showing no "faith" in the promise of amelioration through sex change. More than a typical jibe at the impossibility of homoerotic pleasure, the poem deploys the tropes of social organization—hierarchy, equality—to express is erotic dilemma; in this sense it reverses the project of Benserade and Cubillo by using the social to figure sexuality rather than using sexuality to figure ssocial order. That the poem also refers to the women's relationship as a marriage, and thus an implicitly sanctioned *fait accompli* that will not have an Ovidian rescue, lends an inevitability of impasse to the poem's sexual and social politics. Benserade's own stanzas "Sur l'amour d'Uranie avec Philis," written much later in his life and published posthumously in 1697, renders the sapphic similarly irresolvable: the disgruntled speaker, who has lost out to a woman in a triangular rivalry for another woman, characterizes the sapphic as a "rien du tout," a "mere shadow" lacking force or power ("sans forces et sans pouvoir") and the two women as "zeros" to the male "numbers."[38] Still, he must admit that this nullity has won out over the supposed masculine plenitude. Ironically, the speaker's attempt to secure his superior position in the hierarchy of gender backfires despite the military posture of his words; the poem can ultimately only reduce the male speaker to begging that the women give up "this strange madness [cette étrange manie]" for "solid pleasures [les solides plaisirs]."[39] Here too we see the women's resistance to a metamorphosis the man cannot effect, just as we do in Edward Waller's "On the Friendship Betwixt Two Ladies" (1645), which likewise addresses the sapphic couple in an effort at uncoupling, as the speaker asks why the women are "so careless of our care" and "only to yourselves so dear," and lamenting that they "control" the "power of love." Reversing the meta-

morphic model of a work like the burlesque "Hallándose dos damas" that
I discussed in chapter 2, the poet complains that "the boy's eluded darts"
can "arrive at neither soul."[40] If we think back to the rhetorical questions
about what a woman might do with another woman that characterize the
earlier seventeenth century, we can see, as we see in Benserade's and Cubillo's dramas, that the sapphic is posing a greater challenge to regula-
tory systems that are attempting to put bodies in their proper place and
to the men who rely on those systems. As the next section of this chapter
stresses, putting bodies in their *proper* place also means attempting to
distinguish the bodies and behaviors of Europeans from non-Europeans
on sapphic, as on so many other, grounds. It is illuminating, therefore,
to look at the primary non-European setting for female-female relations
during the period encompassed by this chapter and to consider what that
location might signify.

INTIMATE EMPIRES: TURKEY TO TWICKENHAM

As historians of sexuality have long emphasized and as I noted before,
one of the major moves in the making of modernity is to relocate sexual
behaviors that are undesired or forbidden by one culture to an othered,
sometimes Catholic, more usually non-European, colonial or orientalized
Elsewhere. Indeed, Pamela Cheek argues in *Sexual Antiopdes* that modern
sexuality as constructed in the age of European Enlightenment constitutes
itself precisely on its negotiations with particular, different, and often rivalrous cultural geographies.[41] In the early modern imaginary, however,
different sexual practices occupy different mappings; thus the South Seas
that Cheek examines became imaged as a geography of "free" heterosexual
love. And while American "savages" were sometimes thought sodomitical, probably no Elsewhere carried as relentless a reputation for sodomy,
outside (Papist) Italy, as (Papist) Italy: for one telling example, consider
the title of a mid-seventeenth-century French satire, "La France devenue
italienne avec les autres déréglements de la cour [France become Italian
with the other disorders of the court]."[42] Likewise, no country comes in for
as much sapphic displacement as Turkey and such "Asiatic" neighbors as
Egypt and Morocco, along with the empire for which Turkey often synecdochically stands.

The ethnography of this entanglement between the Islamic Ottoman
world and sapphic subjects invented by Europeans is both physical and
cultural. From at least the late sixteenth century, traveler's accounts like
Busbecq's emphasized Turkish baths as a site of homoerotic as well as eth-

nic promiscuity: "ordinarily the Women bathe by themselves, Bond and Free together," he writes, "so that you shall many times see young Maids, exceeding beautiful, gathered from all Parts of the World, exposed Nacked to the view of other Women, who thereupon fall in Love with them, *as young Men do with us*, at the sight of Virgins."[43] Here Busbecq is already distinguishing what women do in "our" country, and whether that country is the Flanders from which he came or the Holy Roman Empire which he served matters little given the pan-European frequency of this kind of comment. The thread of attribution to Turkey and other Near Eastern countries continues almost unabated across two centuries; indeed, Busbecq's sixteenth-century tale about an older woman attempting to marry a maiden she first saw at the baths is repeated almost verbatim in the 1749 *Satan's Harvest Home*. Turkish baths appear in Nicolay's *Travels into Turkei* as similarly sapphic, as I have already suggested; the "filthie lust" of "woman with woman" is likewise Turkish in George Sandys's *Relation of a Journey* (1615);[44] and the sapphic seraglio will figure, if more sympathetically and in a slightly different (Persian) setting, in Montesquieu's *Lettres persanes* (1721).

Sex segregation is not the only ethnographic pretext, however, for figuring Turkish women as more likely to be homoerotic than their European counterparts. Even as notions of anatomical causality for homoeroticism in European women diminish, they get pushed onto Asian and African subjects. Thus Jane Sharp's *Midwives Book* (1671) comments that "in the Indies, and Egypt" the enlarged genitalia associated with the tribade "are frequent," and then claims, on the basis of a self-deconstructing logic of secrecy, that "I never heard but of one in this Country, if there be any they will do what they can for shame to keep it close."[45] John Marten's *Treatise of the Venereal Disease*, published in several iterations between 1704 and 1711, singles out women of Turkey, Lisbon, Arabia, and Ethiopia for the large clitoris that, he says, leads to sapphic wantonness.[46] Although all the characters figured as "Hermaphrodites and Masculine Females" in the 1718 *Treatise of Hermaphrodites* are French or (mostly) Italian, the text still argues that the planetary influences are strongest in Turkey, where hermaphrodites are thus more numerous "than in the Western Parts of the World, and they are oblig'd to go in different Habits from other People . . . to prevent their lying with any."[47] James Parsons' *Mechanical Inquiry* argues that "Some of the *Asiatick*, as well as the *African* Nations" have a particular propensity to produce women with masculine genitals. That this ethnic logic persists throughout the eighteenth century is vividly illustrated in the libel suit brought in 1810 by two Scottish school-

teachers, Jane Pirie and Marianne Woods, after they were accused of lesbian acts: at least one judge dismissed the possibility that Pirie and Woods
could have been sexually transgressive by nationalizing female anatomy:
"they import the crime of one woman giving another the clitoris, which *in
this country* is not larger than the nipple of the breast and is, furthermore,
immersed between the labia of the pudenda. Therefore . . . it is a crime
which, in the general case, it is impossible *in this country* to commit."[48]
Thus the European sapphic imaginary remains long embedded in distinctions between "their" bodies—especially the bodies of Muslim women—
and "ours." Coupled with images of baths and harems, these orientalized
anatomical fictions render the sapphic particularly suited to Near Eastern
rather than European societies.

It is equally significant that sapphic ethnographies do not connect
female homoeroticism, either through anatomy or cultural practices, to
other non-European sites: except for Catholic Italy, virtually all the specific countries singled out in sapphic ethnographies of the seventeenth and
eighteenth centuries—Egypt, Morocco, Arabia, Bulgaria, and especially
Turkey—are countries within the Ottoman Empire. The absence of other
locations is even theorized in at least one late-eighteenth-century text:
L'esprit des usages et des coutumes de différens peuples (1776) assigns ped-
erasty to the "savages" of the Americas but avows that "travelers never
speak of tribades in describing the manners of savages [Les Voyageurs ne
parlent jamais de tribades en décrivant les moeurs des sauvages]"; this
"disorder" usually begins "in great nations, in seraglios, and in this age
when luxury leads to satiation and disgust [dans les grandes nations, dans
les serrails, & a cette époque ou le luxe amene la satiété & le dégout]."[49]
Note again, here, the sense that in Europe, if not in Turkey, the sapphic is
new, born of modern decadence. And when the New World gets connected
to the sapphic, as it does in Moreau de St.-Méry's *Voyage aux États-Unis
d'Amérique*, the author associates heterosexual license with women of
color (who may be avenging themselves, he said, for the "shocking contempt" with which white Philadelphians treat them), but relegates exclusively to white women the "almost unbelievable" practice of being "not at
all strange to being willing to seek unnatural pleasures with persons of
their own sex."[50]

Certainly the association of the sapphic with Turkey can be read as
an extension of a broader early modern attribution of the oppression of
women to Islamic societies. As Felicity Nussbaum's *Torrid Zones* points
out,[51] Europeans repeatedly singled out Eastern countries as places where
confinement of women and their treatment as "slaves" could be contrasted

to the alleged benevolence of early seventeenth-century England (for example, in Richard Brathwait's *English Gentlewoman*) or late-seventeenth-century France (in Poulain de la Barre's *De l'égalité des deux sexes*) and on to late-eighteenth-century Spain, where Ignacio Lopez de Ayala's defense of women rests on claims of Spanish modernity—"the world is new"—contrasted to "Roman ambition, northern ferocity, the brutal fanaticism of the Mohammedans."[52] Counterclaims were also advanced: the Huguenot humanist Pierre Bayle's influential *Dictionnaire historique et critique* (1696) argues that Turkish women are more virtuous than their Christian counterparts, while Sarah Chapone's *Hardship of the English Laws in Relation to Wives* (1735) "abhor[s]" the comparison between the two, arguing that it is "no excuse for us when the women in Turkey are used harder than we are."[53] In fact, women in Ottoman countries, as is now well supported by historical evidence, fared better both legally and economically, were indeed legal and economic subjects in ways unknown to most European women and especially to wives precisely because of shari'ah law, which fixed women's rights to inherit and testify and supported women's economic enterprise. Mary Wortley Montagu, who lived in Turkey while her husband was a diplomatic representative, understood these distinctions when she claimed that Turkish women "have more Liberty than we have."[54] Most European writers, however, seem not to have recognized or wilfully to have ignored the rights accorded to Muslim women under Ottoman rule.[55]

It seems likely, however, that the singling out of Turkey was also related to the status within the European imaginary of the Ottoman Empire itself. As Donald Quataert reminds us, "throughout nearly all its 600-year history, the Ottoman state was as much a part of the European political order as were its French or Habsburg rivals."[56] The empire had reached the borders of Austria in 1529 and again in 1683; thus the 1694 English translation of Busbecq's *Legation tucicae epistolae* promises in its title to offer "remarks upon the religion, customs, riches, strength and government of that people: as also a description of their chief cities, and places of trade and commerce: to which is added, *his advice how to manage war against the Turks*" (emphasis mine). But even the fearful obsession with the Ottoman Empire clearly exceeded the military threat, especially during the Empire's own desperate political period in the seventeenth century when, as Alain Grosrichard notes, "bloody revolts multiplied," four sultans were deposed or assassinated, and seventeen grand viziers succeeded one another in the twelve years from 1644 to 1656, with "only one of them dying a natural death."[57] Grosrichard sees these events as having encouraged a

European investment in the Ottomans as the displaced site for a fear of despotism; the Orient becomes the "despotic Other held up for us to see" at a time when European countries are grappling with the power of their own absolute rulers.[58]

It seems probable that the entanglements of these countries in the sapphic imaginary, whether framed in terms of moral license or physical difference, has a source in the threat seen to be posed by the Ottoman state and by its state religion. It may not be accidental either that in the early seventeenth century that empire, as Quartaert notes, "shared the world stage" with "Elizabethan England, Habsburg Spain, and the Holy Roman Empire as well as Valois France and Holland"—that is, with world powers where sapphic representations were already in vogue. Moreover, as in the countries where sapphic subjects multiplied, an unprecedented number of women ruled in the Ottoman courts as regents for minor, incompetent, or deposed sultans, as Leslie Peirce notes.[59] It has become commonplace to recognize the ways in which orientalism demands, as Meyda Yegenoglu puts it, the feminization of the East as a veiled and mysterious space,[60] and what more mysterious space than the space of the seraglio with its same-sex relations? It is also possible, especially as the Ottoman Empire itself declined in the late seventeenth and eighteenth centuries, that the putative perversity of Turkey persisted in the European imaginary primarily so that Europe could affirm its own "modernity" on the bodies of women—and eventually of course, justify its conquest of that empire.

It is significant, then, that the sapphic becomes represented not simply as a "Turkish" practice but as an invasive one, a threat to European women and ultimately connected to home turf by the "Turkey" and "Twicken-ham" conjunction in my epigraph. The passage from *Satan's Harvest Home* that makes the move explicit is pirated from William Walsh's 1691 dialogue on women, but Walsh makes no mention of Twickenham: his goal is to silence Sappho's "new Crime" by ordaining that "*Lucian* be forgotten for putting us in mind of it, and let it be Cloister'd up within the walls of a *Turkish* Seraglio; and after that shew you what progresses this Crime has made, not only in the *Turk*'s Dominion, but even in *Spain* and *Italy*." Thus Walsh demurs even as he hints of sapphic practices in England: "were it civil to quote the Lampoons, or write the Amours of our own Time, we might be furnish'd with Examples enow nearer home."[61]

One might indeed argue that the reticence around "Examples . . . nearer home" is just what underwrites the excessive repetition of the sapphic seraglio imagery. But the 1749 addition of Twickenham in the *Satan's Harvest Home* version rejects that reticence with its home-ground reference: Turkey and Twickenham are alliteratively linked, and linked with the sapphic.[62] In a double move, then, the Ottoman Empire and up-start English women can be discredited in a single breath, serving home-grown purposes in both senses of "home" and reinforcing the domestic danger of the sapphic "game of flats." We see a similar allusion in that same year when John Cleland's *Memoirs of a Woman of Pleasure* describes Mrs. Cole's brothel as a "little Seraglio." And by 1749, the year of publication of both *Satan's Harvest Home*, with its alarums over the sexual sins of Great Britain, and *Woman of Pleasure*, which arguably celebrates those same sins, the sapphic is already well conscripted to serve the state. The texts to which I turn now use precisely that horizontal iconography of leveling or "flats" in the interests of English politics.

EXCLUSION POLITICS: THE GAME OF FLATS

By the turn of the eighteenth century, the complications of metamorphic plots like Benserade's and Cubillo's and the recursive evasions of the orientalized ethnographies had together increased the potential of the sapphic to figure "woman + woman" as a logic not easily converted or subsumed. It is thus all the more significant that a number of writings published in England from the 1690s through 1749 grapple, through the sapphic, with the prospects of political leveling. As a case study in the sexuality of history, I turn to a body of texts that span the period, to argue that the sapphic gets embroiled in surprising ways within an urgent and factionalized political project that would seem to have little to do with sexuality: the project of determining the course of British government. It turns out that a surprising number of sapphic representations produced in England during this half century, including some English instances of the "sapphic apostrophes" that I will discuss in chapter 4,[63] are the work of writers with strong partisan politics whether Whig, Tory, or Jacobite. While, as I have said, it is not my interest to tie these writings to biographical causes, the texts themselves clearly take up political questions through tropes of the sapphic, demonstrating dramatically the ways in which sexuality might produce as well as mirror divergent visions of the state.

The diverse texts that I have in mind make connections, often explicit ones, between sapphic relations and contemporary politics. Some of these texts were obviously stimulated by the sexual suspicions surrounding Queen Anne and, before her, King William. The 1708 "New Ballad" attributed to Arthur Maynwaring charges Queen Anne with sapphic motivations in dismissing her longtime intimate—the Whig Sarah Jennings

Churchill, Duchess of Marlborough—in favor of the lesser-born Tory Abigail Hill Masham, cousin to the powerful Tory minister Robert Harley. In making its charges, the ballad deploys the resonant language of "dark deeds," a phrase frequently used against Stuart "enslavement,"[64] to imply that Masham has given sapphic "sweet Service" to the Queen in a leveling of rank as damnable as the shifting of allegiances from Whig to Tory that the Queen's sapphic susceptibility was believed to motivate.[65] From the Tory side, Delarivier Manley's 1709 *The New Atalantis* imagines a "new Cabal" of Whigs that has "wisely excluded that rapacious *Sex*, who mak[e] a Prey of the Honour of Ladies," and in which women may be joining together "in an Excess of *Amity*" to "revive" the "vices of Old Rome."[66] With equivocal irony, *The New Atalantis* posits this female community as a "Commonwealth" of shared property and "invincible" service. This is not a community the text tells us how to interpret: as the *New Atalantis's* mouthpiece Astrea says, the Cabal "is something so *new* and *uncommon*, so *laudable* and *blameable*, that we don't know how to *determine*" whether the women dwell in "*tender Friendship*" or something "beyond what *Nature* design'd."[67] And from the Whig side again, Bernard Mandeville's quirky *Virgin Unmask'd: or, Female Dialogues Betwixt an Elderly Maiden Lady, and her Niece*, also published in 1709, uses a queerly eroticized relationship between the unmarried Lucinda and her niece Antonia to couple the "enslavement" of women with the "enslavement" of Louis XIV's oppressed subjects,[68] offering a rationale for her attachment to women and aversion for men that is also a brief for Dutch over French models of governance. In each of these cases, then, English discourse during the reign of a Stuart queen shapes a politics with sapphic innuendo.

Its later creation notwithstanding, a similar dynamic, more heavily freighted with anti-sapphic vitriol, appears in the Jacobite sympathizer William King's rambling and heavily annotated *The Toast* (1732). Purporting to be the translated Latin epic of one Frederick Scheffer, *The Toast* turns personal venom to political ends as King pillories his cousin's wife as the hermaphrodite and lesbian Myra, who "annexe[s]" male privilege and turns her husband, a milquetoast son of Jupiter and Juno ("or, as others say, of *Juno* alone") into a "God of War" who leads the English army with "little military Skill and less Courage." In an obvious if gratuitous dig at William of Orange (now of course three decades deceased), King pointedly makes Myra's love interest a "little *Dutch* Frow" as well as "a Jewess and a Dwarf" who "gave *Myra* more Pleasure than all the rest of her Lovers and Mistresses. She was therefore dignified with the Title of Chief of the *Tribades* or *Lesbians*."[69] Thus *The Toast* directly entangles the sapphic with political figures as a way to denigrate not simply persons but a political party. It is possible that the presence on the English scene of works such as *The New Atalantis* set the stage for this nastier coupling of sex and politics and that this text, in turn, influenced the plot of the *Sappho-an* that I will take up below.

The texts on which I want to focus more closely, however, lack these obvious explanatory links between the sapphic and the political and would thus seem to have less direct reason for tapping into the potential of same-sex relations. Dating from the turn of the eighteenth century, Catharine Trotter's *Agnes de Castro* (1695) and Nicholas Rowe's brief "Song" (1701) use female-female relations to posit utopias along Whiggish principles. Trotter, who diverged from her Scottish family's Catholic, Tory, and probably Jacobite affiliations though she later married a nonjuring cleric, made her playwriting debut with a drama that reshapes an event from Iberian history to explore the political reverberations of personal desire and the personal reverberations of political intrigue. Although the central conflict revolves around the Portuguese prince, the well-being of the state that is at stake in the drama turns out to depend, far more than is the case for the Tory Aphra Behn's story of the same name on which it is founded, on the loyal love between two women and the politics of integrity they represent.

The triangles at the heart of *Agnes de Castro* raise questions of betrayal and loyalty, submission and resistance to power. The Spanish Princess, aptly named Constantia, learns that her husband the Prince of Portugal has conceived a helpless passion for her beloved friend Agnes. Yet the Princess's love for both Agnes and her husband remains steadfast: "So closely wove by Fate to my fond breast, / That neither can be sever'd from my love, / Without unravelling this Web of Life," and indeed her response to her husband's supposedly unchosen shifting of desire is to refuse rivalry on the claim that "I my self, prefer her to my self, / And love her too, as tenderly as he."[70] Plotting the downfall of both Constantia and Agnes, however, are the state insiders Elvira, sister to the King's ambitious advisor Alvaro, and her sidekick Bianca, who seek revenge for the Prince's having chosen Constantia over Elvira for his wife. Bianca's finding the Princess "leaning on her Rivals Neck" and "mingl[ing] Kisses with the tend'rest Words" (20) only inflames Elvira further: the love between the Princess and Agnes, she insists, compromises the state itself: it is the "Kingdom's Grievance," since "we're all alike neglected for this Stranger," and now "the Spanish Fugitive, is Sovereign here" (18). The challenge to official power that Agnes embodies when she names the Princess "sole

Disposer of my Actions" (14) and insists on loyalty to the (foreign) Princess over submission to the crown has far-reaching implications both within the play and within the politics of an England ruled by a controversial and foreign king.

Agnes's loyalty to liberty is absolute, and it challenges not only one king but the very notion of kingship. When the King attempts to solve the problem of the Prince's illicit passion by ordering Agnes to marry his minister Alvaro, Agnes predictably refuses though the marriage would supposedly make her "the Envy of your Sex": "No, Sir, I value Liberty far more, / Than to forsake it, though for Golden Chains, / A shining Prison, is a Prison still" (13). This refusal the King reads as "contempt," and his helplessness in the face of it, a usurpation of his power: "Am I a king?" he must query, when Agnes "braves my Pow'r, / Disdains my Favourite, slights my Noblest Gifts. / I bear it all, and yet I am a King" (16). In the monarchical model, of course, absolute authority and blind loyalty are the twin, and Stuart-like, evils against which Agnes stands. Once Agnes has resisted the proposal and with it the King's power, the dangers of misbegotten kingship deepen as the King proposes that Alvaro rape Agnes in order to subdue the woman who "treats [the King] as she were some mighty Queen, / And I her meanest, despicable Slave": so "vast" is "Woman's Empire" that "The Conquerers of the World, submit to them" (16). Alvaro's goal, equally venal, is to establish his own supremacy over the prince: Agnes is to be forced into marriage so that "she, and Portugal shall know / That but in Name, [Alvaro] will be more" than "the Prince who loves her" (16). The rapacious competition of the men runs up and down the chain here: Diego, Alvaro's officer, likewise claims, in an admission of double-dealing that would not go unnoticed in the insecure aftermath of the Glorious Revolution, that "to serve my Patron, I'd betray my Father" (19). And Alvaro too manipulates fatherhood, determined to "enflame the King against his Son" and in the end to take revenge for power's sake: "The King's Favour plac'd me above his Subjects, / Revenge on him, makes me above himself. . . . For Desperation's bolder than Ambition. / My Rival is the Pillar of the Nation" (42). There could hardly be a more obvious representation of a struggle for power within a court.

In the end, every character, whether virtuous or malignant, pays the price of this internecine struggle: there is no "private" desire in the world of *Agnes de Castro*. Elvira fatally stabs the Princess, wrongly thinking her to be Agnes; Alvaro stabs Agnes in a misdirected attempt to kill the Prince; and in a fit of madness Elvira kills Bianca to shut her up. Agnes is ready to die once the Princess has died; she is, after all, losing "my Light, my Guard, my All" (25), and she goes to her own death imagining a kind of heavenly intercourse in which "I shall meet my Princess where I go, / And our unspotted Souls, in Bliss above, / Will know each other, and again, will love" (34). Loyalty may be as fatal as jealousy, but loyalty is also here the only ground for a state that is not destroyed by its "rebels"—the word is used repeatedly, especially in the last two acts of the play as things unravel. And the rebels are not the outsider Spaniards, but forces from within, replicating the internal divisions and betrayals associated with the Stuart court and implicitly valuing the foreign William as best fit to reign.

The Prince is willing but weak and survives chastened, but only one relationship, that between Agnes and the aptly named Constantia, holds steady in this play. Moreover, the primary source of rebellion is the lust for power, the fear of being displaced in a hierarchical order: Elvira and Alvaro are undone by their fierce refusal to be bested, and even the King worries that his absolute authority is being challenged by those like Agnes who claim the right of consent over the duty of obedience. Ultimately, then, it is Constantia and Agnes who hold out the possibility of a finer way: a way of trust between equals built on loyal love that cannot be compromised by earthly gain and that must therefore be consigned to an afterlife. With heavy use of a discourse of loyalty, betrayal, and national interest that makes the play's political purposes evident, Trotter relies on a same-sex relationship to model the ideal dynamics of a state.

In a briefer text with more openly sexual meaning, Nicholas Rowe's 1701 "Song" also vividly renders a sapphic liaison as an idyllic parity with implications for the body politic:

> While Sappho with harmonious Airs
> Her dear Philenis charms,
> With equal Joy the Nymph appears
> Dissolving in her Arms.
>
> Thus to themselves alone they are
> What all Mankind can give;
> Alternately the happy Pair
> All grant, and All receive.
>
> Like the Twin-Stars, so fam'd for Friends,
> Who set by Turns, and rise;
> When one to Thetis Lap descends,
> His Brother mounts the Skies.

With happier Fate, and kinder Care,
These Nymphs by Turns do reign,
While still the falling, does prepare
The rising, to sustain.

The Joys of either Sex in Love
In each of them we read,
Successive each, to each does prove,
Fierce Youth and yielding Maid.[71]

In a poem that occasions one of the earliest uses of the term "Game at Flats," in the subtitle appended to the poem from 1715, Rowe encodes not only the corporeal—the sense of two women engaging in sex that involves two "flat" bodies—but a natural dynamic of mutuality that amounts to a political leveling built on a *quid pro quo*.[72] Uniting the Sapho and Philenis who would be best known to English culture by way of Donne, the poem encodes a harmonious, indeed celestial arrangement in which "Alternately the happy Pair / All grant, and All receive." The pair is sufficient unto itself, since they to themselves alone are "What all Mankind can give," and they also mirror the order of nature, in which the "brother" stars likewise rise and set "by Turns." In other words, this is not a model of unnatural practice; it is the natural working of the universe at its most harmonious. The reciprocity represented is complete: the Nymphs reign "by Turns" and do so "with happier Fate, and kinder Care," experiencing the Joys of love both male and female: each woman is able to be both "fierce Youth" and "yielding Maid." Rowe's poem implies a mutuality, a kind of utopian turn-taking, that pointedly suggests a new kind of "reign." Here again, then, a sapphic order of things figures a model of government in which two equal partners move in synchrony for their shared benefit. In the cycle of rising and falling that evokes revolution in the sense still prominent in 1689, the give and take imaged through the sapphic in this short poem readily evokes the ideal relationship between Crown and Parliament.

A well-advertised, four-page, 1728 *Epistle from Sapho to Philaenis* takes a similar approach as it follows along the lines of Donne's original, pilfering, paraphrasing, and embellishing in ways that make for poor poetry but plain politics. In addition to preserving women from "the Till-age of robustous Men" who rob their virtue and leave them with "nine Months growing Load," sapphic intimacy provides "a mut'al Harmony" and "a just Equality of Age and Mind" for couples who "are to the same Desires inclin'd." The poem ends by asking Philaenis for a "sincere and permanent" "Presence" that will "crown my ardent Hope" and give the "utmost Scope" of "Bliss."[73] While the *Epistle* is anonymous and, like so many of these texts, has left little by way of a paper trail, it was popularly advertised in at least four newspapers at the time of its publication, and even if satiric it understands the sapphic as a model of justice, equality, and harmony connected perhaps more than metaphorically to a "crown."

It remains to be understood, of course, why Trotter, Rowe, and the anonymous author of the *Epistle* configure their visions of the ideal state in terms of the sapphic. Certainly the vision itself corresponds with liberal sympathies for governance built around loyalty and mutuality that might have been easier to imagine in tropes of female intimacy during periods when men held the English monarchy and women could stand as figures outside of state power than between 1702 and 1714 when Anne, with her own suspect and politicized intimacies with women, was on the throne. But this condition makes the sapphic available without yet explaining why it might have been desirable. One answer lies simply in the fact of use: if female intimacies could figure the ideal state, than something about the ideal state is already evoked, in the social imaginary, by intimacies between women.

It is telling, however, that the sapphic can also undermine hierarchies in less salutary ways. Such is the case with Jane Barker's "The Unaccountable Wife," an inserted tale within her fictional *Patch-work Screen for the Ladies* (1723) in which a relationship between women that crosses lines of status stands in for the potential destruction of the social order. In Barker's tale, a "gentlewoman of distinction" who is pointedly described as unattractive—a physical defect is also hinted—marries a handsome gentleman who then takes the family's maidservant into his bed, begetting children by her every year. Wife, husband, and servant share that bed, but now it is the wife who gets up each morning to light the fire and make the meals, to wash and scour, while the servant "sits about in her handsome Velvet Chair, dress'd up in very good lac'd Linnen, having clean Gloves on her Hands."[74] Eventually, however, the servant's fecundity begins worrying the husband, who wants to evict her, but to his surprise he cannot persuade the wife to part with her. Though this refusal "offended God, disgrac'd her Family, scandaliz'd her Neighbours, and was a Shame to Woman-kind" (100), the wife insists that her servant is her "dearest friend, indeed the only Friend she had in the World" (101) and that if the servant is sent away she will follow.

Convinced that he can call her bluff, the husband dismisses the servant, but indeed the wife goes too. The women end up in legal custody as

vagrants until a relative recognizes the wife and takes her in. Yet again the
wife insists that she must remain with her "truest Friend in the World"
(104). The husband dies; neighbors get "a Warrant, to have them before a
Justice, in order to prevent a Parish Charge" (103); a relative who is a "Lady
of Quality" offers to help her to no avail; "friends and relations" implore
her to "leave that Creature" and "return to a state suitable to her Birth and
Education" (104); but "all in vain; she absolutely adher'd to this Woman
and her Children" (104) though she was reduced to begging in the streets.
At last, word gets to the Queen of England, who says that she herself will
take care of the wife if she abandons the servant. But this "infatuated
Creature" goes so far as to refuse "the *Queen's* favour" (105) and remains
a beggar for the rest of her days. No one can explain her resistance; they
believe that only some "Spell or Inchantment" (105) or "an Interior thor-
oughly degenerated" (100) could lead a gentlewoman to "oppose her Husband, and all her nearest Friends, and even her *Sovereign*" (105) to follow
her "unaccountable" desires.

In this insistently recursive tale, the cleaving of one woman to another
threatens to topple the entire social order in what is almost a parody of de-
volution. As Antony Upton notes, the "ordered hierarchy of authority, often called the 'great chain of being,'" is still in play in this moment along
with the divine-right theory on which it rests; within its logic, "God's
omnipotence was devolved to his chosen deputies on earth, and through
them it was devolved further to the ground level, to the patriarchal head
of a household of family and servants, which was the basic building block
of society." In this supposedly orderly system, everyone's duty is "to render unquestioning obedience to their divinely ordained superiors and impose it on those entrusted to their charge."[75] But the "unaccountable wife"
abolishes the authority of *all* "divinely ordained superiors" from mistress
to husband to family to queen: a woman's desire gives sovereignty to the
female servant at the bottom of the human chain, creating a resistant
sapphic alliance that its narrator, if not it author, sees as, "a dangerous
threat to a social system" in Kathryn King's words."[76]

Such a representation suggests that women might well be the source of
a cross-class alliance that could undermine the system as a whole. Barker's
"Unaccountable Wife" thus constitutes yet another angle on the powers
and dangers of sapphic desire and the leveling implications of female-
female relations. The wife's clinging to the servant is a conundrum to her
neighbors, "unaccountable" in several senses of the term, and its consequences are disastrous: two women and their children reduced to beggary
by an incomprehensible attachment, yielding the image of social order in

which either an attempt at female resistance or a false notion of equality has set everything awry. Of course one could argue that the demolition began with the husband's displacing his wife for the servant, which intensifies the injunction against changing the hierarchy of class. Whatever Barker's own motives for writing this story into her *Patchwork*, which on the whole upholds women's rights of liberty, this particular tale evokes the concerns about leveling that one might expect from a Catholic Tory with a strong Jacobite history.[77] We see the tensions, then, between different sorts and sites of leveling, tensions similarly evident in the "Tory feminist" Mary Astell's attack on tyrannical husbands on the basis of a Lockean critique of absolutist government to which Astell herself did not adhere.

For a more explicitly Jacobite instance, I turn to a rare and rather mystifying production with almost no traceable history and only two or three copies extant. It has been dated to 1749, though there is no date on the title page, and its putative publisher, Charles Brasier in Fleet-street, seems to be a false name. Its title is *The Sappho-an. An Heroic Poem of Three Cantos. In the Ovidian Stile, Describing the Pleasures which the Fair Sex Enjoy with Each Other. According to the Modern and most Polite Taste* (see fig. 2). Not only is the sapphic yet again rendered modern, but it is also rendered openly political, for the title page tells us that this poem was "Found amongst the Papers of a Lady of Quality, a great Promoter of Jaconitism" [*sic*], an obvious allusion despite the (accidental or deliberate) misprint. Complex and confusing though it is, *The Sappho-an* is certainly taking up issues of British politics in the uneasy wake of the Jacobite rebellion of 1745. While it comes down on the Hanoverian side of the equation, it does so by aligning the sapphic with the Jacobite in a dystopian union of wrongheaded sex and wrongheaded governance. Given its evocation of Juno and Jove, there is a chance that it is also playing upon William King's *The Toast* but reversing the political and sexual onus.

Insofar as the text is plotted, the *Sappho-an* presents a Juno who with her tribe of Amazons seduces women in revenge for Jove's philandering with both women and men. Moving across settings that are variably fanciful, mythical, and historical, the text creates sapphic individuals, pairs, and communities, including a "congress" headed by Sappho herself, to satirize a range of groups, persons, and practices and claim heterosexuality for Englishness. All the more because the text also implicates identifiable events and persons, this elaborate and sexually frank work is much more than an excuse for titillation; it raises issues about nature, power, nation, and liberty that are central to the times and specific to Great Britain in the aftermath of the last major Jacobite defeat.

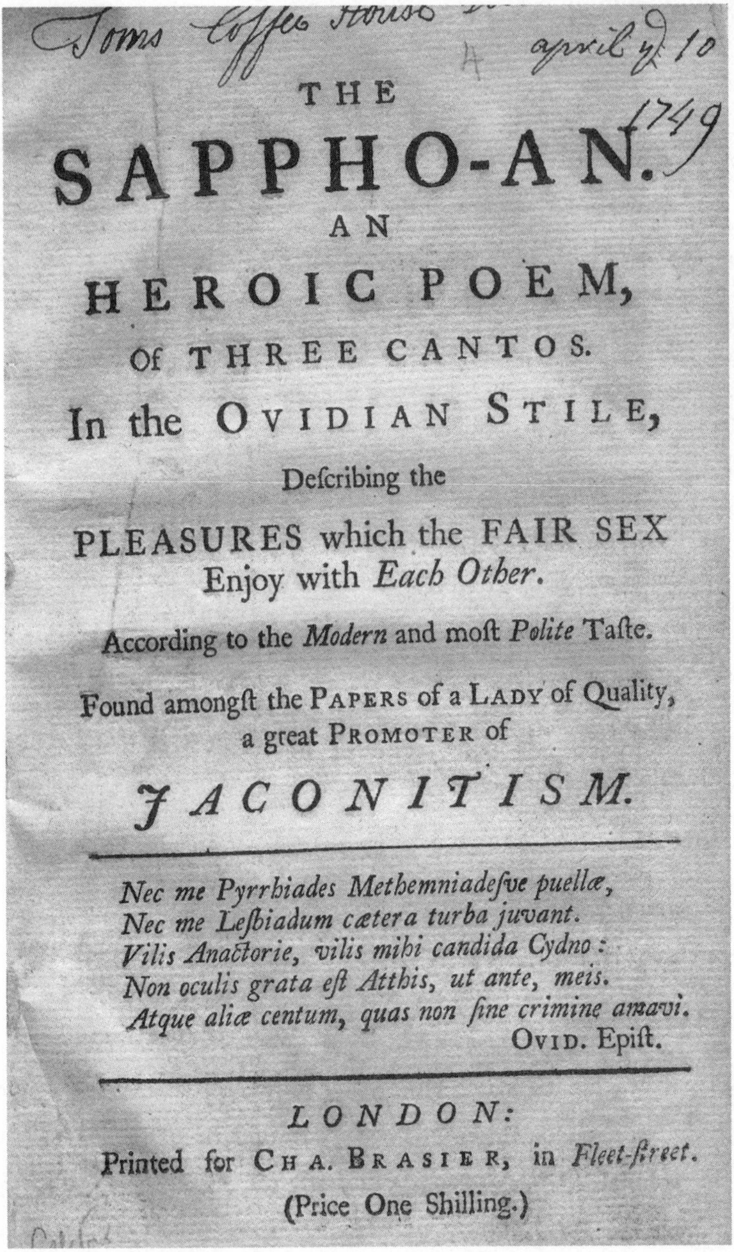

Toms Coffee House   *april y̅ 10*

1749

THE
SAPPHO-AN.
AN
HEROIC POEM,
Of THREE CANTOS.

In the OVIDIAN STILE,

Defcribing the

PLEASURES which the FAIR SEX
Enjoy with *Each Other.*

According to the *Modern* and moft *Polite* Tafte.

Found amongft the PAPERS of a LADY of Quality,
a great PROMOTER of

JACONITISM.

Nec me Pyrrhiades Methemniadefve puellæ,
Nec me Lefbiadum cætera turba juvant.
Vilis Anaɕtorie, vilis mihi candida Cydno :
Non oculis grata eft Atthis, ut ante, meis.
Atque aliæ centum, quas non fine crimine amavi.
                   OVID. Epift.

LONDON:

Printed for CHA. BRASIER, in *Fleet-ftreet.*

(Price One Shilling.)

Fig. 2. Title page of The *Sappho-an* (probably 1749). Courtesy of the Department of Special Collections, Spencer Research Library, University of Kansas Libraries.

The *Sappho-an*'s allusions to events, places, and objects in Stuart history leave little question that contemporary politics are at stake; the text is filled with references *à clef* to Jacobite characters, both Scottish actors and their English supporters ("B—m—d's daughter blushing chaste," "the lady of the Watch," "Westley," "Lady M").[78] But its critique of Jacobite ideology goes deeper than its coded references to the Battle of Culloden or the escape of Bonnie Prince Charlie in the clothes of a serving maid. With echoes of Defoe's 1706 *Jure Divino*, which it also resembles in its Ovidian form, *The Sappho-an* undermines divine-rightism by presenting the gods as the lustful, selfish, and devious authors of tyranny. Between Jove's whoring and Juno's caballing, the divine "chieftains" of the *Sappho-An*— "chieftain" is easily Scottish in 1749—stand as the secretive and vengeful antithesis to the culture of liberty on which a Gloriously Revolutionary England prides itself. "*No god* is honest found" (18), we're told: all engage in "filthy sport" (18) with men and court the "beds" of women: in short, these "deities" are the Stuarts, as references to Charles II as "the baudiest of k—gs" (45), to Nantes as a charged location, and to specific Jacobite supporters makes clear. If Jove is Charles, then clearly the Stuarts are not fit to rule, nor can any king claim the rights of godliness.

Yet it is not Jove but Juno and her female tribe who epitomize Jacobite scheming in their desire for revenge. And revenge is clearly a motivating ethos of *The Sappho-an*, in ways that echo the contention of a text like Fielding's *Jacobite's Journal*, that Jacobite fervor has its etiology in avenging the exclusion of James and his descendants from the throne. At least seven times *The Sappho-an* uses the word "secret"—a term that often modified "Jacobite" in this period—but here always in reference to women, as if the most dangerous, uncontrollable implications of *jure divino* reside in the "congress" of women, who, like the Jacobites, think they are redressing wrongs. And since "two women seldome meet but ills ensue" and thus from twelve "we must expect some plague that's new" (21), these phrases become a pointed reminder of the "plague years" of the early Stuart restoration. Jacobite imposture is also at issue here; the goddesses have "stole" the form of "*British* beauties" (23). But not only goddesses; from its first line, the poem opposes "the Swains of Britannia" to women who steal away the "rich prize" of *their* women "in secret joys," deluding "thoughtless girls," so that "where you expected the long-wish'd embrace; / Your lovely nymph, in private, quench'd her flame / With some experienc'd, well-known, crafty dame" (10). Deploying an "art" that "vy'd with nature" (10), women undermine Britannia's natural, and masculine, state. In effect, sapphists and Jacobites are equated as enemies against

British manhood and, by extension, British government. Jove, Juno, and the Jacobites—and implicitly all women—appropriate what belongs to another, whether young boys, young maidens, or a "pilfer'd crown" (31). And in satirizing the women's recourse to dildos—which, the *Sappho-an* tells us, were brought from France in the Stuart Restoration, the text naturalizes heterosexuality and Hanoverian government in the same breath.

In the end, the sapphic stands as inimical to the model of British government that Georgian England offers as the antidote to Jacobite—and Scottish—"tyranny" by modeling state relations as a mutuality not of women, as Trotter or Rowe imagine it, but of Britannia's boys and girls. On the penultimate page of the poem, the speaker calls for a sexual utopia where "young girls" can "avow your love, confess your flame, / And nature boldly own, devoid of shame." That this nature is heterosexual is immediately made clear: "Woman was made for man, so nature meant, / And ev'ry fibre answers the intent. / Who sins against it the creation wrongs, / Must rank with beasts, nor to mankind belongs" (47). In thus asserting the primacy of an open, faithful, and pleasurable heterosexuality that the text itself does not depict, *The Sappho-an* implies a parallel between two partnerships—men and women, monarch and people—as equivalently natural forms. At the same time, the specter of a female "congress" also legitimates the rule of men *as* men that, as I said at the outset of this book, comes to stand for the eighteenth-century body politic. The sapphic is a product of female spite, and the "false love" of women for women, along with other queer forms of desire, ends up standing in for false and queer forms of government. The scenario could hardly seem more dystopian, and yet the text revels in those women's antics and never shows the "natural" relations that it is ostensibly promoting. Clearly *The Sappho-an* is playing for titillation and satire as much as for politics.

Why might *The Sappho-an* use "lesbians," as it were, to make its case? If the text is critiquing the rule of Jove, why focus on the actions of Juno and throw in a congress of "amazons" that even includes the renowned poet and classical scholar Elizabeth Carter, unmarried and devoted to women as I will note in the next chapter, to be sure, but certainly no Jacobite?[79] It is not only that here again relations between women are seen to stand outside and thus potentially to threaten conventional hierarchies and structures of social control, though surely that project is at work. It is also the case that women have a particular place in the Jacobite story, and not just through the famous cross-dressing subterfuges of escaping kings. As Leigh Anna Eicke notes, "Jacobite political theory itself may have seemed to affirm women's roles in society more than emerging Whig political theories,"[80] and the Jacobite movement quite openly welcomed women's participation on multiple levels; not for nothing did Henry Fielding call them "Amazons in plaid jackets." Tellingly, *Female Rebels*, a political pamphlet published just two years before the *Sappho-an* in 1747, charges that Jacobite women are levelers, masculine in behavior and out to (over)rule:

> It is Time for the Male Part of the Creation to look about them, since a Change of Government might bring along with it more than a simple Change of the legal Constitution. We are not sure, but it is a Plot of that ambitious crafty Sex, to deprive Mankind of their Dominion over the Ladies: It may be a traiterous [*sic*] Conspiracy of our liege Subjects, the Women, against their sovereign Lord Man.
>
> How else can we account for that Number of Petticoats, that have appeared encased in Armour under the Banner of the Chevalier *Charles*? Women, (I had almost said Men) who, regardless of Danger, [are] forgetting the natural Softness of their Sex?[81]

Moreover, these "Female *Jacobites*" do not confine their opinions to the drawing room, but rather "leave the Exercise of the Closet, and sally out upon us in the Field."[82] In its secretive Jacobitish appropriations, Juno's female congress likewise wrests British women from patriarchal regulation to "out-ape the men." Clearly *The Sappho-an*'s ultimate concern, at once sexual and political, is for the well-being of British men. Creating a sapphic coterie thus sets up not simply the titillation to attract readers but the alarm bells that turn political danger into sexual danger and sexual disarray into political turmoil. In *The Sappho-an*, the two turn tandem: Britannia's men are in danger of losing both their "empire o'er the females" and empire itself, through the double perfidy of rulers and wives. Yet the women *as represented* are quite content, and do little harm beyond luring women away from male suitors. And indeed, the heteronormative ideal that the text proclaims is never embodied in the text.

In order to underscore from a different angle the extent to which this interrelationship between the sapphic and the state seems to be fixed in the social imaginary of mid-eighteenth-century England, I want to comment briefly on a novel I mentioned in my introduction, the unattributed, sprawling 1744 work with the equally sprawling title of *The Travels and Adventures of Mademoiselle de Richelieu. Cousin to the present Duke of that Name. Who made the tour of Europe, dressed in men's cloaths, attended by her Maid Lucy as her Valet de Chambre. Now done into English from the lady's own manuscript.* Here it is juxtposition rather than integration of the sapphic with governance that makes the case. Although the novel purports to be "done into English from the lady's own manuscript," no source has ever been discovered and almost surely none exists. The eponymous narrator's name, of course, already evokes (French) affairs of state. But what I find particularly telling is that immediately after explaining her "Design" to turn "Knight-Errant" and make the grand tour, Mademoiselle de Richelieu embarks not on her travels but on a discourse of more than twenty pages, allegedly lifted from another source, on monarchical succession.[83] She prefaces this digression by announcing her intention to treat persons of all stations equally: "my Pen is neither dipt in Gall nor Honey. I have, indeed lashed Vice wherever I found it, even in the Palaces of crowned Heads . . . and if I have dealt impartially on this Side, I have, on the other, equally done Justice to Merit and Virtue from the King to the Cobler" (5). What follows is a sharp critique of hereditary succession, an insistence that kings must serve the "public Good" (11), and a history of the French monarchy that stresses court corruption, the "Blood and Slaughter" (29) of civil war, and struggles over succession that surely implicate the English case. It is as if the "travels and adventures" cannot begin before the narrator sets the text in relation to contemporary debates about governance.

The tone of *Mademoiselle de Richelieu* is certainly satiric, and without undertaking an extensive reading of an extensive text, I would not wish to insist on its ideological commitments even if such commitments were more stable than I believe they are. Susan Lamb has read the text as ironizing its own voice and thus positions its narrator as Jacobite.[84] I would argue for a predominance of leveling sentiment that calls into question hierarchies of gender, power, nation, and belief. But what I want to emphasize is less the text's ideology than the quite literal priority it gives to affairs of state. This three-volume work teems with inserted stories, discourses, and travelogues, so the digression is not in itself atypical. That the first digression focuses on rulership, however, and thus frames what will end up being a picaresque narrative that ultimately brings two transgressive women together for life, suggests the extent to which the social imaginary is already coupling the sapphic and the state even in a work that never explicitly recognizes either causal or homologous relations between them.

In each of these textual instances, then, sapphic relations serve as the ground for exploring or at least evoking, if from different vantage-points, larger questions of political and social responsibility. While clearly the sapphic could fall on either side of a political question and represent a range of qualities both gratifying and troubling, in each of these cases it figures some alternative model of governance and is invested with a degree of power to represent political bodies in which women have no formal part. At the same time, almost all of the texts forge the fearful symmetries not only of leveled same-sex affiliations but also of analogical relations between family and state that underscore the critical place of women in an interrelated whole. I speculate that the sapphic can do this broader cultural work because the position of women itself teeters at this historical juncture on a fulcrum of significance: discursively, women figure as a potential site of power; materially, their position is largely encapsulated by patriarchal structures and strictures. Moreover, since female–female relations did not pose a large material challenge, if only because most women were dependent on heterosocial economies, the sapphic imaginary could become a site for pursuing other horizontal explorations safely displaced, lending itself to both emergent and residual systems for understanding gender and power. And as Walter Cohen among others reminds us, early modern culture operates from a logic of the potential interchangeability of sexual and class oppression, a conjunction vividly evident, he argues, on both the Spanish and English stage.[85] The "game of flats" can thus also stand, as I have been suggesting, for any leveling of status, desired by some and feared by others, that could undermine social foundations.

Insofar as modernity signifies autonomy, mobility, and agency for those conventionally understood as subordinates, the sapphic figures modernity in a particularly dramatic way, with clear implications for the configuration of the body politic. This may help to suggest why, although sapphic representations continue to burgeon in England and France and start to become more prominent as well in the Dutch Republic as they will later in Germany, they seem to fall off in Spain by the end of the seventeenth century. I can only speculate about this diminution—if the diminution I perceive is not simply a lapse in my research; institutions such as the Inquisition and a shift toward more repressive social constraints on women might both be relevant. Many narratives about modernity do see Spain as effectively opting out of new configurations by the end of the seventeenth century; Michael Iarocci goes so far as to say that "in fundamental ways, modern Europe was born out of the material and discursive defeat of early modern Spain," with power drifting to the European north. Within this view Spain, vilified as an axis of (Catholic, colonial) evil, "became a non-European Europe, a non-Western West."[86]

In speculating about the apparent diminution of attention to sapphic subjects in eighteenth-century Spain, I want to suggest a possible homol-

ogy between the decline of the sapphic and the decline of the novel by
the end of the Golden Age.[87] Joan Ramon Resina's analysis of the novel's
Hispanic fortunes is particularly resonant: noting a range of political and
economic pressures, he argues that "Spain did what societies beset with
insoluble problems frequently do: it clamped down on those elements that
it identified as agents of the undesired transformations," by "purging ethnic diversity" and "reaffirm[ing] the aristocratic order." He goes on to suggest that the novel "withered" for the same reason that science "shunned
the country" in this period: neither can "blossom when free inquiry is
impeded and social mobility punished." Indeed, "in the centuries when
the West was developing its modern identity," says Resina, "Spain veered
away from that uncharted horizon."[88] Under what Andrew Ginger calls the
"Bourbon absolutism" of the eighteenth-century, the waning of sapphic
representations might indeed suggest that the efficacy of the sapphic flour-
ishes only where a certain kind of modernity is taking hold.[89]

A conservative turn vis-à-vis gender is doubtless a related reason for the
waning of Spanish-language sapphic discourse. As Sally Kitts has noted,
in eighteenth-century Spain, "even the most fêted enlightened defenders
of women's rationality and fundamental rights are unable to overcome
the limitations imposed upon their thinking by a dominant narrative of
gendered social roles articulated as conformity to nature."[90] Thus Benito
Jerónimo Feijoo starts his important *Defensa de mujer* (1726), the text that
arguably reopened the feminist debate in Spain, by acknowledging that
"to defend all women is going to be the same as to offend nearly all men"
and backs himself into a corner when he asks why, "if women are equal
to men in aptitude for arts, sciences, political government, and economics," God established "the dominion and superiority of man" in Genesis.
The answer, he says, is that God needed to give governance to one of the
sexes, for the implicitly terrible alternative would have been "confusion
and disorder [confusión, y desorden]."[91] Those traits, of course, are exactly
what the dystopic texts attribute to sapphic subjects. It is thus important
to ask, with respect to any particular political crisis, under what conditions the sapphic is available—or unavailable—to serve the state. That I
have focused the last section of this chapter on representations that follow
upon Britain's Exclusion Crisis and the long struggle over regime-change
does not mean that other places and crises were not amenable to sapphic
representation; a focus on the place of the sapphic in relation to the mid-
seventeenth-century French civil wars known as "La Fronde" could likewise produce matter for a sexuality of history,[92] and chapter 6 of this book

will take up the relationship between the sapphic and the state in Revolutionary France.

Yet there is another important if subtler way in which the sapphic figures in forming the political order and in which Spanish women writers, along with women in several other European countries, actively participate: the articulation of a collective subjectivity through erotic friendship. In exploring what I call with a certain liberty the "political economy" of same-sex desire, I argue that a particular relationship between the sapphic and the body politic underwrites seventeenth- and early eighteenth-century women's articulations of a collective female subject understood to have some agency within the public sphere. I turn now to the different if related dynamics of that project.

CHAPTER FOUR

The Political Economy of
Same-Sex Desire, 1630–1765

"The Bishops have their Synods and the Flocks of Monks their Conventicles; the Soldiers their Councils of War, and Thieves and Pick-Pockets their Clubs; . . . and we Women, of all living Creatures, are the only ones that have had no Meeting of Members at all."
—Desiderius Erasmus, *Colloquies* (1518)[1]

The invention of printing is the greatest event in history. It is the mother revolution. . . . It is human thought stripping off one form and donning another. . . . Before print, reform would have been merely a schism; print made it a revolution.
—Victor Hugo, *Notre Dame de Paris* (1831)[2]

It should be eminently clear by now that my exploration of sapphic subjects has not meant that I am looking for lesbians. The last two chapters have concentrated on representations attributable primarily to men, with only occasional attention to writings by women (Fonte, Trotter, Barker). And although the texts I have been discussing differ widely in tone and implication, they would not seem to be encouraging women to write publicly about erotic attachments to members of their own sex. Yet following closely upon the representations that I discussed in chapter 2, we find a plenitude of writings by women, especially in verse, that are amenable to a sapphic rendering. Temporally coextensive with the representations I explored in chapter 3 and geographically even more expansive—embracing Italian, Dutch, English, Spanish, French, Portuguese and (eventually, briefly) German writers—-these texts provide yet another axis through which sapphic representations evoke "fearful symmetries" both between women and women, as a ground of solidarity, and between women and men, as a ground of equality. Nearly all of these representations insist on the "same" in "same-sex," in a horizontal project that in these writings, I argue, is also an elevation of "the sex" to subjectivity, a kind of upward leveling. Many of the texts also couple expressions of intimacy with protofeminist critique. Some deploy a clearly erotic discourse while others render female affiliations in more equivocal language. Some utilize indirect or distancing strategies, but most inscribe their declarations of desire or affiliation in a mode of direct address that I call "sapphic apostrophe." It might seem, then, that we have finally found some lesbians.

It will be precisely the point of this chapter, however, to rupture or reverse the usual scholarly links between private desires and public words. If the history of sexuality typically infers desiring bodies as the impetus for erotic language, the sexuality of history that I propose sees erotic language as an impetus for desiring bodies—or bodies politic. I suggest that the publication of female friendship, enabled by dramatic increases in female literacy during the sixteenth and seventeenth centuries and perhaps also by new material conditions within which friendships could flourish,[3] underwrote the emergence of women as a self-conscious constituency. What interests me here are not women's incentives for creating same-sex friendships but women writers' incentives for making them at once erotic and public, discursively visible in ways that emphasize bodies as well as minds, and in a quantity that we cannot readily assign to individual biographies. Operating primarily in the utopian (and thus horizontal) mode adopted by Fonte, Rowe, and Trotter but with an important elegaic undertone, this discourse operated through tropes of passionate love and physical longing the sheer magnitude of which remains underexplained. I understand such public expressions not only to have social implications, but to have been socially induced. Rather than signifying the private desires of their authors (though such desires need not be ruled out), homoerotic figurations in the writings of seventeenth- and eighteenth-century women have the public purpose of constituting women as political subjects—that is, as persons with claims to rights. The signification of making this claim through the desiring body responds to the structural asymmetries of gender that give female friendship a different social valence from its male equivalent and thus also, I argue, different powers. The sapphic, in short, becomes the economic and economical engine for launching a political philosophy.

In making these arguments, I am recognizing a body of homoerotic discourse as the sign of a collective project, a critical strategy in the project of gender equality and not simply, or even necessarily, as the expres-

sion of individual biography or preexisting desire.[4] Drawing on the political philosophy of Jacques Rancière and evoking the logic of Simone de
Beauvoir's *Le deuxième sexe*, I will argue that women's public inscriptions
of the sapphic, constructed within the gentleclass cultures of seventeenth-
and eighteenth-century Europe, worked to dismantle the logic of male supremacy in order to constitute woman as both body and body politic, that
is, as independent corporeal person and as member of a constituent group.
While most of the textually forged intimacies are, as I have said, amenable
to an erotic reading, I also view them as *epistemically* sapphic, by which
I mean that they insist on the logic of woman + woman as both sufficient
unto itself and equal in subjectivity to man + woman or, perhaps more
importantly, in this period, man + man. In the sapphic dimensions of a
struggle for gendered subjectivity, we can see the "making of the modern self," as Dror Wahrman has called it, working out a project of self-
construction with ramifications for civil liberties and social relations.[5] I
am thus suggesting that the female subject, as early modernity begins to
construct her, is in a deep sense a sapphic subject as well. And insofar as
gentle status became a marker of female virtue, female friendship also advanced class interests that, in turn, helped to protect women friends from
imputations of sexual transgression; the horizontality inscribed in sapphic
apostrophe is of gender, not of class, and elite status is usually sought or,
more often, presumed. That the project of constituting female subjectivity as sapphic forms a definable arc also underscores its historical contingency. To press further, by redefining gender relations in horizontal terms,
erotically inflected discourses of female friendship not only work to construct modern female subjectivity but arguably model the project of modern subject formation itself. Yet if by the end of the eighteenth century,
female friendship could be said to rival and even displace male friendship
as a cultural model for non-kin relations, the arc of sapphic apostrophe
has, perhaps concomitantly, waned.

FRIENDSHIP AS A GENDERED CLASS ACT

It is by now a truism that the early modern practice and promotion of friendship—that supremely horizontal relationship as classically conceived—
was widely understood as an affair between elite men. When Montaigne's
influential "De l'amitié" (1580) makes friendship the noblest human bond,
uniting "one soul in two bodies"—echoing Aristotle's *Nichomachean
Ethics*, Cicero's "Laelius de Amicitia," and the medieval romances that
imagined male friendship as "sweeter than woman's love"[6]—he explic-

itly rejects the possibility of male-female friendship on the grounds of woman's inferior character, and about friendship between women he says nothing at all. This elevation of male friendship is not merely a textual ideal but an emerging practice; as numerous scholars have recognized and as I suggested in chapter 2, one hallmark of early modernity is the promotion of voluntary connections as equal to or surpassing kinship bonds. Though eventually family values will themselves come to rest on affinal rather than consanguineal relations,[7] friendship anchors a society in which men of worth and men of rank could form propitious alliances in an oligarchic system where gentlemen and even noblemen were not only born but made.

We can see the gendering of friendship and its investment in class concerns in a pair of conduct manuals by the English poet Richard Brathwait that offer "rules of direction" for the modern age. Aimed at teaching "the true and new Art of Gentilizing," *The English Gentleman* (1630) and its sequel *The English Gentlewoman* (1631) maintain that "Pedigree" is insufficient for gentility: the "innate Seedes of goodnesse" sown "by lineall Succession" must now be "ripened by instruction."[8] Birth and worth have begun to separate, particularly in countries invested in colonial commerce and encouraged by the "floodtide" of young men to European universities in what some scholars have called a "cultural revolution,"[9] forging a permeable sphere of civil society composed of allegedly worthy upper bourgeoisie and lesser nobility. This elite will come to be defined against a debauched, self-serving upper aristocracy and an ignorant, ill-mannered mass, thereby also marking class, as E. P. Thompson argued, as "a relationship, and not a thing," and a relationship increasingly recognized to be "made rather than merely inherited."[10] In this new atmosphere, conduct books like Brathwait's will insist that the "greatest Signall and Symbol" of status is now not "Pedigree" but rather "goodnesse of Person, [rather] than greatnesse of Place."[11]

Not surprisingly, though, Brathwait's prescriptions for "goodnesse" in gentlemen and gentlewomen diverge: *The English Gentlewoman* stresses appearance and chastity over achievement and activity and uses the word "vertue" almost twice as often as does *The English Gentleman*. As the frontispieces to the two volumes make vividly evident (see fig. 3), friendship is also a point of divergence. Friendship between men, here labeled "Acquaintance," is both social cement and personal affirmation: "whosoever hath had the happinesse to enjoy a true & faithfull friend, to whom he might freely impart the secrets of his brest, or open the Cabbinet of his counsels, he (I say) and only he hath had the experience of so rare a

Fig. 3. Frontispieces to Richard Brathwait's *The English Gentleman* (1630) and
The English Gentlewoman (1631). Note that "acquaintance" (friendship) is
allotted only to the gentleman. Courtesy of the Folger Shakespeare Library.

benefit daily redounding from the use of friendship: where two hearts are
so individually united, as neither from other can well be severed."[12] In contrast to the long discussion of "Acquaintance" in *The English Gentleman*,
friendship is barely mentioned in *The English Gentlewoman* beyond the
quick admission, framed in an exhortation to modesty, that since "love is
the Cement of our life" women should "put on your vailes, and goe into
Company."[13] Taken together, *The English Gentleman* and *The English
Gentlewoman* suggest the extent to which friendship is both a class matter and a gendered one.

   Such friendship, however framed in the lofty language of disinterest, is
clearly a matter of social utility; Carolyn Heilbrun rightly observed that
"what marks all those male friendships" is "reverberation upon the public
sphere. Male friendships were not entirely, or even primarily, private; they
resonated in the realms of power."[14] For Alan Bray "there has never been a
time when [same-sex] intimacy was possible in a space untouched by power
and politics, however much that was desired or rhetorically projected,"[15]
and indeed the first dictionary of the *Académie française* (1694) defines
the friend as one who is ready to "perform all kinds of good offices [rendre
toutes sortes de bons offices]." As an "institutionalized non-institution,"
publicly recognized but shielded "within a structure of privacy," friend-

ship evades public scrutiny yet operates in the public sphere, creating alliances that, as Alan Stewart observes, enable elite men to "negotiate their way into positions of influence and occasional power" without relying on the exchange of women, in effect creating modernity itself as a function of male-male relations.[16] A male-gendered horizontality, in short, becomes the ground of modern civil society.

These articulations remind us that male friendship can be a primary intimacy and raise the question of whether or not the men in question need to have wives. In a sense, intimate friendship sets itself up both *against* kinship and *as* kinship. As terms such as "blood brother" and "wed brother" and the ubiquitous early use of "friends" to signify "family" suggest, friendships are at once "marriages of the soul and of fortunes and interests" and at the same time "brotherhoods," as Jeremy Taylor calls them in a single sentence.[17] This "marriage of the soul" is also an investment in the friend's *person*; even Taylor concedes on the last page of his popular *Discourse of the Nature, Offices, and Measures of Friendship* (1657) that "the love of friends [must] sometimes be refreshed with material & low Caresses; lest by striving to be *too divine* it becomes *less humane*."[18] Bodily intimacy becomes the symbolic capital, the open sign, as Bray puts it, "by which social relationships could be established and given meaning."[19] What matters most is parity; the 1694 dictionary of the *Académie française*, for example, defines friendship as reciprocal affection "between two persons of approximately equal status [entre deux personnes à peu prés d'égale condition]."[20] Thus the codes of gender and gentility combine to make friendship a means for consolidating and performing male dominance while also consolidating and performing the self that, as Peter Goodrich observes, has its counterpart even in the legal maxim of precedent or *procedere ad similia*, in which likenesses are "bound by resemblance."[21] "Another Himselfe," as Francis Bacon wrote in his 1625 essay "Of Friendship," the friend extends the self in time and space "so that a Man hath as it were two Lives in his desires."[22] This sense of extension, of being the self *because* one is also the other, in effect gives intersubjectivity the power of subject formation. Sir Thomas Browne, writing in 1642, describes this process when he articulates friendship as an enigma "wherein two so become one, as they both become two." Browne also articulates the longing that is intrinsic to friendship thus conceived: "when I am from him, I am dead till I be with him; when I am with him, I am not satisfied, but would still be nearer him. United souls are not satisfied with embraces, but desire to be truly each other."[23] If Browne is describing souls here, his language remains corporeal.

Friendships between women are epistemically invisible in this rhapsodic discourse. Even relations between women and men fare better despite the concerns about feminine virtue and masculine honor that attached to non-kin relations between a man and a woman. At the request of the poet Katharine Philips, Jeremy Taylor makes one of the earliest gestures to acknowledge that a woman could be a man's friend. "Grudging" that "vertuous and brave" women can "love as passionately, and converse as pleasantly, and retain a secret as faithfully, and be useful in her proper ministeries; and she can die for her friend as well as the bravest Roman Knight," he still maintains that "a femal[e] friend, in some cases, is not so good a counseller as a wise man, and cannot so well defend my honour," suggesting in a blatantly phallic metaphor that women literally cannot measure up: just as "a Knife cannot enter so far as a Sword, yet a Knife may be more useful to some purposes."[24] Yet of friendship between two women, the relationship that most compelled Philips's own imagination, Taylor says nothing at all.

There are obvious reasons why women would have wanted a share of friendship's cultural capital. But the structural asymmetry of gender does give friendship between women a different social positioning from its masculine counterpart. Friendship between men leaves male dominance intact or reformulates it along new lines; even when friendship transgresses rank, age, or erotic proprieties, it trades upon the rights of men to form alliances, redirect allegiances, control and distribute goods and services—in short, it assumes subjects with the freedom to pledge their fealty. What Francesca Canadé Sautman and Pamela Sheingorn write of the Middle Ages remains normative, as Brathwait's differential conduct books imply: because women were assigned "the obligation to provide vast amounts of unpaid labor within the household," any "strong emotions directed at other women" could be "as dangerous as unauthorized sexual practices, because they would compete with and displace women's allegiance to marriage and their obligation to serve men and the family unit."[25] Alan Bray is doubtless right, then, to assert that "there is no more revealing question about the friendship of traditional society than to ask how it encompassed women."[26]

It is worth pausing at an early eighteenth-century poem by Anne Finch that speaks to the material limits of female friendship and to the epistemic challenge that it posed. Finch's poetry frequently elevates friendship over kinship as a "useful Bliss" and "the Support of Human-kind."[27] But her dialogic "Friendship between Ephelia and Ardelia" makes a subtler and more complicated inference about women friends:

Eph. What *Friendship* is, Ardelia shew.

Ard. 'Tis to love, as I love You.

Eph. This Account, so short (tho' kind)
 Suits not my enquiring Mind.
 Therefore farther now repeat;
 What is *Friendship* when compleat?

Ard. 'Tis to share all Joy and Grief;
 'Tis to lend all due Relief
 From the Tongue, the Heart, the Hand;
 'Tis to mortgage House and Land;
 For a Friend be sold as Slave;
 'Tis to die upon a Grave,
 If a Friend therein do lie.

Eph. This indeed, tho' carry'd high,
 This, tho' more than e'er was done
 Underneath the rolling Sun,
 This has all been said before.
 Can Ardelia say no more?

Ard. Words indeed no more can shew:
 But 'tis to love, as I love you.[28]

Not satisfied with the circular definition that friendship is "to love as I love you," Ephelia presses Ardelia for material meaning. Yet by defining love as a pledge to share, lend, and mortgage, Finch's speaker is necessarily appropriating friendship on men's terms. When Ardelia vows her willingness "to mortgage house and land" lest "a friend be sold a Slave"—or perhaps, given the linguistic ambiguity, to be sold a slave herself, for a friend's benefit—she is pledging goods that women do not conventionally own, let alone bestow, and whether "sold a slave" implies chattel ownership or forced marriage, Ardelia's fulfillment of friendship would interfere with patriarchal prerogatives. When Ephelia answers that Ardelia's pledge is "more than e'er was done," then, she may be recognizing not only the excess but the transgressivity of Ardelia's offer. No wonder that, as Finch writes elsewhere, the "absolute retreat" of friendship requires a utopian withdrawal from the present order into a place of "unshaken Liberty."[29]

Even without its erotic dimensions, then, friendship may be understood as both sign and agent of a feminist politics. Mary Masters pointedly suggests a distinction between friendship and marriage in this regard when she recognizes the crucial factor of choice: the bond of friends is "stronger by far than Tyes of Blood" because "no Force nor Interest can compel" it.[30]

And the Portuguese poet Sor Violante do Céu likewise insists, in a sonnet to her friend Belisa, that friendship must take precedence in women's
alliances because it is "founded on sympathy / from one who prizes loyalty unto death."[31] But the tautological structure of Finch's poem also suggests that female friendship may need to rely on language itself: although
Ephelia says that "this has all been said before," and Ardelia replies that
"words indeed no more can shew," the poem begins and ends with the
same arguably empty claim: friendship is "to love, as I love You."

The structural subordination of women and therefore of women's
friendships, in other words, helps to explain why it is print that bears the
major role in its formation. For women to pledge friendship on men's terms
meant to exercise a dangerous freedom, one without parallel in bonds between men, which rarely reverse hierarchies and may even cement them.
Yet women's writings from the early seventeenth century valorized, with
a persistence that satires against them could not dismantle and abetted by
the new prominence of "the heart" which they were helping to foster,[32]
a discourse of same-sex intimacy that would promote female excellence,
assert intellectual independence, and—most audaciously—to provide a rationale for political wholeness that necessarily imagined women in separation from men. In so doing, they also made clear that the stakes for
female friendship encompassed but also exceeded the desiderata of their
male colleagues and required different strategies both material and textual. This *excess*—what I will describe below, by way of Slavoj Žižek,
as an obscenity—underscores the asymmetry between male and female
same-sex friendships and begins to suggest why women's inscriptions of
subjectivity required friendship and why friendship required an erotic discourse. If this discourse also enabled cover stories for prior relations, the
politics of female intimacy, deeply imbricated with those of class, were
positioned to serve the sometimes conflicting and sometimes converging
needs of gentry hegemony, sapphic sexuality, and feminist agency. The
"political economy" that I am suggesting—and I use these terms with root
meanings that denote the organization or management of civil identity—
thus also illustrates the complex interdependence of status politics and
sexual ideology during a time when both were in flux.

THE (QUEER) PUBLICATION OF DESIRE

The presence of erotic intimacy in seventeenth- and eighteenth-century
writings by individual women is well recognized, and this chapter is deeply

indebted to the archival and critical work of scholars who have plumbed those women's texts far more fully than I will do here. But the European aggregate of these writings, with its geographic breadth and to some extent its shared poetics, remains to be explored as a confluent phenomenon with collective agency. These writings, especially though not exclusively in the form of apostrophic poems addressed from one woman to another, spanned most of two centuries, with a particularly intense concentration in the late seventeenth century along a European map that is close to, though somewhat larger than, the one I described in chapter 2, with writings by women of England, France, Spain, Italy, and the Netherlands especially prominent. Indeed, it is only a mild exaggeration to say that between 1650 and 1730, wherever women wrote literature, some women wrote homoerotically. Since many of their writings advance a critique of male supremacy, such works also intersect with the protofeminist writings of men and women such as Marie de Gournay and Poulain de la Barre that emerged within the same period.

It may already be clear why apostrophe might have been particularly prevalent in this body of writings. As Jonathan Culler has observed, apostrophe works less to describe the other than "to dramatize or constitute an image of the self" and to perform that image publicly for a third party.[33] We already see a ventriloquist version of sapphic apostrophe in the poems of Tyard, Ronsard, and Donne that I discussed in chapter 2, but women's uses of the form often blur the distinction between the poetic persona and the writing self and thus give particular historical force to their representations where authorship is known or surmised. The practice of sapphic apostrophe dates at least from the sixteenth century with poems by Laudomia Forteguerri to Margaret of Austria, whom she calls "mia diva" and whose beloved body she asks God to reveal to her "in parte," and to Alda Torella Lunata lamenting the cruel destiny that has deprived her of to this "angelic face.[34] The Dutch poet Anna Roemers Visscher longs to have as a "playmate" the poet Georgette de Montenay, whose work she has translated, recognizing that "Though in the body this can't be, / Our spirits know no boundary."[35] Amanda Powell sees similar apostrophes to friendship in the works of the Italian writers Tarquinia Molza and Isabella Andreini.[36] Aemelia Lanyer's "Description of Cooke-Ham," the closing poem to a volume that opens with no fewer than ten dedicatory prefaces to women, seeks a female Eden that erases differences of station between the speaker and the woman whose country house she apostrophizes through the moment of a "chaste, yet loving kisse."[37] Anne de Rohan writes that

Cupid's darts have shot "into my anxious heart / the burning desire to love" the woman she names Aimée [Beloved] in a poem that explicitly distinguishes her passions from mere "amitié."[38]

During the middle and late seventeenth century, as more women become published writers or prepare manuscripts that seem to have been intended for print, this pattern of sapphic apostrophe intensifies in quantities large enough that I will only touch on the instances here. Catalina Clara Ramírez de Guzmán's "A la ausencia de una amiga, hablando con ella" declares her "true love" and the deadly "wound" of her separation from the beloved friend.[39] Sor Violante do Céu speaks in several *romances* words "con amor" to figures she variously names Menandra, Celia, and Silvia.[40] Characters in Maria de Zayas's stories address words of desire to one another while her sonnets evoke women such as the beautiful Elisa ("Elisa bella").[41] Marcia Belisarda, the pen name for Sor Maria de Santa Isabel, writes equivocally gendered love poems to women.[42] As Lia van Gemert has demonstrated, similar homoerotic strands characterize the writings of at least three seventeenth-century Dutch poets: Katharina Questiers identifies herself with the Ovidian Iphis in a suggestive poem addressed to the poet Cornelia Van der Veer, who allegedly left a garter in Questiers' room, flirtatiously claiming that she would woo Van der Veer if, like Iphis, she could turn male.[43] Titia Brongersma, whose works include as many as twenty-seven love poems to Elisabeth Joly, writes her "growing desire" for Elise's "kisses" and sends a poem *as* a kiss; and Katharyne Lescailje, who addresses love poems to women in male voices, also writes to at least one woman in a female voice ostensibly her own.[44] Elizabeth Rowe elegizes "Parthenia" as "the Lovely Saint, from my Embraces rent" and evokes (eerily, in a poem published two years after her own death) her "tender passion" for Cleone from an imagined celestial "happy fields," describing a blissful paradise in which the "flames" of their "love" will "swell each heav'nly breast."[45] The less respectable Aphra Behn, who declares herself "bound" in "*Cupid*'s chains" to a "lovely Charmer," more famously imagines "more than woman" the "fair Clarinda, who made love" to her, playfully arguing that their love is "innocent" for the absence of a "snake . . . beneath the fragrant leaves."[46] Katherine Philips creates an extensive corpus of love poems to more than one "dear object of my Love's excess."[47] Margaret Cavendish laces her *Blazing World* with homoerotic scenes, sets up her *Convent of Pleasure* as all female space, and writes *Sociable Letters* professing "more than a Sisters Love."[48] Anne Killigrew describes the "downie" movements and "silken" actions of Eudora, "the Aire of her Face, / Of a gentler Grace / Than those that do stroke the Eare."[49] From her Mexican convent, Sor Juana Inés de la Cruz produces an intense body of homoerotic discourse, in one poem describing her patroness from head to foot and naming herself a "hapless lover," "mad" with a "passion" that is either "love's due" or a crime "of which I will never repent," and in another poem speaking of an "amourous passion" that drives her "mad."[50] Lady Mary Chudleigh's "Marissa" flies to the "lov'd Bosom" of Clorissa "where sacred Friendship gives a Right" to "gentle Passion." Mary Astell agrees to publish her *Letters Concerning the Love of God* only if the volume can be dedicated to her close friend Lady Catherine Jones, whose nearness stirs in Astell, she writes, a heat resembling "Seraphick Flames."[51] Louise-Geneviève Gillot de Sainctonge tells "Madame T . . ." that she had never tasted the pleasures of love before seeing "l'aimable Celimène," proclaims that "this beauty [belle] has changed my soul" and laments that "the more one feels love, the less one can express it."[52] In a somewhat later "epistle" Sainctonge exhorts the widowed Madame la Marquise de C*** not to remarry, admitting that "you have, gentle Lady, / Absolute power over my soul."[53] Pauline de Simiane writes in a "Madrigal" that the kisses of her "nouvelle Diane" are sweet like a sister's yet of an eroticism that must be "condemned."[54] Mary Masters' poem "My Love describ'd to CAMILLA" imagines a "Paradise on Earth" where "social Souls are kindly mix'd, / And in each other live."[55]

These mostly apostrophic writings express admiration, affinity, and a longing that may resemble the always unrequitable desire of friend for friend described by Sir Thomas Browne but that also reverses the tropes of mobility that we saw in previous chapters to suggest a society that keeps women confined and separated by social, domestic, and religious norms. Most of the poems are nonetheless deeply conscious of the beloved's physical being and often speak of the body in loving terms. Some poems express jealousy, many criticize marriage, others lament absence or separation. Some recognize the vulnerability of their own desire to external judgment—note the apparently sincere self-condemnation of Simiane—or express a vulnerability to loss, both of which might account for the elegaic tone of so many of these texts, where poets like Katherine Philips fear to "lose whatever is call'd dear" and "fear that I shall never see thee more."[56] The poems almost invariably single out specific women; these are not paeans to friendship in general or to generic friends. Nor is there anything here that speaks of mere acquaintance in the modern sense: these writings are as intense as, and sometimes more physical than, the Petrarchan love poems that dominate the period. And though the adoption of "classical" eponyms can, of course, be found in women's poetry as in men's—witness

Finch's Ephelia and Ardelia, Rowe's Parthenea, and Philips's Lucasia—the buffers are more minimal. As Bruce R. Smith showed so well in his pioneering *Homosexual Desire in Shakespeare's England*, male writers who addressed poems to men inhabited a canon of classical myths and pastoral models that mediated their apostrophic discourse through distancing, often Virgilian tropes that were less readily available to women.[57]

All the more as the list I have given is not exhaustive, it is plausible to say that homoerotic discourse is a visible feature of women's emergence into European literature.[58] While sapphic interests can certainly be posited for some of these writers, I believe the aggregate demands its own account. For even if it were possible to provide circumstantial explanations for every erotic instance, biography falls short of explaining why private attachments should have been translated into public text or even circulated in manuscript—that is, why women would perform for third parties their expressions of intimacy with other women in discourses whose speakers, given the conventions of lyric poetry, can almost always be taken for themselves.[59] Bereft of the classical buffers, these apostrophic writings are surely as vulnerable to double interpretation as was, say, Shakespeare's sonnet 20, which as Alan Bray notes could be read *"both* as asserting the chastity of friendship in the most transcendent of terms *and* as rejecting it in the most bawdy and explicit of terms."[60] Contemporary responses to such equivocal writings made clear that female-female desires could be perceived as both *"laudable* and *blameable,"* as Delarivier Manley put it in *The New Atalantis*, echoing the "shadow of *Suspicion*" that I have dated back at least to Brantôme: "If only *tender Friendship*, inviolable and sincere, be the regard, what can be more meritorious, or a truer Emblem of their Happiness above? . . . But if they carry it a length beyond what *Nature* design'd, and *fortifie* themselves by these new-form'd *Amities* against the *Hymenial Union*, or give their *Husbands* but a second place in their *Affections* and *Cares*; 'tis wrong and to be *blam'd*."[61] Why, in short, bring same-sex intimacy into the already bold and often troubled project of getting women's writings read, published, and well-received?

Although others have not formulated the question in quite these loaded terms, scholars have tended to account for homoerotic language in women's writings in one of two opposing ways—either as poetic convention or as private expression—with the third alternative of public intervention just emerging. In the first direction lie arguments that these writings are simply appropriating man-made forms or deploying language so conventional as to be devoid of erotic significance. In this view, the writers either take on the dominant (male) subject position by adopting Petrarchan conventions or trade in what are deemed "Platonic" tropes. Thus Dorothy Mermin, for example, has argued that Katherine Philips was simply reproducing a poetic love language in which homoeroticism, whether textual or biographical, plays little part;[62] in the words of Harriette Andreadis, some critics see Philips's love poems to women as "merely clever exercises in courtly convention by a woman seeking reputation and patronage."[63] Such claims eviscerate the text's sapphic potential, rendering the textual homoeroticism in effect heteroerotic without explaining why the female poets did not simply adopt male voices to address women, a practice that only a few women (Katharyne Lescaijle and Catalina Ramirez de Guzmán, for example) seem to have chosen. Such arguments also fall short when faced with texts that explicitly privilege same-sex over cross-sex relationships or call explicit attention to the gender of desire. A related argument holds that expressions of physicality serve purely metaphoric functions as figures of the soul or mind. This position assumes that the vehicle of a metaphor is transparent or inconsequential; I would argue, by contrast, that rather than erasing the body, figuring spiritual feelings in corporeal terms enforces a union of body and spirit and thereby underscores the eroticism of the intense attachments represented in the poems.

In the opposing direction lie the more widespread arguments that sapphic writings emanate from the desiring psyches of their authors, who are assumed, in Lia van Gemert's resonant phrasing, to be "hiding behind words."[64] Elaine Hobby, for instance, insists that not only Philips's poems but Philips herself must certainly be read as lesbian,[65] while in a more nuanced and more persuasive argument, Harriette Andreadis uses biographical material and textual analysis to argue that "the poems that made Orinda famous depended for their creation on Philips's personal affections."[66] To be sure, most scholars today agree that Philips's poetry inscribes homoerotic desires whether or not she herself shared them, though the effort to reclaim for lesbian history not simply the words but the body of Katherine Philips goes on. Still, why women like Philips would want to inscribe those intimate desires beyond their addressees, even in manuscript, remains unclear: surely these desires were not verbally irrepressible, and if these writers wanted to hide relationships, they would be better off hiding the words themselves than attracting attention by attempting to hide "behind" them. Like the argument that women are simply appropriating male tropes to achieve literary acceptance, the autobiographical argument leaves the publication and circulation of such writings underexplained and risks creating lesbian biography in cases where evidence beyond the poems is slim or nonexistent. Approaching women's writings in terms only of private life actually minimizes women's agency while also overlooking the ways in which individual acts may be answering to historical imperatives and collective opportunities.

It is thus worth considering the third alternative: that these writers were engaged in a public project designed to serve more than self-expressive ends.[67] Valerie Traub lays the ground for such a shift in the case of Philips when she argues that "Philips's production of a compelling homoerotic subjectivity" is best understood not as the manifestation of a "deeply interiorized desire" but as a disruption through "erotic similitude" of the teleology of the marriage plot.[68] I want to move farther still in separating interior desire from exterior inscription by asking what collective purposes "erotic similitude" might have served. Such a shift of focus from private life to public imperative might help us account for sapphic elements in writings by women like Elizabeth Rowe and Margaret Cavendish, or Moderata Fonte before them, whose personal histories, unlike that of Philips, do not encourage a lesbian rendering. Biographical difference falls away when we shift the lens of inquiry to the public sphere and examine the possible social effects, rather than the possible personal causes, of homoerotic discourse even when it takes the intimate form of sapphic apostrophe. This move also shifts the focus from experience to discourse and thus to the ways in which literary inscriptions might have furthered social aims, opening connections between sapphic writings and other discourses that might have fostered the epistemic shift toward gender equality that Geneviève Fraisse has labeled a "true conceptual break" with the past.[69] Fraisse traces that break to Poulain de la Barre's important 1673 treatise *De l'égalité des deux sexes*; I would take the conceptual rupture-point back at least to the 1630s and argue for a greater part, both for women and for the sapphic, in creating it.

FEMINISM'S SAPPHIC SUBJECTS

In the introduction to her pathbreaking book *Le Deuxième sexe*, Simone de Beauvoir famously lamented that women "do not say 'We.'" Beauvoir connected the categorical status of women as "Other" to their failure to constitute themselves "authentically as Subjects" standing face-to-face with the normatively human male. The feminist scholarship that Beauvoir's own work helped to foster outlines a more complicated historical picture, but the system Beauvoir identified remains the regulative and arguably the constitutive condition of patriarchy: women "live dispersed among men, tied by homes, work, economic interests and social conditions to certain

men—fathers or husbands—more closely than to other women."[70] Historically and globally, women's material place in a social-political economy
supports the generalization of otherness that *The Second Sex* exposes.

Beauvoir did not allow, however, for the political efficacy of print, an
ironic omission given the political efficacy of *The Second Sex* itself in galvanizing a movement. Without denying the crucial distinction between
circulated paper and lived life that underwrites this entire project, I want
to emphasize the potential of the published word to create a collective female subject, and hence some form of feminist politics, by wresting women
discursively from the matrix of their physical dispersal and intensifying
the imperative for change. It is a power without which twentieth-century
feminism could hardly have flourished, since most women still live "dispersed among the males" and attached to them materially and psychically.
And of course if we consider modern politics in general, from the forming of consensual governments to the making of revolution to the abolition of slavery, discourse has been a crucial if not a sufficient catalyst. My
previous chapters, and particularly my evocation of "the sapphic and the
state," make a milder but relevant argument for the potential or at least
perceived agency of sapphic representations: else why create them at all?

The astute theorizing of the philosopher Jacques Rancière is useful in
illuminating this political potential of words. For Rancière, politics "happens" when a group "with no firmly determined place in the hierarchical
social edifice" inserts itself as a *part* or *party* of humanity entitled to its
full rights and benefits. Political subjects emerge "through a series of actions of a body and a capacity for enunciation not previously identifiable
within a given field of experience, whose identification is thus part of the
reconfiguration of the field of experience." Democracy, then, may be understood as "the way of life in which the voice . . . usurps the privileges
of the logos."[71] In Slavoj Žižek's rephrasing of Rancière, politics happens
when the members of a particular constituency "not only demand that
their voice be heard against those in power" and become "recognized as
included in the public sphere, on an equal footing with the ruling oligar-
chy," but also "present themselves as the representatives, the stand-ins, for
the Whole of Society, for the true Universality." This struggle, says Žižek,
also produces an "excess," a kind of "obscene supplement" that eludes he-
gemonic control and thus has the potential to generate the end of the old
system.[72]

Politics understood within Rancière's framework galvanizes the formation of identities; it calls for a redistribution of the "order of bodies"
through the "order of words" as the mechanism for a new equality. Such

a call will not often originate within formal institutions, Rancière comments, for it is usually the absence of recognition within such institutions that precipitates political movement in the first place. Rather, the process is commonly inaugurated through a "mise-en-scène" that "brings the community and the noncommunity together" through stories or metaphors that expose an absence or a false unity by inserting distinction and difference. Instead of attributing political inclusion to "rational debate between multiple interests," as Habermas does, Rancière sees politics as a "struggle for one's voice to be heard and recognized" in which *who* speaks may be less important than *in whose name* the speaking happens, the effect of which is to expose "the inegalitarian distribution of social bodies" in its dissonance with "the equal capacity of speaking beings."[73] Especially if we accept Rancière's account, we can see why print technologies would afford a powerful machinery for enabling a new part(y) of humanity to stake political claims by constituting a textual "we" that might in time reshape the material conditions under which that part(y) lives. The temporal gap between my two epigraphs is one that print culture begins to fill, as circulated discourses create, across the seventeenth and eighteenth centuries, the representations of those "synods, conventicles and clubs" the absence of which Erasmus's female interlocutors lament. We have already seen those fictional gatherings in the dystopian form of the *Sappho-an's* "congress of amazons" as well as in the utopian gathering Fonte sets in Leonora's Venetian garden.

The plethora of sapphic apostrophe that gathers strength in the mid-seventeenth century intensifies this political project of elevation not only through sheer numbers but through a shared rhetoric of intimate address from woman to woman. In this way, seventeenth- and eighteenth-century discourses bent on creating a female subject that could stand face to face with the masculine subject of emergent humanism took up the project of inserting women as a new part or party to the body politic in what would later become an effort to inject "the rights of woman" into the "rights of man." In underscoring the proverbial (and conventionally phallic) power of pen (*Kiel*) over sword (*Stahl*), Anna Helena Volckmann's "Brief an Mariana Ziegler" (1736), in an early German instance, asks one woman to join what was in effect a print politics:

> Woman! World-famed woman, with ardor I'm aflame,
> Don't let this wanton sex get off without the blame.
> And even if we don't have sharp blades like the men,
> Still let us fight this pack with our sharpened pen.[74]

But as Beauvoir's famous phrasing reminds us and as *Il Merito delle donne* already recognized, this project of insertion that would turn women into the "One" would also require an extraction: wresting women from an androcentric order by revising the discourses that sustained it. As I argued in chapter 2, the conventional *querelle des femmes* could work by comparing women to men and thus usually addressed men, but writings that would claim autonomy for women had, in some sense, to separate women from men and to reflect this separation discursively.[75] Thus Maria de Zayas concludes her *Desenganos amorosos* by sending her female protagonist Lisis, literally arm in arm with her intimates "the lovely Doña Isabel and her cousin Doña Estefanía," to a convent where they will live "with great pleasure," explicitly the "happiest" alternative because the women will not be subject to anyone.[76] Mary Astell, who proposed her own version of a Protestant convent, writes that if women were to acknowledge the immorality of most men, "they wou'd not value themselves on account of the Admiration of such incompetent Judges."[77] Petronilla Paolini Massimi exhorts women to believe in their "gifts" and insists that "the sole oppressor of our worth is man."[78] And in the 1567 *Letter Sent by the Maydens of London*, a brilliant riposte to an attack on women servants, six maids writing as a "we" ("Rose, Jane, Rachell, Sara, Philumias and Dorothie") attempt a solidarity of gender by appealing to their "Matrons and Mistresses" for an alliance across class on behalf of maids' rights that is also a quiet threat to withhold their services.[79] We can already see why apostrophe would be a powerful formal mechanism for enacting what, as J. Douglas Kneale reminds us, its etymology suggests: a turning away, an aversion, from the third party (now a kind of eavesdropper) toward the private "you."[80]

Such an economy, even if only textual, allows women to claim a place in the social contract that the sexual contract, as Carole Pateman has famously called it, denies them.[81] But this move also produces the excess—the obscenity within the existing order—of women who are not only unattached but unattachable to men. Even without homoerotic implications, then, the possibility of women standing together *en face des hommes* becomes obscene. Lady Mary Chudleigh's "To the Ladies," which tells women that a wife is a servant expected to treat her husband "as her God" and sees as the only recourse to "shun, oh! Shun that wretched State," surely stands as one of the harshest-ever critiques of the sexual contract, with nothing sapphic about it.[82] But to call on women in the plural to "value your selves and men despise"—to reiterate Chudleigh's harsh language—is of course to constitute female subjects within a homosocial if not a homoerotic economy. This kind of apostrophic writing creates a

fiction of private communication between women that a male public is en-
joined, in effect, to overhear. As a gesture by emergent writers, such a device might have been especially useful in creating a bulwark against isolation and timidity: I think of Louise Labé's address in 1555 to Clemence de
Bourges that "we must inspire one another" as writers since "women do
not willingly appear alone in public."[83]

But why would *sapphic* apostrophe be constructing this textual politics of subjectivity? Why the corporeal, the passionate, the dyadic, rather
than simply the general call to action that a poem like Chudleigh's "To the
Ladies" enacts? I suggest that sapphic apostrophe allows women to assert a
claim to personal sovereignty that recognizes rights of self-disposition extending at once to the body, the mind, and the soul. More subtly than lay-
ing charges against men, an erotics of friendship discursively separates and
thus protects the female body from its inscription in the sexual contract,
performing not only a claim to independence but its embodiment. Since
women's subordination is constituted through the body, the body arguably
needs to occupy a place within the project of subject formation. The homoeroticism inscribed in women's writings reappropriates the body from
its legal and social status as property by (re)positioning the self within the
one social relationship that is structurally outside male control. Valorizing both one's own body and its mirror image provides a counterweight to
gender subordination, effectively shifting the terms of desire to women and
thus producing the excess that stands against the system. For what more
primary, even primal way to build the self as desirable than to desire its
likeness? One can see this dynamic at work in Philips's "To My Lucasia"
when the speaker imagines a "Union" with the beloved by "forsak[ing]"
the given "self" and seeking "a new / Self in her brest, that's far more rich
and true."[84] When Philips writes to "my excellent Lucasia" that "I am not
Thine, but Thee," and even more dramatically, that she had not "found /
A Soule till she found thine," she is in effect producing the self through
the other. And when the poem then claims to have "all the world in thee,"
the sapphic forges not only self, or self-and-other, but entire universe.[85]

Through the sapphic, then, women could harness, indeed co-opt, what
Laurie Shannon calls the "early modern politics of likeness" for purposes
that exceeded the patriarchal framework of that politics.[86] It seems particularly plausible that for women writers, emerging into print with print
itself, erotic similitude provided a mechanism for establishing at once an
"I" and a "we" and thereby claiming for their sex an autonomy secured by
the (textual) body. Moreover, the emphasis on the union of souls in sapphic
apostrophe cannot be overlooked; insofar as the discourse of friendship el-

evates spiritual bonds (between men) as superior to sexual bonds (between men and women), and insofar as the soul was seen as the seat of person-hood, the elevation of women's souls through mirroring is itself a wresting from religious discourses that equivocate about the equality of souls. Mad-eleine de Scudéry's "Harangue" addressed to Erinne in the voice of Sapho sets up both the move from body to mind and the move from individual to collective when Sapho urges Erinne to seek immortality by writing poetry rather than relying on the fatal transience of beauty ("vous mourrez toute entière, / Si pour vaincre la Parque, & la fatalité, / Vous n'allez par l'estude, a l'immortalité") so that her work, and Scudéry's own *Femmes illustres*, will "persuade our ladies what this beautiful Lesbian persuaded her friend, and more, if I can persuade the whole world that the fair sex is worthy of our adoration so that one day temples and altars will be dedicated to women just as now I dedicate to them this TRIUMPHANT ARCH THAT I HAVE RAISED TO THEIR GLORY."[87] Here the body is the starting point of a similitude that is literary, spiritual, and ultimately political and that extends through Sappho to "our ladies" and "the whole world."

The anonymous poem "Cloe to Artimesa" (1720) which clearly plays upon a poem by the Earl of Rochester,[88] goes a step further in tying female sovereignty and pleasure to same-sex bonds precisely by claiming freedom from bodily subjugation:

> While vulgar souls their vulgar love pursue,
> And in the common way themselves undo;
> Impairing health and fame, and risking life,
> To be a mistress or, what's worse, a wife:
> We, whom a nicer taste has raised above
> The dangerous follies of such slavish love,
> Despise the sex, and in our selves we find
> Pleasures for their gross senses too refined.
> Let brutish men, made by our weakness vain,
> Boast of the easy conquest they obtain;
> Let the poor loving wretch do all she can,
> And *all* won't please th' ungrateful tyrant, Man;
> We'll scorn the monster and his mistress too,
> And show the world what women ought to do.[89]

In Rancière's sense, and whatever the sex of its author, "Cloe to Artimesa" enacts a politics, inciting revolt against the "tyrant, Man" through a fe-male affiliation that is also marked as a superiority of rank: those who "despise" marriage are elevated above the "slavish" precisely by their "nicer taste" for one another. Women who fall in with men are "wretches"; men are reduced to "the sex." It is Cloe and Artimesa who are "selves" and self-sufficient, with authority to "show the world" a different way. Sexual politics here emerges in both senses of the term "sexual"; the erotic ambiguity of "refined" pleasures found "in our selves" opens the possibility that *all* women "ought to" form sapphic alliances. At the same time, however, this apostrophic performance of female affiliation that calls for a separation from men must be performed publicly *within* the heterosocial system in order to produce the resistance for which it calls. That the poem could have been read—and meant—as satire does not diminish its potential efficacy; indeed, the poem's excessive language—its obscenity, in Rancière's terms—might have provided the safety of seeming implausible to some readers while make its pointed case to others.

Similarly, and through the public (though in this case closet) medium of drama, Margaret Cavendish's *Convent of Pleasure* (1668) emphasizes the necessity for the private world of female intimacy also to be represented to men. Foregrounding the links between sapphic affiliation and the conventional "order of bodies," the play requires a man to enter its all-female utopia in the guise of a woman and subjects him, as a stand-in for the third-party audience, to a literal staging of women's miseries. Evoking the scenario that harks back to Pontus de Tyard's "Elégie," the play premises itself on the failings of men and the miseries of marriage, which offers "more crosses and sorrows than pleasure, freedom, or happiness."[90] Rather than living for men, who act only for "their own sake" (4–5) and are "Obstructers" who "produce Pain" and "increase Trouble" (12), Lady Happy determines to create a space of pleasure "incloister'd and retired from the World" (6) where women occupy "every Office and Employment" down to "Women-Physicians, Surgeons and Apothecaries" (12). Pleasure, then, is redefined as possible only in a world of women, and it is rendered corporeal: "a great Looking Glass" is provided in each chamber, "that we may view our selves and take pleasure in our own Beauties" (14), and the play intersperses its scenes of luxurious retirement with vignettes of married women from diverse social classes suffering from abuse, infidelity, and complications of childbirth.

What *The Convent of Pleasure* introduces directly into this setting, however, is an audience of men. Unknown to the cloistered women or to the reader, the space has been penetrated by a "princess" who is really a prince in love with Lady Happy. This gives a politically different character to the contrasts the play sets up, since the prince who stands in for male suitors is placed in the subject position of the women. Because the prince's actual sex is concealed from the audience, the character with whom Lady Happy falls in love is a woman in rhetorical and performative terms. S/he can marry Lady Happy only after s/he has "been" a woman among women and *The Convent of Pleasure* has confronted women's bodily sufferings. In this way an all-female and arguably sapphic space becomes a site of critique and transformation—that is, the site of a politics in Rancière's sense. The scenarios of women's suffering at the hands of men and marriage that constitute the play within the play do not only contrast with the pleasures of the convent; the convent's separate space is what enables that representation of women's burden of suffering.[91] Male transformation is paramount, all the more as the men represented in the play's first scene respond with outrage to Lady Happy's "Heretical Opinions"; she should " be examined by a Masculine Synod," they declare, "and punish'd with a severe" or "de-boist" husband (213). Once "the *Prince* has imitated a Woman," the play implies, there is hope that he will act like one. Although the metamor-phic resolution does, of course, reaffirm heterosexual marriage and indeed pathologizes the sapphic insofar as the lover's sex-change rescues Lady Happy from a desire for the "Princess" that leaves her "pale and lean" and fearing to "fall into disgrace" (40), *The Convent of Pleasure* powerfully illustrates the centrality of the liberated body and the generative role of sapphic space in forging a female political subjectivity.

I also hold it significant that several of these texts, including *The Convent of Pleasure*, deploy a semantics of sovereignty, intertwining the sapphic with the state in continuity with the representations I explored in chapter 3. Lady Happy's male suitor is explicitly a head of state, and the play extends its tropes of sovereignty (46) explicitly to Lady Happy. In this move Cavendish is not alone. Louise de Sainctonge's "Madame la marquise de C***," written in 1714 at the close of Louis XIV's absolut-ist reign, likewise couples same-sex desire with explicitly political lan-guage to pit the homoerotic and the heteropatriarchal against each other within a framework of political relations writ large. The speaker sees her beloved friend's male suitors as enemies wanting to "steal that liberty / that enchants your heart." She reminds the Marquise that, after marriage, an obliging lover becomes a "very importunate master" and exhorts her friend to retain her own "franchise" and live "toujours en souveraine."[92] From a different vantage-point, Katherine Philips uses a similar semantic field to extend royalist dignity to women, who are "both Princes, and both

Subjects too," as her "Friendship's Mystery, To My Dearest Lucasia" typifies. In all of these varied cases, women are exhorting one another to an
autonomy that rings political.

The logic of intimate exhortation to an independence that is both material and spiritual, intricately connected with the eroticized body, not
only helps to explain the otherwise rather mystifying plenitude of female
homoeroticism in seventeenth- and early eighteenth-century women's
writings; it also raises the possibility that personal desire may itself have
been forged out of political impulse, that "erotic similitude" not only abetted, but may have arisen from, feminist imperatives. Such a rendering does
not deny the materiality of the homoeroticism expressed in these writings nor suggest that the erotic tropes are only metaphors (in any case the
word *only*, in my view, never applies to metaphors). Nor does my argument
deny that women who wrote and circulated homoerotic writing might
have been inscribing personal desires. But desires, as historians of sexuality know well, are hardly transhistorical. As Robyn Warhol argues in her
study of popular culture, an anti-essentialist notion of self might usefully
consider the pre-psychoanalytic concept that feelings may not be the outward expression of internal conditions so much as the internal experience
of outward stimuli: not always "I weep because I am [already] sad," but
sometimes also "I am sad because I have been induced to weep."[93] If so—
and Judith Butler's notion of performativity is salient here—then the desires inscribed in sapphic apostrophe may have been produced by the very
process of subject-formation in which women writers were taking part. If
desire does not always preexist its expression, even the "genuinely felt"
and "actually experienced" may be social formations that can have their
source in words as well as in bodies, in political efficacy as well as in personal intimacy.

Rather than looking for desiring bodies "behind" desiring words, then,
I am asking whether desiring words might have inspired an investment in
desiring bodies—or in their representation—in the interests of a similitude that could abet female subject-formation within the constrained circumstances confronting early modern women—and women writers—at
a time when friendship relations carried a strong social resonance. That
male writers in the Petrarchan tradition had already developed an apostrophic and amatory discourse for poetic expression, and one that could
be addressed either to women and/or to a "likeness" of the self, doubtless
further encouraged women's use of it. And of course the familiarity of the
discourse was not irrelevant: as Harriette Andreadis writes of Katherine
Philips, the "use of the conventions of male poetic discourse . . . sanc-

tioned her unconventional subject. . . . Because her discourse was familiar, her subject was acceptable."[94] Both poetic and social conditions, then, enabled the salience of sapphic apostrophe across the seventeenth and early eighteenth centuries.

If my arguments are plausible, then explanations built around the pre-existing desires of individual persons acting from private motives cannot fully account for either the quantities or the qualities of the sapphic apostrophe that becomes a feature of both manuscript circulation and print culture in several European countries between the mid-seventeenth and mid-eighteenth centuries. The privatized analysis that privileges the biographical reading (which fosters a history of sexuality) over the social one (which supports the sexuality of history) may be the less useful and more potentially misleading one, for recourse to the individual subject ignores the public functions of representation and collapses the space of agency between personal feelings or behaviors and what gets inscribed in texts. If sapphic discourses are carrying a more-than-sapphic (though not, I submit, less-than-sapphic) weight, then the history of "lesbianism" as enacted in the public arena is the history not just of a minoritized group but of women in general, a literary and political demand for agency at once over the most private and the most public aspects of women's lives and hence over the relationship between them. Especially in light of the overtly political uses of the sapphic that I discussed in chapter 3, it is also conceivable that in setting the ground for female subjectivity, the sapphic also models a discursive strategy by which other subordinated castes or classes might construe themselves as political subjects.

This formative role of the sapphic and especially of sapphic apostrophe, however, is historically contingent: it arrives, it peaks, it wanes, and differently so in different locations, supporting Traub's proposal that homoerotic representations follow not transhistorical continuities but "cycles of salience." That very contingency supports my argument that the sapphic is as much induced by discourse as inducing it, a product of a particular historical moment rather than a sign of transhistorical desire. We can find many effusive expressions of intimacy between women in personal letters during the later eighteenth century, and yet what I have called sapphic apostrophe in its public formation seems to drop off. I do not mean, of course, that all sapphic representations disappear, nor that women cease to create them; the next three chapters of this book emphatically suggest otherwise. But in the countries I have been studying, the specific form of sapphic discourse in which a woman directly addresses another woman with erotic intensity already seems to wane after the 1730s and, despite some resurgence at the end of the century, does not regain a proportional plenitude until the later nineteenth and early twentieth centuries, and then arguably not again until the 1970s, when the "woman-identified woman" who turns her gaze toward other women becomes a major cultural engine of a widespread political movement.[95]

It may be significant, then, that when Sharon Marcus describes in *Between Women* the normative eroticism in expressions of friendship between Victorian women, her evidence is drawn primarily from private letters and diaries.[96] Equally private is the evidence upon which Elizabeth Colwill draws for her analysis of the tumultuous and not quite egalitarian passionate relationship between the feminist philosopher Constance de Salm and Thérèse, the Princess of Tour and Taxis.[97] The poems written by women during the brief heyday of Spanish Romanticism may provide a similar counterpoint. Those women created an epistolary "circle of solidarity," as Susan Kirkpatrick describes it, indeed a "lyrical sisterhood." They published poems to one another in journals sharp with laments for women's shared fate as "the enslaved sex [el sexo esclavizado],"[98] yet as far as I can tell from Kirkpatrick's examples, the kind of erotic intimacy so prevalent in the poems that I have been describing is simply not there, and the one poem that evokes Sappho, Carolina Coronado's "Cantos de Safo," is wrapped in Sappho's love for Phaon. In other words, it may be the case that although these women were forging a collective subjectivity through an intertextual poetry, mid-nineteenth-century Spain was not a setting where the sapphic could serve that cause; arguably the sapphic would have taken on a greater vulnerability to sexual suspicion as the early modern "politics of likeness" devolved. It is therefore valuable to look more closely at the waning side of this phenomenon, a warning that, paradoxically, accompanies the rise of female friendship as a (class-specific) norm.

COMPENSATORY CONSERVATISM

It is safe to say that despite a continuing strain of satire and suspicion, friendship between women became by the mid-eighteenth century as fully a part of the social imaginary—though of course not part of the formal structure of power—as friendship between men. If we may take the ECCO database for 1700 to 1800 as representative of the English case, it is startling to see that fully 95 percent of writings using the phrase "female friendship" occur after 1750.[99] Once friendship between women becomes more or less a given, it finds its way in conduct books, the emphasis turning to the "discreet Choice of Friends" particularly by the young and unsuspecting.[100] This new emphasis on female friendship highlights its potential to serve purposes both horizontal, vis-à-vis women, and hierarchical, vis-à-vis rank. As I have discussed elsewhere and made clear earlier in this chapter, early modern friendship was always a "class act,"[101] a self-performance of the upper classes, and sapphic apostrophe almost always entailed the address of one gentlewoman to another or to a woman above rather than below her station, so that even as women might be establishing their value, they are also helping to consolidate the privileges of their class; one could argue that female friendship legitimated itself precisely by substituting its class standing for the gender status it lacked. Thus, *The Convent of Pleasure* shows the ills suffered by "mean Women" like the butcher's wife, but membership in Lady Happy's convent is explicitly restricted to "Noble Persons," especially those whose "Births are greater than their Fortunes."[102] As female friendship moves into prominence, it intersects even more directly with the project of establishing a gentleclass consciousness by functioning as a status symbol, marking women as well-connected and well-bred, and thus also lending itself to more conservative purposes.

Writers of sapphic apostrophe may have had particularly strong reasons for valorizing status beyond a typical interest in supporting the system that sustained their own privilege. For in seventeenth- and eighteenth-century Western Europe, status, along with the more obvious criterion of gender conformity, was usually the dominant if never foolproof screen distinguishing virtuous from transgressive persons, acts, and words; if it did not protect the high aristocracy, it did shelter the elite below the top. That is, the imperatives of gentility held in place a range of conventions dividing irreproachable female intimacies from dangerous ones and bifurcating acceptable friendship from transgressive sexuality along class lines. As far as we can tell from the legacy of discourse, women who met the visible proprieties for their gender—in dress, manners, duties—were, if they belonged to the gentle classes, assumed to be chaste. By the late seventeenth century, "lady" had become far more—and less—than a designation of rank; as the counterpart to "gentleman," it moved down the social scale but required the confirmation of earned and learned qualities like those advocated by the new books about the "ladies calling," to evoke Allestree's eponymous prototype of 1673, which claimed that the virtue of gentlewomen now provides them "reason enough . . . to thank God that he made them women, and not men."[103] To the extent that a woman could pass as a "lady," her friendships were more likely to be coded as nonsexual however erotically framed.

But if a woman's presumptive gentleclass status could screen out the
negative vision in favor of the sanguine one, the alternative reading always
lurked, as in Gestalt psychology's famous figure of Rubin's Vase that is also
two faces in profile, or the "ingénue" who turns into a "hag." In an emerging culture of propriety overseen by surveillance, the evaluation of women's
intimacies thus came to rest less on private habits than on public relations.[104] Even or perhaps especially as friendship solidified as a value for
gentlewomen, its public relationship to the homoerotic became more uneasy, a bifurcation between "tender friendship" and the "unnatural" growing sharper by the mid-eighteenth century, and the sapphic becoming ac-
cordingly less available for forging or sustaining a collective project. That
role arguably came to be occupied instead by the construction of women
as learned and the promotion of women's education as the mechanism for
an equality compatible with a gendered separation of social roles. Even
learning, of course, provoked worries: thus a 1762 *Critical Review* about
the "extraordinary" poems of Elizabeth Carter that I will discuss below
opines that "learning is now grown so fashionable amongst the ladies,
that it becomes every gentleman to carry his Latin and Greek with him
whenever he ventures into female company. . . . The men *retreat*, and the
women *advance*. The men prate and dress; the women read and write: it is
no wonder, therefore, that they should get the upper hand of us; nor should
we be at all surprised, if, in the next age, women should give lectures in
the classics, and men employ themselves in knotting and needle-work."[105]

Such cultural anxieties helped to forge what I call a "compensatory
conservatism" in relation to same-sex affiliations. In an earlier essay
that better suits the history of sexuality than the sexuality of history, I
argued that this "compensatory conservatism" enabled women such as
the "Ladies of Llangollen" Eleanor Butler and Sarah Ponsonby, or the self-
consciously lesbian Anne Lister, to manipulate the conventions of class
in what amounted to an elaborate public relations scheme.[106] My purpose
here, however, is to show how a more conservative ethos might also have
muted the practice of sapphic apostrophe by the mid-eighteenth century.
As a way to introduce the intensified threat of the sapphic and its implications for an economy of same-sex desire, I take a moment to consider a letter that the Bluestocking intellectual Elizabeth Robinson Montagu wrote
in 1750 to her sister Sarah Robinson Scott after learning that two of their
women friends were planning to cohabit:

> I must confess I am sorry for [it], as it will add to the jests the men
> made on that friendship, & I own I think those sort of reports hurt us

all. And fall in their degree on the whole Sex: and really if this non-sense gains ground one must shut oneself up alone; for one can not have Men Intimates, & at this rate the Women are more scandalous. So we must become Savages & have no friendships or connexions: I cannot think what Mrs L[ytleton] and Miss R [or K?] can mean by making such a parade of their affection, they might know it wd give occasion to Lies.[107]

Especially because Montagu's is a private communication, this letter reminds us that class is not always a sufficient screen for distinguishing the allegedly chaste from the allegedly sapphic: friendship between gentlewomen may not be presumed innocent nor female cohabitation innocuous. In language as distressed in its way as was Henri Estienne's over the acts of a single couple, the scandal is rendered contagious; it threatens to taint "the whole sex" including the highly respectable wife of a member of Parliament for whom friendship is so important that without it people become "savages." Moreover, the fault of Mrs. L and Miss R is not desire but its display, not private behavior but its public performance, for as Montagu frames it, Mrs. L and Miss R's "parade" of affection reveals not the truth of their intimacy but a "lie." Montagu's concern about this friendship is surely a warning as well to its addressee, her sister, also living in a same-sex partnership with Lady Barbara Montagu.[108]

The poetry of Montagu's own intimate and unmarried friend Elizabeth Carter, the renowned classical scholar, provides a rich site for examining the subtle but pivotal changes wrought to sapphic apostrophe and its political project by mid-century, especially in tandem with other works published at the same moment. I thus want to read Carter's *Poems on Several Occasions* and Scott's *Millenium Hall* against Jean-Jacques Rousseau's massively influential *Emile, ou l'éducation* with the backdrop of Rousseau's *Du contrat social*, all four works published in 1762. Along with Rousseau's wildly popular novel *Julie, ou la nouvelle Héloïse* (1761), which I will discuss in chapter 5, these books advance and reflect the shift that I have in mind.

Because Carter's *Poems* fits the rubric of sapphic apostrophe, its departures from the earlier examples are all the more salient. None of the smattering of poems directed to men in her volume concern friendship, while fully half the volume's thirty-seven poems are apostrophes to women. And certainly they are passionate renderings: Cynthia is the "Dear Object of a Love whose fond Excess / No studied Forms of Language can express," and the "lov'd *Eudocia*'s Image smiles / And gaily brightens all my Heart."[109]

The bodily discourse is more attenuated here; significantly, the most passionate of the poems, the only one that addresses the beloved as "my Love" (55) deploys a male voice, drawn from the poetry of Metastasio, while one that describes a woman "whose voice is Music, and whose Looks are Love" (9) uses the third person. But while the earlier poems that I have been discussing in this chapter almost always gave the addressee a proper name, if only a code name, in Carter's volume not a single addressee is named in a poem's title, so that half the titles are simply the repetitive and privatizing "To ———" or, occasionally, "To Miss ———," highlighting the personal stakes of the poem within an aura of secrecy and thus effectively and paradoxically publishing the very privacy of same-sex relationships.

Moreover, in an intensification of earlier tendencies, Carter's poems to women are characterized by a deep pessimism about the earthly possibilities of female friendship and the legitimacy of desire: beyond the elegaic longing of a Katherine Philips or a Sor Juana de la Cruz, love between women is reserved here for "Beyond the Grave, where vulgar Passions end" (21). The corporeal forms but a state in which "rising Sorrows shake my Breast," where "ev'ry Joy that Friendship gives /Shall fade beneath the Gloom of Spleen" (39). Here death in effect enables friendship: "beyond the Gloom, / Where the short Reign of Time and Death expires, / Victorious o'er the Ravage of the Tomb, / Smiles the fair Object of thy fond Desires" (84). To the extent that Carter's volume is emblematic, it is fair to say that sapphic friendship is effectively being put to death. Her *Poems* thus both enter and disavow the tradition of sapphic apostrophe.

Lest there be any doubt that the volume is not inscribing anything sapphic—or at least Sapphic—the first poem included in the preface, attributed to the statesman and patron Lord Lyttleton, explicitly dissociates Carter's work from Sappho's in a paean to the poet as virtuous and presumably heteronormative Englishwoman. As I have already suggested, earlier women poets were routinely and unqualifiedly compared to Sappho; Madeleine de Scudéry herself adopted that pen name, and her "Histoire de Sapho" (1653) turns Sapho away from Phaon and subtly back toward women in the end. With a bit of equivocation, Feijoo's *Defensa de las mujeres* (1726) marks Scudéry as "the *Sapho of her century*, equal to that most celebrated Greek in the beauty of her writings and much exceeding her in the purity of her habits."[110] But Lyttleton's "On Reading Mrs. ———'s Poems in Manuscript" condemns Sappho unequivocally and replaces her with Carter: "Greece shall no more / Of *Lesbian Sappho* boast, whose wanton Muse, / Like a false Syren, while she charmed, seduc'd / To Guilt and Ruin" (v–vi). The world has no need of Sappho, since "For the sacred Head / Of *Brit-*

ain's Poetess the Virtues twine / A nobler Wreath" (vi). Carter may have benefited from the cover-up; it is worth remembering that she appears in *The Sappho-An* as one of the "manly" and "lusty" sapphic figures. We have here a fine sign of what Harriet Guest has described as celebration of learned women "as the icons of national progress."[111]

The lengthy review of Carter's *Poems* in the *Critical Review* of March 1762 covers over the sapphic at least as much as the volume itself. Citing the passage of Lyttleton's poem that names Carter as the "nobler" version of Sappho, the reviewer comments that "the female muse is seldom altogether so chaste as could be wished, and that most of our lady writers are rather deficient in point of morality. To the honour of Mrs. Carter it may be said, that there is scarce a line in this volume which does not breathe the purest sentiments."[112] The reviewer goes on to single out six of her poems, none of which takes the form of sapphic apostrophe; instead he emphasizes Carter's verses on death, her one ode to a gentleman, her advice in the voice of a guardian angel, and her poems on melancholy and wisdom. In making no mention whatever about the love poems to women that comprise half the book, the review effectively cleanses Carter's volume of any sapphic taint.

It is no wonder, then, that Sarah Scott's female utopia *Millenium Hall*, published in the same year, enacts a similar distancing from the imputations of a physical same-sex desire. The novel sets up female affiliation both as the foundation for Christian philanthropy and as a way for women to escape marriage; in this sense, it is as if Fonte's two-day retreat has become a lifelong and formalized, if also equally sequestered, model for social governance. The community's celebrated foundation is the intense partnership of Mrs. Morgan and Miss Mancel, between whom "*Meum* and *Tuum*" are "watchful and suspicions enemies" of "true friendship." But while we have affiliation here, all traces of physical relationship have been erased except, as in Carter's poems, when the physical is a site of suffering: Morgan and Mancel are "so strongly united" in affection "that one could not suffer without the other's feeling equal pain."[113] Further, the female community lives effectively in hiding; even the gentleman who narrates *Millenium Hall* must agree not to divulge its location, so that its social contract cannot be translated out of the same-sex context: in the novel's sequel, *The History of Sir George Ellison*, a man must take the women's ideas into the world.

In what we might read as a compensatory gesture, *Millenium Hall* does trade on class status to legitimate what I would argue remains a sapphic project. The upperclass paragons live together in the main house of an estate that is class-stratified in its architectural contours and in which no lesser-ranked women are permitted intimate bonds. The less educated "indigent gentlewomen" whom they have rescued from servitude also live under one roof in a separate dwelling, but they find it a strain to cohabit in "comfortable harmony." And the working-class women are provided individual cottages where they get along "better, than if we lived together," for they "used to quarrel" until "the ladies . . . shewed us so kindly how much it was our duty to agree."[114] In this way the text harks back to the elite conceptualization of friendship that I articulated at the start of this chapter, one that promotes the benefits of female friendship as status politics. Not surprisingly, such a representation resoundingly contradicts historical data about materially enabling friendship networks among working women, including evidence of the ways in which, for example, Dutch women accused of tribadism later in the century risked their lives to protect friends and lovers.[115]

As the eighteenth century hardens its gender values and male supremacy increasingly reorganizes itself on grounds of difference, political economy itself is being reconstituted through cross-sex desire. We see this shift dramatically articulated in Jean-Jacques Rousseau's influential writings, *Emile, ou l'éducation* and *Du contrat social*, both published in the same year as Carter's *Poems* and Scott's *Millenium Hall*. In the late (arguably afterthought) chapters of *Emile* that take up the education and status of women, Rousseau shifts the terms of female subjectivity by demolishing any logic of woman + woman (though that logic still haunts *Julie, ou la nouvelle Héloïse*, as we shall see in chapter 5). Rousseau's equal-but-different theory of gender argues that "woman is made specially to please man" indeed "made to please and to be subjugated." Thus "she ought to make herself pleasing to man instead of provoking him," for "the more women resemble men, the less influence they will have over them, and then the men will truly be the masters." By virtue of this asymmetrical symbiosis, "every woman desires to be pleasing in men's eyes." In effect, then, women are not women apart from men, and since this system by which "the woman [must] obey the man" is founded, Rousseau insists, on an "inexorable law of nature," not on "man-made laws," women are effectively powerless to refuse it.[116] Thus Rousseau insists on the necessity for women to be joined to men in arrangements that are not just patriarchal but heterosexual; ultimately, as Christine Roulston argues, marriage becomes for Rousseau "the frame that enables sexual difference to acquire stability."[117] It is thus not surprising that women hardly figure in *The Social Contract*, also published in 1762 and by Rousseau's own declaration a

work meant to be read in relation to *Emile*. Although Rousseau is also unable explicitly to write women out of that conceived form of governance, it
is not insignificant that women appear only twice in the entire document,
once in relation to their fecundity, and the other, more ominously, in
praise of Rome: "Let us judge of what can be done by what has been done.
I shall say nothing of the Republics of ancient Greece; but the Roman Republic was, to my mind, a great State, and the town of Rome a great town.
The last census showed that there were in Rome four hundred thousand
citizens capable of bearing arms, and the last computation of the population of the Empire showed over four million citizens, excluding subjects,
foreigners, women, children and slaves."[118] If Rome is his model, and the
differentiation between citizens and "women, children and slaves" goes
unremarked, then implicitly Rousseau's polity, and its General Will, is
gendered masculine. It would not be an overstatement to say that in Rousseau's philosophical framework, the political economy of same-sex desire
is less than nil: woman without man is woman without the possibility of
even indirect participation in a polity.

It is of course Rousseau's notion of sexual complementarity, and not
the sapphic subjectivity that I have been outlining here, that became the
bedrock for the domestic and political economy that dominated European
thought at least until the turn of the twentieth century. Thus even as Catherine Macaulay asserted in 1790 that educated women would "be glad to
give up indirect influence for rational privileges, and established rights,"[119]
the German philosopher Johann Fichte pressed the Rousseauvian argument that although a woman is a "complete human being," who may of
course "claim . . . all the rights of man and of male citizens," women's
orientation of loving service to their husbands must call into question
whether "the female sex can *desire to* exercise all her rights."[120] Women
are now, in effect, to choose the subordination formerly assumed of them,
resolving the contradiction between female subjectivity and patriarchy by
writing the new economy on the body itself. While there is no evidence
that Rousseau understood himself to be repudiating a sapphic episteme, it
is not farfetched to see his philosophy of gender as a kind of metamorphic
project, a turning of women, from their youth, away from any possibility
of orientation toward other women rather than toward men. Not surprisingly, as Alan Bray laments, same-sex friendship, and arguably friendship
tout court, became a diminished element "of the sinews of 'civil' society
as the eighteenth century constructed it," and "the older meaning that
had once adhered so powerfully to the desire for the body of the friend
slipped finally away" into a "new sexual culture" where "the body of the

friend seems lost."[121] The Dutch poet Aagje Deken, in a poem published in
1775, writes a lament even more intensive than Carter's:

> Oh, the life of women friends who are parted
> Is cruel, bitter, and broken-hearted!
> . . . .
> Let me live with my MARIA, as well I may,
> I'll wish no more, O Friend of Friends, to whom I pray.[122]

In identifying God as the "Friend of Friends"—and thus apparently the
friend of friendship, Deken opens an important avenue for setting female
friendship against civil society but in spiritual terms, a phenomenon particular powerful in late-eighteenth-century Holland and exemplified in
Elisabeth Maria Post's novel *Het Land, in brieven* (1788), which I will discuss in chapter 7. It is important to remember too that the gap between
discourse and lived life may cut both ways. Sarah Scott and Barbara Montagu did not sequester themselves in the shelter of a Millenium Hall, but
lived together in Bath and Batheaston in a quite public if never admittedly
erotic union that Scott described in marital terms,[123] and in 1777 Deken
too formed a lifelong personal and authorial partnership with the writer
Betje Wolff that was widely known and honored across Europe. If friendship was going to be coopted by marriage, then marriage was going to be
coopted by friendship as well, leading to the Victorian scene that Sharon
Marcus and Martha Vicinus describe in which female couples lived together openly and apparently with acceptance in ways that surely would
have distressed Elizabeth Montagu.

Discursively speaking, however, the age in which same-sex desire
could foment a political economy through public writings seems to have
waned, at least for the moment. A brief look at two texts written in the
wake of *Millenium Hall* suggest the alteration that turns a same-sex idyll
laughably dystopic. Anna Williams's poem "The Nunnery" (1766) describes a group of modern-day "nymphs" who decide to "spurn great Hymen's laws" and its "matrimonial fetters." Having "banish[ed] man with
one consenting voice," they start figuring out the ways to sustain their
"bold rebellion" and settle on a Protestant nunnery as a place of "ease and
liberty" not unlike Cavendish's "convent of pleasure" or Millenium Hall.
This nunnery will join the women's "fortunes in one stock" to build a
"pleasing mansion" for thirty "willing vot'ries," wherein the women will
devote their lives "for pray'r, for work, for reading and for tea." But suddenly the planners begin to worry that there will be no visits, no friends,

no dancing partners: "Must no man enter here? Brisk Lucia cry'd: / Then burn the plan, fair Thestylis reply'd: / Let fellows rather stile me Wife than Nun. / And thus the Castle sunk ere yet begun."[124] The very separateness that motivated Fonte, Cavendish and arguably Scott founders on precisely the reason for the separateness in the first place: disdaining "matrimonial fetters," the women decide rather to embrace those fetters than to live without partners for the marital "dance." As in *The Sappho-an* of a few years prior, heteroerotic desire, woman made for man, is the engine that ultimately controls women's choices and ensures the orientation that Rousseau decreed.

Whether or not Anna Williams had *Millenium Hall* in mind, Samuel Jackson Pratt certainly did when he made its eponymous topos the negative blueprint for *Shenstone-Green: or, The New Paradise Lost* (1779). Such a community, says Samuel the "Oracle" to the narrator, "may do very well, sir, in a romance, (like your *Millenium-Hall*) but to introduce them upon *Shenstone-Green* would put all Wales in confusion. . . . Our village shall be of another guess [sic] construction.—No Maynards and Mansells." Women are set up here not as friends but as natural enemies: it is "altogether out of nature" for "Miss Mansell, and Miss Morgan, Lady M. Jones, Mrs. Selvyn, Mrs. Trentham, and all the other Lady Bountifuls," to "live together in the same house without *lovers, husbands,* or *quarrels*."[125] The conjunction would be violent: "times and seasons would come about, if you were *with* them, when Mrs. Maynard would throw her orrery at Mrs. Selvyn, who, like a true woman, would throw her book at Mrs. Maynard, Mrs. Mansell, notwithstanding her being the finest form, and albeit, had beautiful brown hair, would toss her Madona at Mrs. Trentham's carved figure, and away, I warrant you, would go that same carved work to knock off the beautiful brown-haired Mrs. Mansell's Madona."[126] These are harsh and mocking words directed not at the characters so much as at their relationships, which ironically are here rendered aggressively physical; they suggest both the continued specter of same-sex formations and the continued urgency of keeping utopia from going feminine or, we might say, sapphic.

These repudiations suggest the discursive incompatibilities between sapphic subjectivity and the Rousseauvian ideology that becomes widespread during the later eighteenth century. That public sapphic apostrophe begins to diminish in this environment is no surprise. We see yet another sign of the times in the brief brush with the sapphic, and the Sapphic, in the influential poems of the German working-class poet Anna Luise Karsch in the 1760s. As Claire Baldwin elaborates, in fashioning her poetic persona Karsch took hold of the overly (hetero)sexualized image of Sappho prevalent in German culture at the time and effectively tamed it into a femininity through which she could articulate an independent, female poetic voice. This move turned out to be of mixed effectiveness, however, when her self-construction as Sappho was attacked by the young though already distinguished Johann Gottfried Herder; as Baldwin comments, Karsch did not evoke Sappho in her next volume of poems, the 1772 *Neue Gedichte*.[127] We do find two instances of sapphic apostrophe among Karsch's wide-ranging 1764 *Auserlesene Gedichte*: a poem to Frau von Reichmann, "whom my heart recommended to me [der mich mein Herz empfohlen]" and to whom the poet will therefore "tell who I am [dir sagen wer ich bin]," and more pointedly, a poem "An Phillis" asking Phillis to "Come, my Friend! kiss me! [Komm, meine Freundin! Küsse mich]."[128] But Karsch is a pioneer, at this point, in challenging an elite masculinist tradition before the fuller flowering of German women's writing in the later eighteenth century. That as far as I can tell this flowering will not be accompanied by the outpouring of sapphic apostrophe that characterized earlier literary projects may be yet another sign that Europe has moved on, and with it the efficacy of similitude in the context of political apostrophe. Thus Susanne Kord explores the passionate verbal relationships between several pairs of women writers, all of whom, however, kept their expressions of intimacy private. Thus the letters of the mid-eighteenth-century poet and playwright—and wife—Luise Gottsched to the writer Dorothea von Runckel, or the correspondence between the late-century novelist Therese Huber and the actress Auguste Schneider, evoke the tenor of the sapphic apostrophe I have been describing: Gottsched "viewed friendship as the highest form of human interaction" and "considered women more capable of it"; thus she writes that "it would be bad if two souls who love each other as we do should learn the rules of friendship from that deceitful sex"; Huber writes that she loves Auguste "as man and wife, or rather as lover and beloved, we are One."[129] German women writers, arriving somewhat late on the European scene, evince little of the poetic apostrophe that is already waning elsewhere. As we will see in subsequent chapters, however, German novels, including Therese Huber's *Die Ehelosen* (1829), certainly take their place in late-century sapphic representations.

As chapter 5 also makes evident, the decrease in sapphic apostrophe that I have traced schematically to the rising discourse of sexual difference by no means solidifies a "political economy of same-sex desire" during the period encompassed by this chapter. By the early eighteenth century, we can see the novel beginning to take its place as a major "way in which this society speaks to itself," to quote Philippe Sollers.[130] In that conversation, we will see a gathering and testing of nearly all the varied hallmarks of sapphic representation that I have discussed in these past three chapters from tropes of mobility to metamorphic plotting to dialogic apostrophe. But in the rising novel, the sapphic will do more than continue to surface and signify: the genre itself is arguably shaped by the sapphic from the start. It is that queer history of a newly powerful form that the next chapter aims to elucidate.

CHAPTER FIVE

Rereading the 'Rise' of the Novel: Sapphic Genealogies, 1680–1815

By virtue of its initial plan of conquest, [the novel] can only be simultaneously democratic and conservative . . . liberated and despotic, typically middle class, order-loving and restless.
—Marthe Robert, *Origins of the Novel*[1]

In an uprising as in a novel, the most difficult part to invent is the end.
—Alexis de Tocqueville, *Souvenirs*[2]

Franco Moretti has wryly suggested that the more we learn about the history of the novel, the stranger it becomes."[3] If it remains a truism that the novel "rose" with modernity, that truism has indeed been made strange during the past few decades through the contests it has spawned about what counts as a novel; about when, where, how, and why the genre emerged; about whether any specific investments unify the "rising" genre and characterize its touted "realism." In the end, we face what Moretti rightly calls the novel's "polygenesis," which also means recognizing that confluence, far more than influence, governs the early history of a genre about which Mikhail Bakhtin's bold claim still holds: that "experts have not managed to isolate a single definite, stable characteristic of the novel—without adding a reservation."[4] Indeed, it may be what both Bakhtin and Marthe Robert have recognized as the novel's rapacious capacity to engulf and encroach upon the vast multiplicity of its contemporary modes and genres that constitutes its character.

Drawing on the temporal convergence of the novel and the sapphic as hallmarks of the modern, I hope here to "add a reservation" about a key aspect of the novel and, in the process, to render the history of the novel even more strange—or rather, queer. If the novel is the epic of "a world that has been abandoned by God," in which "the extensive totality of life is no longer directly given," as Georg Lukács has famously written,[5] then we can plausibly expect it to emerge in spaces of epistemic fracture. Thomas Pavel argues that "the novel has traditionally focused on love and the formation of couples" to explore the moral tensions between "resisting the world" and "correcting [one's] own frailties" that became the novel's imperative in that abandoned world.[6] Franco Moretti likewise emphasizes the conflict between "self-determination" and "socialization"—or "individuality" and "normality"—that requires renunciation even as it offers what Joan Ramon Resina calls the "illusion of agency."[7] If we merge these observations to see the novel as entangled with negotiations of demand and desire in the formation or prohibition of couples within a social matrix, then it is all the more important to ask where and how the novel's tensions encompass the tension of same-sex desire. In so doing, I argue that even as the genre is "rising," the sapphic is already shaping it. And because of the signal importance of the couple to the novel and of the novel to larger cultural projects, the sapphic as the novel produces it evokes questions about individual liberties, social mobilities, domestic demands, economic imperatives and, not least, the forms and functions of narrative itself. In short, I am asking here—to echo the chiastic imperative of this project— not what we can learn about sapphic subjects from the novel, but what we can learn about the novel from sapphic subjects.

To put it most boldly, I will argue that the history of the ("rising" European) novel can be read as a sapphic plot. Such a claim ought to seem counterintuitive, for scholars have persuasively argued that one underpinning of the eighteenth-century novel is its investment in affirming heteronormative subjects within an emergent system of affective kinship, synchronizing desire and domesticity—to evoke the influential words of Nancy Armstrong—by "creat[ing] the illusion that desire was entirely subjective and therefore essentially different from the politically encodable forms of behavior to which desire gave rise."[8] And to the extent that Thomas Laqueur is right to argue that "some time in the eighteenth century, sex as we know it was invented,"[9] that "invention" was certainly abetted by the novel as a growing genre. That the conjugal family "as we know it" likewise began to take shape during the long eighteenth century cements the focus of the novel not simply on whether marriage shall happen but with whom, in what Ruth Perry recognizes as an "obsessive concern" with the choice of a spouse that I believe holds not only in the English works she studies but in the later-emerging German and Dutch novel and even in the more libertine and tragic fictions that dominate the novel in France.[10]

Moreover, it may be a matter of confluence rather than coincidence that the three countries earliest involved in shaping the modern novel—Spain, England, and France—are also the three countries that pioneer the proliferation of sapphic representations.

It is thus all the more significant to ask to what extent the novel actually does get "cramped into domesticity," as Margaret Doody sees it from the vantage-point of the *longue durée*.[11] This chapter asks what might impede that movement and argues that how the struggle the novel enacts over the place of female agency in the social order turns out to be imbricated with the sapphic in ways that are multifaceted and shifting but also persistent. That is, the "illusion that desire was entirely subjective" depended, among other challenges, on the suppression, management, or transformation of female same-sex bonds: domesticity did not arrive without a struggle that was longer and larger than histories of the novel have yet recognized. That struggle also entangles the sapphic with the dynamics of class and with the national projects to which investments in status attach. Efforts to manage the sapphic entail a complex set of narrative strategies that also resist resolution, as my epigraph from Tocqueville implies. In this chapter, we will see writ particularly large in the novel transformations in several of the key concerns and practices that I discussed in previous chapters: the preoccupation with mobility, pornographic ethnographies, complications of metamorphic plotting, sapphic apostrophe transmuted to narrative structures of confidence, and the horizontality of female resistance—these often entangled with one another in narratives that, in the process of confronting or evading sapphic subjects, are often hoist with their proverbial petards.

Reading the novel as a sapphic story helps to address a gender gap in traditional lineages that herald early works such as *Lazarillo de Tormes*, *Gargantua et Pantagruel*, *Don Quixote*, or that latecomer *Robinson Crusoe*—as fathers of the genre. Feminist critics have argued not only that this patrilineage erases the signal contributions of works by and about women—the *Héptameron*, *La Princesse de Clèves*, *Love Letters Between a Nobleman and His Sister*—but that the standard genealogy effaces the novel's pioneering deployment of female voice and interiority and thus offers little help in explaining forms and functions central to the novel of—and beyond—the eighteenth century. I am not of course denying the continued presence of male-centered novels from *Lazarillo* to *Werther* to *Atala* or anti-domestic plots from *Crusoe* to *Les Liaisons dangereuses* to *Frankenstein* or anti-realist fictions of the kind that Srinivas Aravamudan elucidates in *Enlightenment Orientalism*. But a sapphic history of the novel, which is necessarily a gendered history, illuminates the domestic novel's enabling conditions, its deployment of narrators and narratees, its persistent struggle with picaresque tendencies, and the ways in which its complex negotiations of same-sex desire challenge the heteronormative story that the 'rise of the novel' conventionally presumes. If, as Fredric Jameson argues, the "single great collective story" is the "struggle to wrest a realm of Freedom from a realm of Necessity"[12]—arguably the very project of sapphic apostrophe as I have characterized it in chapter 4— then the collective struggle for female narrators and characters in the eighteenth-century European novel is surely to wrest a realm of alternatives—which includes the alternative of the sapphic—from the sequential necessities of chastity and marriage or their tragic alternatives of transgression and death. Even as the novel is "rising," its arguably heteronormative and domesticating project is sowing the seeds of its discontent; put differently, the sapphic is a sign and agent of the discontent that the novel will be challenged, and sometimes fail, to resolve. The sapphic is thus also a sign that what Nancy Miller described in terms of female characters' refusal or resistance to novelistic "plausibility" is not limited to novels by women, though women writers figure prominently in that project of resistance.[13]

The novel's sapphic subjects confront us with another conundrum: what does it mean to accept, as a claim about the novel, Nancy Armstrong's argument that the "modern individual" is "first and foremost a woman"?[14] How do we reconcile the rise of the female protagonist as what Barbara Johnson calls a "lyric person" with the historical failure to accord women the "rights of man and the citizen."[15] For even if we accept Eve Bannet's compelling argument for a homology between the domestic and the political that would credit the novel for promoting female agency in the public sphere, it would be difficult to deny (and Bannet does not deny) the circumscribed place the novel ultimately gives to its female protagonists.[16] If Moretti is right that marriage is "the novel's definitive and classifying act per excellence," and yet also right that its happy endings come only to "the detriment and eventual annulment of 'freedom,'"[17] surely the implications and intensities of that annulled freedom remain gendered ones I therefore posit novelistic configurations of the sapphic as a primary and not just incidental locus in which the harnessing of desire to domesticity gets contested, subverted, or transformed and in which the question of the "modern individual" takes on new complexities along with the question of the couple as the site where modernity works out the tensions between social strictures and individual imperatives. I suggested

in chapter 2 that sapphic habits evoke the dynamics of alteration, mobility, and self-formation that forge modern narrative; I will suggest here
that those dynamics shape the history of the European novel in ways that
complicate and resist its heteronormative plots, illuminate the dominance
of female voice in eighteenth-century narrative technologies, and underscore the critical place of *means* in both shaping the novel and achieving
its ends. Put differently, I am suggesting that what Michael McKeon has
called the "secret history of domesticity" carries the deeper secret of domesticity's dependence on same-sex desire.[18]

Several scholars have traced sapphic presences in the eighteenth-
century novel. In giving her *Dangerous Intimacies* the subtitle *Toward a
Sapphic History of the British Novel*, Lisa Moore reads challenges to heteronormativity in a range of canonical English works, while George Haggerty has taken up the queer sapphic formations both in novels by women
and in the gothic mode. Chris Roulston has explored the twin dynamics of
marriage and female intimacy in French and English fiction. Novels figure
centrally in Myriam Everard's exploration of "liefde en lust tussen vrouwen" in the second half of the eighteenth century, and Angela Steidele has
shown the emergence of *Frauenliebe* in late-eighteenth-century German
works, a large number of which are novels. I build on such inquiries in
order to argue that ties between the novel and the sapphic are central to
the development of the genre as both literary form and social agent. I hope
therefore to trace a sapphic story not only *in* novels but *of* novels, a story
sometimes embedded more firmly in the telling than in the tale, that is,
in elements of form as opposed to elements of content or in a contest between the two.[19]

In tracing a queerer history of the European novel over the long eighteenth century, I focus first on dialogic structures of narration that emerge
in late-seventeenth-century erotic fictions to make the new practice of female voice an instantiation of sapphic voice as well. I go on to explore a
plenitude of picaresque fictions that treat to the sapphic as an agent of
plot, opening a wide and usually affirmative space for same-sex adventures that challenges heteronormative histories of the novel and shows the
stakes of metamorphosis. The pervasive presence of the female confidante
as narratee, together with queer characters and turns of plot, pose visible
challenges during the very period from the 1740s through the 1770s that
has been associated with the novel's consolidation as a conventional and
heteronormative form. Late in the century, sapphic intimacies attempt
to reconfigure gothic and Romantic plots that ask women to save other
women from patriarchy gone monstrous and, in emphasizing the eco-

nomic underpinnings of rescue, test the terms for effective subjectivity of the kind promised by, if sometimes only longed for in, the discourse of sapphic apostrophe. As the novel reaches a new threshold of domestic realism at the end of the century, shifts in narrative practice contain same-sex relations in ways that become more visible when we read those novels through the lens of the sapphic. The national literatures that will be central to this chapter are those central to the eighteenth-century novel as well—England, France, and eventually Germany, with some presence of Spain, Italy, and eventually the Netherlands; if we construct a sapphic genealogy of the novel in the ways that I am proposing, it is safe to say that in the eighteenth century, where the novel blooms, so bloom its sapphic inscriptions. And if we keep in mind the metamorphic practices so popular some decades earlier, we begin to see that the novel is more likely to enact what I would call "reverse metamorphosis," most blatantly in picaresque manifestations but sometimes even in more domestic plots, that inverts the trajectory of Elizabethan and Golden Age theater by attempting to turn cross-sex into same-sex relations. It turns out, however, that in the sapphic as in the revolution, the "most difficult part to invent" is indeed "the end."

IN THE BEDROOM: THE DIALOGICS OF DESIRE

If we wish to trace the modern novel to sixteenth-century antecedents, then we already have several starting points for a sapphic history. Fernando de Rojas's dialogic *Tragicomedia de Calisto y Melibea* (1499), familiarly known as *La Celestina* and often considered the first Spanish novel, includes a scene in which the eponymous old woman makes verbal and perhaps physical love to the young courtesan Areusa even as she is convincing Areusa to sleep with her son. Late sixteenth-century romances from other national traditions—such as Sidney's *Arcadia*, Ariosto's *Orlando Furioso*, and Thomas Lodge's *Rosalynde*—all play with sapphic desire as they evoke Ovidian tales of gender disguise and metamorphic resolution. As I have already shown, however, such scenarios also appear in poetry, drama, and ethnography and are not unique to the novel in substance or form.

The sixteenth-century antecedent with which I begin my genealogy, however, seems to me to inaugurate what will become a pervasive and specifically novelistic practice. Pietro Aretino's *Ragionamenti* [*Dialogues*] (1534), often considered modern Europe's first erotic fiction, reveals the sapphic potential not only of a single story but of the novel's representa-

tional project itself. I focus therefore not on *Il ragionamenti*'s stories of
women in bed together, but on a scene of narration in which desire effectively circulates among women across textual levels. In this episode, a
midwife-procuress recounts to a wetnurse an illicit encounter she has arranged between a married woman and a man. This conventional tale takes
a queer turn when the midwife rhapsodizes to the nurse about the body of
the wife who is undressing for her male lover. As she watches from a hiding place that effectively replicates the position of the lover, the midwife
sees the woman

> strip herself stark naked . . . for he examined her carefully in every
> nook and cranny. . . . My God, her neck! And her breasts, Nurse, those
> two tits would have corrupted virgins and made martyrs unfrock
> themselves. I lost my wits when I saw that lovely body with its navel
> like a jewel at its center, and I lost myself in the beauty of that particu-
> lar thing, thanks to which men do so many crazy deeds. . . . I swear to
> you . . . that as I looked at her, I put my hand on my you-know-what and
> rubbed it just the way a man does when he hasn't a place to put it.[20]

In this moment, an encounter long delayed and arduously arranged between a man and a woman produces, in effect, a sapphic incident. The
effect is replicated in the act of its reporting, when the nurse who is the
narratee admits that "as you tell me all this" she experiences "that sweet
delight which you feel when dreaming that your lover is doing it to you
and then awake just as you come."[21] The double-layered homoerotic response thus depends on a heterosexual story, while the heterosexual story
depends for its telling on a homoerotic narrative situation that effectively
renders female the proverbial "male gaze."

In an expanded account of the novel's polygenesis, the *Ragionamenti*'s
complication of a heterosexual surface provides an early moment in which
generative specificities of the novel converge. As Bakhtin observes, the
novel is "essentially a literature of snooping about, of overhearing 'how
others live'"; it simulates the kind of peeping and eavesdropping represented in the midwife's account. Sexual behaviors, as among the most
secret aspects of "how others live," make vivid the tension between the
"public nature of the literary form and the private nature of its content"
particularly as these converge in real-seeming time and space.[22] One vivid
consequence of this convergence is the "sex scene," which moves from
private chamber (the site of representation) to public page (the site of reception) by means of a narration that is thus also an erotic transaction. Hence,

says Bakhtin, the disproportionate importance of prostitutes, courtesans, and criminals in the novel's engagement with "the philosophy of the third person in private life."[23]

The *Ragionamenti* augur novelistic practice in yet another central way. If we accept Bakhtin's famous dictum that "the fundamental condition, that which makes a novel a novel, is the speaking person and [his/her] discourse,"[24] then it is significant that early representations of female desire in the novel are heavily wrapped not only in female voice but also in a pattern of female-to-female narration that is structurally sapphic in the way that Aretino's *Ragionamenti* pioneer. That is, eroticized intimacies between women become part of the structural fabric of the genre even when the manifest content of the narrative is heteronormative. Moreover, the novel plays a major role in instantiating dialogue between female speakers as a common practice in modern culture, against a centuries-old tradition of male interlocutors.[25] This will make the birth of female voice in the novel the birth of sapphic voice as well, and at a time that coincides with the emergence of both early feminism and sapphic apostrophe as I discussed in chapter 4.

A group of erotic novels structured as dialogues between women instantiate this formal dynamic. Massively and lastingly popular, and reaching a peak of publication and translation in the late seventeenth and early eighteenth centuries, these dialogues blend homoeroticism with erudition to create what can be read as either a satiric cooptation or a libertine promotion of female voice that potentially turns ersatz lesbian fictions to influential narrative ends. Of these, Nicolas Chorier's *L'académie des dames ou la philosophie dans le boudoir du grand siècle* (1680) and *Vénus dans le cloître, ou, la religieuse en chemise: entretiens curieux* (1683) by the pseudonymous and still unidentified "Abbé du Prat" offer the most obvious convergence of narration and plot into a sapphic formation,[26] but to these one can add similarly prominent works as *L'école des filles, ou la philosophie des dames* (1655), attributed to Michel Millot, and in a more overtly political and less pornographic vein, Bernard Mandeville's *The Virgin Unmask'd* (1709), which I mentioned in chapter 3. Like Aretino's *Ragionamenti*, nearly all of these works continued to circulate widely, in several languages and multiple editions, throughout the eighteenth century. All are structured exclusively as dialogues between women, and as their titles suggest, their erotic and philosophical content is almost always constituted within an instructional setting—a *school* for girls, an *academy* for ladies, a *rhetoric* for prostitutes, *instruction* for nuns—aimed at initiating a younger, less experienced woman into sexual—and more than sexual—knowledge. Structurally, these texts follow the narrative form inaugurated in Aretino's *Ragionamenti*: in a historical change of narrative practice, they make female same-sex narration the frame and filter of representation. But these narratives exceed Aretino's retrospective mode, for here the interlocutors are also the actors and the sexual events become inseparable from their narration. That the works are invested in a certain formal realism also aligns these loosely plotted and recursive episodic fictions to the novel that will "rise" in their wake.

Each of these instances of early pornography works dialogically and wholly or primarily through female voice. *L'académie des dames*, for example, consists of seven dialogues between the newly betrothed Octavie and her more experienced married cousin Tullie, who has come to teach her the sexual ways of the world; *Vénus dans le cloître* uses a similar structure to enact five dialogues between the innocent Soeur Agnès and the sexually experienced Soeur Angélique.[27] Sometimes conversations about male-female sex take an explicitly sapphic turn, as when, for example, a discussion about the size of the male member turns into one woman's examination of the other's amplitude. But throughout, these "entretiens" hold the women in a shared state of intimacy in which each ensuing dialogue is set up as the promise of erotic fulfillment. In ways that show the continued imbrication of the sapphic with intellectual matters, these works place sex within wide-ranging philosophical conversations and deploy narrative strategies that keep same-sex intimacy in motion throughout the text. If heterosexual instruction is the putative starting point of these dialogues, the sapphic intimacies that underwrite them could seem to be their own *raison d'être*.

Through these texts, the time-space relations that Bakhtin calls "chronotopes" and that will characterize the novel in its modern form make sapphic sex available to readers as an experience unfolding in "real time" and thus "materialized in space."[28] The narrating characters effectively perform sex acts through speech acts: they *discuss* sex, *report* sex, and *enact* sex, mostly between one another and sometimes with men in one another's presence, in a discourse that sutures narration to action within a single temporality. This merging of the time of narration (*Erzählzeit*) with the time of events (*erzählte Zeit*), often underscored by the use of onomatopoeic sighs and ellipses to indicate supposed pauses for sex acts, creates a synchrony that makes represented intimacy available as an experience, its temporality "palpable and visible" as events "take on flesh" in a way that the eighteenth-century novel will make normative.[29] Even cross-sex encounters are filtered through sapphic narration, so that in effect all sex becomes queer sex, and heteroerotic pleasure—for both characters and readers—depends on the sapphic word and gaze. Thus in *L'école des filles*, Fanchon follows Susanne's instructions to let Robinet deflower her and then, in a repetition of the model of *Il ragionamenti*, describes the scene in so much detail that Susanne is led to say, "it seems as if I am there [il me semble que j'y suis]."[30] And although *The Virgin Unmask'd* is less sexually explicit than the French texts, reserving much of it erotic content to metaphors and double-entendres, aunt and niece share conversations about sex that place them too in sexually intimate relationships prefiguring the kind that, as I will argue, linger in the structures of female confidence prominent in eighteenth-century domestic fiction.

To be sure, in terms of manifest content, these texts are phallocentric in their assumptions. Yet they accord female characters an authority over more than sexual matters that cannot wholly be reduced to the goal of titillation. The female voices of these novels discuss a broad range of charged subjects, with an emphasis on medicine and science in *L'académie des dames*; religion in *Vénus dans le cloître*, the nature of love in *L'école des filles*; statecraft in *The Virgin Unmask'd*. These works also recognize gender hierarchies and attempt in different ways to outwit them. In *L'école des filles*, Susanne explains to Fanchon that intercourse with the woman "on top" is Love's way of inverting the gender hierarchy, indeed a "metamorphosis" that gives a man the sense that "he has changed his sex, and the woman reciprocally imagines becoming a perfect man," such that "if you were to see them coupling from afar, you would mistake them for one another."[31] And *The Virgin Unmask'd* sets up a dialogue about marriage and politics in which the erotic enters, however queerly, from its opening scene, where the spinster (and virgin) aunt Lucinda, asks her niece (and virgin) Antonia to "cover your Nakedness. . . . I can't abide your Naked Breasts heaving up and down."[32]

For all their artificialities, then, these texts carry a formal power that is gendered female and rendered sapphic through a dialogic narrative structure that exceeds what are clearly also androcentric imperatives.[33] Elizabeth Wahl suggests a utopian element to the *Académie* that fits these other exempla as well, insofar as they relocate knowledge, authority, agency, and action to women. Most of them also offer a radical epistemology of pleasure: in a utilitarian language that presages Diderot's "Entretien" of a century later, for example, the *Académie*'s Tullie claims that "nothing is fair or unfair in itself, no customs good or bad, use qualifies everything."[34] As Manuela Mouráo observes, the text's erotic orientation also places men in the position of sexual object,[35] enacting a displacement not entirely different from the kind I associated in the previous chapter with *The Convent of Pleasure* or "Cloe to Artimesa." Lynn Hunt has similarly argued that many early modern pornographic texts "validate" female desire, militate against misogyny, and operate subversively in feminist ways that she considers unintended.[36] To be sure, these texts also perform a kind of double-entendre by celebrating male access to women, and scholars have rightly been suspicious of what Nancy Miller called "feminocentric" fictions in which men pretend to be women in order to exert control.[37] But the surfaces of these erotic fictions authorize female voice and female response, in sapphic tandem, to an unprecedented degree. Like the apostrophes through which the body becomes a logical site for constituting female subjects, though in ways probably directed much more to male than to female readers, they begin to level the authority of both sexual and narrative agency. In most of these texts too the sapphic remains entangled with social concerns. Indeed, one could argue that the sapphic stands here for a radical rethinking of sexual norms and practices and, with it, a rethinking of the underpinnings of traditional morality.

That this dialogic structure soon disappears from erotic fiction is plausibly a sign of its potency. But it is possible to see a connection between the seventeenth-century erotic fictions and at least three of the primary novelistic modes—libertine, domestic, and picaresque—that shape eighteenth-century fiction. In their representational content, of course, these works find their clearest heritage in the libertine novels that proliferate during the middle and later eighteenth century: Diderot's *La religieuse* (1770/1796) can be easily read as an implicit revision of *Vénus dans le cloître* and Sade's *Philosophie dans le boudoir* (1795) titles itself as an explicit revision of *L'académie des dames*. Sexual initiations or encounters between women make momentary appearances in most of the famous libertine fictions of the mid-eighteenth century; the Marquis d'Argens's very popular *Thérèse philosophe* (1748), for example, introduces a Madame Bois-Laurier who twice entices the narrator Thérèse to sleep with her, and similar moments occur in Diderot's *Les bijoux indiscrets* (1748), in the anonymous *New Atalantis for 1758*, and fleetingly in Laclos's *Les liaisons dangereuses* (1784). In most of these instances, however, the sapphic has the status of anecdote that I have marked as pervasive among early modern representations of sapphic subjects: it functions in detachable episodes rather than underpinning the form or function of the whole. Except for John Cleland's *Memoirs of a Woman of Pleasure* (1749), a hybrid outlier that I will discuss later in this chapter, none of those sexually explicit fic-

tions of the eighteenth century perpetuates either the sapphic structure or
the gender-leveling possibilities inscribed in the 1680s works.

Yet even as libertine fiction is opting for non-sapphic structures of narration—often, however, retaining sapphic episodes of plot—the narrative
structure forged by female intimacy will find a central place in the domestic novel. If the main stream of the eighteenth-century novel eventually foregoes its most overtly pornographic "snooping," then it seems even
more significant that the structure of sapphic interlocutors set in motion
by erotic fiction will find a muted counterpart in one of the novel's most
common narrative devices: the use of confidantes whose letters, journals,
or conversations place two women in a *structurally* erotic relationship
in which same-sex secrets become the narrative vehicle for representing
cross-sex desires. The sexual genealogy of the novel thus argues for a line
of continuity between the libertine dialogues of the late seventeenth century and the novels of courtship and domestic desire that become the eighteenth century's most heavily produced and canonized form.

I will explore below this proliferation of female narrative intimacy. But
the sapphic dialogues of the late seventeenth century also show a continuity, in privileging both female voice and the sapphic subject, with another
mode that plays a pivotal role in the novel's development: the picaresque,
which like the erotic novel relies on an episodic structure, though one that
effectively moves the sapphic subject of the novel from the bedroom to the
road in a challenge to both heteronormativity and domesticity and thus to
the main stream of the novel and its emergent ideologies of sexual difference. Indeed, I will be arguing that mid-century contests over the form and
function of the novel are also struggles between picaresque and domestic
models in which the sapphic figures with surprising centrality and with a
persistence well beyond the arc usually alleged of the picaresque. Implicit
conversations between these two modes are formative for both the European novel and for the societies that produced and consumed them.

ON THE ROAD: SAPPHIC PICARESQUE

Almost every history of the modern novel acknowledges the picaresque as
a founding mode; Marthe Robert characterizing the genre itself a *pícaro*,
an "upstart, even a bit of a swindler," a "commoner made good."[38] Scholars
have characterized the picaresque by its deployment of a rogue hero, most
often but not always lowborn, whose "fortunes, dangers and adversities
[fortunas, peligros, y adversidades]"—to quote the Ur-pícaro Lázaro—form

the episodic structure of eponymous adventures. These adventures are most often narrated in the first person and represented with an "aggressive realism" by protagonists who survive and thrive by outwitting masters and other authorities.[39] Launched in mid-sixteenth-century Spain and thus contemporary to early pornographic fictions like Aretino's, the picaresque took shape in novels such as *Lazarillo de Tormes* (1554), Mateo Alemán's *Guzmán de Alfarache* (1599–1604), Francisco de Quevedo's *Historia de la vida del Buscón* (1626), and Miguel de Cervantes's *Don Quixote* (1605) and continued across Europe though exemplars like Thomas Nashe's *The Unfortunate Traveller* (1594), Charles Sorel's *Vraie histoire comique de Francion* (1622), Hans Jacob von Grimmelshausen's *Abenteuerliche Simplicissimus Teutsch* (1669), and Nicolaes Heinsius's *Den vermakelyken avanturier* (1695). Although the picaresque has been defined in both narrow and broad terms, it is almost always associated with geographic mobility, class struggle, social satire, episodic structure, and the chronotope of the road as a site of both movement and unlikely encounter.[40] As my list suggests, the picaresque has also been seen as a male-centered form even though some of the earliest examples of the genre—Francisco López de Ubeda's *La pícara Justina* (1605) and Alonso Jerónimo de Salas Barbadillo's *La hija de Celestina* (1612)—testify to a flourishing female strain that also travels across Europe by way of Defoe and Marivaux, for example, and will continue in novels prefixing "female" to words like "wanderer," "traveler," and "spy."[41]

But the genealogy of the picaresque also encompasses a sizeable body of narratives spanning the mid-seventeenth to the mid-eighteenth century that challenge the gender configurations both of male-centered picaresque and of the female-centered domestic fiction that arguably came to define the novel *tout court*. These works that I call sapphic picaresque are usually built around upstart women whose stories follow motifs of adventure and cunning to challenge encroaching norms of class, gender, and domesticity through same-sex affiliations. Like classic *pícaros*, the characters rove from episode to episode and place to place, outwitting or outrunning authorities through socially transgressive and often morally ambiguous acts that rely on wit or subterfuge. Some present women as actively sexual and in pursuit of partners; others set up adventures undertaken by faithful erotic friends; others use same-sex relations to resolve dilemmas involving fathers or husbands; many send off their female characters in male disguise. Most of these texts allow relations between women to be surprisingly viable: in the terms that I have used earlier in this project, they are more often modally ethnographic or horizontal than metamorphic. And whether the sapphic *pícaras* resemble lowborn, ingenious outsiders like Lazarillo or aristocratic, eccentric idealists like Don Quixote, nearly all of them expose the material underpinnings of affective economies. With a generic longevity that spans the century, these fictions—some of which claim auto/biographical status—resist the formal and ideological pressures on the novel to confine women in heteronormative spaces that are often, however, represented as freely chosen, and thus also to "cramp" the novel itself into domesticity, as Margaret Doody lamented. As such, the picaresques propel "questions of virtue" and "questions of truth" that Michael McKeon has deemed basic to the origins of the early eighteenth-century novel,[42] and their logic provides a further key to understanding the path of the novel's development.

As I implied in chapter 2, the sapphic lends itself well to picaresque tropes of adventure, repetition, and movement: Estienne's and Montaigne's accounts of girls turned husbands could easily have been drawn out into episodic fictions, Catalina de Erauso's posthumously published *Vida* adheres well to the Spanish conventions of the form, and the iterativity that I associated with habit in chapter 2 finds an ideal medium in picaresque structure. Even the apostrophes that I examined in chapter 4 suggest by way of their tropes of longing and their frustrations at female confinement or separation that same-sex relations demand a mobility not conventionally afforded elite women. Although I will of course focus on the novel in this chapter, it is worth recognizing that picaresque elements filter into other genres of the period. We find an early instance of the picaresque in Madame de Villedieu's *Mémoires de la vie de Henriette-Sylvie de Molière* (1671–74), whose eponymous narrator moves repeatedly from place to place and country to country as she is pursued by suitors and detractors through the vagaries of "Fortune: and repeatedly tests her erotic appeal to other women. Two seventeenth-century French pseudo-memoirs involving women fleeing their pursuing husbands, Marie Mancini and Sébastian Brémond's *L'apologie ou les veritables memoires de Madame Marie Mancini* (1678) and Henriette de Murat's *Mémoires de madame la comtesse de M**** (1697), likewise carry sapphic resonance. Picaresque elements characterize "The Apparition of Mrs. Veal" (1706) which spurred the title of Terry Castle's *Apparitional Lesbian*,[43] in which the unhappily married Mrs. Bargrave receives the caresses of a long estranged friend who has returned from beyond the grave, and then goes off in search of her. The women in Delarivier Manley's "female Cabal" (*The New Atalantis*, 1709) come and go in episodic fashion, while the pseudoscientific *Treatise of Hermaphrodites* (1718) traces the adventures of three more and less female

couples or varying anatomy. The apocryphal "Epistle from Signora F——a
to a Lady" (1727), in which the famous Italian singer Faustina declares her
love for an English beauty but affirms her continuing need for sexual ad-
venturing, could stand as a picaresque manifesto: Faustina styles herself
a "living *Aretin*" to "Ladies, unpractis'd in the Art of Love" and must
continue roving "like the industrious Bee" who "suck'd the Honey, then
forsook the Tree."[44] Picaresque modalities and sapphic intimations characterize several of Eliza Haywood's short novels. In *The British Recluse*
(1723), two women of very different backgrounds end up together after they
discover they have been wronged by the same man, while in *The City Jilt*
(1726), Glicera, with the help of her "exceeding intimate" friend Laphelia,
takes revenge on the faithless suitor Melladore and, having ensured his
"Humiliation"—and greeted his death with "happy Indifference"—vows
an "Aversion to that Sex," and lives happily with Laphelia until the latter exchanges "the Pleasures of a single Life, for the more careful ones
of a married State."[45] In *The Rash Resolve* (1724), the most elaborate of
Haywood's versions of this dynamic, the shamed and pregnant Emanuella, after betrayal by her cousin Berilla, is wooed and rescued by Donna
Jacinta. The two women end up living together as an inseparable couple,
so that when Emanuella's now repentant seducer Emilius turns up—to become an object of exchange between the women—the now primary bond
between Emanuella and Donna Jacinta is affirmed "till Death inforces
a Separation," as indeed it does.[46] The movements I have already traced
in Jane Barker's "Unaccountable Wife" (1723) likewise create a recursive
picaresque pattern that keeps two women on the move, and certainly
the sapphic potential of Defoe's *The Fortunate Mistress* (1724), with its
equivocal relations between Roxana and her servant Amy, has not gone
unremarked.

While my discussion here will draw upon many of these more and less
classic examples that cluster in post-Fronde France and in early Georgian
England, I will be most interested in the sustained narratives that appear
during the 1740s and 1750s, precisely the time when many scholars have
considered the novel to have taken on its more domestic shape. This chronology makes sapphic picaresque not simply a predecessor but a companion to the domestic novel, but a companion necessarily in contest with the
more confining fictions of that form—a sign of the continued restlessness
of the genre, its pull between the democratic and the conservative, that
Marthe Robert describes.[47] The most elaborate of the sapphic picaresques
from this period is the anonymous three-volume *Travels and Adventures
of Mademoiselle de Richelieu* (1744) that I discussed briefly in chapter 3,

in which the young woman Alithea, touring Europe in male disguise and "mak[ing] Love to every Woman I meet with,"[48] becomes passionately attracted to the young widow Arabella, who then dons male disguise herself so that the two might adventure together, until they abandon their breeches for petticoats and live together alternately at one another's estates. Several allegedly true histories that also follow the picaresque model are Giovanni Bianchi's *Breve storia della vita di Catterina Vizzani Romana* (1744), which recounts the heroine's escapades with other women, her death from a gunshot wound, and the autopsy that proves her to be an anatomically ordinary female, and F. L. Kersteman's *De Bredasche Heldinne* (1751), the ostensible as-told-to autobiography of Maria van Antwerpen, twice convicted for passing as a man and marrying a woman. Sarah Scott's tale of the devoted cousins Louisa and Leonora in her 1754 *Journey Through Every Stage of Life* also entails picaresque, as the two women run off to an "irregular life" together to save Laura from a forced marriage, with Leonora disguised as a clergyman. The autobiographical *Narrative of the Life of Mrs. Charlotte Charke* (1755) details Charke's adventures while seeking a living in man's dress and also reports suggestive liaisons with women, and the 1760 *Life and Imaginations of Sally Paul* recounts the adventures of a successful cross-dresser who woos women supposedly to prove that she is not a "molly," ends up marrying a woman until the law catches up with her, and then shows the law, and not the marriage, to be inadequate. The vast majority of these texts use the dominant picaresque practice of first-person narration and thus of female voice, and all show sympathy for their central characters. Also picaresque in genre though of decidedly different tenor and—not incidentally, narrative method—is Henry Fielding's *Female Husband; or, the Surprising History of Mrs. Mary, Alias Mr. George Hamilton* (1746), a case history turned a cautionary tale as the woman masquerading as a doctor named George marries women, is repeatedly suspected of imposture, and finally ends up in jail condemned to a public whipping. Milder in manner but sharing a concern for the dangers of sapphic adventure is John Cleland's English translation and amplification of *Catterina Vizzani*, published under different titles in 1751 and 1755 with a cautionary afterword that shares with *The Female Husband* the class anxieties that underlie what may be particularly English concerns about female-female relations.

Across obvious differences of form, length, and motive, the texts I am gathering under the sapphic picaresque umbrella trade in resistance to patriarchal schemes. Unlike the erotic fictions that allow the sapphic to coexist with marriage, they usually make relations with women an alternative rather than an adjunct to relations with men. Villedieu's Henriette-Sylvie de Molière laments that every man, even the one she long loved with passion and eventually marries, has betrayed her. Mrs. Veal's ghostly visit to Mrs. Bargrave brings solace to a miserable wife. The *Treatise of Hermaphrodites'* most "feminine" women come together because both have been jilted. Alithea de Richelieu refuses to be "a domestic Tool designed for no other Use but to satisfy the brutal Inclinations of her Lord and Master Man," and the widowed Arabella who becomes her lover has already had a "fatal Experience" in the "married State."[49] Yet even where same-sex relations are a refuge, they are a refuge born not of convenience but of desire. Thus Belinda and Cleomira are drawn to one another well before they learn they had the same seducer: "each found, at first Sight, so much to admire in the other, that it kept both from speaking," and eventually "there grew so entire a Friendship between these Ladies that . . . Belinda quitted her Chamber, being desir'd by the Recluse [Cleomira] to take part of her bed."[50]

As is typical of picaresque, repetitive encounters and narrow escapes serve as the agent of plot. This recursivity underscores the power of desire to propel narrative action and multiplies the number of women receiving the overtures of protagonists who are sometimes visible as women and sometimes disguised as men. And if the women courted by cross-dressed suitors engage in same-sex flirtations unwittingly, the unquestioned success with which the protagonists not only fool but magnetically attract other women testifies to the fluidity of both gender and desire, setting up the protagonists as women who can outman men. Catterina Vizzani is called "the best woman's man" on earth [il maggior donnajuolo di quella Terra],"[51] and Henriette-Sylvie's "good looks" teach another young woman "to love a man."[52] Mademoiselle de Richelieu delights in the success of her amorous transvestite wooings. Here, in a dazzling reversal at once of novelistic convention and metamorphic plot, the act of revelation that usually shuts down an erotic encounter between a cross-dressed woman and an unsuspecting one becomes the very move that enables the plot of *Mademoiselle de Richelieu*: when Alithea, disguised as the chevalier de Radpont, bares her breasts to show Arabella that she is a woman, the formerly resistant Arabella rushes to embrace her, explaining that she has sworn off men. In many of the texts as in this one, the question of physical intimacy is titillatingly raised and skirted; embraces are exchanged, and terms of endearment—in this case extending to "Husband" and "Lover"—are evoked. Similarly, *The Rash Resolve* uses the language of courtship to emphasize the love between Donna Jacinta and Emanuella. Such gestures work at making women's relationships normative; Alithea and Arabella even consider finding a priest to marry them.

Clearly such narratives are firmly invested in tropes of movement, arguably in movement for its own sake. In contrast to the fixed interior spaces of both erotic dialogues and domestic novels, the picaresque binds sapphic desire to adventure: whether by choice or necessity, all of these women leave a home space to move into a public space, a borrowed space, or a space of movement such as the road, roaming or escaping from town to town or country to country and usually well aware of the gender-transgressivity of their own movement. Catterina Vizzani wanders "from one Country to another, in Quest of the desired Object."[53] Mrs. Veal travels from the next world to kiss Mrs. Bargrave who, thinking her friend has come only from Dover, then goes off in search of her. Scott's virtuous and accomplished Leonora relocates whenever a sticky amorous situation with a woman might disclose her sex. Henriette-Sylvie is constantly pursued and constantly running; Sally Paul becomes an itinerant painter and a seaman who moves about to earn her keep. Yet movement emerges from the sapphic picaresques as a positive value and not only as a mechanism for evading pursuers or avoiding scrapes; the immobility of a Princesse de Clèves or the imprisonment of a Clarissa are gender-inflicted evils to avoid. Faustina has "rov'd about" "Inconstant as the Wind, free as the Air" and vows to continue in "perpetual Motion."[54] Manley's female Cabal is said to be headquartered at a "little lodging about twelve furlongs from Angela" but is textually represented as a parade of coaches along the road.[55] Alithea and Arabella, having found one another halfway through the novel, nonetheless decide to adventure on, passing as male comrades, sheerly for the titillations of travel and masquerade; even at the novel's close the women are moving back and forth between one another's properties. Movement, in short, becomes a mechanism for wresting freedom from necessity and thus also an exposure of the price paid for the heteronormative resolution of the courtship plot. If we want to think in terms of Certeau's distinction between "space" and "place" as elaborated by Shlomith Rimmon-Kenan,[56] then the sapphic seeks space, while the very goal of the domestic is place, a home of one's own, all the more as so many heroines and heroes of domestic fiction are dis-placed, orphaned, or dependent.

Most strikingly, and across the temporal range of my examples, when closure does put a stop to the recursivity of the picaresque, most of the women live out some kind of sapphic possibility: metamorphic resolutions are almost nonexistent here. Faustina remains on the fly, Alithea and Arabella alternate seasons at each other's French estates, Haywood's female couples opt for rural seclusion. *The British Recluse* gives its protagonists a life together of "perfect Tranquillity."[57] Catterina Vizzani surpasses the "lesbian Nymphs [donzelle di Lesbos]" in courting "great disasters [grandi disastri]" to pursue her passions" literally unto her death.[58] and Maria of Antwerpen, the "heroine from Breda [Bredasche Heldinne]," is three years married to her Joanna before she is recognized by a neighbor and jailed. Henriette-Sylvie, drawn to both sexes but in flight from men, planned to retire to an abbey where a beloved nun resides but ends up in more ambiguous retirement with the wherewithal to lead "a peaceful and comfortable enough life in whatever situation I might want to choose."[59] Even in the rare metamorphic case when a heroine marries—for example, in *Journey through Every Stage*—the same-sex bond is sustained with the same apparent intensity and often accompanied by an exposure of marriage as economic rather than emotional need. And although Sally Paul is ordered to stop cross-dressing, nothing prevents her from living once more with her "wife" Hetty as the novel's conclusion suggests. Even Fielding's hostile account cannot eradicate the sapphic habit: on "the very evening she had suffered the first whipping," the narrator tells us, Mary Hamilton "offered the gaoler money, to procure her a young girl."[60] What's more, the women who pursue other women find no dearth of willing partners, suggesting that same-sex relations can happen anywhere and to anyone; the universalizing models so rarely represented around 1600 are in full play here.

Like conventional picaresques, the sapphic picaresques usually turn their judgment against the system rather than against the rogue adventurers who are subverting it. That the women are central characters, often their own narrators, and usually successful in both their conquests and their escapes, confers on them a certain heroic status; even Mary Hamilton can be seen as rather heroic for her victimization at the hands of the crowd, the law, and—textually speaking—the narrator. *The Travels and Adventures of Mademoiselle de Richelieu* admits not a word of condemnation for the sapphic couple, even though the women are explicitly united on "Terms, more proper for a Lover than a Friend."[61] Not in the least repentant, the "unmanned and divorced" Sally Paul laments only the come-down, "after so long wearing the pre-eminence of man," in being "precipitated into the natural subjection of my sex," which "sat as uneasy as my stays."[62] And turning the law to her advantage, she reminds her readers that "the law could not say anything to the matter, consonant with its own maxims, which are grounded in reason; as there is no reason for two women marrying, there could not be any law consonant with reason to prevent it, consequently no law about the matter"; indeed, addressing her visitors from Bridewell Prison, she assumes the presence of other "ladies" who "have such like husbands."[63] Except in the 1718 *Treatise of Hermaphrodites*, aberrant anatomy is nowhere in play and is indeed discounted by Bianchi's insistence on Catterina Vizzani's normalcy, though these texts certainly valorize in women masculine attributes of independence, courage, and erudition. Nor do most of the texts attempt to explain women's preferences within rubrics of influence or contagion: some women cross dress while others do not, some bodies are rendered mannish while others are feminized, some pairs of women are represented as explicitly sexual, others only as affectionally bound, some women have been disillusioned by men while others prefer women for reasons that go unnoted. If we were to map these texts along the three modalities I introduced in my second chapter, they would be in aggregate ethnographic in their mostly noncommittal portrayal of same-sex habits, leveling in adhering to horizontal affiliations, and only occasionally metamorphic except where they are metamorphic in reverse.

What *is* in often play—as in the picaresque *tout court*—is social resistance. Thus the one metamorphic marriage among these texts, that of Leonora, not only seems motivated by enabling her nearness to Louisa but gets negatively framed by an external, female narrator and narratee: at the conclusion of Leonora's story, they jointly deplore the "Custom, not Nature" that "obliges" women to depend on "the Industry of Man for our Support" and laments that Leonora has "done so common a Thing as marrying, and made herself dependent on one of the other Sex."[64] Perhaps the most dramatic resistance to formal powers comes when Sally Paul's trial for "the crime of committing matrimony" is overturned: as everyone must acknowledge that "no injury took place," the law itself stands condemned for "perpetually diving into carnal secrets," leaving Sally free to return to the woman with whom she had lived "as happy as two angels, that know not the distinction of sexes," as long as she remained in women's clothes.[65] Thus several of these texts openly revise and reject the long textual and legal tradition by which death becomes the consequence of same-sex marriage, putting marriage itself into contest.

The texts I have been describing under the aegis of the sapphic picaresque, with their evasions of law, their usurpations of social order, and their refusals of constraint, enact in their form a resistance to any domestication that is built upon the foreclosure of desires or indeed any limitations on women's movements literal or figural. Almost universally, if to a greater or lesser degree, they reject both gender and sexuality as social constraints, complicating Michael McKeon's speculation that in this period biological difference is the stable and inalterable ground against which "the alterability of socioeconomic situation" becomes the mobile figure.[66] For in eighteenth-century Europe, the class mobility of women is itself structured primarily in sexual terms: women's upward mobility is conventionally achieved through marriage, while downward mobility is the most common effect of sexual transgressions publicly known. This makes gender, sexuality, and class mutually constitutive, with any element able to anchor or to compromise the others. The sapphic picaresques deny sex and sexuality any stabilizing power, while also rendering economic status and social class as crucial determinants of a woman's future.

Indeed, the sapphic picaresques underscore the tight relationship between sexual liberty and economic means, prompting me to argue for the economic subject as a third category in Barbara Johnson's opposition between "lyric" and "legal" subjects.[67] Nearly all the texts expose affective relations as economic ones by making clear the necessity of resources to sustain female alliances. At one pole, sapphic affiliation renders Barker's "unaccountable wife" and her servant-lover indigent, as I described in chapter 3. At the other, more common pole, female alliance is enabled by the liberal fortunes of the women in *The British Recluse, The Rash Resolve*, and especially *Mademoiselle de Richelieu*, where both young women are financially and legally independent and can ally themselves where they will. Cross-dressed female husbands conventionally ply a trade in order to sustain themselves and sometimes their spouses; Sally Paul works as a sign painter; Maria of Antwerp enlists in the army to avoid earning her living by prostitution and is thus able to support a wife; even the genteel Leonora, in the guise of a cleric, must hire out her services as a tutor to sustain herself and Louisa. And Charlotte Charke laments the "horrible Disappointment on both Sides" when, in her guise as a "well-bred Gentleman," she meets—but is revealed as unable to marry—an "Orphan Heiress" of "forty thousand Pounds in the Bank of England" and "Effects in the Indies" who would have provided "an excellent Remedy for Ills."[68] The attention to income, employment, and economic security in these texts also makes clear, then, that if women can live comfortably apart from men, the gender system that underlies capitalist (re)production is compromised.

This may be why several of these texts, particularly the "backlash" *Female Husband* and the English elaborations to *Catterina Vizzani*, are so heavily preoccupied with questions of class. It is difficult to know whether any of these novels is speaking directly to another, but it may not be irrelevant that *Mademoiselle de Richelieu* and *The Female Husband* share a publisher, and while *The Female Husband* is the better known of these texts in the present, *Mademoiselle de Richelieu* went through at least four editions between 1744 and 1758, while Fielding's short novel appears to have been published only once during the eighteenth century. Although Fielding's is a fictionalized account of an actual legal case, it invents freely, and shows its agenda in deeming Mary Hamilton as "monstrous" and "unnatural" (29) for her economic opportunism as well as for her sexual practices. Moving Mary from one locale to another—the Isle of Man, Dublin, Bristol, Dartmouth, Totness, Asburton, and Wells—the text is able to set up the sapphic as a danger to the entire kingdom; she is prosecuted explicitly "for having by false and deceitful practices imposed on some of His Majesty's subjects" (21). Those deceitful practices are also economic, for Mary Hamilton plots to marry women of fortune while also making herself renowned as a doctor of physic and thus in a man's role. No surprise, then, that *The Female Husband* emphasizes Mary's femininity: she is the only adventurer whose efforts—according to Fielding—are repeatedly undermined by her failure to "pass." Each time she courts or marries a woman, her "effeminate squawl" (33), her "odd" shape, her lack of beard (42) and her unmanly "bosom" (47), mark her as a queer specimen of manhood, a "Farinelli" at best. Even the flogging she receives for her imposture arouses pity because her skin is "so lovely" in its femininity. Ironically, such an effort to fix Mary's gender detaches the sapphic from an anatomical origin: in a way that Fielding cannot explain except with recourse to the influence of an early Methodist seducer, this woman is a biological female with the "wrong" desires.

A similar anxiety about class inflects John Cleland's translation and elaboration of Bianchi's *Catterina Vizzani*. Bianchi rejects anatomical masculinity as the cause of same-sex desire, but Cleland's Vizzani, like Bianchi's original and unlike Mary Hamilton, succeeds in passing as a "Woman's Man," and Vizzani's father considers her a "Son" though she is "in all Respects, a Female, as the Woman who bore her."[69] Wounded and hospitalized during one of her amorous adventures, Vizzani contracts a fatal infection and confesses her sex. After her death she is discovered to have "prominent breasts" and, most importantly, a clitoris that "was not pendulous, or of any extraordinary Size," even "so far from any unusual Magnitude, that it was not to be ranked among the middle-sized, but the smaller."[70] Thus, as Paula Findlen notes, "with a stroke of his pen, Bianchi dismissed two centuries of anatomical lore about the size of the clitoris and its relation to female sexual desire."[71]

Anatomical intervention may have been Bianchi's objective, but Cle-

THE TRUE

HISTORY

AND

ADVENTURES

OF

Catharine Vizzani,

A YOUNG

Gentlewoman a Native of *Rome*, who for many Years paſt in the Habit of a Man; was killed for an Amour with a young Lady; and found on Diſſection, a true Virgin.

With curious Anatomical REMARKS on the *Nature* and *Exiſtence* of the HYMEN.

By GIOVANNI BIANCHI, Profeſſor of Anatomy at *Sienna*, the Surgeon who diſſected her.

With a curious FRONTISPIECE.

What odd fantaſtic Things, we Women do!
Ep. to CATO:

L O N D O N:

Printed for W. REEVE, *Fleet-ſtreet*, and C. SYMPSON, at the *Bible-warehouſe, Chancery-lane.* 1755.

(Price One Shilling.)

Fig. 4. Frontispiece and title page to the second edition of John Cleland's version of *Catterina Vizzani*, emphasizing the transmutation of Bianchi's narrative into an object lesson about class. Courtesy of the British Library.

land's English edition of Catterina Vizzani's story does a different kind of work. Translated in 1751 as *Historical and Physical Dissertation on the Case of Catherine Vizzani*, the work was reissued in 1755 with the more novelistic and picaresque title, *The True History and Adventures of Catherine Vizzani* (see fig. 4). Although relatively faithful in spirit to, if verbally embellishing, the Italian original, the English editions append an afterword that chastises Bianchi for not "assign[ing] any in Cause whatever, or so much as advanc[ing] any probable Conjecture" about Vizzani's sapphic propensities. Since Bianchi has acquitted "Nature"—i.e. the body—"of any Fault in this strange Creature," the translator locates causality in Vizzani's mind, which he reads as the site of "more monstrous Productions" than "strange Births, and such like Prodigies," and proceeds to tell disastrous stories of other cross-dressing sapphists and the women they victimize. The dangerous marker of the sapphic woman is still her masculinity, but a masculinity now transferred from clitoris to clothes: women are therefore cautioned to avoid cross-dressing, as if that alone could make them sapphic, and to beware of other women in disguise, though the translator also implies that a "real" woman will be able to spot a "real" man.[72] Most importantly, while Bianchi's (actual) Catterina Vizzani was "the runaway daughter of a Roman carpenter" who for eight years worked as a manservant,[73] the English editions make significant moves to change her class identity. In the 1751 version, Vizzani is simply "a young Woman" involved in "an Amour with a young Lady," but in 1755 she has become a "Gentlewoman a Native of Rome," and the picture added as frontispiece now shows her dressed in a gentleman's habit and duping a woman equally well dressed. Such class-conscious representations seem to suggest that if wellborn women forsake the patriarchal system, social order will indeed be jeopardized.

I have belabored the qualities of these picaresque fictions, and particularly their long and late history in relation to the "rise" of the novel, to dramatize an alternative genealogy to the domestic productions that will be equated by the later eighteenth century with the novel *tout court*. I would argue that just as the sapphic is often picaresque, the picaresque is often sapphic. The picaresque fictions that proliferate across the long period from the late seventeenth to the late eighteenth century instigate a broader contest around gender, economics, and desire that will take new forms in the classic domestic fictions of mid-century. If we read the genealogy of the novel through a sapphic lens, then, we see the weight of challenge that domestic novels face: to contain not simply the sapphic but the economic, legal, physical, and social liberties that the sapphic picaresque inscribes. The challenge of containment is also a function of form: the picaresques are notably invested in giving direct voice to their protagonists, who are thereby represented as independent—in effect textually free and mobile subjects—on the level of narration as well as of plot. Together, these resistant dynamics make the place and the voice of women in the novel more contested terrain than histories of the novel have tended to recognize.

AT HOME: RITES OF RETURN

The plenitude of sapphic picaresque challenges the assumption that the 1740s marked an easy turning point toward domestic realism and complicates the contests over just what the new genre was to become. The contest is often figured in the rivalry between Richardson and Fielding that took on international contours as so-called sentimental fiction prolifer-

ated across the Continent, and though that will not be my focus here, it is
worth noting the picaresque priorities of a Fielding and the ways in which
they do and do not enable the mobility of women, as opposed to the female
confinement that generates Richardsonian plots. The struggle I have in
mind, though, has always been about more than Richardson and Fielding,
of course; it is ultimately about different approaches to representation and
the divergent moral and social positions that underwrite them. We can
shed new light on these contests if we acknowledge both the challenges
that sapphic picaresque poses and the opportunities that sapphic dialogue
facilitates for fiction focused on the intersections of homeland and home.
I suggest that the sapphic picaresques put a certain pressure on the novel
to *become* domesticated not only so that the agency of female characters
can be contained within familial structures but so that containment can
be represented, through narrative strategies, as the effect of women's own
desires.

I have already observed that by mid-century the sapphic potential of
libertine fiction has become more limited; in the libertine context, instead of the hegemony of sapphic interlocutors we now see a reduction
of the sapphic to anecdote. The closest analogue to the sapphic dialogics
of the 1680s is Cleland's *Memoirs of a Woman of Pleasure* (1749), which
is structured—without explanation—as a sexual confidence from one
woman to another: each volume begins with a salutation to an anonymous
"Madam"—a particularly double-edge word, as Hal Gladfelder notes,
given the book's primary setting in brothels.[74] Moreover, the telling itself
has the air of a sexual service: Fanny considers the Madam's "desires" as
"indispensable orders" to provide the "stark naked truth," even though
she wishes her narratee would be "cloyed and tired" with the "repetition
of near the same images, the same figures, the same expressions" in re-
counting the *"joys, ardours, transports, ecstasies"* in a narrative of which
"the *practice of pleasure* . . . professedly composes the whole basis."[75] This
female-to-female "practice of pleasure" thus provides an analogue on the
level of narration to the relationship between Fanny and, at different moments, both Phoebe and the "madam" Mrs. Cole on the level of plot: it is
Phoebe who engineers Fanny's initiation and who suffices for her until
Fanny discovers "finer" pleasures, and yet Phoebe herself remains a resistant sapphic presence and perhaps so does Fanny given what John Beynon
rightly sees as her infatuation with Mrs. Cole, madam of a brothel that, as
I noted in chapter 3, is also described as a "seraglio."[76] The extent to which
the text goes to backpedal its sapphic implications is evident, for example, in Fanny's description, filled with perhapses and double negatives, of

Phoebe's "secret inclination" for women, attributed to "one of those arbitrary tastes for which there is no accounting" (49), after which statement, however, the narrator rushes to assure the "Madam" that Phoebe did not hate men or might "even prefer them to her own sex," yet a possible "secret bias, inclined her to make the most of pleasure wherever she could find it, without distinction of sexes" (49–50). As a novel at once libertine, picaresque, and ultimately domestic, *Memoirs of a Woman of Pleasure* would seem to be just the text that proves the rule, showing how, in the 1740s, the novel itself gets domesticated to a heterosexual, indeed heteropatriarchal project. But as that earnest double-talk makes evident, this text that is structured as an intimate epistolary narrative from one woman to another, *Memoirs of a Woman of Pleasure* also has difficulty leaving the sapphic behind.

This is the claim I am also making for other mid-century novels, novels as popular as Cleland's and more respectable. For even as libertine fictions are limiting the homoerotic to the isolated episode, some of the most popular domestic novels remain entangled with the sapphic in ways that implicate both formal practices and plot designs. Some novels introduce sapphic characters that they then need to evict. Others use structures of narration to create attenuated forms of the kind of intimacy I associated with the erotic dialogues of the late seventeenth century. Still others take that structure of intimacy into the plot, sometimes creating a struggle within a metamorphic story that shifts a woman's allegiance from erotic female friend to male partner, and sometimes almost literally representing the sapphic as a kind of death throe. By tracing these temporally coexistent patterns, we can see the novel's continuing reliance on the sapphic even as we might expect to see the genre putting same-sex relations to rest.[77] Indeed, some of these novels engage in a subtle form of what I have been calling reverse metamorphosis insofar as their cross-sex narratives gets undermined or overwritten by a same-sex affiliation.

If we take the basic metamorphic project to involve the elimination of the sapphic threat in favor of a heteronormative order, then we can see the instrumentality of the gratuitous sapphic figure working quite blatantly in at least two important mid-century novels, Richardson's *Sir Charles Grandison* (1753) and Diderot's *La religieuse* (1760–96).[78] In each case, an explicitly sapphic character becomes a plot device bearing a distinctive message that takes on more power if we consider the traditions of sapphic fiction that preceded these works. Richardson's novel sets itself as a guide to national conduct, ensuring that the proper Englishman will marry a proper Englishwoman (rather than the Italian Catholic to whom he is engaged), that Protestant values will be upheld, that the family will become a model for national virtue, and that Harriet and Sir Charles will be worthy exemplars of their sex. Such a utopia has no place for a woman in search of a wife, which makes it all the more significant that Richardson introduces one. The explicitly sapphic Miss Barnevelt—indeed one of the most explicitly sapphic figures in eighteenth-century fiction—appears early in *Sir Charles Grandison*. In a novel whose heroine believes that "a woman out of wedlock is half useless to the end of her being," Richardson inserts Miss Barnevelt, "a lady of masculine features" who values learning and speaks her mind; she is "loud, bold, free, even fierce when opposed." Her sexual inclinations are not in doubt: "No-body . . . thinks of an husband for Miss Barnevelt. She is sneeringly spoken of rather as a young fellow, than as a woman, and who will one day look out for a wife for herself."[79] Barely a woman and yet not a man, Barnevelt is a "mortal of a doubtful species, hardly owned by either, and laugh'd at by both." Her sexuality, like that of Harriet's kidnapper Sir Hargrave, is predatory rather than mutual: almost as soon as she meets Harriet, she beholds her "with the eye of a Lover" and, "clasping one of her mannish arms round me, she kissed my cheek" and "only laughed at the freedom she had taken."[80] Instead of aligning herself with other women, Barnevelt is, paradoxically, an outspoken misogynist who "affects at all times such airs of contempt of her own sex, that one almost wonders at her condescending to wear petticoats."[81] Indeed, with strange illogic, Barnevelt proclaims herself "satisfied with being a woman" because if she were a man she would have to marry one, though the text has just told us that she will look for a wife. Yet Barnevelt also lays claim to certain rights and freedoms that link her to the sapphic picaresques: independent judgment and movement, an assertion of difference, sexual license and, most notably of course, the right to seek a same-sex spouse. Marked with the metonyms of masculinity that substitute, in this era, for the anatomical deviations of the previous century, she is clearly also not a character to be converted.[82]

And thus the novel must be rid of her, in effect turn her from plot element to anecdote. When Harriet not only rejects Barnevelt's advances but vows to her confidante that she will not let Barnevelt have a wife or even a female correspondent, she foretells what the novel itself will accomplish. Having taken pains to introduce and satirize Miss Barnevelt through the eyes of Harriet, Richardson drops her from the novel before any plot involving her can develop or a single letter appear in her voice. Indeed, it is the dropping that does the work: to introduce a presence that the world of the novel cannot sustain—and a presence vividly marked as a masculine and sapphic woman—and to give that character a "possible world" that is then rejected make for a powerful denial of the possibility of sapphic plot. At the same time, Miss Barnevelt's presence leaves a remainder, suggesting that the social order of the novel, and implicitly of the nation, needs to acknowledge the sapphic in its midst even though—or because—it cannot through any acceptable narrative development resolve its presence. We might think back to the letter that Elizabeth Montagu wrote just three years earlier about two women choosing to cohabit to see how that same sort of plot gets truncated here.

A similar logic in refusing a sapphic story can be attributed to Diderot's *La religieuse*, which is equally bent on national reform through its creation of a Catholic dystopia. Diderot's novel savages the ecclesiastical powers and clerical practices of the Church particularly as they affect young women, using the conventions of sentimental fiction to demand the rescue not only of Suzanne but of France itself from a corrupt and powerful Church in collusion with a self-serving aristocracy—all of which, of course, was threatening in 1770 but belated at publication in 1796. This novel too is rather picaresque in structure: Soeur Sainte-Suzanne is shunted from convent to convent, at the mercy of a mother superior who subjects her to episode upon episode of cruelty, in each new circumstance becoming the scapegoat for a different and progressively more objectionable set of "adventures." But although Suzanne is abused both physically and psychologically by the cruelest of the abbesses, what is set up as the last straw for Suzanne and for the novel, and as the strongest sign of the evils of convent life, is the sexual interest of a lesbian mother superior (see fig. 5).

Unlike Miss Barnevelt, Diderot's lesbian mother superior—she has no proper name—is a relatively sympathetic figure. The convent over which she presides is effectively a convent of pleasure, where at first the "unknowing" Suzanne, as Eve Kosofsky Sedgwick has called her, finds respite from the cruelty of her previous convent.[83] Yet physical punishment, isolation, and deprivation turn out to be weaker plot motivators than lesbian sex. Suzanne has been suffering literally for years from convent cruelties, and she has hoped to be released from the cloister throughout most of the novel, yet it is not until she alerts a priest in confession that she has received advances from the lesbian superior (who, like Barnevelt, is represented as a predator) that there is some traction to her pleas for freedom from the life to which she has been consigned against her will. Her confession seals the fate of the mother superior as well, who descends into madness as the ultimate sign of what an unnaturally all-female environment

Fig. 5. Illustration from an early edition of Diderot's *La religieuse* (1796): Suzanne
subjected to the advances of her mother superior, the catalyst for her release from
the convent after twenty years of suffering. Courtesy of the Granger Collection.

can do—and a sign too of the limits of Enlightenment tolerance. Diderot
and Richardson thus provide inversions of the same plot, both of which require the removal of the sapphic subject so that the social order can thrive,
and both of which suggest that the sapphic remains a force of disorder that
is resistant to resolution. Here too metamorphosis is not a plausible op-

tion: the sapphic mother superior, like the sapphic Miss Barnevelt, is who she is, and she must either be accommodated or, in both these instances, removed.

But even as sapphic figures are evicted from these two novels, female intimacy finds its more subtle way into the "mainstream" domestic novel through its narrative structure and, in the case of what are arguably the century's two most famous domestic novels, *Clarissa* and *Julie, ou la nouvelle Héloïse*, into a kind of postlude to the plot. If we attend to narration rather than only to textual events, female homoeroticism underwrites the eighteenth-century courtship novel in ways as deep and pervasive as, if less obvious than, the erotic fictions of the late seventeenth century. For as I suggested earlier, the dialogic narrative pattern set in motion by those early erotic fictions finds a muted counterpart in one of the eighteenth-century's most common narrative devices: the device of the confidante that places two women in a structurally eroticized relationship in which same-sex secrets become the vehicle for representing cross-sex desires.

We find an early and cautionary version of this structure of confidence in Eliza Haywood's *The Masqueraders or, Fatal Curiosity* (1724). In a fiction situated like so many of Haywood's novels between the libertine and the domestic, the rake Dorimenus seduces a willing widow named Dalinda, to the apparent bliss of both. Yet for Dalinda, sex requires the supplement of its *telling*:

> Whatever Company she happen'd to be in, she always found some pretence to make [Dorimenus] the Theme of her Discourse, and even among those who were the greatest Strangers to him, would invent some way to introduce his Name. But all this fell short of the Satisfaction she wanted:—Her Soul, full of his Charms, wild 'twixt Desire and Transport, could not contain the vast Excess.—She long'd to impart the mighty Bliss."[84]

Here Haywood in effect sets up the primacy of narration over story as a *sexual* practice. When Dalinda "pour[s] out the overwhelming Transport" (7) to her friend Philecta, her account of her own sexual encounters is not merely mentioned but transcribed, and it occupies far more textual space than the heterodiegetic narrator's initial reporting of those acts. Moreover, the narration is explicitly represented as an erotic re-experience: while Dalinda "related to [Philecta] the particulars of her Happiness," she "felt in the delicious Representation, a Pleasure, perhaps, not much inferiour to that which the Reality afforded. . . . She no sooner parted

from [Dorimenus's] Embraces, than she flew to her fair Friend, gave her
the whole History of what had pass'd between them—repeated every tender Word he spoke—not the least fond Endearment was forgot—describ'd
his Looks—his melting Pressures—his Ardours!—his Impatiences!—his
Extasies!—his Languishments!—and endeavour'd to make her sensible
how different he was from other Lovers!—how much beyond his Sex!—
with what a God-like Sublimity of Passion he ador'd her!—and what was
more prodigious than the rest, assur'd her, that each Enjoyment but en-
creased Desire" (14).

Here we have a sapphic supplement that turns sex between a man and
a woman into sex "between women" at the level of discourse in a way that
echoes the practices I described in Aretino's *Ragionamenti* and the erotic
fictions of the seventeenth century, so that the narrative becomes a story
of the pleasure both of (hetero)erotic act and (homo)erotic reporting. That
the sapphic structure is enclosed within a heterodiegetic (third-person)
narrative, however, alerts us that this intimate female confidence may not
prove worthy of trust. And as it turns out, Dalinda's need to tell her sexual
secrets to another woman has negative implications for the plot: Philecta
uses what Dalinda has told her to lure Dorimenus to herself, so that the
consequence of same-sex confidence, in this case, is same-sex betrayal.
Philecta's own ruin is, in turn, effected by Dalinda, who vows that Philecta's affair with Dorimenus "shall be no Secret—I will, at least, have the
satisfaction of Revenge" (44). The tragic outcome of this particular structure of narration takes us far from the collusive eroticism of the libertine
fictions to a dystopic and cautionary tale. Still, *The Masqueraders*, like
L'académie des dames and *Vénus dans le cloître* before it, is entirely dependent on a structure of same-sex erotic intimacy that is also an erotic rivalry. Were it not for Dalinda's narration of sexual secrets to Philecta, the
entire narrative of *The Masqueraders* would halt: the plot is built around
the ugly consequences of Philecta's *use* of Dalinda's sexual secrets. *The
Rash Resolve* creates a similar structure of confidence when Emanuella's
cousin Berilla uses Emanuella's sexual secrets to destroy her relationship
with Emilius, though the novel recuperates that structure with the positive intimacy between Emanuella and Donna Jacinta in its second half.

By mid-century, the novel's reliance on this structure of female confidence has become so pervasive as to count as one hallmark of the domestic novel. In its most common form, a female narrator tells her own story
to a female listener who is either active within the novel or simply a silent
narratee. We have seen this structure in *Mémoires de Henriette-Sylvie de
Molière* and in *Memoirs of a Woman of Pleasure*, and it recurs in the most

canonical European fictions: in Marivaux's *La vie de Marianne* (1728–42), in Richardson's *Clarissa* (1747–48) and Rousseau's *Julie, ou la nouvelle Héloïse* (1761), in Sophie von La Roche's *Geschichte des Fräuleins von Sternheim* (1771), in Aagje Deken and Elisabeth Wolff's *Historie van Mejuffrouw Sara Burgerhart* (1786), in Elisabeth Maria Post's *Het Land* (1788), and in myriad other epistolary and memoir novels featuring a female protagonist who confides her secret story or her secret feelings to a friend. I suggest that this pervasive narrative structure creates an eroticized intimacy at the level of discourse that calls even more deeply into question the extent to which we can think of the novel as a heteronormative project *tout court*. It is also significant that the eighteenth-century novel genders feminine both these structures of desire and the mechanisms of their narration; the pattern I am describing does not, I think, have a male parallel until Goethe's *Die Leiden des jungen Werther* (1774).[85] But the consequential strand of female narrative intimacy effectively reverses the eviction of the sapphic undertaken by *Sir Charles Grandison* and *La religieuse*: instances in which an erotic intimacy between female confidantes disrupts narrative closure and, in so doing, calls into question the security of the heteronormative social order on which the text seems to be built. These particularly potent deployments of same-sex narrative confidence in Marie-Jeanne Riccoboni's *Lettres de Milady Juliette Catesby á Milady Henriette Campley, son amie* (1759) and Francis Sheridan's *Memoirs of Miss Sidney Bidulph* (1761), but they are even more significant elements of *Clarissa* and *Julie, ou la nouvelle Héloïse*—and doubly so given the enormous impact and influence of these two novels. Here is where what I call reverse metamorphosis begins to enter: in each case, some aspect of closure resists the trajectory of cross-sex desire that has already been filtered through same-sex affiliation.

Like many mid-century novels in letters, Riccoboni's *Juliette Catesby*, which went through multiple editions including six London imprints alone, is effectively a one-way correspondence from Juliette to her confidante Henriette, narrating Juliette's flight from Lord Ossery, to whom she had once been secretly engaged but who had abandoned her to marry another woman. Ossery's wife has died, and he is now pursuing Juliette in an effort to explain that he did not love his wife but married her as the honorable response to a peccadillo. After Juliette yields to her own desire and marries Ossery, it is he who writes the news to Henriette, appropriating Juliette's pen even as he reduces Juliette's "liberté" and "droits" to the trivial opening of a letter, and attempts, effectively if ostensibly playfully, to silence his new wife: he tells Henriette that "there is no longer a Lady

Catesby," but "if in place of this friend so dear to your heart you'll accept a new one, then Lady Ossery is ready to receive your warm congratulations." Ossery is emphatic: Juliette is now "mine, forever mine. No more Lady Catesby; she's my wife, my friend, my mistress."[86]

Ossery's insistent need to appropriate—which is effectively to rupture—the relationship between his wife and Henriette is itself a sign that female intimacy, an intimacy in which the erotic figures as content, is a threat to his control. But this control is precisely what the text ends up disavowing. For Juliette recovers her pen from Ossery and in the process not only reappropriates narration but gives it a swerve back toward her confidante, so that the novel's last words of desire are not for the husband but for the friend: "We await you impatiently here: no parties, no balls, without my dear Henriette; I would say no pleasures, if the person who is following my pen with his eyes were not already a little jealous of my *tendre amitié*."[87] In the final narration, then, in marked contrast to the apparent plot, it is the husband who gets figuratively abandoned and the female friend who receives the last avowal of love in language that evokes a tradition of female intimacy dating from the seventeenth-century.[88] The novel thus lends itself to a dual reading: on the one hand, the plot achieves its conventional ending and the heteronormative compact is sealed; on the other, the very moment of marriage, already playfully called into question when Juliette quips in that same letter that it happened so quickly it may not be valid, becomes the moment of its resistance, and female intimacy the very *requisite* for the "pleasures" of the balls, parties and, implicitly, marital satisfaction.

The same-sex intimacy sustained by narration overtakes the cross-sex intimacy of plot even more vividly in Frances Sheridan's *Memoirs of Miss Sidney Bidulph*. Constructed as a journal written for her friend Cecilia, for whose "embrace" Sidney "longs" and to whom, in conventional fashion, "she revealed all the secrets of her heart," *Sidney Bidulph* is built upon blatant trade-offs in the object of desire: just as Cecilia leaves to *go* abroad, Sidney's brother returns *from* abroad to introduce Faulkland, the man who will eventually become Sidney's husband, though not before complications and unions on both sides. The metamorphic task of this novel is embedded clearly in its design if not in its language. Here plot is exchanged for narration, in effect, since Faulkland's arrival inaugurates a plot of desire that Cecilia's departure inaugurates as narrative confidence. At the end, in a reversal of the opening drama, Cecilia returns from the continent just after Faulkland again leaves for it. And although she is newly married to Faulkland after literally years of delay and an unhappy first marriage,

Sidney still writes to Cecilia that she "shall not be sorry if I am detained from Mr. Faulkland till I have the happiness of first embracing you, as our separation may be afterwards of a long continuance" (455). As it turns out, the separation of long—indeed permanent—continuance will be from the new husband, who dies almost immediately after the marriage. It is Cecilia who narrates the end of the story, having "immediately on [her] arrival in London . . . fl[own] to the dear friend of [her] heart" and "found the dear Sidney alone, in her bed-chamber . . . prepared to receive me." (459). It is as if Faulkland's death enables a new kind of "marriage" effected through the novel's structure and affirmed by the fact that after this scene of reunion, Cecilia herself takes over as narrator and completes the telling of Sidney's tale, entrusted as "her bosom friend" to "more tenderly disclose" the "melancholy" news of Faulkland's death (461–62). In the end, Sidney takes refuge in a country retreat, with Cecilia "accompanying" her "into her solitude" (465). In yet another exchange of narration and story, then, heterosexual marriage dies off to be replaced by a kind of female textual union. The novel's last pages, though, leave both Sidney's fate and the fate of the narration unsettled; "the lady's narrative," liked the truncated marriage plot, "breaks off" and reduces to "fragment" (467), so that the confidante's tale mirrors the heroine's story.

If it is possible to read a novel like *Juliette Catesby* or *Sidney Bidulph* as an attenuated and sanitized sapphic dialogue, then the domestic novel is entangled with female intimacy as a routine practice. Moreover, the distinction between narration and plot in these novels is not absolute: the interactions between narrators and narratees that might seem artificially separable from the story end up becoming textual events that revise the plot or set up substitutionary relations between cross-sex and same-sex desires. This trajectory in which sapphic narration ends up complicating a heteronormative plot turned tragic characterizes what are arguably the eighteenth-century's two most acclaimed, popular, and influential domestic novels, Samuel Richardson's *Clarissa* (1747–48) and Jean-Jacques Rousseau's *Julie, ou la nouvelle Héloïse* (1762). Each of these epistolary novels, though structured through multiple voices, includes a female confidante for the female protagonist (Anna Howe for Clarissa, Claire for Julie) who is openly resistant to marriage and professes an excess of love for the heroine. At the close of both novels, the confidante attempts to reclaim the heroine's dead or dying body for herself in a bedroom scene that is also a failed attempt at reverse metamorphosis, but one that compromises the eighteenth-century novel's ability to sustain a heterosexual trajectory.

Anna Howe's pledges of love for Clarissa are threaded throughout

Richardson's text: "I love thee as never woman loved another," she professes repeatedly, and increasingly so as Clarissa is dying. However, these speech acts are never permitted to affect the course of the novel's events: Clarissa does not run off with Anna though Anna proposes this option more than once, nor does Anna effectively come to Clarissa's rescue. The novel thus effectively rejects the potential of Anna's love for Clarissa as a solution on the level of plot while requiring that love as a central feature of the novel's narrative strategy. Separated from Clarissa through the long months of the heroine's ordeal, Anna turns up to make good on her loverly pledges only when Clarissa is a corpse. With heaving bosom, in what she herself calls a "wild frenzy," Anna repeatedly kisses Clarissa's lips, attempting "by her warm breath" to bring Clarissa back to life. When Anna twice asks "is this all . . . of my Clarissa's story!"[89] she suggests that this *isn't* all, that the female affiliation that has structured the *narration* cannot be killed off by the apparent closing of the plot or even by Clarissa's death, that there will be a story beyond the story, and one in which she herself is paramount. If Richardson's novel has been unwilling to integrate Anna's passion for Clarissa into the novel's events during Clarissa's lifetime, insisting thereby on the dangers of heterosexuality and the inability of women to save women from men, now it is as if the novel itself has an afterthought, as if it cannot close itself without marking the failure of a same-sex relationship. The effect is a kind of sapphic utopian impulse that is already foreclosed: a way of naming what realist fiction cannot allow—but seems nonetheless determined to posit. Julie's cousin Claire is likewise set up early on as an intimate, in a complex design of desire that triangulates the relationships of Claire, Julie, and Julie's lover Saint-Preux and that culminates in Claire's excess of grief and passion when Julie contracts a fatal illness after rushing into cold waters to rescue her child. Rousseau makes sapphic after-love even more explicit than does Richardson when Claire shares the dying Julie's bed after exiling both the husband and the chambermaids. Unexplained "comings and goings" precede the moans that draw Julie's husband, Monsieur de Wolmar, to the chamber, where he sees "the two friends motionless, locked in each other's embrace; the one in a faint, and the other expiring." Claire has to be dragged and locked away to keep her from "throw[ing] herself upon [Julie's] body, warm[ing] it with hers, endeavor[ing] to revive it, press it, cl[inging] to it in a sort of rage, call[ing] it loudly by a thousand passionate names," and literally going mad with grief.[90] Here again, it is as if the ending of the novel is rehearsing a plot it never enabled: one in which Claire herself becomes the center of Julie's affections. It is as if, having demonstrated the failure of the utopian system set up at Clarens—it is, after all, motherhood that kills Julie in the end—the text reaches for the trope of the sapphic to hint at an alternative that is even more utopian since it has no place even in the world of the novel.

Both Anna and Claire attempt to create, then, and both Richardson and Rousseau instantiate, a kind of sapphic after-plot: in the novel's very last letter, Claire insists that Julie lives on, that indeed she hears Julie "murmuring" to her "Claire, O my Claire, where art thou? What doest thou far from thy friend?" The next words conclude this very long novel with the promise of a posthumous union not of Julie and St-Preux, her former lover, but of Julie and Claire: "her coffin does not contain all of her . . . it awaits the rest of its prey . . . it will not wait for long."[91] And although Anna Howe will survive as Claire apparently will not, she likewise imagines a heavenly union in which she and Clarissa "may . . . meet and rejoice together where no villainous *Lovelaces*, no hard-hearted *relations*, will e'er shock our innocence, or ruffle our felicity."[92] Thus two of the eighteenth-century's most widely read and widely imitated novels embed a sapphic structure in which a confidante writes beyond the plot's ostensible closure, indeed beyond the death of the heroine herself, implying the possibility of a union between two women that has clear erotic overtones. To be sure, these elements work only as supplement; a plot summary might not even notice them; but that is precisely the point. In both instances, the text stages a return of the sapphic "other" who has no official place in the domestic novel and in so doing produces a site of resistance that threatens to ravel the whole.

In a sense, the effective sequel to both these novels—the mid-century utopia though well sanitized of physical passion as I remarked in chapter 4—is Sarah Scott's *Millenium Hall* (1762). For *Millenium Hall* repeats the gesture incipient in these other novels: it introduces female intimacy as the aftermath to a series of courtship and marriage plots that come to less than successful ends,[93] and in so doing, it challenges the project of the mid-century novel by exposing its tragic underside. Scott's book refuses the novel's apparently unified plot structure as well, returning the novel to a recursive picaresque in which different women alternately occupy the position of the heroine, with rescue effected not by a hero but by the community of women led by Mrs. Morgan and Miss Mancel. Especially when they are read in light of *Millenium Hall*, more conventional novels from the mid-century of the novel's "rising" are exposed as caught in the limitations that the women of Millenium Hall are so happily evading. And all the more as the overwhelmingly strong trajectory of the eighteenth-century English novel is comic, it is striking to note that with the exception of *Juliette Catesby*, in which the confidante plays little or no role in the novel's events, three of the four novels I have described as fostering a kind of return of the sapphic end tragically, just as do the inserted stories that lead each of the ladies to Millenium Hall, while novels such as *Sir Charles Grandison* and *La religieuse* are able to secure a happy ending only after removing the sapphic figure from the text—Miss Barnevelt from the discourse, the lesbian mother superior from the plot. Both comic and tragic iterations of these novels suggest, then, that the story of the domestic woman and the attendant blueprint for the nation that the eighteenth-century novel seems bent on consolidating is also the story of the failure or at least incompleteness of that consolidation. That sapphic structures of narration persist through the second half of the eighteenth century in numerous English and French novels, especially by women, testifies to the continued significance of female erotic intimacy and the continued need for, or failure of, its management.

In linking the eighteenth-century domestic novel to the blatantly sexual dialogues of seventeenth-century erotica and the adventure tropes of the picaresque, I am not claiming a direct lineage, any more—or even less—than I would argue for the influence of other eighteenth-century novels and novelists on one another. I am suggesting, however, that the sapphic gets put in motion as a problem that is intimately tied to the project of the novel and especially to the novel's important role in regulating gender and sexuality in and as institutions. Particularly if we read canonical novels through the pressures established by erotic fictions and sapphic picaresques, we see that in mid-century the discursive project of fixing a gendered subjectivity through the novel was growing not simpler but more complex, and that around the edges of apparent consolidation, queer formations are erupting in queer forms. These forms morph into rather fascinating and often more dramatic shapes in the 1790s, through projects of rescue in which structures of confidence, picaresque strategies, and domestic dramas converge. In the aftermath of that decade, I see sapphic subjects taking more muted forms in English and French fiction even as they are emerging quite forcefully in the German novel—a phenomenon that underscores the uneven developments wrought by the novel's polygenesis.

IN THE WORLD: RIGHTS OF RESCUE

Histories of the European novel often see the 1790s as a period of gothic intensity especially in England, the turn of the century as a flourishing of

Romantic fictions especially on the Continent, and the early nineteenth century as one of realist consolidation pioneered by Austen, Edgeworth, and Scott on the English side, by the Goethean *Bildungsroman* in Germany, and a bit later by Stendhal and Balzac in France. It is thus worth tracing the sapphic through that same admittedly schematic trajectory to see where and how it continues to figure—and fails to figure—in these decades around the turn of the nineteenth century and to ask whether the story of the novel remains what I have been calling a sapphic plot. I begin with a quasi-gothic formation that seems particularly significant because it also entangles the sapphic with questions of revolutionary politics and women's rights. Each in a different manner, but all three with a marked and arguably excessive intensity, Eliza Fenwick's *Secresy: or, the Ruin of the Rock* (1796), Charles Brockden Brown's *Ormond; or The Secret Witness* (1799), and Caroline Fischer's *Die Honigmonathe* (1802), create grotesque versions of domesticity from which the sapphic becomes a means of rescue—a kind of reverse metamorphosis whether successful or failed. These novels share a single project: a woman who loves a woman is bent on saving that woman from male tyranny. They also share a narrative method insofar as each makes one woman the primary narrator and the other the primary, and more vulnerable, character, underscoring and making more interactive the structure of erotic confidence that I have been discussing. Such a structure forges yet another narrative strategy for modeling the sapphic, for the novel's focus of meaning thus necessarily resides not in the single character but in the relationship, and indeed the relationship becomes the instrumental emphasis of plot. These novels also grapple explicitly with women's rights and set themselves against confining institutions and restraining practices, so that the sapphic seems to stand in these novels for Revolutionary liberties, and the agency of a woman who loves a woman becomes invested with an authority that allows it to stand against the social order with a new force. They thus go beyond the model of the erotic confidante to create a kind of double structure, with the confidante, rather than the ostensible protagonist, carrying the primary narrative voice in ways that reinforce the interdependence of the two female figures on the level of discourse as well as the level of plot. In each case too the primary narrator, who is also the rescuer, is the stronger and more culturally resistant figure, one who pushes the boundaries of domesticity by using public-sphere agency, enabled by economic privilege, in the service of the friend.[94]

Secresy makes no secret of the "romantic friendship" between the putatively rational but deeply passionate Caroline and the fanciful Sibella, forging a convoluted plot of multiple desires: Sibella's fatal passion for the libertine and penniless Clement, who also turns out to be her cousin, the sensitive Arthur Murden's noble passion and the rake Lord Filmar's venal one for Sibella, Caroline's unrequited love for Murden and, in one more gothic turn, Clement's ultimate marriage to Caroline's mother for economic gain. The whole of this convoluted system, moreover, is organized beneath and against the parental tyranny of Sibella's uncle and Clement's natural father, Valmont, a name already rendered (in)famous by Laclos's *Liaisons dangereuses*. Valmont's notions of gender, influenced by Rousseau, have denied Sibella an education and kept her confined to his castle in good Gothic style. The relationship between the two women, which reinforces the crucial place of correspondence—that is, text—in any plot of rescue—is manifestly eroticized through Caroline's overtly physical rhapsodies over Sibella and more or less reciprocated in Sibella's eroticized dependence on Caroline. As the convoluted plot thickens, Caroline enlists Murden's aid in rescuing Sibella from her uncle's castle, but Sibella has already become pregnant from a secret liaison with Clement. The sapphic is arguably the ultimate open secret in *Secresy*, Caroline's primary passion for Sibella coexisting uneasily with the heteroerotic entanglements yet effusively, even excessively, represented. And although she musters her wit and her economic privilege against Valmont's self-serving machinations and the various weaknesses and infidelities of the men, Caroline is finally powerless to save Sibella from the multiple evils of Rousseauvian education, paternal cruelty, and libertine masculinity: Sibella will ultimately die in Caroline's arms after bearing a stillborn child. Fittingly, the novel's last words conjoin the intimacy of narration with the intimacy of plot, as Caroline grieves both Sibella and Murden: "I loved them both as I never loved man nor woman beside."[95]

Secresy posits sapphic love as the fierce passion that would go to extremes to rescue the beloved, extremes that are also in keeping with Caroline's radical stance for the rights of women. A similar, more successful pattern characterizes one of the earliest American novels, *Ormond; or The Secret Witness*, which I include for its close ties to Europe in both theme and setting. Constantia, daughter of a man done in by a swindler and prey to the murderous genius Ormond, is eventually rescued by Sophia, who also narrates the text in a structure that again marries narrator and main character as female intimates. Although unlike Fenwick's Caroline, Sophia is herself already married, her husband poses no emotional threat to the primary relationship between the two women nor stands in the way of Sophia's transatlantic rescue: as Christine Roulston notes, Sophia's marriage to Courtland is dispensed with in a sentence, "obliterated" by the "attention to female friendship," and Courtland is left at home in England while Sophia returns to New York in search of Constantia. By contrast, Sophia describes her union with Constantia after a three-year separation in ecstatic terms as embodying "the impetuosities of a master-passion. To look and to talk to each other afforded enchanting occupation for every moment. I would not part from her side, but eat and slept, walked and mused and read, with my arm lock'd in hers, and with her breath fanning my cheek."[96] In *Ormond* men are either ineffectual stay-at-homes or rapacious murderers; women, including not only Sophia and Constantia but Ormond's Revolutionary sister Martinette, for whom Constantia had conceived a passion, are the active figures who unite to rid the world of tyranny.

But the contest embedded in *Ormond's* sapphic intimacies extends to those sapphic intimacies themselves, for the most enduring triangle in the novel is the mostly unarticulated struggle between Martinette and Sophia for Constantia's affections. The struggle is also deeply ideological, the cross-dressing Martinette representing radical French and feminist politics, Sophia embodying a more conventional and conservative middle ground. That this political struggle is enacted through sapphic competition makes same-sex desire a kind of normative practice in the world of this novel, where a woman's passion for another woman cannot be located simply in a single political space. In ways more successful than is true of *Secresy*, *Ormond* affirms the agency of women, the value of their intimate relations in setting the world right, and the dangers of male interests both economic and amorous. In light of these values, however, it is striking that Sophia's narrative is framed as a message to one "I. E. Rosenberg," who appears to be a man romantically interested in Constantia. That the reasons for Sophia's disclosure of the intimate story of her friend are never given destabilizes the intimacy between the women, which could be read as a performance for the man to whom Sophia seems to want to marry Constantia. In this sense, Constantia is still bereft of agency; she is a figure in *Sophia's* story rather than an agent of her own.

Neither of these novels goes as far as Caroline Auguste Fischer's *Die Honigmonathe* in conceptualizing rescue by way of what is effectively a same-sex marriage, although—or perhaps for this reason—this novel, like *Secresy*, affords no rescue for its doomed heroine. In this novel in letters in the tradition of *Clarissa* and *Julie, ou la nouvelle Héloïse*, the aptly named tragic protagonist Julie marries the tyrannical soldier Olivier, whose jealousy finally leads him to murder his rival Antonelli. From beginning to end, however, the emphasis falls on Wilhelmine's efforts to keep Julie first from marrying Olivier and then from staying with him when that marriage goes badly awry. In the end it is Julie's own ascription to feminine caregiving—abetted by her mother's interest in her daughter's making a financially sound match—that ties her to Olivier until it is too late. Julie herself realizes, too late, that she should have stayed with Wilhelmine, who does find marital happiness in the end—though an end that is not textually developed—while the widowed Julie's own life is tragically short. What makes this novel particularly transgressive is the extent of its representation of passion between the two women and its brief for what is effectively a marriage between Julie and Wilhelmine. Although it is Wilhelmine who lays out the material strategies for living together, there is clearly passion on both sides. Julie, for example, writes on one occasion, "You, my true one and only! I press you in thought to my heart, and cover your beloved angry face with a thousand kisses" and "feel how much you love me."[97] Wilhelmine's love for Julie is all-encompassing, "a passion in her soul," and "the hope of [her] life."[98] Not surprisingly, Olivier regards Wilhelmine as "an Amazon" with "Revolutionary principles!" (Letter 11). The rivalry is an open one, as Wilhelmine pits her love for Julie against Olivier's need to possess her. The "marriage" between the two women is not to be; ultimately Julie cannot wrest herself from the heternormative model. Thus she asks Wilhelmine: "Do you believe these hopes would have ever been fulfilled? Don't you believe Nature would have sought revenge? Did she create two women to be everything to each other, and to ridicule her laws, which cannot be changed?"[99] Wilhelmine's retort is bitter: "Who is mocking the laws of nature now and who is going to suffer for it? Two women cannot be all to each other? Bad enough? Bad enough that the creatures who are supposed to be this everything, represent everything so miserable."[100] The denouement of *Die Honigmonathe* is a tragic one— the rescue fails—but the plot itself becomes the vindication of Wilhelmine's apology for female friendship as women's best hope. Moreover, the novel's extensive consideration of female union, as Angela Steidele notes, makes Wilhelmine "the first figure in German literature to strive for an exclusive union with a woman."[101]

While authorial biography need not be a recourse in this any more than in prior instances, it is probably not coincidental that Fenwick, Brockden Brown, and Fischer all allied themselves with liberal and Wollstonecraftian if not always Revolutionary politics. Yet in deploying strategies of rescue, each of these texts also exposes the boundaries that the novel places around women's capacity to act in the public sphere. Two of the three women in need of rescue end up dying, and the third, Constantia, is being set up in what might amount to an arranged marriage. I would argue that the narrative structure in which these novels embed the project of rescue, which privatizes the relationship between the women, also suggests the limitations of the private in addressing the larger social problems that the texts themselves engage. I have written elsewhere about Mary Wollstonecraft's uncharacteristic struggles in bringing her last work, *The Wrongs of Woman; or, Maria* to a conclusion, in good part because the legal problems the novel raises cannot readily be solved within the confines of fiction. The "rights of rescue" in *Secresy, Ormond,* and *Die Honigmonathe* likewise show dramatically, as much in their failures as in their successes, that women's options for the kind of friendship I described in chapter 4, the friendship in which one woman could intervene on behalf of another, also cannot easily be resolved within the space of realist fiction at this historical juncture. And as the realist imperatives of the novel itself intensify and put pressure on narrative voice, we will also see an attenuation in certain forms of sapphic presence. This is by no means the end of the story, even for the eighteenth-century; in chapter 7, several novels will appear among a group of Romantic works that naturalize female couples in ways that render them monumental, if at a price, and of course novels will continue through the nineteenth century to represent both female intimacies and arguably sapphic characters from Théophile Gautier's Romantic *Mademoiselle de Maupin* (1835) with its queer central figure and its equally queer Romantic triangulation to Charles Dickens's *Little Dorrit* (1855) with its equivocal Miss Wade and her equally equivocal relationship with Tattycoram. At the same time, it is worth looking further, by way of concluding this chapter, at the changing landscape at the end of the eighteenth century to continue testing my argument about the rising novel as a sapphic plot.

THE ENDS OF A NOVEL CENTURY

If we were mapping the sapphic in the novel around 1800, it might be fair to say that it is more visible in Germany than in countries such as France and England where it had been flourishing in the century before. In a convergence that may not be coincidental, the novel and the sapphic emerge in German literature more or less in tandem in the last decades of the eighteenth century. As I have mentioned, structures of same-sex confidence characterize both of the novels that propel German fiction into international prominence: Sophie von La Roche's *Geschichte des*

Fräuleins von Sternheim (1771), uses a *Clarissa*-like structure that incorporates female confidence within a multi-voiced novel that moves its heroine around Europe in the manner of picaresque; and Goethe's *Die Leiden des jungen Werther* (1774) is perhaps the first prominent novel to adopt a manly equivalent of same-sex confidence. Not surprisingly, then, as the German novel begins to flourish around the turn of the century, the sapphic emerges within it. In addition to Fischer's *Die Honigmonathe*, a spate of novels written around 1800 primarily by women and explored by Angela Steidele would seem to bear this out. Particularly significant are the novels of Friederike Unger, several of which repeat the pattern of sapphic picaresque. In *Rosalie und Nettchen*, for example, two women kidnapped by the same man escape from him together, with one of the women cross-dressed much as Leonora and Louisa escape in Sarah Scott's *Journey Through Every Stage of Life*. Unger's *Albert and Albertine* also plays with lesbian desire, and Elisabeth Krimmer sees lesbian currents in Unger's 1806 memoir, *Bekenntnisse einer schönen Seele* (1806). In ways doubtless abetted by the 1790s culture of lively political debate, female intimacy is born with the German novel in a way that makes *Bildung* itself a contest—or a compatibility—between same-sex and cross-sex intimacies at a time when what Goethe will call "elective affinities" (in *Die Wahlverwandtschaften*, 1809) have become a particularly dominant thread in German—and Romantic—thought.

The mainstream English novel, however, seems to me to be moving toward more conservatizing and realist ends, as a look at works by Maria Edgeworth, Frances Burney, and Jane Austen might suggest. In Edgeworth's *Belinda* (1801), a figure rather like Richardson's Miss Barnevelt is satirized not only for her mannish and implicitly sapphic behaviors but for her politics. *Belinda* offers as this sapphic figure the gun-toting Harriot Freke, whose "wild oddity" of countenance, "dashing audacity," "bold masculine arms," and comfort "in male attire" all mark her as "a young rake" with nothing "feminine about her."[102] Freke is Richardson's Miss Barnevelt intensified, and in language that sometimes repeats *Sir Charles Grandison* almost verbatim; she flatters Belinda about her beauty as Barnevelt had flattered Harriet Byron, she recalls the years "when I was a schoolboy—girl—I should say," and she is clearly a woman that "no man of any taste could think of" for a mistress or a wife. But Harriot Freke is also a political campaigner and a "champion" of the "Rights of Woman," and perhaps for these reasons, while Miss Barnevelt simply disappears from Richardson's novel, Harriot Freke must get her comeuppance: after she is injured in a "man-trap" during one of her mean-spirited escapades, it is "hinted, that the beauty of her legs would be spoiled, and that she would never more be able to appear to advantage in man's apparel."[103] Once Lady Delacour has disavowed Harriot as a bad influence, it is the more decorous friendship of Belinda that will sustain and indeed reform her. Female friendship remains efficacious in this novel, then, but its intimacy is carefully sanitized of acknowledged desire.

It would of course be a disservice to Edgeworth, as to Frances Burney and Jane Austen, to align them simply with a conservative rejection of same-sex relations. Yet if we read through the lens of the sapphic strategies I have been describing, there are ways in which their novels do perform some muting of previous practices. *Evelina*, for instance, creates in Mrs. Selwyn a far more benevolent "masculine" character than Miss Barnevelt or Harriet Freke, yet she is largely a comic figure whose satiric propensities conflict with a feminine ideal; when *Evelina* needs rescue, it is not Mrs. Selwyn or any other woman but Lord Orville who usually saves her; and her confidant, of course, is also not a woman but her foster father the Reverend Villars. Burney's *The Wanderer* (1814), turns aside other tropes that could well have carried sapphic inflection: titled with the language of picaresque, and indeed forcing its heroine to move from place to place and even to wander the countryside disguised as a peasant, *The Wanderer* creates in Juliet an isolated Romantic figure who cannot rely on any of her friends, even on the benevolent Lady Aurora who turns out to be her sister and with whom she is, to be sure, physically effusive. Most often, Juliet is, even more than Evelina before her, the immobilized prey both to more powerful women and to a panoply of men, while Eleanor Jodrell, the novel's eccentric, histrionic, and ultimately ineffectual Revolutionary feminist, is too busy being hopelessly in love with the man who loves Juliet to give Juliet much help. It is as if the tropes of the sapphic are present here through their absence, in a kind of epitaph.

To the extent that form and function are related, narrative method might explain the muting of the sapphic in this period. With Edgeworth and Burney—and also the giant of the era, Walter Scott—we see in the English novel not only a more conservative project but an arguably more conservative narrative strategy. Unlike most of the novels that have formed the history embodied in this chapter, *Belinda* and *The Wanderer* are heterodiegetic narratives: they use the distanced authorial voice of a third person to render female characters and their relationships, a practice that Austen's novels, of course, will repeat. Both John Bender in *Imagining the Penitentiary* and Nicola Watson in *Revolution and the Form of the British Novel* have linked the shift to authorial narration to a more conservative politics for a more conservative age. This certainly seems the case for a sapphic history of the novel; homodiegetic narrative allows direct representation of female intimacy in a way that heterodiegetic narration more readily attenuates. Certainly heterodiegesis turns the novel away from the dialogic structure of female confidence, walling off same-sex narration along with same-sex event. And so although it would be a stretch to argue for any causal relationship between the turn to third-person narration and the diminution of the sapphic in the novel, these moves do happen more or less in tandem, particularly in the English case.

In France, on the other hand, it is the masculinization of the first-person narrative that is striking. Homodiegesis undergoes a strong resurgence after the turn of the century in a spate of Romantic fictions, but not in forms conducive to female confidence. The slight exception is Staël's *Delphine* (1802), which Joan DeJean calls France's "last major epistolary novel," and which does create female structures of confidence in a formal sense.[104] Yet the confidantes betray or fall short of reliable friendship, and no rites of rescue prevent Delphine from swallowing poison when her lover Léonce is condemned to die before a Revolutionary firing squad. Certainly the novel makes its feminist statement, condemning a society "that imposes on men and women nearly opposing laws" and "requires women to submit to the power of public opinion."[105] Most other turn-of-the-century French fictions are either predominantly male-centered—I think here of René de Chateaubriand's *Atala* (1801) and *René* (1802) and Benjamin Constant's *Adolphe* (1816) as examples that will be followed by Alfred de Musset's *Confessions d'un enfant du siècle* (1836)—or heavily heteroerotic—as are Isabelle de Charrière's popular *Caliste* (1787), with its male narrator, or her *Trois Femmes* (1796), which focuses on women but is narrated by its putative author, the "Abbé de Tour," or Staël's heterodiegetic *Corinne* (1807), which builds its plot on rivalries between women. My exploration in chapter 6 of the trajectory of sapphic representation during and after the Revolution may help to explain the relative absence of the sapphic from French romantic narratives, though a sapphic formation will certainly characterize Revolutionary-era Europe's extremely popular novel, Bernardin de Saint-Pierre's *Paul et Virginie* (1788), which I will discuss in chapter 7. At the outer edge of my study, we do see two Romantic French fictions of 1835, Théophile Gautier's *Mademoiselle de Maupin* and Honoré de Balzac's *La fille aux yeux d'or*, formed around decidedly queer couplings. Clearly each national tradition has its own history of the novel, though it is also the case that, with few exceptions, by 1820 virtually every European tradition will have reached a phase of quiescence in the particular arc of sapphic history that I have traced here.

As an emblem for a major path that the novel ends up taking for its sapphic subjects at the turn of the nineteenth century, I turn to Jane Austen, the novelist classically seen, thanks especially to Ian Watt, as consolidating the strands of eighteenth-century formal and ideological imperatives into the nineteenth century's realist mode. I want to ask whether we can find analogues in Jane Austen's work to the modes of female intimacy that I have been tracing in this chapter that include but are not limited to those suggested by such scholars as Terry Castle.[106] We might well begin with Austen's first lengthy juvenile fiction, *Love and Freindship*, all the more relevant for being dated to 1790 in Austen's hand. Writing to her friend Isabel's daughter—already an attenuated form of confidence—Laura describes an instant friendship with Sophia, wife of her husband's friend:

> After having been deprived during the course of 3 weeks of a real freind (for such I term your Mother) imagine my transports at beholding one, most truly worthy of the Name. Sophia was rather above the middle size; most elegantly formed. A soft Languor spread over her lovely features, but increased their Beauty.—It was the Characteristic of her Mind—. She was all Sensibility and Feeling. We flew into each others arms and after having exchanged vows of mutual Friendship for the rest of our Lives, instantly unfolded to each other the most inward Secrets of our Hearts.[107]

Clearly *Love and Freindship* is a double spoof, at once on narrative conventions and on the foolish belief that intimate friendships can be formed on the spot, yet it still embeds same-sex desire in attractions of body as well as mind. *Northanger Abbey* too cautions against quick sympathies when Catherine Morland discovers the treachery of Isabella, but the novel affirms Catherine's more lasting bond with Eleanor Tilney. Significantly, the closest bonds of female intimacy in Austen's novels end up being those between sisters or sisters-in-law rather than unrelated friends, in a pattern that dovetails with the valorization of female intimacy as familial intimacy that I will discuss in chapter 7. Relationships between non-kin friends—Fanny Price and Mary Crawford, Emma and Jane Fairfax, even Emma and Harriet—are strained even at their best moments. Certainly Emma Woodhouse can be understood to have homoerotic desires for both Harriet Smith and (with a rivalrous eroticism) Jane Fairfax, as both Terry

Castle and Susan Korba have argued.[108] But only confidence between Anne Elliot and Mrs. Smith provides a lasting friendship between two women who are not also kin; otherwise, the most loyal friends, who are sometimes also loyal rescuers, are siblings, siblings by marriage, or trustworthy elders such as Jane Bennet's Aunt Gardiner or Mrs. Weston, Emma Woodhouse's former governess. In Austen's novels, non-kin peers who confide secrets to other women are usually either deceivers (Lucy Steele) or deceived (Harriet Smith).

Indeed, reading the history of the novel as a sapphic plot offers a new look at the closest female relationships in Austen's novels, revealing a diminution of confidence even between seemingly intimate sisters. It is worth remembering that Elinor Dashwood says almost nothing to Marianne of her feelings for Edward, and even the ebullient Marianne speaks only what—and when—she must about her relationship with Willoughby. Elizabeth Bennet likewise holds back so much of her belated desire for Darcy that her ostensible confidante Jane is as surprised as Mr. and Mrs. Bennet when Elizabeth agrees to marry him. It may be no accident either that the strongest affirmations of sisterly intimacy in *Sense and Sensibility* and *Pride and Prejudice* occur after the sisters are safely married off; at the close of each novel, the narrator tells us of the pleasures the sisters experience in living near one another.

I am not arguing that the sapphic disappears from the novel or even from the arguably more conservative English novel, but I am suggesting that the novel's "arrival" at the turn of the nineteenth century, such as it is, brings the sapphic plot, which threads through its "rise" in the multiple and interrelated ways that I have been describing, to some sort of conclusion or at least a resting point. If the sapphic continues to work on and in the novel as it moves across the next two centuries, it will need to take new forms as the novel itself turns toward different structures and forges different kinds of engagements with different worlds. Although the nineteenth-century European novel will yield its share of new sapphic characters and new forms of female-female intensity, I would maintain that it will take a modernist aesthetic, in a very different moment in the history of both sexuality and the novel, to give the sapphic the prominence it bears during the novel's "rise." But that, of course, is another story.

CHAPTER SIX

Sapphic Sects and the Rites of Revolution, 1775–1800

Saved during your tender youth from the seductions of men, taste the
happiness of finding yourself in the bosom of your kind.
—Pidansat de Mairobert, *Confession d'une jeune fille* (1778)[1]

This is what the Nation has had to face in our century: a woman beyond every restraint.
—Restif de la Bretonne, "La duchesse ou la femme-sylphide" (1783)[2]

In November 1775, the following item appeared in the influential underground journal *Correspondance littéraire, philosophique et critique*:
"There exists, they say, a society known as the *Lodge of Lesbos*, but whose
gatherings are more mysterious than those of the Freemasons have ever
been, with initiations into all the secrets that Juvenal described so frankly
and openly in his Sixth Satire. . . . One would have to be Juvenal to dare
to say more." The *Correspondance* identifies the priestess of this *loge* as
the renowned actress of the Comédie française, Mademoiselle de Raucourt
("our superb Galathea"), and the rites of Lesbos as "the only mysteries our
century seems tempted to renew."[3] The passage makes the sapphic at once
a closed realm and an open secret, a phenomenon that excludes men but
about which men alone are authorized to speak, a modern concern that is
also an antiquarian revival. The source of the Lodge's existence is public
rumor; its historical validation, the proper name of a well-known person;
and its currency, a pointed reference to eighteenth-century Europe's most
powerful secret society. In a year of revolutionary ferment in North America and a recently crowned young king and queen at home, the *Correspondance littéraire* announces the relevance of the sapphic for contemporary
politics.

Far from an isolated instance, this textual tidbit encapsulates both the constellation of concerns and the discursive practices that will dominate European representations of the sapphic for the last quarter of the eighteenth century, that Dickensian best and worst of times. Well before the upheavals of the French Revolution could have been foreseen, the sapphic begins to stand for a secretive realignment of power. The appeal to gossip as the best source of fact—"Il existe, dit on"—signals the mechanism by which the late *ancien régime* propels individual women onto the scene of history, rightly or falsely "outing" them in print at a time when the technologies of rumor—newspapers, journals, scandal sheets, secret histories— are among Europe's most flourishing genres. Most importantly, the 1770s mark an intensification of interest not only in sapphic *sex* but in sapphic *sects* that underscores the political agency of same-sex alliances. Turning their focus to all-female groups and gatherings rather than primarily to individuals and couples, the representations I will examine in this chapter take up, often even more directly than the texts I examined in chapter 3, the potential intersections of the sapphic with the state. They configure same-sex alliances on a notion of similitude pulled to its ironic extreme, in a reverse discourse that appropriates the emergent popularity of sexual difference: if men and women are incommensurable by nature, then woman's place may indeed be with her *pareilles*, her "kind," forging alliances toward the potential reconstruction—or destruction—of the status quo. The metamorphic scenario all but disappears from this discourse: its primary preoccupation is at once with the resistance of the sapphic to heterosocial integration and the pliability of the sapphic to horizontalizing aims.

In this way, the sapphic becomes a potent force in the social imaginary of a geopolitically unstable environment, one in which elite women's public-sphere participation, if nowhere formalized, is on the discursive agenda almost everywhere in Western Europe; when the influence of clubs and societies is growing; and when expanding notions of rights open questions about group identities and their influence. In chapter 4 I traced, through the framework of Jacques Rancière, one strategy by which disenfranchised persons might forge a politics. During the late eighteenth century, the possibility emerges more strongly that new polities might become not simply *a* party but *the* party, gaining rulership as well as rights. Bolstered by references to known women that stoked the fires of credibility, discourse about the sapphic dating from the 1770s already imagines that some women who are not under male control might indeed become that party, the sect that rules. In tandem with fears and fantasies about the potential for conspiracy of clubs in general and the Freemasons in particular, specters of sapphic sects gain new currency, signifying a closed space that those in power, or aspiring to power, were imagined to be unable to penetrate. The sapphic thus also stands for a partiality of interest, for faction in the Rousseauvian sense: parties formed "at the expense of the whole association"—but also parties that could also create a new social blueprint for that larger body politic. While we confront the most dystopic manifestation of this dynamic is the well-known virulence toward Marie-Antoinette and her female favorites, a scholarly emphasis on the queen has tended to obscure more complex and sometimes more sanguine uses of the sapphic particularly in the fifteen years before the fall of the Bastille.

I thus read sapphic sects as leveling double agents both of revolution and of *the* Revolution. In ways that already began to brew by the 1770s, imaginary sapphic sects became imbricated with reformist and counter-reformist politics both in and beyond France as newspapers, pamphlets, scurrilous poems, and secret histories grappled with the broader threat of groups and their social powers in a world of political turmoil and potentially radical change. On the one hand, the utopian potential of the sapphic intensifies; on the other, the sapphic fuels fears of female faction that help to justify the configuration of the man as citizen and the citizen as man and to hasten the demise, if not of club culture in general, of female association in particular. In short, a discourse of similitude, attached to intensifying conversations about rights, puts the sapphic at the heart of a politics of class, of concerns about conspiracy, and of hopes for collectivity. In positing the possibility of sapphic sects, writings of the 1770s and 1780s work out hopes *and* fears for a different future, but by the1790s these representations turn dystopic through concerns not only for a bourgeois sexuality grounded in difference but for the imagined transparency of a panoptical politics. By the end of the century, explicitly sexual representations will be more or less foreclosed from polite discourse even as romanticized and more sanitized notions of the female couple become the elegaic site of pastoral family ideals, as I will explore in the next chapter. In this chapter, we will see an alteration between 1775 and 1800 of discursive fields as simple and as widely visible as the use of terminology, and especially in changing definitions of the word "tribade" that had ushered the sapphic into modernity two centuries earlier.

ACTS OF NAMING

If late-eighteenth-century writers are more likely to see the sapphic as an ancient practice widely renewed than as a new invention, images of vestal virgins, amazons, secret cults, and esoteric practices link the sapphic with the modern through the mysterious workings of power now attributed to the present-day "tribade." Thus Mirabeau's *Erotika biblion* (1783) reminds the public that in the ancient world tribades had "high privilege" and "limitless power."[4] The 1788 *Choix de mémoires secrets* claims that "tribaderie" has always been in vogue but "never flaunted as blatantly as today," when "our most beautiful women give themselves to it, boasting about it, making it a badge of glory!"[5] The *Almanach des honnêtes femmes* (1790) avers that women who prefer one another to men must be particularly happy since their numbers are now so numerous.[6]

Of course it is these very publications that are effectively creating and promoting the scandal they claim to lament. Rather like the burst of concern about the sapphic and the modern after 1560, this new discursive production is also making the sapphic a more prominent sign of the times. We see a dramatic increase in the explicit use of terms such as "tribade" (mostly in France, the only country routinely to include "tribade" in official dictionaries and in the new *Encyclopédie*), "sapphic" (mostly in England), and "lesbisch" (emerging in Germany) during this last quarter of the eighteenth century.[7] In England, for example, "sapphic" appears in contexts as diverse as a discussion of "Sapphic passion" in the *Genuine Memoirs of the Celebrated Miss Maria Brown* (1766); the "Sapphic love" claimed by William Dalrymple to be commonplace in Spain and Portugal (1777); the "Sapphick Epistle" meant to discredit the sculptor Anne Damer (1778); the "Sapphic taste" mentioned in the *Anecdotes Recorded by the Police of Paris* (1794); the "Sapphic affection" "indulged" by the rather masculine women of Aleppo in W. G. Browne's *Travels in Africa, Egypt, and Syria* (1799); and even the "Sapphic oppression" allegedly wrought on youthful breasts by stays that ward off the embraces of (male) lovers.[8] A cross-national conversation of shifting terms is also a sign of the times: while it is not new that English and German discussions of the sapphic emphasize French connections—and "tribade" has become a French-associated term despite its Greek origin—French sapphic texts now also often presume a connection with things English, not only claiming English imprints but setting sapphic scenes on English soil.

This increase in explicit naming is more than definitional; it accompanies both a proliferation of proper names and a preoccupation with clubs and collectives. In a practice that spans Western Europe but occurs most intensively in France, ephemeral and underground publications mark both individual women and classes of women—especially actresses, artists, and aristocrats—as sapphic. Marie-Antoinette, along with her friends the princesse de Lamballe and the duchesse de Polignac, is of course the best known of those accused in public discourse, but the canvas is far broader; it includes Marie-Antoinette's sister Carolina, queen of Naples, and Carolina's English friend Emma Hamilton, Louis XVI's sister Elisabeth; Marie-Joséphine de Savoie, wife of the comte de Provence and her lady-in-waiting Marguerite de Gourbillon; the English actresses Eliza Ferren, Mary Ann Yates, and Kitty Clive; Madame Joly de Fleury, whose father and (to be divorced) husband were members of the Paris Parlement; the lesser known noblewomen Madame la Prieure and Madame la Vermeille, Madame Nicolet, and Mademoiselle Verneuille; Georgiana Cavendish, Duchess of Devonshire; Cecelia Tron, the Princess of Belmonte; the sculptor Anne Damer, Lady Harrington, and the writer Mary Berry. No woman is as ubiquitously present as the French actress Raucourt, whom I mentioned in conjunction with the Lodge of Lesbos, and the women with whom she is connected—Sophie Arnauld, Madame Souck, Mademoiselle Contat—who are often mentioned as a group. Within the new ethic of exposure, to take a few examples, the 1778 *Sapphick Epistle* by "Jack Cavendish" fingers Damer and her putative lovers, especially Kitty Clive, with only the thinnest of typographical veils; the *Fureurs utérines de Marie-Antoinette* (1791) lists thirty-four persons of both sexes and a range of social classes with whom the French queen has allegedly had liaisons; and lesser-knowns from countesses to market women are named for a range of alleged proclivities in the *Almanach des honnetes femmes* (1790), which devotes the month of November to "Tribades." The other "woman" named most frequently is actually a man: "Mademoiselle d'Eon," the channel-crossing *chevalier* believed until her/his death in 1810 to be a woman passing as a man, but who was in fact that rarer person, a man passing as a woman. Acts of naming are also accompanied by threats to name; thus an anonymous poem, *The Adultress* (1773), boasts that "I know a thousand *Tommies* 'mongst the Sex" and warns that if they don't "relinquish" their "Crime," the speaker will "give their Names to be the scoff of Time."[9]

The late eighteenth century is not, of course, the first time that individuals are being named publicly as sapphic. We can think back two centuries to Brantôme's suspicions about Laudomia Forteguerri and Margaret of Austria and to murmurs about sixteenth-century women rulers such as Catherine de Médicis and Elizabeth I or the seventeenth-century *précieuses*.[10] And as I discussed in chapter 3, there were more than murmurs in 1708 when England's Queen Anne appeared to throw over the Sarah Churchill in favor of Abigail Masham. Indeed, the use of sapphic representation for political ends during the English Exclusion Crisis and

its Jacobite aftermath may have been a brewing ground for the later eruption, establishing the potency of the sapphic in relation to the state. But
during these last decades of the century, as never before, a sizeable number of women are getting identified in print as sapphic, and repeatedly so,
whether pruriently, vitriolically, or matter-of-factly, within a network of
published gossip and scandal sheets rife with *historiettes*.[11] This new ubiquity of naming individual women as tribades and providing gossipy details
of their liaisons does more than compromise the reputations of the women
in question; the practice serves equally as authentication, giving credence
to the larger claims about sexual—but also more than sexual—behavior.

A wider, looser, and less controllable print culture is doubtless one
major reason for this increase in scandalous gossip, but I argue that concerns about female faction are at least as significant. For not only are more
women explicitly named as sapphic, they are most often named as members of sapphic groupings, coteries, and secret societies. A 1779 *Mémoire
secret*, for example, lists six "famous tribades" who have collectively "infected the capital" (155); a 1799 British newspaper report identifies Raucourt as a "distinguished Member of the celebrated Vestal Club."[12] Johann
Wilhelm von Archenholtz's travel narrative, as Emma Donoghue records,
likewise claims the existence in London of "small societies, known as
Anandrinic Societies . . . of which Mrs Y——, formerly a famous London actress, was one of the presidents."[13] It is not implausible to suggest,
therefore, that to be seen as a "tribade" in the late eighteenth century is in
effect to be seen as a member of a club. Conversely, the idea of all-female
clubs often implicated the sapphic; Emma Donoghue notes the sapphic in-
nuendos about specific women in at least two English publications, *The
Whig Club* and Charles Pigott's *The Female Jockey Club* (both 1794) along
with references to "blue stockings" who refuse submission to "that *odious
monster man*."[14] A 1776 issue of the London *Morning Post* acknowledges
the "neological" term "Tribadarian," which the writer claims to have read
in the *Post*'s pages, but announces his own preference for *"Tribadists,"*[15] a
suffix that emphasizes shared identity and a kind of party membership.

Designating the tribade as the member of a sect lends a different valence to sapphic representation, turning the emphasis from sexual pairings toward collective interests that dovetail quite firmly with the social
and political preoccupations of the period. Even when they sensationalize
their subject with obscene words and lewd images, these writings are preoccupied with the ideological investments they attribute to women's alliances. It is this banding for purposes of sect rather than only for sex that
seems in these texts to be the primary cause of concern. The tribade is not

simply a woman who desires a woman; she is a loyal member of an imagined "lodge of Lesbos." She thus evokes a concern not only about women beyond male control but about a larger phenomenon: the rise, and rise in fear of, exclusive clubs and private societies.

GROUP SECTS: THE POLITICS OF SIMILITUDE

It is widely recognized that the eighteenth century was not simply an age of sociability; it was an age that conducted its sociability through a myriad of groups and associations whether formal and individualized or informal and status-based. As one *Mémoire secret* puts it epigrammatically, "nos héros, nos beaux esprits / Forment mille compagnies, / Salons, clubs, académies."[16] These various organizations, though often praised or condemned for bringing together people of diverse classes and religions, were almost always premised on some form of similitude: shared identities, shared values, shared interests. As many of these groups were male-only operations, they also often reinforced an unacknowledged similitude of sex. Numbering across Europe literally in the thousands, these institutions ranged from coffee-houses, loose associations where nearly anyone (male) could enter, to literary and music clubs, commercial associations, professional academies, private (usually heterosocial) salons, and secret societies of which the Order of Freemasons, which I discuss later in this chapter, was of course the largest and best known and both revered and feared. Most eighteenth-century clubs were in some sense closed: invitational, purposeful, class-bound, and often political. Secret, often all-male organizations were especially important to revolutionary activity in Boston (the Sons of Liberty), to reform in Bavaria (the Illuminati), and to rebellion in Ireland (The United Irishmen); Jacobitism continued through secret societies long after the '45, and of course the French Revolution's political parties were nested in clubs. Exclusive clubs were particularly widespread among those of more liberal inclination—the emblematically named Select Society of Scotland, for example, took a critical role in forging the Scottish Enlightenment. These groups were also suspect, not only by those who might disagree with their values but by intellectuals upholding the ideals of Rousseau's *Social Contract*, in which transparency and unity were high values and faction and cabal ongoing concerns. Thus, writing in 1788, the Hanoverian Adolf Freiherr Knigge, himself a former member of both the freethinking Illuminati and the Freemasons, lamented the "rage for Secret Societies" as a "fashionable folly" and marked such groups as "extremely dangerous to social happiness" despite their promulgation of enlightened thought, for enveloping important ideas "in mysteries," concealing the power of secret leaders "behind the scene" and thus licensing "perverted geniuses and rogues," and ultimately promoting "cabals, discord, persecution, intolerance, and injustice against good men."[17] In short, exclusivity was perceived as much a social concern as a social benefit.

Not surprisingly, then, the idea of clubs specifically for women stirred both anxiety and derision. In what may be a first English print usage of the phrase "exclusive club," in Arthur Murphy's *Gray's Inn Journal* of 1753, a young woman proposes a coffee-house entirely for women; since "men are always contriving places for their own accommodation," such a club "would be the sweetest revenge. I would have it an exclusive club; no man to be admitted.'" This suggestion occasions from the narrator a rather strong critique of coffee-houses in general, followed by an alarum over the sexual license that would be fomented in an all-female club: "I tremble for the consequences. . . . The graces of the sex, I fear, will be laid aside. The town will swarm with pretty libertines, and masculine beauties." Female clubs would "threaten a revolution of the manners, in its nature violent" and therefore "probably, be found intolerable."[18] These are strong words for what could have been read as a modest proposal and is certainly not a proposal for more exclusivity than English men enjoyed; the sapphic is not mentioned here, but it is arguably implicit.

Ironically, however, the differentiation of men and women fostered by Rousseauvian philosophy by which, as I described in chapter 4, "a perfect woman and a perfect man ought not to resemble each other in mind any more than in looks,"[19] has the ironic effect of encouraging just this kind of separatism on the ground of a same-sex similitude that is arguably fostered by the ideology of incommensurable sexual difference. The ribald *Sapphick Epistle* (1778) sees women of all types and classes as united by similarity: a writer's sapphic "quill" could equally seduce matrons, widows, whores and bawds and girls dark, fair, or olive brown. These "Lesbian maids" range from England's Queen Charlotte and "Russia's Kate" (leveled here even in the naming) to the ordinary Moll, or Peg, or Nan.[20] Far more rhapsodic examples of collective similitude abound, offering synonyms and euphemisms—"votre espèce," "mes semblables," "mes pareilles," "soeurs," and "sosies," to take the rich range of French usages— that reaffirm the aggressive female similitude we saw in works like "Cloe to Artimesa" in chapter 4.[21] Marie-Jeanne Riccoboni's private—but in 1781 published—account of her twenty-five-year relationship with Thérèse Biancolelli provides the typical excess: the partnership is "as sweet as heaven could in its goodness have given me. Independent, free, living for twenty-five years with a friend whose intelligence, equanimity, and lovable character spread a continual accord over our relationship, I taste a peaceful repose. We know neither quarrels nor boredom; the word *no* is banished between us. The same principles guide us and naturally make our desires alike. Thus a perpetual peace reigns in our little household."[22] Revolutionary women will also exploit this similitude to exhort other women to join their clubs; as Madame Brillat of Bordeaux, for example, exhorts: "You French women who are kept far apart from us by the error of your ways, tear away your blindfolds. . . . Come into our midst, you will find tender sisters worthy of friendship; leave behind your fanatic priests who fool you. . . . Listen to a citizen who prefers the sweetness of liberty to vile slavery. Tear off your chains and save yourselves in the bosom of free women."[23]

If refuge in the "bosom" of "tender sisters" sounds a bit sapphic, a sapphic source may have been its provenance. For one text of the 1770s, far more than any other, shaped the late-eighteenth-century European image of women as adherents to a secret society with a specific political philosophy: the extremely popular *Confession d'une jeune fille* that first appeared in the 1778 *Observateur anglais*,[24] a *chronique scandaleuse* almost surely created by the journalist and government censor Mathieu-François Pidansat de Mairobert. The story's narrative segments were subsequently gathered into a single text and reprinted at least eight times between 1779 and 1797 under more explicit titles such as "Confession de Mademoiselle Sapho," "Anandria," and "La jolie tribade." A strong example of what Robert Darnton calls "political pornography" and an *exposé de clef* that names several alleged tribades including the famous Raucourt, the *Confession* describes the daily life, secret rituals, and political philosophy of a "Society of Anandrynes" in ways so detailed that some scholars have taken the account for fact; the preface to a 1920 Spanish translation, for example, called it "incontestable" and "beyond doubt" that the work describes an actual sect of Parisian sapphists and further claimed a counterpart secret society in London.[25] It is also from the *Confession* that the term "anandryne," which literally defines the sapphic as "without men," emerges as a particularly popular moniker for women sexually and socially aligned to one another in what are presumed to be exclusively female groups or networks.

The narrator-protagonist of the *Confession* is a young woman from the provinces who enters the sapphic community through the brothel of the famous Madame Gourdan, where she has taken refuge after her provincial parents discipline her for sexual precocity. Endowed with a "diabolical clitoris," she is judged better suited to women than to men and sold off to Madame de Furiel (the name an obvious anagram for Madame Joly de Fleury). Groomed in dress and manner to enter the upper class, "Mlle. Sapho," as she gets dubbed, is expected to join the "secte anandryne." In part compelling personal narrative, in part pseudo-ethnography that names names, in part prurient peepshow, the *Confession d'une jeune fille* also offers a revolutionary manifesto, a long inserted "Apologie de la secte anandryne," attributed to the society's president Raucourt and ostensibly delivered on 28 March 1778.[26] Set within a description of the Society's esoteric Freemason-like rituals, evoking a noble history of the sect from ancient Greece, Rome, and China through monastic Europe, the "Apologie" describes a harmonious, peaceful, and disciplined community responsible for the well-being of all its citizens, built upon the virtues of respect, wisdom, loyalty, and generosity, and living together in "tranquility, unity, concord and peace" (218). Benevolence toward the unfortunate is a distinctive trait: all goods are held in common, and all distinctions between rich and poor abolished. Intemperate language is forbidden, manners are gentle, wisdom and discretion are promoted, and all must follow the community's laws. As in Cavendish's *Convent of Pleasure*, no men may enter, not even as servants, and so women are employed in every capacity from teacher to hairdresser to gardener. Women of every class are admitted to this society, from *femmes de qualité* to philosophes, actresses, and girls of low birth or fortune; young apprentices from poor backgrounds are taught to read, write, dance, sing, play the harp, and other accomplishments as each person's "tastes or talents are revealed." Relationships between the women are enthusiastically sexual and tenderly mutual; the society safeguards the virtue of girls and widows and offers consolation in old age. Since philandering, sexual and physical violence, and the dangers of pregnancy and childbirth are unknown here, there are "no contradictions between feelings and faculties: the soul and the body work together."[27] The society's manifesto reads like a feminist-separatist *Social Contract*, and it seems no accident that some of the members are described explicitly as *philosophes*. The community's model is the large happy family, with "no other hierarchy than that [of age or talent] established by nature itself for its preservation, and necessary for its governance."[28] In short, this is a rather radically class-leveled sexual and social utopia—though one that retains certain prejudices of the period—and as Raucourt makes clear, it can thrive only because it is exclusively female.[29]

Like the beliefs attributed to actual secret societies flourishing in late-century Europe, then, the "apologie de la secte anandryne" promotes

Enlightenment ideals, social benevolence, and new forms of governance. Sexual passion is wed to an intellectual and spiritual commitment to the well-being of all women and to the belief, already evident if less openly sexual in the sapphic apostrophes of the previous century, that women's troubles stem from their mistreatment by men. The commitment is built into the new definition of the tribade as one who, "convinced of the excellences of her own sex, finds in women the true and pure pleasures of the flesh, devotes herself entirely to them, and renounces that other sex who is as treacherous as it is seductive."[30] And rather than seeing the sapphic as either unnatural or illegal, the *Apologie* declares the State itself, with its insistence on propagation, to be at fault. In what could be argued to be either a model for the state or an extreme instance of faction, the Anandrynes adhere to their own moral law, the law that valorizes what is deemed good for women.

Like secret societies such as the Freemasons, the Anandryne is a community with a private culture that claims to serve public purposes. The walls of its temple are engraved with images of women's bodies, the wine is Greek, the songs are Sapphic. Incantations parasitic of conventional structures abound; there is an analogue to the "domine non sum dignus" of the Catholic mass, for instance, and Raucourt's words are said to be drawn from the "Second Letter to the Women" by Mademoiselle d'Eon (208). At a time when Enlightenment philosophy, art, and architecture are taking cues from ancient Greece and Rome—one need think only of the Pantheon or of Jacques-Louis David's *Oath of the Horatii*—the *Confession d'une jeune fille* uses antiquity to dignify not only its sapphic but its social purposes. And although the Anandrynes have their secret rituals (see fig. 6), they are urged to be proud public members of their sect, representing the community so well that outsiders will say with admiration, "there's a student of the Anandryne sect; that's what it means to sacrifice to Vesta!"[31] Through the happiness and beauty of its pupils, the group will propagate itself through example, since as the women appear in public with their genteel manners and regal dress, they will attract others to the sect; "in the hearts of those who are like you [vos pareilles] and admire you, you will plant the desire to imitate you by sharing your destiny."[32]

Mademoiselle Sapho herself, groomed, educated, and indulged, thrives in this lap of sapphic luxury for fifteen months, believing herself "the happiest of women" until a "strange adventure" leads her to experience an even more "supreme happiness" that, however, "soon plunged me into an abyss of evils."[33] A young male hairdresser named Mille, disguised as a woman, conceives a passion for Mademoiselle Sapho and seduces her.

Belle présidente et vous cheres compagnes, voici une postulante.

Fig. 6. A "postulant" is initiated into the "anandryne sect." The image, taken from an excerpt from the *Confession d'une jeune fille* reprinted as the *Histoire de la secte anandryne* (1793–94), inscribes some of the iconography described in the prelude to the "Apologie." Courtesy of the Bibliothèque Nationale de France.

Evicted from the sect when her pregnancy is discovered but soon abandoned also by the faithless Mille, sent for a stint to prison and disowned
by her outraged father, Mademoiselle Sapho ends up back in the brothel
where her Parisian journey began, again rescued by women. Now, she says,
she "understood, but too late, the truth of what my benefactress told me"
about the "insouciance, the inconstancy, the perfidy, the wickedness of
men, and I resolved never to attach myself to another in my life."[34] Ironically, the message of the Anandrynes is not overthrown by her departure
but confirmed; that Mademoiselle Sapho is much worse off in the heterosexual regime to which she is evicted only underscores the sapphic ideal.

Clearly the *Confession* imagines the sapphic not just as sexual coupling but as interpellation into a collective subjectivity, indeed an alternative body politic. If early representations of the sapphic implicated habit—
what one does—the "Confession" sees the sapphic in terms of what one
believes—and belief, of course, implies the possibility of conversion. In
dramatic distance from the minoritizing model so dominant in the seventeenth century, the sapphic becomes a universal female ideal. What I
called in chapter 5 "reverse metamorphosis" is exactly what is promoted
here; indeed, the result is disastrous when Mademoiselle Sapho's sentimental story moves in the Ovidian direction. In short, and for all the potentially satiric and pornographic implications of this text, the sapphic is
represented as the social order that works.

As I have already noted, the *Confession d'une jeune fille* with its inserted "Apologie de la secte anandryne" was widely circulated and pervasively mentioned both in and beyond France, oft cited, and imitated in
sequels and parodies; sometimes the "Apologie" was excerpted and published independently or appended to another text. As perhaps the most
widely reads sapphic representation of the late eighteenth century, the
Confession remains curious in its moment for presenting a society of tribades as thoughtful *philosophes* yet also as an explicitly sexual, separatist,
and proselytizing elite. In biographical terms, it is as difficult to account
for Pidansat de Mairobert's creation of this text as it is to explain the "Sapho to Philaenis" of John Donne; while it is easy to imagine his decision
to produce a pornographic secret memoir that would sell, it is harder to
imagine why he would create or transmit a separatist utopian vision.[35] As
we will see, there is an ironic resonance between the societal qualities advanced by the Anandryne manifesto and the agenda of the French Revolution in its late Jacobin, welfare-state form, even though the public uses of
the sapphic after 1789 will render the association between the Revolution
and the sapphic untenable.

The *Confession d'une jeune fille* is the most elaborate but not the only text that represents a sapphic sect as a utopian community. We see a similar emphasis on sapphic similitude in a 1789 compilation of anecdotes titled *La curieuse impertinente*, in which the narrator describes convent life as a no-man's-land where women turn out to be superior lovers who understand what other women need and want. As the narrator, Madame E., sees it, men are "always occupied by business, irrelevant matters, and pointless speculations" and thus "incapable of those attentions that the heart requires." Here again the very dynamics of sex-role differentiation that are supposed to cement cross-sex relations undermine them. Madame E. herself has experienced with her convent lover "more tenderness, more ecstasy, more pleasure, than I have ever experienced in the arms of a man. With what attentiveness and tenderness did my little friend take care of me! with what concern every morning for the state of my health! what pleasure in teaching me everything she knew!" Similitude defines this erotic pleasure: "when she would see that she had warmed my imagination to the same degree as her own, when she would observe that my chest was heaving and had felt my heart racing, she would take me in her arms with the greatest transports of tenderness, and imitate with me all the movements that produce desire."[36] While it is no more chaste than the convent of the 1683 *Vénus dans le cloître*, this cloister promotes consideration and tenderness, harmony and happiness. Speaking "out of attachment to my sex," Madame E. also explicitly defends the Sect of Anandrynes: its many adherents are not at all absurd, she insists to her male interlocutor, nor is it criminal or unnatural for women to withdraw from the commerce of the world and find pleasure in one another.[37] Here again the sexual and the political converge in women's interests.

This idea of sapphic utopia is also, however, reconfigured in a novel, likewise published on the eve of the Revolution, that aims to defuse the *Confession d'une jeune fille*. Set in England, *Les chevalières errantes, ou les deux sosies femelles* (1789) is sapphic only by innuendo, yet it incorporates the Anandryne initiation ritual with a similarity of detail that could be no coincidence. It also works to deny the validity of that society and to create in its place a heterosocial utopia that retains some of the Anandryne principles. The Raucourt figure of the *Chevalières errantes* is Miss Eleanora Finch, an "Amazon" who hunts, shoots, and preaches "disdain [mépris] for men," whom she sees as "women's natural enemies." She is thought to have unduly influenced her niece Clara and Clara's intimate friend Bella against marrying: "Who takes a husband takes a master," Clara declares, and Bella agrees that wives are no better than "white slaves exposed to the market, and bargained for by men."[38] Midway through the novel, Miss Finch does indeed induct Bella and Clara into a secret sect dedicated like the Anandrynes to Vesta, though billed as an Order of Chastity—explicitly of the heart rather than as vulgarly conceived—and one so class-leveled that Miss Finch's servant Polly presides as its "Sovereign." This sect, however, is explicitly described as but a tiny remnant of the past, with only thirteen members worldwide, effectively dismantling the robust sapphic genealogy on which the *Confession d'une jeune fille*'s manifesto relies. Revising the separatist agenda as well, Miss Finch stresses that the group never proselytizes and does not accept women who are likely to become mothers.[39] That Clara and Bella are inducted despite their highly marriageable status, then, already augurs a marital turn of the plot.

Ultimately, then, although Clara and Bella have joined this society of what Bella's nurse calls "crazy virgins [vierges-folles]" (2:102) who are also "Don Quixotes in petticoats" (2:105), and although in good sapphic picaresque fashion they run off to France to escape the men who are pursuing them (thereby earning their double-entendre identity as wandering and wayward *chevalières errantes*), the two young women end up renouncing their vows and marrying their suitors after Miss Finch reveals that the sect into which she initiated them does not exist. It was merely an invention, she claims, to humor the young women and to forestall any possibility that they might decide to enter a Catholic convent. Yet even as the novel denies the power of the Anandrynes, it perpetuates some of its values by creating a new, heterosocial Order of Chastity in which the prospective male-female couples swear to be faithful, loyal, and benevolent. In this way, the text takes a pivotal early revolutionary moment and quietly turns its gender dynamics back toward heterosexual domesticity while building that domesticity on the values of similitude and concern for the fate of women advanced by the Anandrynes. And Miss Finch, still the unmarried Amazon, remains visible as the singular resistant figure who has, in fact, orchestrated much of the plot. Although the *Confession d'une jeune fille* claims a true sect of sapphists and the *Chevalières errantes* works to deny that possibility, then, the dialogic implication of these texts is that the sapphic is at once a separatist plot and a blueprint for happiness.

In an age of enlightened re-invention, when questions of societal well-being are paramount and the position of women under scrutiny, it makes sense that female communities might loom as both appealing and threatening. At a time when French Freemasonry had begun to admit women, the similarities of both ritual and value between the Anandryne society

and the Masonic Order suggests yet another reason for the double valence
of this story: the specter of a "Lodge of Lesbos," with rites "more mysterious than those of the Freemasons," has already arrived.

WOMEN AND THE ORDERS OF BROTHERHOOD

Of all the voluntary associations and secret societies that came to prominence in the eighteenth century, most prominent by far was the international and fast-growing Order of Freemasons. As Robert Beachy notes,
freemasonry emerged in the eighteenth century as "a pan-European fraternal association, committed to Enlightenment ideals of religious and social
tolerance. Important associational venues for mercantile and professional
elites, the lodges instantiated not only an incipient bourgeois social and
political order but also its corresponding definitions of gender."[40] It is not
necessary to rehearse here the various concerns that Freemasonry raised in
both politically conservative and Catholic circles; in one extreme formulation, an *Apologie de Franc-Maçons* reiterates the objections to Masonry's
"assembly of people of all sorts of states, religions, ages, nations, professions, etc." as forming a *mélange* "contrary to the laws of separation that
God and nature have establishing among men" showing "a criminal indifference to all religion" and "all the more dangerous for extending across
the entire world."[41] The danger was not trivial, since Freemasonry seems
to have been one of the most vigorous institutions not only in spreading
Enlightenment ideas and expanding the boundaries of political and social
power but in fomenting reform. It is no wonder that as early as the 1730s,
just twenty years after the order's founding, multiple European governments, including those of France, Sweden, Switzerland, Spain, Italy, and
Portugal, attempted to outlaw it.

Although most eighteenth-century clubs and societies were created by
and for men, all-male groups were usually considered simply normative
rather than being recognized as the separatist organizations they clearly
were. But what Beachy calls the "exclusionary fraternalism" of the Masonic Order did not go unchallenged within Freemasonry itself.[42] As Janet
Burke and Margaret Jacob have demonstrated, France was a leader in au-
thorizing female "lodges of adoption," officially in 1774 amidst widespread
debate, but according to James Smith Allen perhaps as early as the 1740s.[43]
By the last quarter of the eighteenth century women were being admitted
as well in England, Denmark, Germany, and Austria in female "Lodges of
Adoption" overseen by men. As their name implies, these women's lodges
were never wholly independent; they were supervised by male clubs, and

men seem always to have been present in the women's gatherings. Indeed, the 1775 *Adoption, ou la maçonnerie des femmes* uses Adam-and-Eve language to promise "a succession of pleasures [une suite de plaisirs]" in the joining of "soeurs" with "frères." But strict codes of behavior were apparently also enforced; one popular "manual" says that women can be initiated only if they are in good health and neither pregnant nor menstruating,[44] which rather implies that women members should call as little attention to their sex as possible—or, in an ironic similarity, makes the women eminently suitable for the Sect of Anandrynes. Despite the paternalist structure of the Lodges of Adoption, the inclusion of women was a sign of Freemasonry's leveling tendencies, as was the instantiation in March 1775 of the first African-American Masonic lodges, known as the Prince Hall Freemasons, which were organized like the women's lodges into separate groups. Separation of course also supported the ideology of gender similitude that legitimated the Sect of Anandrynes, on the one hand, and would legitimate the French Republic, on the other; as Beachy writes, the "precocious 'modernism'" of eighteenth-century Freemasonry "also theorized a remarkably 'modern' ideology of the alleged character differences that divide men and women."[45]

It makes sense, then, that in November 1775, soon after the official creation of French lodges for women, an alarm might be raised about a "Lodge of Lesbos" and that in 1778 a high-class gossip sheet such as the *Observateur anglais* might foment the fiction of a sapphic secret society, all the more as male Masonic lodges were subjected to charges of sodomy and alleged to incorporate mysteries and indecencies associated with Saturn, Bacchus, and Priapus; esoteric male-bonding rituals alone made the "brotherhood" suspect and laid the ground for similar concerns about all-female groups.[46] Women's lodges resembled the men's in their ethos of friendship and exclusivity as in their Enlightenment philosophy, and as Burke notes, "the powerful rituals, the emotional bonds of sisterhood, the assertiveness of their incipient feminism and the novel feelings of friendship as a union of virtuous souls made their impact on these women and altered the way they faced their day-to-day tasks."[47] Moreover, the rhetoric of some women's lodges sounds suspiciously like that of the Anandrynes. The highest Masonic degree for women in at least one lodge was called the Amazonnerie Anglaise and its leader the Queen of the Amazons, and this body indeed exhorted women "to throw off the yoke of the men and regard as tyrants those who refused to submit to the female order; it would be shameful for a woman to submit to those whom she put on Earth."[48] An elite Parisian Lodge, the La Candeur, similarly argued that women had "the right to serve the State."[49] Such claims on behalf of women's lodges, then, do stir the specter of a "Lodge of Lesbos."

It is not clear, of course, that Freemasonry gave women effective power; where Burke and Jacob see agency, Dena Goodman sees a mechanism for maintaining patriarchal authority.[50] For my purposes, however, the real power of Masonic women's lodges is less important than the public perception that separate-seeming female alliances might be dangerous. Clearly the single-sex sociability of Freemasonry challenged the heterosocial culture of the salons; since there were no totally female formal organizations in eighteenth-century France, the lodges were themselves close to an aberration.[51] It is probably no coincidence that Lodges of Adoption sprang up during the same period when the *Confession d'une jeune fille* and most of the texts I have been citing appear. The rites of Freemasonry are blatantly evoked by the "Apologie de la secte Anandryne," with its emphasis on secrecy, mystery, and initiation even to its test of the applicants' virtue—in the Anandryne case an imperviousness to phallic images—along with its commitment to equality and community; the "Apologie" reads like any number of eighteenth century Masonic constitutions and manifestos.

If the *Confession d'une jeune fille* was promoting a Masonic sort of female society, and representing its members as aristocrats, then it would be doubly vulnerable to backlash against both aristocratic women and Freemasonry. By 1789, when the *Chevalières errantes* was already using fiction to turn a same-sex sect into a heterosocial Order of Virtue, the Freemasonry that was arguably formative in fomenting the values that underwrote the Revolution was falling to the Revolution's anti-factional spirit and its rejection of secrecy. Although it is estimated that a full quarter of the representatives to the new National Assembly were Freemasons, the Masonic Order itself was fading in effective power not least because so many of its known members were also aristocrats (the most famous being the duc d'Orléans, dubbed Philippe Egalité, but others doubtless far less enthusiastic about the new regime). The combined hostility to aristocracy and hostility to female rule was to make the notion of female societies doubly troubling, and it was surely no advantage that one of Marie-Antoinette's best-known intimates, the princesse de Lamballe, was admitted to a Lodge of Adoption in 1777 and, as Janet Burke has shown, was strongly committed to the values of Freemasonry.[52] Nor is it irrelevant that on 30 November 1775, and thus at end of the very month that the "Loge de Lesbos" was so named in the *Correspondance littéraire*, Lamballe apparently wrote to her mother about "an epidemic of satirical songs" concerning her relationship with the queen, nor that earlier that year a *Mémoire secret* had for the first time made a "suggestive allusion," as Antoine de Beacque puts it, to this relationship.[53] It is but a short step from the combination of suspicions about secret societies as sites of *ancien-régime* power to suspicions about the queen to a Revolutionary backlash against the sapphic as the epitome of the secretive, regressive, aristocratic, woman-powered, and counter-revolutionary social faction. And the primary cause and effect of hostility was, of course, the reputation of the queen, on whose putatively sapphic, promiscuous, and acquisitive head were laid the sins of the old regime and thus the reasons for Revolution. But the queen was far from the only casualty as the potential of "woman + woman" turned heavily dystopian and the sapphic came to signify the antithesis of the social order imagined by the Anandryne manifesto. As we will see in chapter 7, it will take a very different and rather queer convergence of family values, irregular prosody, and elegaic poetics to recuperate the sapphic for further positive use.

ENEMIES OF THE PEOPLE

It is difficult to know whether the popular *Confession d'une jeune fille*, which names several well-known French women as tribades, fomented or was fomented by emerging rumors about the queen. That the two strands of sapphic representation were sometimes conjoined is evident, for example, when we see the *Confession* appended to the *Cadran des plaisirs de la cour* (1795), a satire directed against the (executed) queen. Known connections between Marie-Antoinette and the actress Raucourt, connections that also turn up in some of the pamphlet literature, also tied the notion of a sapphic sect to court culture. Whether or not the two phenomena are directly connected, negative images of the queen and her circle circulated with a vengeance in the 1780s in what amounts to a national hysteria about the potential of aristocratic female power. These writings are frank in suggesting that women of sapphic leanings want to overrule men and rule the state, and though the writings are fictions, it is actual women whom they name. I suspect that the popularity of the *Confession* combined with rumors about the queen and the female intimates of her Petit Trianon, where men were allegedly not welcomed, along with a backlash toward Freemasonry and a distrust of the women's lodges, all overdetermined the increasingly negative status of the sapphic during the years leading up to and embracing the Revolution.

We already see a critique of the politics of sapphic similitude in Restif

de la Bretonne's novella, "La duchesse ou la femme-sylfide" (1783). Beautiful and brilliant, the duchesse Maclovie is persuaded that men are "monsters whom women are supposed to serve without esteeming them or being attached to them" and calls on women to "love persons of your own
kind [aimez les personnes de votre espèce]."[54] Though required to marry,
the duchess retains her powers and indeed her powers of sexual refusal:
"we are not equal, Sir, . . . if you have your rights, I have mine; . . . No, Sir,
I will not be the submissive victim of your whims; the wife is mistress of
her favors, and a wife like myself is doubly so."[55] Instead of welcoming her
husband to the bedroom, Maclovie creates a coterie of six demoiselles who
(allegedly) share a "contempt for men," and she insists not only on approv-
ing their male lovers but effectively supervising their sex life. The duchesse alone has a "natural taste" for women; the other women are banding
together as a political rather than sexual group. Eventually, in a scenario
that echoes Mademoiselle Sapho's experience among the Anandrynes, the
duchesse succumbs to heterosexuality when one of her supposedly female
servants, Mélanie, turns out to be a man in disguise. But the lesbian accusation sticks once it has been leveled, the duchess's relentless reputation
as "une Safo" underscoring the novel's insistence that the sapphic is entangled more with separatist politics then with sexual deeds. Ultimately,
though, what condemns the duchesse is an elitist and self-serving arrogation of power that subordinates everyone and everything to her desires.
Thus the duchesse's story concludes with an homage to Rousseau's *Emile*,
the book that presumably could have set her on a better path:

> This is what the nation has had to face in our century: a woman be-
> yond every restraint, even the most useful ones, perverse in the eyes
> not only of the purist, but of the most lenient of decent men, yet who
> nonetheless had the most brilliant and most citizenly virtues, the
> queen of virtues, generosity! As for good qualities, she possessed all
> of them to the most eminent degree. Who then made her so lost? Who
> turned her scandalous, even dangerous to so many people? Her situ-
> ation alone; the manner in which a child of the upper class is raised,
> a manner pernicious for society, criminal, punishable, and so rightly
> prohibited in the immortal *Treatise on Education* of J.J.R.[56]

Here the sapphic becomes a philosophy, a set of aristocratic values dangerous to the nation itself: the duchesse, though capable of virtue, is "a woman
beyond every restraint [une femme audessus de toutes les entraves]." Although this duchess is a fictional figure, it is possible that Restif meant

to satirize the queen's intimate, Gabrielle de Polignac, made a duchess in 1780 by the queen herself and reviled even more intensely than Lamballe as the queen's lover and co-conspirator. The savaging of Marie-Antoinette and her intimate women friends, particularly Lamballe and Polignac, is widely known, thanks to the important work of Chantal Thomas, Lynn Hunt, and Elizabeth Colwill—and, a century before them, Hector Fleischmann.[57] In keeping with the specific aims of this book and of this chapter, I want to emphasize here not the vilification of the queen but the extent to which these representations are embedded in notions that France's power is vested in a sapphic sect secretly bent on destroying "the people."

Pamphlets naming Marie-Antoinette, her sister Caroline of Naples, the duchesse de Polignac and the princesse de Lamballe as dangerous sapphists with secret plans against the kingdom begin as least by the mid-1780s and run for a decade along shared themes. Although sex between women is represented in these text and images, what is emphasized is the instrumentality of the sapphic is instrumental in the destruction of the state. Thus, in *Les imitateurs de Charles IX*, the duchesse de Polignac is ready to wipe out millions of French citizens in exchange for power; the women Arest from our fatigues of lovemaking" only by Aworking with ardor to destroy a people who have the insolent pride to despise us." Their hatred of the people is paramount: "who cares, indeed, if thousands of men are destroyed? Paris is overflowing with inhabitants; let's purge them from the kingdom and ensure our bliss."[58] A male character in the *Cadran des plaisirs de la cour* (1795), seduced into libertinage by Marie-Antoinette and Polignac, reports hearing from them that Amen are like oranges; when I have sucked the juice, I toss the peel far away."[59] Even texts that ostensibly blame men ultimately turn the fault on a sapphic "cabal": thus in the false "Confession générale de son altesse sérénisimme" the king's brother d'Artois admits that "the horrific condition of France is my doing [l'état affreux de France est mon ouvrage]," but then traces his perfidy to sexual liaisons with sapphists: the actress Contat, Marie-Anoinette, and especially the "execrable" monster, the "Tribade Polignac," with whom he and the queen form an "affreux trio" of "enemies of the people and of liberty."[60] In an apocryphal *Confession et repentir de Mme de P**** probably dating from 1789, Polignac blames herself for having Apoisoned" Marie-Antoinette "through my perverted advice": "It is I and my kind [mes semblables] who have collaborated in swelling the national debt; it is our doing that the State has for so long now been turned upside down."[61] The princesse de Lamballe is said to have delivered "advice dictated by a truly diabolical politics."[62] *Les bordels de lesbos* (1790) has Lamballe rejoicing that she and the queen have no need of men because they could simply take their place. Marie-Antoinette's sister Caroline is charged not only with "squander[ing], on her lover, on her tribades, on her favorites, the blood of the Neapolitan people, whom she delights in destroying as did her sister Antoinette in France," but with having murdered "her male children and kept only the girls."[63] In all these instances of what we might call the politics of similitude gone mad, it is the queen's role as perpetrator, participant, or dupe of an erotic liaison that leads to national ruin. Thus the entire complicated financial and political mess of late *ancien-régime* France is blamed not simply on Marie-Antoinette—even Thomas Jefferson did that[64]—but on sapphic alliances.

Clearly by 1789, the sapphic was explicitly coded as an aristocratic, anti-male and anti-progressive vice no matter who practiced it, and thus a practice with no place in a virtuous republic: the *Chevalières errantes* is daring enough in attempting to recuperate the social blueprint of the Anandrynes without recovering their sexual practices. It is significant, then, that while working-class revolutionary women were sometimes called "Amazons," they were to my knowledge never called "tribades" even by those who stood against them. This unavailability of the sapphic as a social model is all the more interesting if we notice that the Anandryne social contract of the *Confession d'une jeune fille* yields a welfare state *avant la lettre* that is not so different in spirit from the one Robespierre was engineering before Thermidor. We might consider as evidence the resonance between the Anandryne apology's high value on social cooperation in the interests of happiness and the first article of the never-implemented constitution of 1793: "The purpose of society is mutual happiness [le but de la société est le bonheur commun]." That constitution guarantees all French men not only equality, liberty, and security, but property rights, free education, the means of survival, protection against despots, the right to assemble, and the enjoyment of all the rights of man; the Anandryne sect claimed similar rights translated to gendered terms. Yet the Anandryne vision, *as* Anandryne, is simply no longer available for revolutionary purposes.

We can see the dramatic gap between the "before" and "after" of Revolution in the differences between the "Apologie de la secte Anandryne" that appears in the 1778 *Confession d'une jeune fille* and the scurrilous 1791 pamphlet *La liberté ou Mlle Raucour à toute la secte anandryne assemblée au foyer de la comédie française.* A far more ribald piece of sensationalist slander that uses political language for shock value, this later piece pits "whores" against the Anandrynes. In the ensuing battle, the actress Adeline declares a proud alliance with men—"I love men, and I have no use for women hanging around me"—and unites herself to heterosexual women against both sodomites and tribades.[65]

The Raucourt of this pamphlet has recourse in her rebuttal to the same arguments about men's mistreatment of women used in the 1778 "Apologie," and she repeats the noble history of tribades from the ancient Amazons to recent and respectable authorities. But what is vowed here is an everlasting hatred for the Anandryne sect: "With all the intelligence that is attributed to Mademoiselle Raucourt, with all the insight with which she is truly endowed, it must be admitted that her reasoning is sometimes faulty," Adeline begins, and she goes on to accuse Raucourt of criticizing the "August National Assembly and present[ing] all the events that the Revolution has engendered, in a hateful and frightful light" (207–9). Raucourt is now an enemy of liberty and patriotism; accustomed to living with the agents of aristocracy, she has "swallowed their principles with their fuck."[66] The whores are now set up as the natural women: "in the eyes of the public, we are less degraded, less contemptible" than the tribades. For not only do the whores "fulfill the design of nature," they are workers rather than aristocrats, "the sweat of [their] asses being comparable to the sweat of others' brows."[67] Heteronormativity and labor go hand in hand, and queer is irredeemably aristocratic.

Although scholars continue to explore the complex legacy of the Revolution in relation to the status of women, pamphlets like *La liberté ou Mlle Raucour* stir anxieties about female collective power that may well have shaped the course of government; as Lynn Hunt has eloquently argued, the Revolution did create a kind of separatist government—but of men, a fraternity in which women had the right to go to the guillotine but not the right to vote and by 1793 not even the right to assemble in women-only organizations.[68] Certainly the anti-aristocratic sapphic texts fueled fears about all-female association that would help to justify the republican reconfiguration of female civic participation in domestic terms. So did the refusal of anything resembling a secret society; as Suzanne Desan writes, the women who formed republican organizations "were self-consciously aware . . . of the need to be public. In part, they sought like their husbands or brothers to transact the factionless, transparent politics that Rousseau had called for; they also knew that to be public could help protect the organization from accusations of back-room machinations and slander." Yet "even the most docile women's provincial clubs," she notes, faced criticism and satire.[69] Women club members were repeatedly warned to avoid circumstances that might risk the appearance of sexual impropriety; in one instance, men who defended the women's clubs were themselves de-nounced as "Jacobin hermaphrodites"; and women club members were on at least one occasion called *chevalières errantes*. Jean-Baptiste Amar's view that "the social order results from the differences between men and women" of course took hold when, on 30 October 1793, the Convention decreed that all "clubs and popular societies of women, under whatever denomination" must close. The efficacy of similitude would continue, but only men could continue it—in clubs, societies and, most importantly, the public sphere of politics. A party had indeed become *the* party, the sect that rules: as R. R. Palmer reminds us in *Twelve Who Ruled*, France was now governed by "nobodies," nobodies "who first introduced a universal male suffrage on a national scale, projected a national system of public schools, and decreed the abolition of slavery,"[70] but, I add, who also refused women the rights of active citizens. I am not alone in speculating that the sapphic specter was one catalyst for this position.

Even in countries where Revolutionary dicta did not hold force, we see the after-effects of the discrediting of the sapphic as secretive and aristo-cratic that makes it unavailable for horizontal values. Anti-sapphic dis-course also extended to liberal efforts to recuperate a feminist politics from the Revolutionary aftermath. We can see the shift in a contrast be-tween two other parallel texts, much milder and more allusive than the dramatically different representations of Raucourt in 1778 and 1791: I have in mind here the ways in which the sapphic plays out in Mary Woll-stonecraft's 1788 novel *Mary, A Fiction* and in her 1792 *Vindication of the Rights of Woman*. *Mary, a Fiction* represents an intense though not en-tirely reciprocated relationship between its eponymous heroine and her friend Ann; Mary's "friendship for Ann occupied her heart, and resembled a passion"; Ann was "all the world to Mary," who "wished so continually to have a home to receive her in, that it drove every other desire out of her mind; and, dwelling on the tender schemes which compassion and friend-ship dictated, she longed most ardently to put them in practice." She cares for the dying Ann with intimate tenderness, and when Ann succumbs, "the first string was severed from her heart."[71] To be sure, this is an elegaic representation of the kind that in chapter 7 I will explore further in texts of the same period, and it is also the case that Mary's passion for Ann is in some ways superseded by her subsequent passion for Henry. But female intimacy is here a primary signifier of sensibility.

In the *Vindication*, however, intimacy between women becomes car-nal and worrisome. Wollstonecraft targets servants and boarding schools as particular causes for alarm: "I should be very anxious to prevent [girls from] acquiring nasty, or immodest habits; and as many girls have learned very nasty tricks, from ignorant servants, the mixing them thus indiscriminately together, is very improper." Wollstonecraft thus recommends that girls be taught to wash and dress alone and laments that women, unlike men, "tend to obtrude on notice that part of the animal economy, which is so very disgusting."[72] On that account, Wollstonecraft also "object[s] to many females being shut together in nurseries, schools, or convents. I cannot recall without indignation, the jokes and hoiden tricks, which knots of young women indulge themselves in, when in my youth accident threw me, an awkward rustic, in their way. They were almost on a par with the double meanings, which shake the convivial table when the glass has circulated freely" (131). Even more dramatic because disproportionate is the fear that "with respect to both mind and body, women are too intimate, too familiar with each other," and she calls on them to keep up between them a decent personal reserve: "Why in the name of decency are sisters, female intimates, or ladies and their waiting-women, to be so grossly familiar as to forget the respect which one human creature owes to another. . . . Why women in health should be more familiar with each other than men are, when they boast of their superior delicacy, is a solecism in manners which I could never solve" (131). Wollstonecraft worries about intimacies between women even when these appear to be merely verbal: "The greetings of affection in the morning are . . . more respectful than the familiar tenderness which frequently prolongs the evening talk, and when a woman friend turns up in the morning with her clothes huddled on because she chose to indulge herself in bed till the last moment" (132). The excess of Wollstonecraft's fears of the sapphic in the *Vindication*, particularly in contrast to the romanticization of female intimacies in *Mary, a Fiction*, suggests a kind of overcompensation that is not unlike the excessive language that surrounds the French aristocrats in the pamphlets. These gestures on both sides of the channel affirm what Katherine Binhammer has called the "sex panic of the 1790s"; as Binhammer notes, 1790s feminism relied on a firmly heterosexual model of gender as a way to advance feminist goals; while standing against the sexual exploitation of women, these feminists nonetheless reaffirm "a rational and reproductive sexuality" as "a prerequisite to an equal and just society." In short, "to have a masculine understanding is one thing; to have a masculine sexuality is another."[73]

Nor is this anxiety exclusive to Wollstonecraft or to early feminists. Boarding schools, for example, grew up rapidly in late-eighteenth-century Europe under the new impetus for educating women, thanks in part to the advocacy by women such as Wollstonecraft herself, whose own first book was the *Thoughts on the Education of Daughters* (1786). Like convents before them, however, boarding schools became a common site of sapphic concern. *The Cherub: or, Guardian of Female Innocence*, a 1792 text notable for its complex engagements with colonialism, devotes its longest chapter to boarding schools as a particular threat to female innocence. In giving girls access to obscene reading and "especially in permitting the more grown girls to sleep with the younger pupils," boarding schools promote "a species of *unnatural practice*, by which, though *unknown* to man, they enter into life without that *important requisite* to which mankind are so much and so laudably attached." *The Cherub* even uses one of the rare English references to "tribade" in when it mentions a woman whose "niece of about twenty years old was as expert a proficient in the art of *tribade* as in the natural enjoyments of the male sex," and who beds with an "innocent and ruddy Creole" who "was but half a virgin" by morning.[74] As I noted in chapter 3, the French Créole Moreau de St.-Méry proclaims himself similarly appalled to discover that young women in Philadelphia "give themselves early to self-pleasuring, and [seek] the *jouissances* of a wayward imagination with persons of their own sex." He is particularly shocked that gentlemen's daughters sleep with their servants, "so that from her eighth to tenth year she may have shared the bed of fifty or sixty creatures of whom nothing is known except their names and who may be possessors of habits that could be disastrous to young persons."[75]

Two other events of the mid-1790s, one legal and repressive, the other textual and transgressive, suggest even more sharply that the tribade has acrrued a kind of monstrous excess. In the first instance, as Theo Van der Meer has documented, Amsterdam saw between 1795 and 1798 an unprecedented prosecution of middling and poor women as lesbians; that some of these women were accused of singing patriotic Orangist songs during a time of French occupation extends in a different direction the conjugation of the sapphic with the state already so active in Revolutionary France.[76] In the second instance, the Marquis de Sade's *Juliette*, with its "veritable phalanx of tribades," as Elizabeth Colwill rightly puts it, bursts onto the sapphic scene in this same period (1797) with an excess of pornographic violence.[77] Notwithstanding Sade's explicit mission to dismantle sexual and political codes in tandem, however, I would argue that *Juliette*, for all its claims to recuperate queer sexualities, reinforces an emerging horror at the sapphic and renders it even less viable for advancing revolutionary aims. Arguably, all of Europe was uniting around the rejection of the sapphic, and especially of the sapphic sect, in a "gender panic" that Dror Wahrman identifies vis-à-vis England but that can be seen in wider scope.

UNDEFINING THE DEFINABLE

What James McMillan notes of France is true of Europe (and the new United States) in general: "across the ideological and political divide, there came to exist a remarkable degree of consensus among both women and men with regard to the new gender order of the post-Revolutionary period." Although Suzanne Desan and Carla Hesse have shown the ways in which the Revolution gave women new paths for advancing their legal and political interests respectively through the courts and through the press,[78] it remains the case that an insistent postrevolutionary discourse of sexual difference reinforced the conjugal family as the site from which those interests would be advanced. It is "in direct response to the Revolutionary experience," McMillan argues, that "the stability of the social order was now seen to depend in no small measure on the maintenance of differences between the sexes and the avoidance of any confusion of sexual roles."[79] Sylvain Maréchal's equivocal 1801 essay that proposes "a law forbidding women to read," taken by some as spoof and by others as serious, stands in vivid contrast to his 1790 *Almanach des honnêtes femmes*: if listing actual women according to the sex acts they had allegedly performed taps into the libertine mood of 1790, the 1801 essay taps an anxiety about women's place in print culture and reinforces the new domesticity by addressing itself "to heads of household, fathers of families, and husbands" as if to cover every patriarchal base.[80]

It is thus not surprising that by 1800 public discourse about the sapphic had moved primarily into more subtle, pastoral, and familial forms, as chapter 7 will explore. When Geneviève Fraisse asks whether there is a necessary link between founding a democracy and the exclusion of women,[81] we might also ask whether there is a link between both of these and the fear of sapphic sects. For it is not simply difference that underwrites the new societies but the assurance that women will remain materially "dispersed among the men," dependent, loyal, and effectively unable to form same-sex alliances beyond the aegis of print that I have recognized in my fourth chapter. That, of course, will not be the end of the story, not even of the eighteenth-century story, as both the last sections of chapter 5 and the whole of chapter 7 show. But it is important to see what begins to happen to the explicitly sapphic as a public phenomenon around 1800, and

for a snapshot I turn to a very simple place: changing dictionary definitions of the tribade. Such an inquiry seems a fitting way as well to mark
the temporal arc of this project from the evacuation of meaning that marks
Henri Estienne's unnaming of the tribade in 1566 through a plethora of
converging and conflicting definitions by the mid-eighteenth century, particularly in the French context, to a sudden and self-contradictory attempt
to restore that space of silence in the Revolution's wake.

In the middle of the eighteenth century, those few European dictionaries that define the tribade do so in language that is harsh and prurient. In
the 1742 *Zedlers Universal-Lexicon*, for example, the "tribade" is a woman
with a "large and long" clitoris that can be "inserted into a woman's body"
as a man does his "rod."[82] The 1755 *Manuel lexique ou dictionnaire portatif* designates the tribade more cynically as "the name given to lascivious
women who try to obtain among themselves pleasures they can receive
only from the other sex."[83] The 1762 *Dictionnaire de l'Académie française*
considers the tribade a woman "who violates another woman [qui abuse
d'une autre femme]," making the sapphic predatory rather than consensual.[84] The influential *Encyclopédie* calls sapphic desire "a type of peculiar perversion as inexplicable as that which inflames a man for another
man,"[85] and Peyton's 1764 *Compendious Dictionary of the French Language* calls her "a woman that plays a man's part with another woman."

This persistent pattern will undergo some telling alterations in the
1780s. Displaying the international influence of the *Confession d'une jeune fille*, the 1784 *Krünitz's Lexikon* makes the definition both more collective and more separatist: tribades are "Anandrynes, a whole sect of lustful women, who mix only with their own sex."[86] Successive versions of
Thomas Nugent's *New Pocket Dictionary of the French and English Languages*, published respectively in 1774, 1781, 1787, and 1799, are especially
illustrative of divergent definitions that they tell us how much confusion
overlays the sapphic at this point. In both 1774 and 1781, Nugent defines
tribade simply as a "female sodomite," emphasizing the sex act. Yet six
years later in 1787, the definition changes to "a woman loving her own
sex," a phrasing that may be euphemistic, but is also more ethnographic
than critical and more collective (loving her sex) than individual (loving
another woman).[87] In 1799, however, both specificity and potential positivity disappear, as Nugent's *Dictionary* defines tribade euphemistically and
negatively as a "bad woman," substituting moral judgment for denotation
and making no reference whatever to sex, love, or sects.[88] In 1798, in a
similar spirit and more bluntly, the *Dictionnaire de l'Académie Française*
repeats its earlier and persistent definition of the tribade as "femme qui

abuse d'une autre femme," but it adds for the first time this warning: "on évite ce mot" (this word is to be avoided). The era of explicit sapphic representation, along with the sapphic as sect, has begun to pass, and I would argue that in its passing we can see its long reach of significance for figuring, and propelling, a politics. If sapphic sects needed an epitaph, they would find one in the English periodical essays of 1815 and 1816 about "that infamous club of Tribades," the "vestal club" that forswears "natural" relations and proves the longstanding evil of the French—but that can no longer be discussed publicly because of the "delicacy of the topic."[89] Yet this "delicacy" notwithstanding, the potential and potency of the sapphic will not disappear but be reconfigured, not as sect or secret society but in the seemingly innocuous yet irregular form of the sapphic family.

CHAPTER SEVEN

"Sisters in Love": Irregular Families, Romantic Elegies, 1788–1830

Wretched trellised tree! For, tethered tightly
To your chilly wall, you languish there, . . .
And imagination . . . brings the plight
Of a human shape before my gaze,
Who, forever severed from the liberal ways
Of nature, is coerced by alien norms,
Just as you are, into rigid forms.
—Sophie Mereau, "To a Trellised Tree" (1801)[1]

The "Bluestocking" Hester Thrale had a nose for lesbians. In April 1789 she wrote in her diary that "the Queen of France is at the Head of a Set of Monsters call'd by each other *Sapphists*, who boast her Example; and deserve to be thrown with the *He* Demons that haunt each other likewise, into Mount Vesuvius." In December 1795 she recorded similar suspicions about other women including her neighbors, Lady Eleanor Butler and Sarah Ponsonby, the "Ladies of Llangollen" whom I discussed in chapter 1: "Witness Cæcilia Tron, & Principessa Belmonte—and hundreds, *hundreds* more: while French and English Women are now publicly said to practise Atrocities . . . 'tis now grown common to suspect Impossibilities—(such I think 'em)—whenever two Ladies live too much together; the Queen of France was all along accused, so was Raucoux the famous Actress on the Paris Stage; & 'tis a Joke in London now to say such a one visits *Mrs Damer*."[2] Given Thrale's language, which in naming names echoes the gossip I discussed in chapter 6, one would think that Butler and Ponsonby would have been shunned. In fact, they were celebrated in print and in pilgrimage during the same years that the sapphic had grown "monstrous":

if "visiting Mrs. Damer" was an accusation, visiting Butler and Ponsonby was a privilege.

This does not, of course, mean that Thrale was alone in speculating about the Ladies' relationship. But nearly all the speculations were private ones. In 1790 one well-distributed newspaper piece did proclaim Butler and Ponsonby to "bear a strange antipathy to the male sex" and, in a metamorphic effort, to characterize Butler as "tall and masculine" and Ponsonby as "polite and effeminate,"[3] but most public language about the "ladies," as the epithet "ladies" itself suggests, allowed mainstream culture to recuperate a sanitized homoerotic formation rather than cede sapphic subjects wholly to the "Monsters" of the French court. This strategy placed the female couple at the crux of a tension between values of intimate domesticity and liberatory individualism, both underwritten by affinities with "nature" and harnessed to utopian ends. At a time when homoerotic relations were under suspicion, and public discourse, as I noted in the last chapter, had yielded considerably to the "delicacy of the topic,"[4] intimacies between women became conscripted for seemingly antithetical purposes: to figure family harmony and individualist transgression as if these were a natural pair. This move helps to underwrite something of a sex change in the social imaginary surrounding intimate friendship that even the proliferation of sapphic apostrophe did not quite accomplish. Thus, writing privately to Elizabeth Pigott in 1807, Byron can boast that his love for John Edleston will "put *Lady E. Butler* and *Miss Ponsonby* to the blush, *Pylades* and *Orestes* out of countenance, and want nothing but a catastrophe like *Nisus* and *Euryalus*, to give *Jonathan* and *David* the 'go by,'" effectively recognizing the turn in the genealogy of same-sex relations that Tyard's "Dame" only imagined in 1573.[5]

The reconfiguration of the sapphic in terms of family values gives it a new agency in the complex convergence of industrial capitalism and Romantic idealism that allows it to "queer" both conservative and transgressive aims. It also suggests a limit case for the Romantic investment in the "notion of sexual pleasure that is separable from reproduction and marriage" that Richard Sha identifies, for the homoeroticism of the same-sex couple is muted or even repudiated in the texts I will be examining.[6] In the convergence of tropes of domesticity with tropes of irregularity inscribed formally as well as thematically in representations of the sapphic around the turn of the nineteenth century, we can see the use of the sapphic— almost always now articulated in a horizontal mode that emphasizes similitude—to figure intimacy as a fragile balance between convention

and transgression in landscapes where the domestic coexists with the untamed. If the sapphic threatened the undoing of the patriarchal family in a
work like Benserade's *Iphis and Ianthe* or Cubillo's *Añasco el de Talavera*,
and if sapphic mobility forged resistances to the domesticated couple in
the eighteenth-century novel as I described in chapter 5, here the sapphic
provides the pastoral foundations for a new kind of family value. But the
fragility of the sapphic as an anchor for antithetical aims—a fragility that
characterizes so many other Romantic configurations, to be sure—is borne
out by the elegaic quality of these representations and indeed by the ubiquity of death in both image and event. At the same time, what may appear
as a textual impasse also enables the idealization of one sapphic formation
that does the work of marrying antithetical impulses within the social
imaginary at a time when bourgeois interests and revolutionary resistance
converge.

It is a commonplace, of course, that Romanticism celebrated transgression in the service of what Harold Bloom long ago described as a "my-
thology of the self,"[7] privileging singularities over categories to challenge
the hegemony of reason, order, and social conformity. We see these challenges in the wild rhymes of Byron's *Don Juan*, in the enjambments of
Hugo's *Hernani*, in the privileging of Goethean "elective affinities" over
prescriptive ties, in Sophie Mereau's abhorrence of the "coercion" figured
in the "trellised tree" of this chapter's epigraph. It is no surprise that Anne
Lister, the early nineteenth-century diarist who left ample evidence of her
sapphic relationships, aligned herself with the Rousseau of the *Confessions*, quoting in her journal the opening passage that became a Romantic
watchword: "I know my heart, and I know people; I am not made like anyone that I have seen; I dare to believe that I am not made like anyone who
exists. If I'm not more worthy, at least I am different."[8]

Lister's cathexis to Rousseau notwithstanding, Romantic culture
never fully embraced the sexual liberty of women and arguably relies on
the domesticating social imaginary that propelled republican strategies
everywhere in Europe after the most radical promises of revolution faded.[9]
Romanticism indeed has been well recognized for what Alan Richardson
calls its "colonizing" of the feminine as the repository of sensibility in the
service of the natural.[10] In this light, Romantic male subjectivity already
embraces the feminine, whether in the men who "seem to be becoming
more and more like women," as Margaret Waller puts it,[11] or in the binding
of woman to man as twin, double, mother, sister, or muse: in other words,
similitude in the context of Romantic ideology is itself rendered heterosexual and thus, within the framework I have been adopting, metamor-

phic. If such representations do not erase patriarchy but merely rewrite it in subtler terms, they also seductively figure the feminine as essential in both senses of the word.

This Romantic re-formation gives the sapphic couple a generative potential, binding woman to woman in ways that both intensify the feminine and queer it, allowing the same-sex couple to figure at once as domesticated and transgressive and thus as a site for reconciling contrary imperatives—if, as I will show, at its own expense. Stuart Curran has quipped that "there is little sex, seldom an actual body, and virtually no romance in Romanticism";[12] if so, then Romanticism's allusive relationship to sexuality well suits the representational demands of a moment in which explicit female homoeroticism has been subjected, especially but not only in France, to virulent attack followed mostly by (injunctions to) silence. Importantly, in the Romantic inscription of the sapphic, it is neither the individual nor the sect that now becomes the site of possibility, but the couple, figured as harmonious pair whose shared sensibility might also bridge differences of class or background. At the same time, though, the heterosocial imperative of Romantic similitude—a similitude that departs dramatically from the homosocial similitude of a century earlier—together with the gendered limits of Romantic ideology, converge to figure that idyllic harmony of the female couple as a kind of death knell, with the sapphic ushering, as it were, the era of a family formation in which it has no future of its own.

I begin this analysis with recourse to a work written just before the eve of the French Revolution by exploring the sapphic underpinnings of the period's most popular novel, Jacques-Henri Bernardin de Saint-Pierre's *Paul et Virginie* (1788). The idealization of a female couple in and as natural harmony takes related but distinctive forms in Elisabeth Maria Post's novel *Het Land* (1788) and in two tribute poems to Butler and Ponsonby— Anna Seward's "Llangollen Vale" (1795) and William Wordsworth's much later sonnet, "To the Lady E.B. and the Hon. Miss P." (1824). I then take up the deployment of irregular prosody as a significant feature of several poems that figure the sapphic, including Dorothy Wordsworth's "Irregular Verses," Percy Bysshe Shelley's "Rosalind and Helen" (1818), Therese Huber's pastiche novel *Die Ehelosen* (1829) and, as a particular limit case, Coleridge's "Christabel" (1816), which I explore both on its own terms and as the site of a contest around "family values" in conjunction with its excision from the 1800 *Lyrical Ballads*. Together, these texts create elegiac contours that enable a certain instrumentality of signification for same-sex intimacies, though at a cost to those intimacies themselves.

SAPPHIC FAMILY VALUES

Published on the eve of the French Revolution, Bernardin de Saint-Pierre's
Paul et Virginie (1788) is possibly the single most popular work of the
late eighteenth century, running through over thirty French editions and
twenty translations in the 1790s alone, including fifteen printings of three
different English translations, and producing stage adaptations in English
and Spanish and a song by the composer of "La Marseillaise."[13] That popularity is worth noting given the irregular family values on which the text
is founded: while the quasi-incestuous relationship between Paul and Virginie is the most obvious of these transgressions, the intense intimacy between their mothers did not go unnoticed at the time. This intimacy is all
the more significant given that *Paul et Virginie* was not just an extremely
popular novel but a social blueprint read and debated as such. The work's
preface leaves no doubt: the novel was aimed at a "several great truths—
among others, this: that our happiness consists in living according to nature and virtue."[14] And the basis for "nature and virtue" in this novel is
what I will call a sapphic motherhood grounded in a critique of the wrongs
of woman.

Indeed, *Paul et Virginie* carries a certain unexpected continuity with
the *Confession d'une jeune fille* and may even bear traces of its influence.
Like the anandryne utopias I discussed in chapter 6, the plot of *Paul et
Virginie* is motivated by the tragic consequences of women's cross-sex relationships and their determination to create a world that safeguards virtue, embraces worth over birth, and promotes universal happiness. Marguerite has been seduced and abandoned by a gentleman; Madame de la
Tour (as the text persists in naming her) was widowed after she and her
lesser-born husband escaped her family's wrathful response to their marriage. Both women have crossed boundaries of rank and convention that
Paul et Virginie is bent on dismantling: "the misfortunes of one mother
had arisen from having neglected marriage, those of the other from having
submitted to its laws: one had been made unhappy by attempting to raise
herself above her humble condition of life, the other by descending from
her rank."[15] In the isolated pastoral setting of the Ile-de-France (Mauritius),
they find a perfect sympathy with one another that rejects Europe's "cruel
prejudices [cruel préjugés]" for the horizontal values that they also vest
in their children, who are to "enjoy at once the pleasures of love, and the
blessings of equality" (22) [des plaisirs de l'amour, et du bonheur de l'égalité
(19)]. It cannot go without saying that this world of "equality" does not extend to the liberation of slaves but only to their "fair" treatment: even as

it denounces the cruelties of some slave-owners, *Paul et Virginie* fails to support abolition despite its author's own belief in a cause that was then reaching a peak of intensity. It is in the two white families that relative equality and freedom rest.

The intimacy between Marguerite and Mme. De la Tour is effectively conjugal, a marriage of natural affinity. The love that underwrites both the narrative and the utopia is as much theirs as their children's; Mme. de la Tour finds in Marguerite "more goodness" than she has "ever experienced from my own relations!" (10).[16] The narrator, godfather to both children, puts it thus: "United by the tie of similar wants, and the sympathy of similar misfortunes, they gave each other the tender names of companion, friend, sister.—They had but one will, one interest, one table. All their possessions were in common."[17] And in the kind of demurral we see so often when female intimacy is idealized, but here with an elegaic quality already in evidence, he assures us that "if sometimes a passion, more ardent than friendship, awakened in their hearts the pang of unavailing anguish, a pure religion, united with chaste manners, drew their affections towards another life; as the trembling flame rises towards heaven, when it no longer finds any aliment on earth" (18).[18] Yet the physicality of their shared maternity is presented in queer and arguably prurient detail: "They delighted to place their infants together in the same bath, to nurse them in the same cradle, and sometimes changed the maternal bosom at which they received nourishment, as if to blend with the ties of friendship that instinctive affection which this act produces." The children are thus in some sense the offspring of a same-sex marriage, figured textually in an elaborate image: "we shall each of us have two children, and each of our children will have two mothers. As two buds which remain on two trees of the same kind, after the tempest has broken all their branches, produce more delicious fruit, if each, separated from the maternal stem, be grafted on the neighbouring tree; so those two children, deprived of all other support, imbibed sentiments more tender than those of son and daughter, brother and sister, when exchanged at the breast of those who had given them birth" (21–22).[19] As "mères de lait," so to speak, Madame de la Tour and Marguerite are physically intimate through the mediation of their children. Motherhood here configures not only a new kind of sapphic family but a new kind of conjugality.

In deploying the joint images of an "untamed" island and a fatherless family, *Paul et Virginie* cements a relationship between the sapphic and supposedly uncorrupted nature that doubly distances this world from patriarchal "civilization." Clearly this utopia covers over a range of disturbances to conventional family life; if class is the spoken one, sapphic the covert one, and incest the one the text must struggle to overcome, slavery is the openly displayed worm in the bud that is never acknowledged as such; Madame de la Tour and Marguerite are benevolent slave-owners whose single slaves likewise join in marriage. Everyone is paired up, but the Adam-and-Eve that begins this little family is a female couple in a reverse-Edenic paradigm restored to prelapsarian purity after the Fall. Such a conjugal grouping clearly undermines the longstanding notion of a family as a paternal and hierarchical arrangement: although the narrator lends a grandfatherly presence as the godfather of both children, it is paternal absence that makes this family possible. What we have here is the kind of "botanic family" that Bendta Schroeder describes with respect to a set of contemporaneous English novels as rejecting "'artificial' forms of traditional consanguineal and affinal kinship" in favor of a "natural" affiliation supported by the "dynamism" of "organic forms," building family "on the basis of sympathy rather than the ties of family, class, and nation" in a way that seems to be "offered as a starting point for the transformation of the social body."[20]

Unlike the heteronormative familial models of the novels by Radcliffe, Smith, and Owenson that Schroeder studies, however, Bernardin de Saint-Pierre's sapphic family is denied its reproductive, hence future, force. After Virginie is sent to the corrupting metropole and drowns in shipwreck on the return when she is too modest to throw off her clothes, the utopia moves to the graveyard, where Paul, the two mothers, and their enslaved servants follow Virginie in death. The setting that forged a harmony of wild and carefully cultivated landscape as the ground for a new society becomes a literal burying ground, a memorial to the progeny that could have been. Thus the sentimental novel that gripped Europe from the eve of the French Revolution through the new century owes its foundation to a same-sex marriage that nourished the boy and girl whose tragic fate was the primary focus of popular investment. But what the story buries, the text renders iconic. The sapphic is necessary for wresting the family from its European contours, and must be paid homage, but it must be rendered obsolete.

Monumentalizing female intimacy is the direct object of another version of sapphic utopia published in the same year as *Paul et Virginie*. Explicitly anti-reproductive and elegaic from the outset, Elisabeth Post's *Het Land* [The Country] (1788), which I mentioned in chapter 5 for its use of epistolary confidence, gathers its religious and rural values to erect same-sex intimacy on a landscape that becomes the setting for a shared tomb

Fig. 7. Illustration from Elisabeth Post's *Het Land, in Brieven* (1788)
emphasizing the imbrication of female intimacy, landscape, and death. The
caption reads simply, "There appeared a graveyard, to which you brought
me." Courtesy of Harry Elkins Widener Collection, Harvard University.

(see fig. 7). Eufrozyne, the city-dweller, and Emilia, doyenne of the countryside, commit themselves to one another rather than run the risks of
relationships with men. Expressions of their intimacy are plentiful and
effusive as Emilia and Eufrozyne vow a friendship "stronger than love"
and "fall into each other's arms."[21] But their relationship, bound to the
natural landscape of the countryside as the title suggests, is always one of
melancholy, of "somber desire [sombere wellust]."[22] Indeed, at a moment
when the two friends are reunited, they literally walk the path to their

future grave, and in the moment most emblematic of the friendship, they choose a gravesite and plan for a tomb that they will share, making their strongest vows at the site where their bodies will be interred together. Eufrozyne says to Emilia, "Oh, how you move my heart! The grave of my Emelia must be mine as well; one gravestone should cover us both while the willow tree will weep over our slumbering ashes." The account of Eufrozyne's death closes the novel, which ultimately suggests that friendship not only extends beyond the grave but is meant for the afterlife: as Eufrozyne promises, "as in life, we will never be separated in eternity. Our beautiful friendship can thus last forever."[23] We have here not simply a marking of same-sex affiliation as transcendent; we have its marking as *only* transcendent: it cannot be of this world.

In *Het Land* we have a stark rejection of reproductive relations in favor of an idealizing same-sex "marriage" that sees its futurity in both a heavenly union and an earthly tomb. The union through motherhood that is effected in *Paul et Virginie*, which likewise ends without future in a grave shared by parents and children, is simply short-circuited in Post's novel on a direct and indeed literal path from friendship's embrace to the embrace of the grave. But the project of monumentalizing here is significant and powerful. *Paul et Virginie* remarks explicitly on the *absence* of "monument"—that symbol of civilization—upon the communal grave at Ile de France: as the narrator says here, "No marble covers the turf, no inscription records their virtues; but their memory is engraved upon our hearts, in characters, which are indelible"—and engraved as well, of course, in the novel's own words. But Emilia and Eufrozyne are determined that their relationship be inscribed on the very earth they claim to be so eager to abandon.

Such a memorializing gesture, however fictional, is worth attention, all the more as it will be shared by so many other Romantic-era texts. We know from Alan Bray's *The Friend* the importance of joint burial both for couples themselves and for the public preservation of a history of sexuality. Bray himself found only two tombs, across the long period before 1800, in which female friends are interred together. That the fictional characters of Elisabeth Post's novel are bent on this form of futurity is thus significant, all the more at a historical moment when, doubtless stimulated by Thomas Gray's famous memorial to a male intimate in "Elegy Written in a Country Churchyard" (1751), the graves even of fictional characters such as Susanna Rowson's Charlotte Temple were becoming sites of sentimental pilgrimage.

A seemingly more earthly paradise that will also turn elegiac characterizes poetic representations of the Lady Eleanor Butler and Sarah Ponsonby—another status-crossing female couple—whose pastoral idyll at their Welsh cottage, aptly named Plas Newydd (New Place) in one more marker of the sapphic as innovation—became a celebrated site of literal and literary pilgrimage. It is possible that a work like *Paul et Virginie* (and, if only in the Dutch context, *Het Land*, which was apparently not translated) may have helped to encourage the idealization of couples like Butler and Ponsonby or the renowned Dutch literary couple Aagje Deken and Betje Wolff, who were similarly idealized in relation to their pastoral home "Lommerlust";[24] such an idealization surely preserved both couples from what could have been a public pillorying like that given in print to Anne Damer in England and in body to the princesse de Lamballe in France. Notably, the shared gravesites both of Butler and Ponsonby (erected in St. Colen Churchyard, Llangollen) and of Deken and Wolff (in Scheveningen) would soon add to the scant number of actual memorials to female couples, creating family plots that bear out what Sha calls "the Romantic disregard for reproduction" or, put differently, turn monument itself into reproduction of a different sort.[25]

In Anna Seward's "Llangollen Vale" (1795), Butler and Ponsonby are heroized within a wild utopian pastoral not unlike that of *Paul et Virginie*. Claudia Kairoff rightly sees in "Llangollen Vale" Seward's critique of European politics as "Sara" and "Eleanora" transform a site of war into a site of peace.[26] In the process, Seward naturalizes the "sacred Friendship" of Butler and Ponsonby even as she evokes a "Vestal lustre" that could easily implicate the ambiguous history of sapphic "mysteries" that I discussed in chapter 6.[27] Butler and Ponsonby become heroes for resisting the "stern Authorities"; the women are "High-born, and high-endow'd" but—in a nice pun—"peerless" as they "scorn" the "Pride, Pomp, and Love" of the fashionable world for a "Fairy Palace" that is protected from "the storms of Winter" where their "Energy and Taste" (6–7) creates an idyllic setting perhaps more conventionally European than that of Bernardin's novel but similarly self-forged. Portraying the natural surroundings much more than the cottage or its inhabitants, Seward naturalizes a same-sex marriage much as Rowe did in his 1701 "Song" (see chapter 3) but with much more elaboration. Standing as a model to "the prouder sex," this "pure Friendship" carries the "steadiest lustre" of "Virtue" in woman's "own soft sex" (9). The pair who were in reality heir to the strongest prejudices of their class are here presented as without any "withering influence" of envy or bigotry and as paragons of "endowment" and "Charity" (11).[28] In this way, the women's lives are set at one with the "luxuriant Vale" (1) itself.

Yet in a turn of temporality, the poem's final stanzas turn once again toward the immortality that mortality alone ensures. The first part of "Llangollen Vale" has traced a long and bloody story, but once the poem rescues the vale for female friendship by settling Sara and Eleanora into domestic bliss, it turns to tracing the more minute diurnal rhythms of the couple's retired life. In so doing, though, it intensifies the images of shadow and darkness that permeate the poem, affirming in the landscape itself a "gloom," a "shadowy elegance," "dark woods," "dark expanse," "dark cowl" (8–11) until, in a rather startling move, the poem celebrates not the continuing life of the couple but their death. In this way what amounts to an apostrophe to Butler and Ponsonby, to whom the poem is "inscribed," becomes an elegy, even an epitaph. In the last two stanzas, the speaker imagines the couple's deaths—or rather death, since the end is presented as Romantically singular, a shared fate in which "lengthen'd Life" will simply "subside in soft decay" without pain or sorrow until "one kind ice-bolt" puts an end to it (11). The poem's final image is not of the two women, but of their grave and the memorializing that of course requires their demise: "While all who honor Virtue, gently mourn / LLANGOLLEN'S VANISH'D PAIR, and wreath their sacred urn" (11) (see fig. 8). In other words, in an idealizing tribute to a female couple, women at the time aged forty and fifty-six who will live for more than thirty years are, poetically speaking, killed off;[29] Seward preserves the idea of the couple at the expense of the couple's life. As we will see, this trope that also characterizes *Paul et Virginie* and *Het Land* will have a persistent place in Romantic representations of the sapphic, but its presence in this text, inscribed as it is to the women whose death it imagines, has a particularly disconcerting resonance. Perhaps not incidentally, Anna Seward's late-published poems to Honora Sneyd, the foster sister whom she loved, are likewise elegiac, and far before Sneyd's death in 1780.[30]

William Wordsworth's sonnet of 1824, "To the Lady E.B. and the Hon. Miss P," provides yet another idealizing representation of Butler and Ponsonby, with memorializing but also normalizing implications:

> A Stream, to mingle with your favourite Dee,
> Along the Vale of Meditation flows;
> So styled by those fierce Britons, pleased to see
> In Nature's face the expression of repose;
> Or haply there some pious hermit chose
> To live and die, the peace of heaven his aim;
> To whom the wild sequestered region owes,
> At this late day, its sanctifying name.

Glyn Cafaillgaroch, in the Cambrian tongue,
In ours, the Vale of Friendship, let this spot
Be named; where, faithful to a low-roofed Cot,
On Deva's banks, ye have abode so long;
Sisters in love, a love allowed to climb,
Even on this earth, above the reach of Time![31]

Titled to convey nothing so much as title itself, the poem creates an idyll of the natural to displace sexual intimacy and foreignness through re-naming and metaphor, turning the couple named only through initials into an English family. Its addressees appear only twice, and only as pro-nouns, before the thirteenth line, like Seward's "Llangollen Vale" sub-ordinating Butler and Ponsonby to the landscape, as an elaborate set of synecdoches substitutes the place for the persons rather than evoking the persons by the place. Instead of the "mingling" of Butler and Ponsonby, we get the "mingling" of stream and river; the women "favour" the river rather than one another; they "have abode so long" not with each other but "on Deva's banks." These images both naturalize and neutralize the marital relationship, and when their love is finally proclaimed twice over in the closing couplet, it arrives in the safe trope of sisterhood. The domes-ticity of the pair is emphasized in their fidelity not to one another but to "a low-roofed Cot," a "flat" image oddly dissonant with the imposing enough gothic home of whose improvements Butler and Ponsonby were so proud. In the sonnet's last couplet, however, the love is "allowed to climb," lan-guage that perhaps suggests its transgressive struggle, and in transcending "the reach of Time," it receives immortality and perhaps even sublimity.

In this process, William Wordsworth's sonnet also reclaims a queer and, by 1824, elderly Anglo-Irish couple settled in Wales for normative Englishness. Although "fierce Britons" have already supplied a sanctifying place-name, Wordsworth displaces the "Cambrian tongue" to rename the Glyn Cafaillgaroch as the Vale of Friendship, in effect engulfing whatever is fierce or wild into English gentility. That the sonnet *is* a cover story is underscored by the private account of William Wordsworth's only visit to Llangollen, which was later published with the poem. There Butler and Ponsonby appear to him a bizarre and rather gothic pair: "so curious was the appearance of these ladies, so elaborately sentimental about them-selves and their 'Caro Albergo,' as they named it in an inscription on a tree that stood opposite," and "so oddly was one of these ladies attired that we took her, at a little distance, for a roman Catholic priest. . . . They were without caps, their hair bushy and white as snow, which contributed to the mistake."[32] Such a passage makes clear the selectivity of the images in the sonnet and the project of substitution that erases Butler and Ponsonby's strange, curious, odd, old, and foreign style. What Wordsworth achieves, then, is to normalize and pastoralize what is clearly a transgressive relationship in a way that allows the love of two women to "transcend" fierceness and foreignness—and time itself—to embody a domestic English ideal.

This taming of the sapphic and its engagement with bourgeois notions of family are clearer if we compare William Wordsworth's sonnet to the "Irregular Verses" that Dorothy Wordsworth composed and revised during the same period. Although the poem was not published in Dorothy Wordsworth's lifetime and is thus technically tangential here, she did make at least three fair copies of the text and may have sent the poem to the daughter of her beloved friend Jane Pollard, whose loss she grieves. I address it for its value as a bridge to exploring the "irregularities" that other texts and even William's slight sonnet build into their prosody in the engagement with the sapphic couple. While "Irregular Verses" may not have been responding directly to William's sonnet, it revises some of his images as it imagines a sapphic pastoral much like the one at Plas Newydd: a life "exquisite and pure" in "a cottage in a verdant dell" enveloped by plenitude.[33] But Dorothy infuses sexuality into the scene. Where William described Butler and Ponsonby as faithful to a "low-roofed Cot," Dorothy and Jane raise "a tower / Of bliss" (lines 14–15). Their stream does not merely "mingle" but "foams"; their wanderings "to the topmost height" are invited rather than simply allowed; there is no "lack" (22, 34) This project of "hope untamed" (36) is not "vexed" by "maxims of caution" or "prudent fears" (17). In "A Holiday at Gwerndovennant," a poem written during the same year for which "Irregular Verses" is the subtitle, Dorothy sets this same kind of woodland cottage against the phallic sublimity of a "Kubla Khan": "the shelter of our rustic Cot / Receives us, & we envy not / The palace or the stately dome."[34]

Like so many of these texts, if for reasons more closely resembling the elegaic in a poet like Elizabeth Carter or Katherine Philips, "Irregular Verses" turns toward loss, in this case toward the barren reality of separation; suddenly "the cottage fled in air" (39) and the "streamlet never flowed" (40) as Jane is "by duty led" (44) to trade the "brighter gem" of same-sex pastoral for a "prince's diadem" (55) and a daughter who is "placid" and "staid" (96). Here we have a stark contrast between sapphic coupling and the reproductive family. This love too transcends its moment, but even more elegaically: in the last two lines, the poet claims that her heart "has

still kept time / With every pulse of thine" (106–7). Here again, the sapphic
is at once the idyllic figuration of perfect intimacy and an intimacy that
can flourish only in memory or, one might add, in textuality. For although
I will argue for a less sublime reason beneath the elegizing in so many of
these texts, George Haggerty is surely right to see the elegy as the form
par excellence for enabling the sublimity and futurity of the queer couple,
something nowhere clearer than in his own essay "Love and Loss: An Elegy," that is also built around a Romantic poem, Shelley's "Adonais."[35] It
is perhaps significant that Dorothy Wordsworth's poem is the only one of
these late instances in which the elegizing is performed by the lover rather
than by an external voice. It is also the only one of these not published at
the time of its composition, and even this poem does not enact the sapphic
apostrophe of the earlier period since for most of the poem Dorothy is
speaking not to Jane but about Jane to that "staid" daughter Julia. In one
draft, however, the poem does end with five lines directed to Jane herself
(now deceased), in eerie resonance with the ending of William's poem in
terms of its evocation of the temporal: Dorothy speaks of herself as "one
whose heart has still kept time / With every pulse of thine." Here too,
even as time is eulogized, the sapphic is consigned to afterlife.[36]

THE POETICS OF IRREGULARITY

In titling her poem "Irregular Verses" and using "irregular" in the titles
of three other poems that also express loss and longing, Dorothy Wordsworth may have had nothing sapphic in mind. But it is worth noting
that in the eighteenth century the word "irregular" was used frequently
enough to describe individuals whose sexuality might not conform to expectations. Irregularity turns up in this sense as early as Manley's *New
Atalantis* in 1709, figures in the 1755 autobiography of the cross-dressing
Charlotte Charke, and describes the "fancy" of the sapphic Miss Hobart in
the 1811 English translation of Anthony Hamilton's *Memoirs of the Count
de Grammont*. It is thus interesting and perhaps significant that claims of
irregularity characterize more than one poem with sapphic content and
perhaps significant that in Dorothy Wordsworth's "Irregular Verses," the
most glaring (though far from the only) metrical aberrance—a single line
of heptameter—breaks the poem in two at just the moment of breach in
the speaker's relationship: "Though in our riper years we each pursued a
different way" (line 43).[37] It is thus especially interesting that both claims
and practices of poetic irregularity characterize more than one sapphic
representation, possibly signifying a more than metrical departure from

the rules. For "irregularity" turns up as an explicit practice not only in several of Dorothy Wordsworth's poems but in at least two other long poems with female intimacies as central content, Coleridge's "Christabel" (1816) and Percy Shelley's "Rosalind and Helen," and characterizes the narrative form of Therese Huber's novel *Die Ehelosen* as well.[38]

Subtitled "A Modern Eclogue" (1818), a phrase that, whatever its intentions, repeats the link between female same-sex relations and modernity that has been so persistent over the period of this study, "Rosalind and Helen" also appropriates the Virgilian pastoral for female intimacy. A rather obvious reinscription of *Paul et Virginie* and one in which incest is likewise and more horrifically entangled, Shelley's long poem reunites two unhappy women, previously estranged, now effectively exiled and without familial resources, mothers who will together raise Rosalind's daughter and Helen's son. The poem is also prefaced by a disclaimer, rare if not unique in Shelley's *oeuvre*, that "the impulse of the feelings which moulded the conception of the story, determined the pauses of a measure, which only pretends to be regular inasmuch as it corresponds with, and expresses, the irregularity of the imaginations which inspired it."[39] Irregular imaginations arguably abound in "Rosalind and Helen," given the persistent motif of illegitimate desire in the tragic histories that Rosalind and Helen tell one another: of Rosalind's unwitting love for her half brother and Helen's passionate relationship outside wedlock with Lionel, of the cruelty of Rosalind's unhappy marriage and the horrific legendary incest written into the history of the place itself—all signs of mismatch between social institution and personal desire. But "Rosalind and Helen" also projects a sapphic family resolution that, as John Donovan argues, "transforms into a critical and revisionary feminism that is plotted so as to close on an image that marries the domestic and the sublime."[40]

While this sublime and domestic union of two women is never articulated as sexual—though the Shakespearean "Rosalind" is suggestive—there is a notable marking of the early tension between the two women as a bodily phenomenon, and they end up living together in maternal-marital harmony like the mothers of *Paul et Virginie*. When Helen and Rosalind meet after a long estrangement, although Helen asks her "sweet Rosalind" to "come sit by me" and recalls the "cherished token" of Rosalind's "woven hair" (36–37) that she still keeps, Rosalind speaks of Helen's "tainting touch" (42) and Helen of Rosalind as "strange" (91). When Helen finally takes Rosalind's hand at evening, the text makes a point to say that Helen is now "*un*repelled" (my emphasis). While this "taint" and "repulsion" can be explained on one level by the friends' painful history, it sits upon the text as a queer obstacle that the text itself must overcome before the two women can settle with their children in the "clean and white" "English home" (1261) that has effectively been transported to the "solitude" of an Italian lake.

As in the previous texts I have been describing, the "marriage" of the two women is in narrative terms eclipsed and short-lived, for the poem devotes much less attention to Rosalind and Helen's union than to their deaths. To be sure, the final message attempts to move the sapphic, yet again, beyond "the reach of time": "if love die not in the dead / As in the living, none of mortal kind / Are blest, as now Helen and Rosalind" (1316–18). Shelley does not follow Bernardin de Saint-Pierre in killing off the children; Helen's son and Rosalind's daughter, unnamed and thus all the more iconic, like Paul and Virginie "fed / From the same flowers of thought," unite "like springs which mingle in one flood" to give their mothers "peace" "in their union" (1289–91). And in a word that eerily echoes the image of Butler and Ponsonby's death in "Llangollen Vale," a tomb of "lasting ice" is raised upon a hill for Rosalind first, and then Helen, led there "slowlier." The poem's last line sustains the union: no longer among the living, but again the progenitors of a new kind of family, Helen and Rosalind are "blest" in death (1318). A poem that could have ended simply with the creation of the happy family of two women and their children, once again insists on taking its female couple to and beyond the grave. The good sapphic couple, we may start to be surmising, is the dead one. That couple is instrumental only insofar as it can be relocated to posterity.

Once again, prosody embodies this configuration. In "Rosalind and Helen" as in Dorothy Wordsworth's poem, "irregularity" marks the distinction—though in the reverse direction—between a tragic history of patriarchal family and a happy same-sex union. The dominant metrics of the poem change at just the point where both women have finished relating their sad histories and Rosalind is being led off to Helen's home: from over 1,200 lines in which tetrameter has been dominant the poem moves to pentameter, retaining, however, the irregular rhyme scheme, which varies widely throughout the poem. And without reducing metrics to sexuality, I would note that even William Wordsworth's sonnet to Butler and Ponsonby is irregular within the context of his *oeuvre*: while the overwhelming majority of his sonnets are Petrarchan, "To the Lady E.B. and the Hon. Miss P." is mainly Spenserian, with an oddly Petrarchan third quatrain, and its final rhymed couplet is a rarity among Wordsworth's 500-odd sonnets.[41] One could argue that this couplet—"Sisters in love, a love allowed to climb, / Even on this earth, above the reach of Time!"—puts both the poem and the "sisters" to a rather emphatic rest.

Therese Huber's late and rather convoluted novel *Die Ehelosen* (1829) provides an even more dramatically mortal articulation of sapphic coupling. In one major and elaborately recounted strand of a longer work, *Die Ehelosen* makes the case that marriage is simply not good for women. Marie, for example, refuses an arranged marriage for a chosen one, yet finds her life far from blissful and dies young. Justine and Zoe are similarly unhappily married, and Anna, already disillusioned by the two unhappy marriages of her mother, finds happiness in raising her half-siblings and later in nurturing the daughter of a friend. Throughout the novel, charity and nurturance are posted as the highest good, though a good that, it is made clear, must not come at the cost of personal happiness.

It is thus significant that the most enduring relationship in the novel, and the one that forms the basis for the happiness of its most positive character, Elisabeth, is an intimate friendship presented as clearly superior even to a promising love between a woman and a man. Elisabeth finds herself deeply attracted to the ill and "angelic" Sophie—so attracted that the novel itself shifts from third- to first-person narration when it articulates Elisabeth's fascination with Sophie's frail but beautiful body: "her first youth was already vanished" and she was even emaciated, yet "she was still the most attractive being that my eyes ever came upon. Thin as a lily stem, and such a perfect physique that her thinness robbed none of her beauty."[42] In acknowledging the depth of her feelings for Sophie, Elisabeth realizes that marriage to Hugo, to whom she is engaged, will never fulfill her. Even Hugo himself recognizes that "her bond as friend is much more intimate than her devotion to him."[43] After Sophie's death, therefore, Elisabeth determines not to marry and creates a life of what the text describes as "geistige Mutterschaft," a spiritual motherhood realized in founding a school, in a pastoral setting, that educates working-class women and girls. In a departure from the other texts I have been describing, Sophie and Elisabeth are not even allotted a full earthly life together, yet it is their love, and Sophie's catalytic presence, that allows Elisabeth to thrive. Here too, however, death shadows the same-sex couple, and here too, the novel changes its narrative dynamics in ways that underscore the primacy of this relationship.

In all of these texts from *Paul et Virginie* through *Die Ehelosen*, then, relations between women sit at a point of negotiation between the transgressive and the utopian, the fatal and the familial. To be sure, loss and dying permeate much Romantic discourse especially in the context of love that is unrequited, misbegotten, or disallowed. Nor, as I have suggested earlier, is elegy new to sapphic representations at the end of the eighteenth century. But in every case except Dorothy Wordsworth's, these relationships are presented as fulfilled and fulfilling. The mothers of Paul and Virginie die because they lose their children, but the more gratuitous moves of taking Eleanora and Zara, Eufrozyne and Emilia, Helen and Rosalind, and Elisabeth's Sophie to the grave seem to be serving other purposes. I read this practice as simultaneously marking a limit case for the Romantic confrontation with sapphic subjects and an acknowledgement, in the way that Haggerty rightly sees as so significant, that same-sex relations should not be allowed to pass from memory. In a sense, female relations are creating utopias in which they themselves turn out to have no place but in memory—truly, then, *utopic* for the women themselves even as *place* becomes a memorial setting. All of them, however, wed same-sex intimacy to a natural order in ways that recuperate its positivity in some progeny or movement. This will not be the case with Coleridge's "Christabel," which arguably perverts those familial tropes in what is probably the most controversial of sapphic Romantic texts. It is not surprising, then, that "Christabel" also became enmeshed in the family politics of Wordsworth and Coleridge's *Lyrical Ballads.*

ALL IN THE FAMILY

If "Christabel" seems a jarring intruder into this conversation, then this chapter is mirroring the response that was not uncommon when the poem was finally published in 1816. Although the encounter between Geraldine and Christabel in part 1 of the poem is shrouded in mystery, the poem makes clear as much through its silences as through its images that something sapphic happens in Christabel's bed on the fateful night of Geraldine's appearance. Geraldine herself and the scene of seduction are represented metonymically: we know Geraldine as a "faint and sweet" voice, as white garments and a whiter neck, as bright eyes, a "bosom" and "half [a]side."[44] We know that both women undress and become the objects of one another's gaze; that Geraldine "had" her "will" with Christabel after a psychic struggle with Christabel's dead "wandering mother"; that Geraldine's "spell" becomes "lord" of Christabel's "utterance"; and that the "touch" of a "bosom" reveals a "mark" of "shame" that creates a tightness "beneath [Christabel's] heaving breasts." We know that Christabel later recognizes that she has "sinn'd," but experiences only "perplexity of mind" about its occasion. Of what passes in the bed we know only that Geraldine held "the maiden in her arms" and "worked" her "harms." The scene carries images of both pleasure and danger; that it is "a sight to dream of not to tell" suggest that the unspeakable may also be irresistible. And in a perverse doubling, it will be Sir Leoline, the father, who becomes infatuated with Geraldine, as Geraldine's presence among women in part 1 of the poem shifts, in a kind of queer metamorphic instance, to her figuration among men in part 2. As family romance, especially in relation to the pattern I have been describing, "Christabel" is itself a shadowed and disturbing "sight." We are far already from the family values of *Paul et Virginie* or the Llangollen "ladies" or Therese Huber's "geistige Mutterschaft."

Like "Rosalind and Helen," which it probably influenced, "Christabel" also announces itself as potentially "irregular": Coleridge prefaces the poem with a statement that its meter was "not, properly speaking, irregular, though it may seem so from its being founded on a new principle, namely, that of counting in each line the accents, not the syllables." "Nevertheless," he continues, "this occasional variation in number of syllables is not introduced wantonly, or for the mere ends of convenience, but in correspondence with some transition in the nature of the imagery or passion."[45] Much has been written about the metrics of "Christabel," and it is not my intention to argue that Coleridge's meter (which, as several critics have noted, he himself does not accurately describe)[46] is simply a function of the text's queer eroticism. But the preface does suggest some connection between the text's "imagery or passion" and its prosody, and Coleridge's choice of the term "wantonly" underscores the possibility that the "passion" in question is sexual. Certainly sexuality is here placed squarely in the nexus of family dynamics: relations among daughter, father, suitor, dead mother, and close friend are all complicated by Geraldine's appearance in the textual world.

It is not surprising that Coleridge never finished this poem, given the burden the first two parts would place on a resolution and given the reception the poem received. That reception begins as early as 1800, when the Wordsworths and Coleridge were revising the *Lyrical Ballads* into a new edition for which the completed parts of "Christabel" were to serve as the final poem. The oddly last-minute distress that the poem caused the Wordsworths, a change literally from one day to the next if Dorothy's journal is to be trusted,[47] led to its excision from the volume even though page proofs had to be destroyed and a new poem hastily written. While scholars continue to speculate about the reasons for the substitution, that new poem, Wordsworth's "Michael," offers an indirect answer. As Susan

Eilenberg notes, "Michael" appropriates many of the concrete details of "Christabel": "oak tree, faithful dog, troubling dream, and morally emblematic lamp," the alienation of children from parents, an old friend's evil to which a child is sacrificed.[48] It also revises "Christabel's" constructions of gender and sexuality to reinstate a safer family model, a heteronormative pastoral that is a paean to male bonding purged of foreignness. If "Christabel" offers us unholy aristocratic alliances forged by a queer woman, "Michael" recreates the poor but honest holy family of loving father, loving if hardly present mother, and beloved son. Michael himself is as much mother as father, doing "female service" to the child; as Michael rocks Luke's cradle "with a woman's gentle hand," the poem subordinates the need for the actual mother as much as the works on sapphic motherhood erase the father.[49] Of course insofar as Michael himself is feminized, we could also argue that his relationship with Isabel, though so little represented by the text, is rather like a marriage of two mothers. But at least on the surface, in substituting "Michael" for "Christabel," Wordsworth restores the dignity of the paterfamilias and privileges filial alliances between men over erotic relations between women. If Geraldine is a shapeshifter agent of domestic havoc, Michael is an agent of domestic happiness. "Michael" thus also recuperates the idealized maternal family of a *Paul et Virginie* for a differently gendered pastoral. Yet "Michael" too is elegaic; the beloved son must be sent to the "dissolute city" (line 444) to earn the family's way and, there corrupted, is forced to hide abroad; the property is sold "into a stranger's hand" (475), the parents die, and only the oak and an unfinished sheepfold remain in monument. In a sense, then, "Michael" replicates the family as queerly configured but without the sapphic transgressiveness of "Christabel."

In the early responses to "Christabel" when it finally was published in 1816, we can also read the status of more sexually disturbing sapphic representations during the first decades of the nineteenth century. Andrew Elfenbein reports that one anonymous reviewer called it "the most obscene poem in the English language," and another fretted that Geraldine's seduction of Christabel resembled "the spells of vicious example in real life."[50] Some of Coleridge's reviewers also imagined the proverbially "monstrous" sapphic body in Geraldine's hidden side, calling it "terrible and disgusting" and "all deformity."[51] Given such responses, the Wordsworths' substitution of "Michael" for "Christabel" was prescient. Intriguingly, Alaric Alfred Watts recounts his mother's report of a visit with Wordsworth in 1824 or 1825 in which the subject of "Christabel" came up; Wordsworth, she said, "'did not dissent from my expressions of admiration of this poem, but rather discomposed me by observing that it was an indelicate poem, a defect which it had never suggested itself to me to associate with it."[52] Wordsworth, in short, held over that quarter century to the dominant conservative view of "Christabel."

If we think back to the plethora of ribald public discourse about the sapphic that spans the two centuries from the 1590s to the 1790s, it becomes even clearer that public tolerance for overtly homoerotic discourse had waned by the early nineteenth century. I mentioned in the last chapter that the 1798 *Dictionnaire de l'académie française* added to the definition of "tribade," for the first time, "one avoids this word [on évite ce mot]." Even more emphatically, the Academy's 1832 Dictionary announces, "one avoids *using* this word [on évite *d'employer* ce mot]" (emphasis mine). We see a similar contrast in responses to Donne's "Sapho to Philaenis": as I noted in chapter 3, the poem engendered an elaborate imitation in 1728 that was well advertised in at least four newspaper editions. Yet in 1823, the scholar Joseph Spence argued that Donne's "Sapho to Philaenis" should not even be quoted because of its offensive subject, even though he conceded it to be "perhaps the most poetical" of Donne's epistles.[53] In this same period, two German plays that made a splash, Franz Grillparzer's *Sapho* (1818) and Adolph von Schaden's parody, *Die moderne Sappho* (1819), discredit Sappho with mockery, in the second instance including a sharp satire both on Sappho's homoerotic desire and on her literary aspirations.[54]

Particularly significant, in view of the emphases in this chapter, is the repeated evocation in the period between 1810 and 1830 of a dying, often suicidal, Sappho—that is, a Sappho who, though not necessarily sapphic, must like so many of the sapphic figures in the texts I have been discussing, be killed off. To be sure, the suicidal Sappho has a much longer life than this Romantic one, but the clustering in the early nineteenth century bears some scrutiny. French poetry is particularly rich in these representations. Magalon and Barginet's "La mort de Sapho" (1817), for example, effects a telling reversal of the notion of Sappho or the sapphic as modern, the suiciding Sappho marks herself as a figure of the nation's past, as if she is in the way of republican progress: evoking Greece to "be always free" and never be done in by discord, Sappho is to throw herself "into the past": in death lies hope.[55] Similarly and sapphically, Alphonse de Lamartine's "Sapho: élégie antique" (1815) bids farewell to a dying Sappho who pays the price for illicit love and who leaves behind the "cult" and its "virgins" who must now go into a future without her, again suggesting that the death of Sappho is the requisite for the next phase of modernity.[56]

These representations also suggest that the efficacy of the sapphic was waning. To be sure, female-female relations themselves were quietly taking their place in European culture at large. In the mid-1830s, as I suggested in the last chapter, the sapphic was to be particularly resonant in French Romantic writings such as Théophile Gautier's *Mademoiselle de Maupin*, George Sand's *Lelia*, and Honoré de Balzac's *La fille aux yeux d'or*. These texts were to begin to create a different history of sexuality, and to mark an end to one long era in the shaping of a sexuality of history.

We Have Always Been Modern

In the countless quarrels between Ancients and Moderns, the former come out winners as often as the latter now, and nothing allows us to say whether revolutions finish off the old regimes or bring them to fruition. . . . As I have suggested, however, we do not wish to become premoderns all over again.

—Bruno Latour, *We Have Never Been Modern*[1]

In the two hundred sixty-five years this book has spanned, the sapphic has repeatedly presented itself as modern even when it has entangled itself in ancient tropes. From Henri Estienne's French "girls" and Pontus de Tyard's "Dame enamourée" to Adolph von Schaden's "modern Sappho" and Shelley's "Modern Eclogue," the logic of woman + woman reappears as unexpected, unprecedented, or unaccountable whether it is welcomed or reviled. I take this recurrent novelty as a sign of the degree to which sapphic subjects continued to confound epistemic assumptions and yet kept demanding attention because modernity could not set their logic aside. This perverse inability of the social imaginary to resolve or reject the sapphic signals its complex potential to mark both social upheaval and social harmony. During the epoch of powerful transformations that I described in this book's first paragraph, the social imaginary struggled to sustain gender hierarchy as a still point of the turning world; this struggle gave the sapphic a particularly charged potential for engaging the confrontations that shape modernity as I have been conceiving it.

If we review the texts and trends encountered in these pages through my opening litany—consensual governance coexisting with colonial slavery; a print culture of increasing power; entrepreneurial mobility; challenges to hierarchical structures and class fixities; rising individualism;

deepening conjugality; and a stasis with respect to women's rights—we can see that sapphic representations are entangled in many of the phenomena that I believe the seventeenth and eighteenth centuries bequeathed to a later age. Looking at whether and where the sapphic has been engaged with those weighty changes may help us to understand what it means for sapphic representation to have traveled in circuitous pathways from the longings of Sapho for Philaenis to the romps of the *Sappho-an*, from the pornographic anecdotes of Aretino to the picaresque union of Mademoiselle de Richelieu and her Arabella, from the threat of a "Lodge of Lesbos" to the idyll of "sisters in love" and on to the different disturbance of a Christabel. That backward look may also illuminate some vexing questions. What changes, if any, can we chart in sapphic representation as national priorities and cultural dynamics shift? Even if we accept the link between the sapphic and the modern that I have posited, can we speak of progress or regress? How do metamorphic, ethnographic, and horizontal renderings fare respectively across the span of two centuries? Is it more than fanciful to think of modernity as a "sapphic episteme," and if so, at what cost? In sum, what does happen to or through sapphic subjects in the long early modern period, and with what significance for studying the past?

In framing this project within two periods of political upheaval, I was not, of course, suggesting that the sapphic fomented Dutch revolts and French revolutions, but rather that these events mark a long period of intellectual and social ferment in which questions of rights, power, and governance, mobility and stability, personal desire and collective imperative, are repeatedly subjected to textual and material pressure. In confronting the ways in which those challenges are figured through same-sex female relations, I have uncovered an unexpectedly tight alliance between the history of women and the history of the state. Certainly the emergence of social contract theories underscores the extent to which, despite some gestures toward equal standing, women ultimately lie outside them, bound as Carole Pateman has persuasively argued in a sexual contract from which the sapphic often figures as an attempt at extrication.[2] That print culture emerges during this period to create a potential leveling force against traditional hierarchies of state and religion also gives the sapphic a power that it could not have accrued on other terms. It seems to me particularly illuminating that the sapphic gets entangled on both sides of debates about governance and especially about the place of consent within a polity, for the logic of consent is itself deeply gendered across this period.

In representations of sapphic formations as viable human arrange-

ments, we see the radical implications of the new understandings of nature and desire that also challenge orthodoxies both religious and secular. These challenges will be cemented in a post-Romantic ideology of
the individual's right to the proverbial pursuit of happiness, although
counter-tendencies toward the regimentation of bourgeois subjects, and
ideologies of female service, will take equal hold of the social imaginary
to produce, across the next century, the complicated negotiations between
"individual" and "society" that continue to form the crux of the novel. My
revisionist history of that genre suggests that well before the Romantic
moment, picaresque and even domestic fictions were confronted, through
the sapphic, with the irrepressibility of desire and the instability of its
social management that undermine heteronormative projects. That even
domesticated versions of sapphic affiliation get bound up in the pastoral
and the elegaic at the turn of the nineteenth century, however, also suggests that the sapphic may have become instrumental to reconfiguring a
natural order in which it is not meant to have a place. The queer convergence of the sapphic with the "rising" novel, in settings as disparate as
late-seventeenth-century France, mid-eighteenth-century England, and
late-eighteenth-century Germany, provides an impetus for a broader and
deeper investigation of a confluence than my single chapter on the novel
has been able to embrace.

I have emphasized throughout this project, and especially in chapter 4,
the ways in which print could render the sapphic a mechanism for political pressure if not political power. I have not quite been willing to suggest
that the sapphic might have influenced rather than only exploited the possibilities of print that, to evoke the words of Victor Hugo which preface my
fourth chapter, turn schism to revolution. Only in the realm of the novel,
where I take on directly the force of female relations for shaping an emergent genre, have I declared this kind of agency for the sapphic as a print
phenomenon. But the very fact that the sapphic became inscribable, that
it appears so frequently in gratuitous contexts and functions through the
portability of anecdote, may have helped to foment a textual economy in
which rumor, secret history, newspaper account—all the stuff of the emergent sphere of public opinion—become a powerful discursive field. That at
the end of the eighteenth century we see injunctions toward silence—to
"avoid" the word "tribade" as the 1798 *Dictionnaire de l'Académie française* enjoins—does testify to the difficulty of silencing a discourse once
it is in play.

Thus, while a few key texts have been disproportionately lasting and
probably influential in shaping cultural production, I am speculating that

in most cases it is the aggregate rather than the individual instance that may have intervened in history. As I said at the outset of this book, there is rarely an easy way to prove the efficacy of any text. We are most likely to see suggestions of effect when texts refer to one another: surely one would be hard-pressed to doubt the influence of Genesis 3 and the figure of Eve in (mis)shaping centuries of theology, law, and culture in the Christian West. Many of the texts I study here, by contrast, leave few traces in the historical record. In that context, confluence and repetition are promising signs of effectiveness, and so where the texts I study have shown repeated patterns, allusions, or interrelationships, there their efficacy arguably dwells. And where this book has raised questions it did not answer, I hope that other scholars will see ways of interrogating further the patterns, constellations, and individual representations that I think deserve fuller scrutiny.

Surely contradictions and conundrums will abound. The shift from consanguineal to conjugal kinship, for instance, plays out in relation to the sapphic in conflicting ways. On the one hand, the specter of female erotic friendship so insistently inscribed may have encouraged a preemptive move within the social imaginary to reconfigure marriage as an ostensible union of friends. On the other hand, the changing marital model may also have opened the way for representations of lasting affiliation between women that we see both in novels like *The Travels and Adventures of Mademoiselle de Richelieu* and in the romanticized couplings of "sisters in love." In this regard, it may not be irrelevant that in so many of instances the same-sex couple is formed after, and often because, women have been rejected or betrayed by consanguineal ties. The conjugal is itself a mixed blessing; as Ruth Perry observes, "the weakening of consanguineal ties" left women "more dependent than ever before on the goodwill of their husbands" and deprived them of "power as sisters and daughters" even as "they gained social importance as mothers and wives."[3] And it is as mothers that Bernardin de Saint-Pierre's and Shelley's female couples, for example, form families. At the same time, however, the imaginative possibility that women could form independent households, a phenomenon that emerges into representation in the mid-eighteenth century in settings from Eliza Haywood's plots of rescue to Sally Paul's same-sex marriage to the educational project of the Anandrynes when they shelter girls in need, testifies to the ways in which textual preoccupation with the separation of women from consanguineal families may have enabled, and been enabled by, sapphic formations. The tragic implications of obeying parents that are played out in such novels as *Secresy* and *Die Honigmonathe* provide another brief for female intimacies as superior to those engineered by family.

Here, as in many of the sapphic apostrophes, we see the ways in which an emergent sense of the distinctiveness of persons and their desires helps to underwrite the primacy of choice as a modern imperative. If Mary Masters idealizes female relations in assuming that the bonds of friends are "stronger by far than Tyes of Blood" because "no Force nor Interest can compel" them, still the overwhelming dynamic of representation across the vast differences among my texts is precisely the sense of the sapphic as a voluntary tie, a dynamic that must also set itself against scenarios of duped women who have fallen for a woman in disguise. In this way too, the sapphic thus readily figures the individualist ethos long associated with modernity.

Modernity also figures as mobility, and throughout these chapters the sapphic subject has emerged as a signifier of mobility both social and geographic, and in both directions: mobility enables the sapphic, on the one hand, and the sapphic inscribes its consequences, on the other. Movement also embroils sapphic figures in the struggles of class difference, a repeated thread within the texts I have studied, whether utopically, in ways that celebrate cross-class alliances, or dystopically, in ways that make the sapphic the source of dangerous liaisons. Hence the intimate relationship between sapphic and picaresque not only in the literal sense of the novel but in the dynamics of forced or chosen movement, of upward mobility, and of the class disturbances that relations between women are understood to entail. The threat or promise of the unattachable woman, the woman who refuses to be anchored to the heterosocial status quo, is repeatedly configured in relation to class movement whether upward, as in stories of women who become men and marry better-positioned women, or downward, as in the few stories of women who forsake their status for sapphic affiliation. Where gender disguise or sex-change is entwined with the sapphic, it is of course the usurpation of male privilege that enables movement in space and status; in such instances it is arguably the metamorphic scenario of change in social gender that carries the most radical possibility. Despite the utopian potential of horizontal representation, metamorphosis is a much shorter circuit, even in representation, than the leveling project that would raise women to the status where they do not have to "be" men in order to partake in human rights or male privilege.

In the end, however, we probably cannot know whether sapphic representations aided or retarded women's rights. Certainly some such representations, from Fonte's *Il merito delle donne* in 1600 through the sapphic apostrophes of chapter 4 to Therese Huber's *Die Ehelosen* in 1829, insist on engaging the question of woman's place and thus participate in the

long slog towards female enfranchisement that will not occur formally
in any national government until the early twentieth century. The persistence of patriarchy indeed helps to explain the persistence of sapphic
discourse, particularly in forms that promote some form of sex separation
as one of the few ways by which women might experience a limited form
of freedom, wrested from that realm of necessity of which Fredric Jameson writes,[4] either within the space of the individual household, within
the utopia of a single-sex community, or only within the space of print.
As I have suggested, that quest for freedom keeps sapphic subjects on the
move, and thus the tropes of the picaresque invade more than the novel as
sapphic representations move through textual space and place.

Representations of the sapphic do engage with questions of colonialism and empire; the discourse around both bodies and customs often locates the sapphic in an orientalized space, as I have discussed especially
in chapters 2 and 3, and sometimes sapphic characters are associated with
colonial conquest. A related observation worth further pursuit is the way
in which the sapphic often enough appears in texts that also evoke other
others—Jews, for example—though without making direct connections
between the two—a sign, perhaps, of shared ways in which both Jewish
and sapphic textual subjects confound conventional social assumptions.
But there is relative silence within sapphic discourse around the practice
of slavery. That a novel like *Paul et Virginie* can build a pastoral utopia on
an island that is actually a slaveholding French colony of sugar plantations
and without questioning the idealized family's holding of slaves already
points to the fracture lines that dissolve one kind of hierarchy while promoting another. The frequent elitism of sapphic settings also suggests the
ways in which even in its utopian framings the sapphic relies on existing hierarchies of race and status more than it tries to dismantle them. In
this behavior, I suggest, eighteenth-century sapphic representations bear
some resemblance to eighteenth-century novels, where servants rarely
have voices or even names and where, with few exceptions, the problem of
slavery is not directly confronted. On the whole, then, I think it possible
to argue that the history of the eighteenth-century European novel is also
the history of the repression of slavery *from* the eighteenth-century European novel. The same seems to be true of the sapphic, and this similarity
strikes me as one more argument for suggesting, as I have done in passing in earlier chapters and in this coda as well, that the sapphic and the
novel share some deep similarities, worth further interrogation, in their
relationship to the modern.

In elaborating a temporal arc for this project, I have been suggesting

that "cycles of salience," to retain Valerie Traub's resonant phrase, characterize nearly every pattern of sapphic representation: there is no one textual formation that spans even a single country over these two and more
centuries. It is also clear that different genres and modes of representation
foster that temporally and geographically limited salience. If my research
is representative, only in England and France do we see a relatively consistent plethora of texts interacting within multiple discursive spheres
in some tandem with the ebb and flow of genres, across the full period,
though were we to graph these after the fashion of a Franco Moretti, they
too would reveal highs and lows. I find Spanish texts prevalent at the early
end of my time frame and German texts at the later end, Dutch texts on
the increase and Italian on the wane, for reasons that I have only begun
to examine and that I hope other scholars will pursue or, if my mapping
is inaccurate, correct. The purposes of sapphic representation likewise
vary across this long period: it is only, for example, in moments of intense
political turmoil that I have encountered direct interactions between the
sapphic and the state. At the same time, utopian figurations of sapphic relations cross through the centuries, if with differential tenors and effects.
One phenomenon that may have been elided by my use of the sapphic as
so large an umbrella is the distribution between explicitly and covertly
sexual representations. Utopian formulations come in both forms: there
is as much social blueprint in Donne's "Sapho to Philaenis" and Pidansat
de Mairobert's *Confession d'une jeune fille* as there is in Moderata Fonte's
more chaste *Il merito delle donne* or Anna Seward's still chaster "Llangollen Vale." Clearly, however, the compatibility of the sapphic with the
institutional is reliant on a certain elision of sex. Clearly too, texts that
imply sexual activity are more likely to engage in satire than in sentiment, especially in the English and German contexts though not necessarily in the French. The above-ground or underground status of a text
matters: much more can be made explicit in clandestine forms.

But perhaps the varying fortunes of metamorphic, ethnographic, and
horizontal representations tell the fullest tale. I have been suggesting
through the course of this book that metamorphic modes are already troubled by the early seventeenth century and that by the early eighteenth the
explicitly metamorphic has tended to wane. This is not quite the case in
the subtler formations of the novel, where female intimacies are supposedly set aside at the time of marriage, in that infamous formulation that
"marriage is the tomb of friendship" articulated by the heroine of Hannah
Foster's *The Coquette* (1797) but expressed often and earlier in other, non-
fictional settings.[5] On the whole, however, the eighteenth-century social

imaginary is more invested in figuring out the implications of same-sex relations than in dissolving them. Whether this shift signifies simply the fatigue of metamorphic conventions more broadly, or the shift of sapphic representations from public stage to private page, or the demise of scientific faith in sex change, it is more likely by the later eighteenth century that we will see reverse metamorphosis—in a genre like the picaresque or in the scare-tactic pamphlets of the French Revolution—than scenarios of women turning away from one another into cross-sex bonds. Hence, perhaps, the need to evict such unrecuperable figures as Miss Barnevelt, Harriot Freke, or Diderot's lesbian mother superior; hence too, however, the misery of Mademoiselle Sapho when she leaves the safety of the Anandrynes.

As I have already suggested here, the waning of the metamorphic also entails the rise of the horizontal with its insistence on the "same" in same-sex. I don't mean to overstate that "sameness": it is not that metonyms of masculinity disappear from sapphic representations or that male/female (or butch/femme) dynamics do not get configured within sapphic representations. But insofar as female-female relations are rendered irreducible, they provide opportunities to explore forms of leveling, similitude, and mutuality—as well as forms of exclusion, power appropriation, and faction—that stem from the assumption that the logic of "woman + woman" cannot simply be transformed to the logic of "woman + man." From the mid-eighteenth century, most representations take this form, even when they are also function ethnographically through exploratory and interrogative modes. At the same time, the ethnographic tends to move into home territory; by the end of the period, we see less emphasis on the sapphic as a foreign phenomenon and more attempt to explore its workings on home ground. The "acts of naming" that I detailed in chapter 6 are ethnographic projects meant to map individuals and groups of women in local space. One might argue too that the sexological moves of the later nineteenth century reinvigorate ethnographic practices as the ground of the new scientia sexualis.

It is arguably the (temporary) irreducibility of the horizontal that helps to account for what I believe is a waning legibility for sapphic subjects in the early nineteenth century. I have posited a decrease in explicit sapphic representation almost everywhere by the 1820s, when Europe was settling into a modern order underwritten by solidified and panoptically policed inscriptions of class- and gender-specific identities, though of course countermoves and resistances, including queer resistances, remained. There will be resurgences of public discourse about both female similitude and its contrary, the "inversion" of the "third sex," in the later nineteenth century, just as there will be extensions of sapphic publicity to other geographic settings that also bear scrutiny within a "sexuality of history" beyond the scope of this book. I would attribute the decrease in part to the one major change that, as I have already suggested, I can claim about sapphic representations across the long period: their growing resistance to metamorphosis and thus their unassimilability in a social imaginary increasingly invested in heteronormativity. The closing section of each of my last four chapters points to a time when representations are waning in the particular formations that chapter is studying. Whether the larger arc of this book will hold up to scrutiny is not mine to judge: clearly, it will be up to those who work at the edges of this book's long period to provide the more informed view. I reiterate, however, that it is a view about *public representation* of the sapphic and not about private writings or lived lives; my study in no way conflicts with the important work of Martha Vicinus or Sharon Marcus about female intimacies in the nineteenth century, and indeed I hope that my fifth and especially seventh chapters help to support their brief for challenge and change in the next century.

At the same time, the waning of the sapphic as public preoccupation—for a while—deepens the question of what difference those representations that I have studied might have made. I do not mean here to ask whether sapphic representations made the world safe for sapphic *people*: as Martha Vicinus writes of the women she studies across the long period from the 1770s to the 1920s, women living in sapphic formations "fully understood the dangers of same-sex intimacy" and adroitly "used and deflected the public gaze upon their more private relations."[6] If that is true across the period, then in one sense Radclyffe Hall and Una Troubridge were no better off than Eleanor Butler and Sarah Ponsonby, except that Butler and Ponsonby lived in a world of innuendo from which they had to dissociate themselves, while the women of the 1920s "had a public discourse and a set of recognized stereotypes with which to shape their conversations."[7] And of course the world is still not safe for lesbians depending not only on what country or culture one inhabits but, to put it metonymically, on whether one's legible existence threatens the person next door.

While I am making no claims for the effects of the sapphic discourses I have been studying on lived lives, then, I do think that modernity (as I have used the term) has entailed an epistemic struggle about the possibility of the sapphic and thus a movement into what I have been calling a sapphic episteme, an epistemological and therefore discursive framework in which the logic of female-female erotic relationships makes imaginative sense.

Having raised a Foucauldian framework for such a claim, I am perhaps en-
joined to return to Foucault's formulation, which argues for rupture rather
than continuity in the period I have been studying. Foucault's "Renaissance" episteme is a function of resemblance and similitude, and arguably
in that sense horizontal; his "Classical" episteme, in contrast, insists on
hierarchy and ordering, on categorization and control. Foucault's primary
interest here is in the nature of signification, of course, in perceived relationships between signifiers and signifieds, and it would be an exercise
in itself—arguably one that this project could have undertaken—to map
sapphic representations in terms of such Foucauldian categories as analogy
and microcosm and representational logic. But in terms less philosophical, I would pose the possibility that a Renaissance similitude does make
sapphic logic thinkable even as material hierarchies render it impossible,
while a Classical episteme relocates the sapphic into an anterior space
that requires it to reformulate its strategies of resistance. Throughout this
process, however, sapphic representations are both reflecting and shaping
the ways in which a social imaginary can recognize, or refuse to recognize, female homoerotic relations as viable. One way of looking at the arc
of these representations is to see where they hold firm and where they get
pushback that ends in a silence. The pushback seems to happen earliest
in Spain but to have extended across Europe by the 1810s and 1820s. I am
not, then, positing a steady progress of the sapphic into epistemic power
but rather seeing these centuries as a kind of first wave for advancing a
certain logic that will hold for a while and then cease to be widely available. Charting—worldwide, in the end—the places where that epistemic
logic can happen seems to me, however, to be charting a move into a kind
of modernity that could ultimately demolish the hegemony of gender over
all aspects of political economy and social life. I see the representations I
have gathered in this project as configuring that logic perhaps for the first
time on a wide scale, at least in the European context. I am not, however,
arguing that this modernity is necessarily European or that it necessarily
originates in Europe or takes a European form; I am simply representing
seventreenth- and eighteenth-century Europe as one place where sapphic
logic became an idea to reckon with.

In *The Other Enlightenment*, Carla Hesse comments that "in a modern Republic, the real liberation for women comes not when their sex is
represented (although this is an important and necessary part of the enterprise), but when they are perceived as capable, as well, of representing
something larger than gender alone."[8] I'm not sure that counts as liberation, but we might say something similar about the sapphic. During the

period when European modernity has been forging itself, the sapphic has almost always represented "something larger" than the sapphic, and in this sense, the sapphic has always been modern. But there has often been a qualification, a price to pay, even for what is only textually sapphic: a death, a moral judgment, a social cost, a provisionality, a desexualization in the interests of recuperation. As the "Sapphist" became an iconic figure at the turn of the twentieth century, that figure too becomes subject to cost; we need think only of Radclyffe Hall's *The Well of Loneliness* (1928) and its legal struggles to recall some of the devastating implications of female same-sex desire even as literary modernism was managing to forge queer formations in subtler veins. Certainly the story of the sexuality of history I have hoped to tell, like the sexuality of history that might come after it, is not linear; it is entangled with its own past.

It is possible that some national and local cultures are now reaching a historical moment when the logic of woman + woman has transformed the social imaginary and is beginning to transform the social itself. I have no illusions that the transformation is permanent, but certainly this book could not have been written had what I am calling modernity not become in some sense sapphic, and in this sense I would not, as Latour put it, "wish [us] to become premoderns again." That a same-gender logic remains to be realized in much of the world, but that the conversation is widely beginning, should remind us of the power of print—and now of social media—to open new possibilities. In this context, it is worth recalling that, as Sahar Amer argued, "explicit and detailed" descriptions of lesbian sexuality, offered with no critical comment in ethnographic accounts of "the tradition between women in the game of love," can already be found in medieval Arabic texts of the twelfth century (by al-Tifāshī): sapphic modernity thus arguably came far earlier to Arabo-Muslim countries than to Christian Europe.[9]

One question remains: if I am touting modernity as a place where the sapphic is epistemically viable, if I insist on modernity as a sapphic episteme, if one that emerges unevenly and can perhaps never be secured, then do we not need to ask what might be lost in such a formulation? Making the world safe for the sapphic, as I have bluntly put it, is surely only one of many of modernity's urgent imperatives. Is there a cost to reading modernity in sapphic terms? I have implied that even beneficent sapphic representations may screen out aspects of modernity that are devastatingly dangerous and resistant to change, slavery not least among them. Does my own focus on the sapphic likewise risk screening these out?

I raise the question through a convergence that I do not believe to be accidental though it occurred technically through the simple difference of a single vote in a context that reminds us how unpredictable modernity's alliances and misalliances can be. On 26 June 2013, the United States Supreme Court dismantled the Defense of Marriage Act signed into law by a liberal Democratic president and thereby paved the way for full marriage equality for same-sex couples. If we think back through the first text I discussed in this book, Henri Estienne's account of a woman put to death by the state for marrying a woman, we may recognize even more vividly the changes not only in discourse but in material life that were unimaginable—though not always unimagined—for centuries. If legal same-sex marriage is not a modern paradigm, I am not sure anything could qualify.

Yet on 25 June 2013, the day before handing down this momentous decision, that same Supreme Court also gutted key sections of the Voting Rights Act signed into law by another Democratic president in 1965. That act enfranchised millions of Americans who had been denied the rights of citizenship, changed the character of American politics, and allowed the country to elect its first Black president. Its defeat in 2013, it is predicted, will hamper the civic participation of nonwhite Americans, the poor, and the elderly, and this at a time when the income differentials in the United States have grown vaster than they have been for almost a hundred years: when 1 percent of the people earn 40 percent of the wealth, where the 400 richest individuals have more assets than the bottom 150 million put together, where the earnings of white women and all people of color still trail the earnings of white men by 20 to 40 percent. Subsequent Supreme Court decisions such as an April 2014 judgment that strikes down limits on personal campaign spending will surely exacerbate the potential damage wrought by the Voting Rights Act decision of June 2013.

It is difficult to celebrate this trading off of right for right. If the logic of "woman + woman" is now arguably viable in the United States of America as in much of Europe—for now—the logic of race and class equality is not. And if as my opening epigraph from John Melon proclaimed, "there is such an intimate relationship among the different parts of society that none of them could receive a blow without repercussions on the others,"[10] do we not need to ask not only whether but how these two court decisions are related? What does it mean that racial inequality, indeed racism itself, has been wrought and continues to be perpetuated by the same "modernity" that now gives us same-sex marriage? Bruno Latour, proclaiming the crisis of the modern, argues that "we are going to have to . . . distinguish between [modernity's] durable characteristics and [its] lethal ones."[11] Latour means "durable" to signify what should be kept, but unfortunately what has been lethal has also been durable.

Some day, a scholar may be writing a paragraph about the twentieth and twenty-first centuries that articulates the "truths (almost) universally acknowledged" in the legacies of our own time. I hope that the new and radically horizontal separation of marriage from gender will be among them. But I also hope that as that story gets recorded in whatever print or digital form of the future, it will recognize that our own era's "intensified interest in lesbians" needs to be set, as I have tried to set the interests of the past, in the larger and not always comfortable sphere not only of the history of sexuality, but of the sexuality of history.

CHAPTER I

1. Melon, *Essai politique sur le commerce*, 709: "Il y a une liaison si intime dans les parties de la société, qu'on ne saurait en frapper une, que le contre-coup ne porte sur les autres." All unattributed translations in these pages are my own.

2. I recognize that "the West" is a contested as well as a geographically relative term. While "global North" might be more appropriate to describe hierarchies of power and prosperity in the present, I retain "West" for its historical salience.

3. In choosing the freighted word "subject" I have multiple valences in mind, but I mean the term primarily in its most bland and basic senses: as a topic of inquiry, as a grammatical focus on which predications are made, as a figure with the potential for action. I am not making claim here to sexual *subjectivity* on the part of actual or textual persons, though I would not insist that such a subjectivity is historically impossible. I discuss my preference for the word "sapphic" later in this chapter.

4. I address below the vexed nature of the terms "modern" and "modernity."

5. I use the term "social imaginary" to denote the amalgam of symbolic inscriptions of a culture's beliefs, values, and self-understandings. For inaugural if somewhat different conceptions of the social imaginary, see especially Castoriadis, *L'institution imaginaire de la société*, and Taylor, *Modern Social Imaginaries*.

6. Foucault, *The History of Sexuality*. It is important to remember, however, that Foucault did not inaugurate this academic field; it existed *avant la lettre*.

7. Vicinus, "Sexuality and Power," 135.

8. Foucault, *History of Sexuality*, 23, 26.

9. In *Erotic Subjects*, Melissa Sanchez brilliantly effects the turn I have in mind by reading heteroerotic literary dynamics in tandem with English Renaissance politics.

10. Babcock, "Introduction" to *The Reversible World*, 32.

11. See Halperin, *How to Do the History of Homosexuality*. Halperin's article, from which he draws the title for his book, includes an important qualification: "How to Do the History of *Male* Homosexuality" (emphasis mine).

12. Jeffreys, "Queer Disappearance," 459; Castle, *Apparitional Lesbian*, 12.

13. Martin, "Extraordinary Homosexuals and the Fear of Being Ordinary," 101.

14. See Scott, "Gender: A Useful Category of Historical Analysis."

15. Wiegman, "The Desire for Gender"; King, *The Gendering of Men*, 1:11.

16. Binhammer, "Thinking Gender with Sexuality," 670, 686.

17. Valentine, "The Categories Themselves," 219–20.

18. Watt, "Why Men Still Aren't Enough," 452; Sedgwick, *Epistemology of the Closet*, 36.

19. Brooten, *Love Between Women*, 24.

20. Halperin, *How to Do the History of Homosexuality*, 78.

21. Bennett, "Confronting Continuity," 73.

22. Bray, *The Friend*, 10–11. As Lorna Hutson has noted in "The Body of the Friend and the Woman Writer," Bray himself neglects the important seventeenth-century instance of Katherine Philips.

23. See Lanser, "Of Closed Doors and Open Hatches."

24. On the eighteenth-century roots of heteronormativity, see Lauren Berlant and Michael Warner, "Sex in Public."

25. Bennett, "'Lesbian-Like' and the Social History of Lesbianisms," 4.

26. Scott, "Gender," 1054.

27. Laqueur, *Making Sex*, 156–57.

28. Fraisse, *La muse de la raison*; Honegger, *Die Ordnung der Geschlechter*.

29. Parker, *Sexing the Text*, 1, emphasis mine.

30. See McKeon, "Historicizing Patriarchy" and, for my counter-argument, Lanser, "Sapphic Picaresque." McKeon reiterates his position, without adjustment, in "The Seventeenth- and Eighteenth-Century Sexuality Hypothesis" and again in a *PMLA* forum in 2013.

31. Dabhoiwala, *The Origins of Sex*, 128.

32. See Duberman, Vicinus, and Chauncey, eds., *Hidden from History*.

33. Abelove, "The Queering of Lesbian/Gay History," 49.

34. Doan, *Disturbing Practices*, 81, 12.

35. Hill, "Introduction," *Crisis in Europe, 1560–1660*, 3.

36. See Spurlin, Hayes, and Higonnet, eds., *Comparatively Queer*. Elizabeth Wahl's *Invisible Relations* is exceptional in working evenly across English and French cultures.

37. See Dekker and van de Pol, *The Tradition of Female Transvestism in Early Modern Europe*.

38. Indeed, at least one national culture that could address some geographic and political conundrums raised by this project—Sweden—is absent from this conversation simply by virtue of my own linguistic limitations atop the paucity of English-language scholarship on early modern sapphic representations that may have circulated in Scandinavian languages. The reputation of Queen Christina (1626–89), suspected of intimacies with both women and men, might well have stimulated public discourse in her home country, but I have not been able to excavate such evidence myself nor to identify scholars who are doing so. See also note 161 to chapter 2.

39. Traub, "The Present Future of Lesbian Historiography," 126.

40. Latour, *We Have Never Been Modern*, 10.

41. Ferguson, *Modernity and Subjectivity*, 1–2, 4.

42. Giddens, *The Consequences of Modernity*, 1.

43. Traub, "The Present Future of Lesbian Historiography," 127.

44. Sanchez, "'Use Me But as Your Spaniel,'" 504.

45. See Lanser, "Befriending the Body"; "Bluestocking Sapphism and the Economies of Desire"; and "Tory Lesbians."

46. Landes, *Visualizing the Nation*, 6.

47. See, for example, David Robinson's call for scholars to hunt "for traces of closeted lesbian and gay lives and closeted lesbian and gay writings" ("The Abominable Madame de Murat," 63).

48. Vickery, *The Gentleman's Daughter*, 11.

49. Hunt, "The Sapphic Strain," 277.

50. For decoded selections from the diaries, see Lister, *I Know My Own Heart*; *No Priest but Love*; and Jill Liddington, *Female Fortune*.

51. The "sapphic" in this sense does not always implicate Sappho herself; as Joan Dejean (*Fictions of Sappho*) has well established and as my own research bears out, the early modern Sappho is often associated with (wanton or fatal) heteroeroticism rather than with lesbianism.

It is also worth acknowledging that my conceptual framework does orient this project toward the "frankly female" rather than the "gender-queer." I have not, on the whole, engaged the challenge of representations that might be better accommodated by rubrics of transgender or intersexuality.

52. Brooten, *Love Between Women*, 18.

53. Bennett, "'Lesbian-Like,'" 11. I do not mean, nor does Bennett, that a lesbian identity figures in discourses of the tenth century. It is the adjectival "lesbian" that has changed surprisingly little over time. Note also, however, the cautions of Harriette Andreadis (in *Sappho in Early Modern England*) against the belief in a continuous etymological history for any term associated with sexuality.

54. Butler, "Imitation and Gender Insubordination," 14.

55. Andreadis, "The Sapphic-Platonics of Katherine Philips," 59.

56. Vicinus, "Lesbian History," 57, 59.

57. For those who might consider "romantic friendship" a useful term for its origins in the period, I recall that Samuel Johnson's *Dictionary of the English Language* (1755) defines "Romantick" as "wild," "improbable; false," and "fanciful" and that the period's references to "romantic friend" are almost all pejorative, evoking youthful impetuosity at best and dishonor at worst. On the long-recognized conceptual problems with the term "romantic friendship," see Stanley, "Epistemological Issues."

58. Lady Eleanor Butler, Sarah Ponsonby, and Caroline Tighe Hamilton, *The Hamwood Papers*, 27.

59. See Traub, "The (In)Significance of 'Lesbian' Desire."

60. See Castle, *The Apparitional Lesbian*.

61. Carolyn Woodward deserves the credit for unearthing this novel; see "'My Heart So Wrapt.'"

62. Materialist theorists have long argued that the Hegelian notion of Zeitgeist mystifies the specific forces that create a shared mentalité. A Zeitgeist model also

assumes a single, homogeneous mind-frame rather than recognizing, as Foucault has argued and subsequent scholarship has shown, that competing discourses are in play at any given time. On this issue, see Denise Gigante, "Zeitgeist."

63. Guillén, *The Challenge of Comparative Literature*, 70.

64. Foucault, *The Order of Things*, xxi–xxii.

65. Cohen, *Drama of a Nation*, 16–17, 120.

66. Wahrman, *The Making of the Modern Self*, 47 and passim.

67. Williams, *Writing in Society*, 210.

68. Turchi, *Maps of the Imagination*, 44.

69. Calvino, *If On a Winter's Night a Traveler*, 244.

70. The exception is Susan Lamb ("'Be Such a Man as I'"), who argues that the text deploys a "Jacobite politics," a claim that I will discuss in chapter 3. I discuss Lamb's reading of the novel's sexual ideology, thought not its political philosophy, in "The Author's Queer Clothes."

71. See especially Moretti, "The Slaughterhouse of Literature."

72. See Abelove, "Some Speculations on the History of Sexual Intercourse."

73. For key texts in this debate that has been flourishing in Renaissance studies—but, perhaps significantly, not in eighteenth-century studies—see Jonathan Goldberg and Mhadavi Menon, "Queering History," and Traub, "The New Unhistoricism."

74. Sanfeliú, *Juego de damas*, 13–14.

75. Lister, letter to Sibbella MacLean (3 August 1822), in *I Know My Own Heart*, 210.

76. Hume, *Reconstructing Contexts*, 71.

77. Loselle, "Introduction," 3; Campell, *Wonder & Science*, 46.

CHAPTER 2

1. Swetnam, *The Araignment of Lewd, Idle, Froward, and Unconstant Women*, 14.

2. Estienne, *L'introduction au traité*, 110: "Je vien de reciter un forfaict merveilleusement estrange: mais j'en vay reciter un autre qui l'est encore d'avantage, (non pas toutesfois si vilain) advenu aussi de nostre temps, il y a environ trent'ans. C'est qu'une fille native de Fontaines, qui est entre Blois & Rommorantin, s'estant desguisee en homme, servit de valet d'estable environ sept ans en une hostelerie du faux-bourg du Foye, puis se maria à une fille du lieu, avec laquelle elle fut environ deux ans, exerceant le mestier de vigneron. Apres lequel temps estant descouverte la meschanceté de laquelle elle usoit pour contrefaire l'office de mari, fut prise, & ayant confessé fut là brunlee toute vive. Voici comment nostre siecle se peut vanter qu'outre toutes les meschancetez des precedens, il en ha qui luy sont propres & peculieres. Car cest acte n'ha rien de commun avec celuy de quelques vilaines qu'on appeloit anciennément tribades."

3. The first European instances of "tribade," found by Marzio Barbagli, are passing uses in two ribald Italian satires. Annibale Caro's *Commento Di Ser Agretso* (1538) marks the genitalia of tribades as deviant, deploying the slang "fiche" (figs) that is still in the Italian lexicon. In the same year, Niccolò Franco's *Le pistole vulgari* uses *tribadi* to designate Sappho's disciples (222). The adjective "tribadique" appeared in French in 1565, in Tahureau (see note 10 below). By this time, a correlative term for "tribade" had

already occurred with some frequency in Arabic literature, as Sahar Amer reports in "Lesbian Sex and the Military," 187.

4. Anne Lake Prescott, "Male Lesbian Voices," 124.

5. In *The Literature of Lesbianism*, Terry Castle reads the poem's attitude toward love between women as "disgust" and "catastrophe" and argues that Tyard "invokes the history of male homoeroticism . . . precisely in order to disparage female-female eros" (74). My reading departs significantly from Castle's as does my translation of the poem. For readings more consistent with mine, see Robert Griffiths, "'Les trois sortes d'aimer,'" 116–17, and Prescott, "Male Lesbian Voices," 121.

6. Tyard, "Elegie," *Oeuvres poétiques*, n.p.:

Qu'en vain j'avois pensé que le temps advenir
Nous devroit pour miracle en longs siecles tenir :
Et que d'un seul exemple, en la françoise histoire
Nostre Amour serviroit d'eternelle memoire,
Pour prouver que l'Amour de femme à femme épris
Sur les masles Amours emporteroit le pris.

7. Proclaiming the modern instance far worse than the ancient case may be abetting Estienne's claim that antiquity is superior to modernity, or it may simply reflect what Winfried Schleiner has called "polemical Protestant homophobia"; see Schleiner, "Linguistic 'Xeno-homophobia.'" Tyard's poem may be connected to a protofeminism that is evident in the 1552 preface to the first edition of his *Premier Solitaire*, which he later suppressed; see John C. Lapp, "Pontus de Tyard and the Querelle des Femmes."

8. That there is no *necessary* novelty tied to Estienne's anecdote is clear when we consider the Latin account of this incident that appeared just a year earlier in Theodor Zwinger's *Theatrum vitae humanae*: "A certain *Galla* who disguised herself as a stableboy worked for an innkeeper in Blois for seven years. She married the daughter of a citizen, and had tribadic relations with her for two years. When the crime came to light, she was burned alive." For Zwinger this case forms but the latest example in an enumeration that starts with Sappho; in his rendering, this is an *old* story: "here we say nothing which has not been said before." The English translation by Faith Wallis is found in Kenneth Borris, *Same-Sex Desire in the English Renaissance*, 223. Later in this chapter I discuss the differential—indeed, minimal—place of the sapphic in the cultural imaginary of the German states in the sixteenth century, in contrast to its emerging prominence in France, Italy, Spain, and England. Zwinger's handling of the anecdote provides small but telling supporting evidence for that larger claim.

9. Firuenzola, *On the Beauty of Women*, 17. The full Italian passage: "E questi tutti, o volete i buoni o gli scelerati, fuggono per lo più il consorzio di voi altre donne; che ben so che eziandio al di d'oggi ne conoscete qualcuno. Quelle ch'erano femine, o discendono da quelle che erano femine in ogni parte, amano la belleza l'una dell'altra, chi puramente e santamente, come la elegante Laudomia Forteguerra la illustrissima Margherita d'Austria, chi lascivamente, come Safo la Lesbia anticamente, e ai tempi nostri a Roma la gran meretrice Cicilia Viniziana; e queste così fatte per natura schifano il tor marito e fuggono la intrinseca conversazione di noi altri; e queste debbiamo credere che sien quelle che si fanno monache volentieri e volentieri vi stanno, che sono poche;

percioché nei munisteri le più vi stanno per forza e vivonvi disperate" (734). Firenzuola does acknowledge that there are men who love men "even in our own day" (17), but the "even" is telling.

10. Tahureau, *Dialogues*, 58–59: "quand elles se verroient en si peu d'estime, eu égard en celle-la, qu'elles sont pour le iourd'huy, elles accorderoient à peu de peine ce que les longues prieres, sottes harengues, dons superflus, & autres telles caresses qu'elles ont accoutumé de receuoir, ne peuuent faire, si d'avanture il ne s'en trouuoit quelques-vnes, qui eussent le coeur tant vertueux, & assis en si bon lieu qu'elles aimassent mieux en vser à la tribadique."

11. Ronsard, "Elegie [Pour vous monstrer]," in *Oeuvres complètes*, 2:889f.

12. L'Estoile, *Registre-Journal edu règne de Henri III*, 3:185. An unpublished contemporary German manuscript, the *Zimmerische Chronik*, likewise blames the age, and specifically "the evil mores of rotten nations plagued by sins [den bösen sitten deren verderbten und mit sünden geplagten nationen]" for the sapphic behavior of a servant named Greta. On this text, see Helmut Puff, "Toward a Philology of the Premodern Lesbian," 148.

13. Nicholas de Nicolay's widely circulated *Navigations, pérégrinations et voyages faicts en la Turquie* (1568) does make that linkage that Estienne refused, but tellingly in an orientalist context; he sees Turkish women in the baths as "fervently in love with one another as if they were men" as "in the past did the Tribades among whom was Sappho the Lesbian." See *Les quatre premiers livres des navigations et pérégrinations orientales*, 73: "entre les femmes de Leuant y a tres grande amitié , ne procedant que de la frequentation & priuauté des bains. Voire quelque fois deuiennent autant ardamment amoureuses les vnes des autres, comme si c'estoyent hommes . . . comme jadis estoyent les Tribades, du nombre desquelles estoit Sapho Lesbienne."

14. *The Laughing Philosopher*, 90–91. The conjunction of "very Jews" with "Tommies" is atypical in its specifics but one of many reminders that in the seventeenth and eighteenth centuries, homoeroticism often gets coupled—and, as in this case, gratuitously so—with other vectors of degradation.

15. Walsh, *A Dialogue Concerning Women*, 103; *Satan's Harvest Home*, 18; *Correspondance littéraire* for November 1775, 11:159; *Mémoires secrets*, attributed to Mouffle d'Angerville (1784), 116.

16. Erauso, *Lieutenant Nun*, 3; *Historia de la Monja Alférez*: "a la noche del 18 de marzo de 1600, víspera de San José" (11). The text is fairly explicit; for example: "I had my head in the folds of her skirt and she was combing my hair while I ran my hand up and down between her legs" (17); "estando en el estrado peinándome acostdo en sus faldas y andándole en las piernas" (25).

17. See Velasco, *The Lieutenant Nun*, 51–52.

18. Lodge, *Rosalynde*. In language very like that of Tyard's lady, Alinda vows that "I will ever be thy Alinda, and thou shalt ever rest to me Rosalynd: so shall the world canonize our friendship, and speake of Rosalynd and Alinda, as they did of Pilades and Orestes" (14).

19. Denise A. Walen's *Constructions of Female Homoeroticism* characterizes over seventy Elizabethan and Jacobean plays as having some female homoerotic content (157–59).

20. McKendrick, *Women and Society*, 311. For a discussion of Church concerns about the *mujer varonil* expressed in 1600 by Fray Jose de Jesus Maria, see Velasco, *The Lieutenant Nun*, 36–37.

21. Moreto y Cabaña, *El desdén con el desdén*, 9. McKendrick notes that "every year from about 1590 to 1660 witnessed the appearance of at least one new play featuring a *mujer varonil*" (*Women and Society*, 311).

22. Brooten notes a Roman gravestone, dating about 27 BCE to 14 CE, that depicts two women with hands clasped in a typical marital posture, see *Love Between Women*, 59–60 and fig. 7. Judith Bennett has discovered in England a somewhat more elliptical "lesbian-like" brass image of two fifteenth-century friends. See Bennett, "Remembering Elizabeth Ethingham and Agnes Oxenbridge."

23. See Bray, *The Friend*, 109 and passim.

24. Fonte, *The Worth of Women*, 29, 47, 49; *Il merito delle donne*: "noi non stiamo mai bene se non sole e beata veramenta quella donna che può vivere senza la compagnia de verun'uomo" (17).

25. Leo Africanus, *A Geographical Historie of Africa*, 148–49.

26. Bodin, *De la démonomanie des sorciers*, 99: "quand le diable leur manqué [les sorcières] cherchent les ieunes femmes et filles dont elles abusent, common on disoit de Sapho." The connection likewise surfaces in two 1597 Inquisitorial reports from Mallorca, where Esperanza de Rojas and Catalina Lebrés were separately convicted of lesbian-motivated sorcery. See Velasco, *Lesbians in Early Modern Spain*, 50–53.

27. On the "Duval-Riolan Debate," as she calls it, see Katharine Park, "The Rediscovery of the Clitoris," 179–84.

28. Du Laurens, *Toutes les oeuvres*, 223. These texts had legal impact: when the famous "hermaphrodite" Marie/Marin le Marcis was condemned in 1601 for seeking to marry a woman, s/he was saved by Duval's avowal that despite her feminine anatomy s/he had ejaculated male seed. The onetime wife and mother Elena/Eleno de Céspedes, tried in Toledo in 1587 for marrying a woman, also probably escaped punishment because she convincingly used her knowledge of modern science to explain both the alleged appearance and the subsequent disappearance of her male genitalia.

29. Torquemada, *Jardin de flores curiosas*, 115.

30. Brantôme, *Oeuvres complètes*, 2:275f.

31. Serna, "El sueño de la viuda," lines 23–24. Further references will appear as line numbers within the text. For my introduction to this work, I am indebted to Martín, "The Mediation of Lesbian Eros."

32. "Hallándose dos damas," poem 30 in *Poesía erótico del Siglo de Oro*, ed. Pierre Alzieu, Robert Jammes, and Yvan Lissorgues, 46.

33. Dekker and Van de Pol, *The Tradition of Female Transvestism*, 59.

34. See Paola Lupo, *Lo specchio incrinato*, 199–200; Louis Crompton, "The Myth of Lesbian Impunity," and Ruthann Robson, "Lesbianism in Anglo-European Legal History."

35. Andreadis, *Sappho in Early Modern England*, 46.

36. [Ben Jonson], "The Forest," in Robert Chester, *Love's Martyr*, 181. "Go, crampe dull Mars, light Venus, when he snorts, / Or with thy Tribade Trine, inuent new sports, / Thou, nor their loosenesse with our Making sorts." The 1878 editor of this

volume, Alexander B. Grosart, seems clearly nonplussed when he comments that "one may hope [Jonson] used this word as 'artful only" (245).

37. Jonson, "Epigram on the Court Pucell," in *Poems*, 195–96. Jonson also offers what is probably the first indigenous usage of "fricatrice" in English print in his play *Volpone* (1607), though the meaning here is not necessarily sapphic; a female character describes her rival as "a lewd harlot, a base fricatrice, / female deuill, in a male outside" (4.2, n.p.).

38. See Giffney, Sauer, and Watt, eds., *The Lesbian Premodern*.

39. See Amer, "Lesbian Sex and the Military," 192ff.

40. Puff, "Female Sodomy," 41.

41. I am aware that "caste" is a controversial term to apply to women, and I use it sparingly in this book. In the early modern context, I would argue, words such as "class" and "group" do not adequately represent either the hierarchical order of gender or the extent to which gender operates, in both the social imaginary and material life, as a "system of rigid social distinction" based on perceived identity at birth, to take one of the *Oxford English Dictionary*'s definitions for "caste."

42. Andreadis, *Sappho in Early Modern England*; Bonnet, *Un choix sans équivoque*; Martín, *Erotic Philology*; Traub, *The Renaissance of Lesbianism*; Velasco, *Lieutenant Nun and Lesbians in Early Modern Spain*; and Walen, *Constructions of Female Homoeroticism*.

43. See Gilbert, *Early Modern Hermaphrodites*; Graille, *Les hermaphrodites*; Harris, *Hidden Agendas*; and Daston and Park, "The Hermaphrodite and the Orders of Nature."

44. See Dugaw, *Warrior Women and Popular Balladry*, and Schwarz, *Tough Love*. Neither I nor these other scholars suggest that female transvestism is unknown in the medieval period, of course. But Valerie Hotchkiss seems right to suggest that the medieval transvestite is exceptional and usually in some sense heroic; see *Clothes Make the Man*.

45. Hunt, *Governance of the Consuming Passions*, 214. Hunt notes that medieval sumptuary laws were aimed mainly at men and argues that legal attention shifted to women with the rise of an "urban mercantile class" (235).

46. Dekker and van de Pol, *The Tradition of Female Transvestism*, 9.

47. Gisela Bock, *Women in European History*, notes that "roughly a thousand such works were written in the fifteenth and sixteenth centuries," not even including translations, reprintings, and passing comments in other works (4).

48. See Foucault, *Les anormaux* and *The Order of Things*.

49. Men did, of course, sometimes dress as women for carnival, political action, or sexual chicanery, but these were usually temporary moves rather than life choices, and men were rarely considered guilty of fraud for doing so. Even the famous seventeenth-century exception, Abbé de Choisy (1644–1724), lived "habillé en femme" only for portions of his life and indeed was admitted to the Académie française, an honor not given to a woman for another three centuries.

50. Anna Klosowska, *Queer Love in the Middle Ages*, 111.

51. As Sahar Amer notes by way of contrast, the Arabic words *sahq* (lesbianism) and *sahiqa* (lesbian) were not unusual in medieval Arabic literature; see *Crossing Borders*, 16–19.

52. For excellent discussions of the word "tribade" respectively in antiquity and in early modernity, see Brooten, *Love Between Women*, and Bonnet, *Un choix sans équivoque*. Thus far, I have not found a Dutch instance of "tribade" before 1650, a belatedness that is not surprising given the strong sexual censorship in Golden Age Holland and the attendant tendency for public discourse to resort to euphemisms, as Rudolf M. Dekker notes in *Humor in Dutch Culture*, 106.

53. Several related terms also come into vernacular usage around this time. "Dildo" makes its earliest entry into English in 1593, the French (*godemiché*) and Spanish (*baldrés* or *baldés*) having appeared a decade or two earlier. The verb *travestir*, from the Italian *trasvestire*, enters French in the mid-sixteenth century and quickly narrows from denoting all disguise to its current gender-crossing meaning. Like the use of "tribade," however, these terms do not appear simply as the effect of a rising "sexual science." The word "vagina," to make a relevant contrast, does not seem to have entered vernacular usage until a century later (1676 in French, 1682 in English), significantly later than "clitoris," for which the first *OED* attribution is Crooke's *Microcosmographia* of 1615.

54. By amalgamating the research of Crompton, Robson, Puff, Martín, Velasco, Bennett, and others, we can point to at least the following nonexhaustive list of legal cases: 1405 (France), 1444 (Rottweil), 1477 (Speier), 1480 (Italy), 1482–83 (Bruges), 1502 (Valencia), 1533 (Toulouse), 1536 (Foye), 1547 (Freiburg), 1555, 1560 (Hapsburg Spain), 1567 (Basel), 1568 (Geneva), 1580 (Montier-en-Der), 1597 (Mallorca), 1603 and 1620 (Castile), 1623 (Florence), 1624 (Seville), 1625 (Glasgow), 1656 (Aragon), 1641 (Holland), 1661 (Ireland), 1682 (London), 1688 (Leiden), 1702 (Hamburg), 1721 (Halberstadt), 1724 and 1737 (France), 1745 (Colombia), 1746 (Wells), 1786 and 1788 (France), 1795 (Amsterdam), and 1801 (Mexico). Not all of these cases resulted in capital punishment.

55. Dekker and Van de Pol, *The Tradition of Female Transvestism*, 83.

56. Anne Lane Prescott makes this speculation, but conjecturally, in "Male Lesbian Voices."

57. Fiction and Friction" in his *Shakespearean Negotiations* (Berkeley and Los Angeles: University of California Press, 1987), 66–93. Greenblatt's discussion begins with Montaigne's account of the hanging of a "female husband" in 1580 in Montier-en-der and then slides into discussing the dynamic of cross-dressed same-sex desire in *Twelfth Night* by claiming that "Shakespeare almost, but not quite, retells" this story. Montaigne's 1580 journal was not even published in Shakespeare's lifetime, but one has to look closely at Greenblatt's strategy to realize that while readers might infer an influence of Montaigne on Shakespeare, Greenblatt makes no such claim. Greenblatt's juxtaposition suggests influence; what is actually at stake is confluence.

58. Bray, *The Friend*, 139.

59. Firenzuola, *Of the Beauty of Women* [*Dialogo delle bellezze delle donne*]: 38, 45. Brantôme, here in the translation by Merrick and Ragan, 107; see also *Oeuvres*, 2:279–80.

60. Ronsard, "Elégie [Je suis un demi-dieu]," in *Oeuvres complètes* 1:161f. Interestingly, this "Elegie" was redacted out of Ronsard's *Oeuvres* in 1584 but restored in 1609.

61. For a different reading of the relationship between Helena and Hermia, though, see Sanchez, "'Use Me But as Your Spaniel.'"

62. Lyly, *Gallathea*, 2.2.

63. Thevet, *Les vrais pourtraits et vies d'hommes illustres* (Paris: I. Keruert et Guillaume Chaudiere, 1584), ch. 27: "mais qui voudroit de là tirer quelque presumption du crime detestable à elle imposé, faudroit par mesme moyen confesser que l'autre Sappho, qui avoit aussi bien des compaignes que nostre Lesbienne, seroit coulpable d'une telle & si execrable abomination, & generalement toutes les femmes qui se trouvent en bandes & compaignies."

64. Traub, *Desire and Anxiety*, 128.

65. Rojas, *Tragicomedia de Calisto y Melibea*, 94 (7.2).

66. Valverde, "Governing out of Habit," 218–19.

67. See Halperin, "Forgetting Foucault."

68. Upton, *Europe, 1600–1789*, 14–15.

69. "El Sueño," 209: "Estoy de mi figura tan mudada / Que no puedo a mi misma concerme. / De lo que gora soy, yo no se nada, ni quien baron de hembra pudo hazerme."

70. DiGangi, *The Homoerotics of Early Modern Drama*, 92.

71. "El Sueño," 208: "su fortuna le ayudase, / o tal planeta entonces ynflyuyese"

72. Puff, *Sodomy in Reformation Germany and Switzerland*, 35.

73. Park, "The Rediscovery of the Clitoris," 174.

74. Torquemada, *Jardin de flores curiosas*, 117. Paré repeats the story almost verbatim. A similar case publicized in 1617 is that of María Muñoz, discussed, among other places, in Velasco, *Lesbians in Early Modern Spain*, 28–29.

75. In this period, however, female masculinity is still more likely to be allied with excessive *hetero*-eroticism than with the sapphic. The 1620 pamphlet *Hic Mulier*, for example, accuses women who wear men's clothing of whorishness: the woman's mannish French doublet is "all vnbutton'd to entice" men, not women. In such cases, whatever homoeroticism we can speak of is effectively a homoeroticism between "men."

76. Serna, "Hallándose dos damas," in *Poesía erótico del Siglo de Oro*, ed. Alzieu, Jammes, and Lissorgues, 46.

77. Ferrand, *Traicté de l'essence et guérison de l'amour, ou mélancholie érotique*,14: "je croirois qu'il faut entendre ce changement, non du sexe, mais de temperament & habitude du corps."

78. Brantôme, *Oeuvres*, 2:276: "La femme donc, selon cela, qui contrefait ainsi l'homme peut avoir reputation d'estre plus valeureuse et courageuse qu'une autre, ainsi que j'en ay cogneu aucunes, tant pour leur corps que pour l'ame."

79. Montaigne, *Journal de voyage*, 1:13–14: "sept ou huit filles . . . complottèrent, il y a quelques années, de se vestir en masles, & continuer ainsi leur vie par le monde"; "*elle disoit aymer mieux souffrir que de se remettre en estat de fille.*" I have not focused closely on this rich text because of its much later circulation date, but the account is fascinatingly dialogic.

80. See Campbell, *Wonder & Science*, 44–50.

81. Aquinas, *Summa Theologiae*, Prima pars, Q. 92, Art. 1, obj. 1; Abelard, *Commentary on Saint Paul*, quoted in Edith Benkov, "The Erased Lesbian," 108. The Latin: "contra naturam, hos est contra naturae institutionem, quae genitalia feminarum usui virorum praeparavit . . . non ut feminae feminis cohabiterent."

82. Stallybrass, "Patriarchal Territories," 127.

83. Fourquet, *L'idéal historique*, 20 : "le désir est le mode même de la vie."

84. Quoted in MacCulloch, *The Reformation*, 598.

85. For a discussion of this poem, see Jane Farnsworth, "Voicing Female Desire in Poem xlix."

86. Thomas, "Women and the Civil War Sects," 332.

87. Shannon, "Nature's Bias," 191.

88. See Kuhn, *The Structure of Scientific Revolutions*, 62ff.

89. Niccholes, *A Discourse on Marriage and Wiving*, 36.

90. Goddard, *A Satirycall dialogue*, n.p. It is tempting to link this rhetoric with the Jacobean anxiety about female behaviors expressed in the famous *Hic Mulier* of 1620.

91. *The Passionate Pilgrime. By W. Shakespeare*, n.p. The poem is widely agreed not to be Shakespeare's and has been attributed by one source to his friend Henry Willobie.

92. L'Estoile, "Dialogue surnommé la frigarelle": "Sache que je suis femme, et que je n'ai en moi / Rien qui soit différent des femmes comme toi, / Mais j'ai entière-ment tout le désir d'un homme"; "Elle gouste un Plaisir, que nul autre n'egale, / Et je l'embrasse aussi, tout ainsi comme un Masle."

93. Brantôme, *Oeuvres*, 2:273–79, passim: "contrefaisoit d'homme," "ne veulent pas souffrir les hommes," approach women "ainsi que les hommes mesmes," conjoin "comme les hommes" and "ainsi que font les hommes," "imiter les hommes," "les servoit plus que les hommes," keep other women from "aller aux hommes," "ne leurs servent qu'à faute des hommes," "comme avec les hommes," "ne jamais font entrer les hommes."

94. In Ovid's version, Iphis has been raised as a boy from infancy because her father had planned to destroy the child were she a girl. She falls passionately in love with Ianthe and a wedding is planned; the potential disaster is averted when the goddess Isis changes Iphis into a man before the wedding night.

The strong popularity of Ovid's *Metamorphoses* in general, and of renditions of Iphis and Ianthe from book 9 in particular, arguably stems from the same early modern preoccupation with alteration that I have already described. While an Italian translation of Ovid appeared as early as 1497, most vernacular versions of the *Metamorphoses* saw print between the mid-sixteenth and early seventeenth centuries; by 1600 there were already two German, two French, one Italian, one Dutch, and five English editions.

95. Ariosto, *Orlando Furioso*, canto 25.

96. Traub, *Renaissance of Lesbianism*, 288.

97. Robinson, *Closeted Writing*, 188 and passim.

98. Garber, "Foreword: The Marvels of Peru," xv. Sapphic ethnography arguably creates an even more resistant version of "categorical confusion" than simple cross-dressing, for while cross-dressing temporarily confounds the sexes, it carries the possibility that a "wrong" sartorial signifier can be removed from the "right" body so that, as Valerie Hotchkiss notes of the medieval context, "the woman's body is finally relocated in its cultural place" (*Clothes Make the Man*, 128).

99. Traub, *Renaissance of Lesbianism*, 180.

100. Upton, *Europe, 1600–1789*, 16–17.

101. I am not suggesting that all of these claims were embodied in social or politi-

cal action or carried equal threat or promise at this point. But all are on the theoretical table by 1600.

102. Aylmer, *Harborowe for Faithful and Trewe Subjects*, sig. C4v.

103. Davis, *Society and Culture in Early Modern France*, 78.

104. The term comes from Babcock, ed., *The Reversible World*.

105. Crouch, *Loves Court of Conscience*, n.p.

106. Kunzle "World Upside Down," 88–89.

107. Davis, "Women in Top," 153.

108. Quoted in Davis, *Society and Culture in Early Modern France*, 74, emphasis mine.

109. Pizan, *Cité des dames*, 274 (3.18): "un nombre infini de dames de toutes conditions"; see also section 2.69, when Christine speaks to "femmes de toutes conditions" (238).

110. Ibid., 276: "ne vous indignez pas d'être ainsi soumises à vos maris, car ce n'est pas toujours dans l'intérêt des gens que d'êtres libres."

111. Pizan, *Trésor de la cité des dames*, 114v.

112. Marinella, *The Nobility and Excellence of Women*, 80.

113. Fonte, *The Worth of Women*, 59. Further references to the English translation will appear within the text.

114. Fonte, *Il merito delle donne*: "Lodato sia Dio," says Cornelia, "poiché pur possiamo dire delle piacevolezze così per rider tra noi e far ciò che più ne aggrada, che qui non è chi ci noti o chi ci dia la emenda" (16–17): "senza aver rispetto di uomini che le notassero, o l'impedissero" (47).

115. Ibid., 260: "E come alcun mortale / Viver senz'alma e senza cor no vale, Tal non pon senza d'elle / Gli uomini aver per sé medesimi aita, / Che è la donna de l'uom cor, alma e vita."

116. Ibid., 17: "noi non stiamo mai bene se non sole e beata veramenta quella donna che può vivere senza la compagnia de verun'uomo."

117. Ibid.: "Non servo alcun, né d'altri son che mia" (18); "tante diversità di sangui et di costumi, evvi però una pace ed equità incredible. Il che tutto procede dalla accurata profvidenza e valor de chi la governa" (14); "più tosto morrei che sottopormi ad uomo alcuno; troppo beata vite è quella che io passo cosi con voi senza temer di barba d'uomo che possa commandarmi" (17).

118. Ibid., 80: "la vera amicizia e cagion, d'ogni bene, per l'amicizia si mantiene il mondo."

119. Ibid., 80–81: "in terra le città per la pace se construggono, I regni si accrescono e tutte le creature si consolano"; "le provincie e la famiglie s'esterminano, gli stati si mutano e I popoli si consumano."

120. Ibid., 14: "fra le più chiare e reputate famiglie si trovarono, non ha gran tempo ed ancor si trovano alcune nobili e valorose donne di età e stato diferenti, ma di sangue e costumi conformi, gentili, virtuose et di elevato ingegno, le quali, perciolché molto si confacevano insieme, avendo tra loro contratto una cara e discreta amicizia."

121. Ibid., 13–14: "e sì per questo, come per molte rare e sopranaturali eccelenze in nobiltà e dignità avanza tutte le altre città del mondo, così antiche come moderne, onde drittamente può chiamarsi Metropoli dell'universo. . . . in tutte le arti e professioni

convengono, tutte le virtù vi regnano, le delizie e piaceri si gustano, I vizi si estirpano e vi fioriscono tutti I buoni costumi. . . ."

122. Ibid., 143–44: "Che avemo a far vi prego con magistrati, corti di palazzo e tali disviamenti? Or non fanno tutti gli uomini questi iffici contra di noi? Non ci domandano se ben non gli siamo obligate? No procurano per loro in nostro danno? No ci trattano da forestieri? Non fannosi proprio il nostro mobile?"

123. Ibid.: "eleggiamo tra noi una, che commandi alle altre e sia ubidita; perché invero la ubidienzia cosi' in una casa, come in una città è non pur utile, ma necessaria" (23). The word "city" is lost in the English translation, which substitutes "private" and "public sphere" for "house" and "city" (56). Translation mine in this instance.

124. Mueller, "Lesbian Erotics," 107. Mueller does rather overgeneralize the representation of Sappho here.

125. Readings of "Sapho to Philaenis" are highly contested and frequently polarized; my view arguably view sits near one such pole.

126. Donne, "Sapho to Philaenis," in *Poetry*, 2:409–10.

127. Bates, *Masculinity, Gender and Identity in the English Renaissance Lyric*, 234, 227–28, and passim.

128. Meakin, *John Donne's Articulations of the Feminine*, 124.

129. Some scholars have suggested that a key motivation for Fonte might have been the changed practices of inheritance in sixteenth-century Venice, which left many daughters without dowries, increased the number of unmarried women, and encouraged forced claustration. See, for example, Cox, "The Single Self."

130. At least one scholar, George Klawitter, sees the poem as inscribing an autobiographical male-male desire. See *The Enigmatic Narrator*, 47ff.

131. *Il merito delle donne*, 260.

132. Smarr, *Joining the Conversation*, 227–28.

133. Holstun, "'Will You Rent Our Ancient Love Asunder?'" 838, 847.

134. Blank, "Comparing Sappho to Philaenis," 359.

135. Shannon, *Sovereign Amity*, 101–2.

136. Carlyle, *The French Revolution*, 2:304.

137. As I already suggested, prosecutions map differently from imaginative representations, the former being most common in northern, Reformationist settings, with France a particular strong exception where prosecutions and non-juridical representations converge. Conversely, German states prosecuted some women as tribades, but German discourse does not show the public interest in sapphic subjects so prevalent in England, France, and the Mediterranean even though, as Helmut Puff argues, Reformation Germany and Switzerland "disseminated notions of [male] same-sex sexuality on a grand scale" as "notions of power and masculinity intersected with intensified religiosity and a revived interest in ancient literature." Puff, *Sodomy in Reformation Germany and Switzerland*, 172.

138. Cameron, *The Sixteenth Century*, 207.

139. Upton, *Europe, 1600–1789*, 31.

140. Konnert, *Early Modern Europe*, 314, 41.

141. Black, "Society," 114.

142. Konnert, *Early Modern Europe*, 54.

143. Nauert, "The Mind," 140.

144. Knox, *Enthusiasm: A Chapter in the History of Religion* (1950), quoted in Thomas, "Women and the Civil War Sects," 345.

145. Davis, "Women on Top," 176.

146. Puff, *Sodomy in Reformation Germany and Switzerland*, 172.

147. On sexual censorship, see Dekker, *Humour in the Dutch Culture*, and Israel, *The Dutch Republic*.

148. See Frieda, *Catherine de Medici*, xxi.

149. Bock, *Women in European History*, 30.

150. Barzun, *From Dawn to Decadence*, 86.

151. On the *Europa regina* phenomenon, see Schmale, "Europa: Die weibliche Form."

152. Paola Malpezzi Price, *Moderata Fonte*, 17.

153. Lope de Vega, *Fuente Ovejuna*, 91; English translation is from *Three Major Plays*, 55.

154. Price, *Moderata Fonte*, 43.

155. Ambrosini, "Toward a Social History of Women in Venice," 422.

156. J. L. Price, *Culture and Society in the Dutch Republic*, 44.

157. Grise, "Depicting Lesbian Desire," 41–57.

158. Stephens, "Into Other Arms: Armoret's Evasion," 211.

159. Cited in Braudel, *Wheels of Commerce*, 472.

160. Ibid., 556.

161. As I mentioned in chapter 1, I have not had the linguistic capacity to explore the possibility of Danish, Norwegian, or Swedish writings. Attention to the arguably lesbian Queen Christina (1626–89), whose sexually suggestive comments raised more than eyebrows at home and abroad, created at least a private discourse about the sapphic in Sweden; on this topic see Buckley, *Christina, Queen of Sweden*. Certainly Denmark by the 1620s and Sweden by the 1630s were parcel to the colonial project, but their place in the "sexuality of history" that I am outlining must be left to scholars of Scandinavian history. Norway, of course, has a much longer colonial history, but its union with Denmark in 1536 ceded its independent colonizing power.

162. See Foucault, *The Order of Things*, 17–23.

163. Cameron, *The Sixteenth Century*, 8.

164. Braudel, *Wheels of Commerce*, 565.

CHAPTER 3

1. *Satan's Harvest Home*, 18.

2. Campbell, *Wonder and Science*, 6, 19.

3. Wanley, *Wonders of the Little World*, 52–54 (book 1, ch. 24).

4. Editions of Wanley appeared at least in 1704, 1774, 1788, 1790, 1791, 1796, and 1806. I also find interesting the large reprint gap between 1704 and 1774. I cannot, of course, substantiate my proposed rationale for the disappearance of this chapter among others.

5. I am not suggesting that humoral accounts are magical nor that accounts of hermaphrodites disappeared; the eighteenth century is notorious for its interest in what it perceived as oddities. But belief in a sudden alteration in the sexed body certainly diminished.

6. Campbell, *Wonder & Science*, 8.

7. Traub, *Renaissance of Lesbianism*, 164, 181.

8. Hume, *The Development of English Drama*, 30. Sanchez, *Erotic Subjects*.

9. See Michael McKeon, "Historicizing Patriarchy."

10. The dates of *Añasco's* performance and publication remain uncertain. Shirley Whitaker (in *The Dramatic Works of Álvaro Cubillo de Aragón*, 98), argues for a date before 1637; most recently, on internal evidence, Elena Marcello sees 1635 as a *terminus ante quem*.

11. Traub, *Renaissance of Lesbianism*, 180.

12. Sollers, *Logiques*, 268: "Le roman est la manière dont cette société se parle." Sollers makes this claim about the novel in the twentieth century, but his insight raises a question for any age: what is the medium through which a particular society speaks to itself?

13. Foucault, *The Order of Things*, 44.

14. See note 95 of chapter 2.

15. Benserade, *Iphis et Iante*, 42: "Iante a sur mon âme une entière puissance, / Et je n'ai pour vous deux que de l'obéissance." In this case, of course, Iphis cannot obey both parents, since they stand opposed.

16. Ibid., 85: "vous allez faire un crime, au lieu d'un mariage."

17. Ibid., 92: "un coeur que la nature a fait contraire aux autres."

18. Ibid., 113: "j'oubliais quelque temps que j'etais une fille"; "je touchais, je baisais, j'avais le coeur content."

19. Ibid., 105: "Ce mariage est doux, j'y trouve assez d'appats."

20. Ibid., 105–6: "Si la fille epousait une fille comme elle, / Sans offenser le ciel et la loi naturelle, / Mon coeur assurément n'en serait point faché, / Je me contenterais de n'avoir pas péché; / Mais puisque la nature et le ciel même ordonne / Que la foi d'une fille à des hommes se donne, / Et que c'est seulement un homme qui l'obtient, / Iphis ne l'étant pas, c'est où le mal me tient."

21. Ibid., 104–5: "Si l'on n'en riait"; "si l'on ne profanait le noeud qui nous assemble"; "si nos bons parents n'abusaient à leur gré"; "si la fille epousait une fille . . . sans offenser le ciel et la loi naturelle"; "ceux qui sont contents de ma triste fortune"; "jugeant rien que par l'extérieur"; "fire parler les théâtres de nous."

22. Ibid., 117, 119: "Quoi donc, mon gendre est fille? . . . ce n'est pas comme on traite avec d'honnêtes gens."

23. Ibid., 109: "Mon sèxe eût étouffé l'amité paternelle, / Mon sèxe qui déjà me rendait criminelle."

24. In making this claim, I diverge from David Robinson's reading of the play in *Closeted Writing and Lesbian and Gay Literature*, which sees in the ending only a mild reprimand of Lidge and which argues that "condemning abuse of patriarchal authority" is emphatically not "one of the play's aims" (226). Although I agree with Robinson that the play must sacrifice heavy condemnation to its comedic end, I see the treatment

of Lidge as harsher, and the instability of the community as more ominous, than he does. I am not, of course, suggesting a deliberate anti-patriarchal agenda on the part of Benserade.

25. Benserade, *Iphis et Iante*, 114: "Mon Dieu! Que les enfants nous donnent peu de joie."

26. Ibid., 121: "Je veux vous obliger dans l'ardeur qui vous presse."

27. The other is Luis Vélez de Guevara's *La Serrana de la Vera* (1613), in which the *mujer esquiva* Gila declares her love for Queen Isabella and indeed her predilection for women, asserting herself a man "by inclination" ("Por inclinación soy hombre," 138). That Isabella is queen, however, sets this relationship on a different level of attainability and idealization; Dionisia's love for Leonor, by contrast, is presented as a real-world possibility, indeed one that Leonor must ward off.

28. Álvaro Cubillo de Aragón, *Añasco el de Talavera*, 1.207–8. I am grateful to Elena E. Marcello for providing me with a copy of her edition in progress. Further references are to act and line numbers as marked in this edition; there are no page numbers in the original text.

29. Ibid.: "yo, aunque hembra nací, soy diferente" (1.49); "aunque nacio mujer, no lo parece" (1.106); "vuestra prima no es mujer" (1.132).

30. As Sherry Velasco reminds me, Dionisia fails the contest because her portrait lacks a nose—clearly a metaphor for her own lack, and one that leads her to vengeance with her phallic sword.

31. Ibid. 3.2042–44: "Mi padre es el ofendido, / y yo ciega y torpemente / a quien le defiernde injurio / y defiendo a quien le ofende."

32. *Ibid.*, 3.2061–63: "si defiendo a don Juan, / es por matarle y beberme su sangre."

33. Ibid., 3.1975–79: "aunque yo / le he acuchillado dos veces, / me he de poner a su lado, / si ocasión se le ofreciere."

34. Velasco, *Lesbians in Early Modern Spain*, 141.

35. Antoine de Torche, *La Toilette galante de l'amour*, 107: "Pour vous rendre satisfaite, / Je voudrais bien avoir ce que vous n'avez pas."

36. Ibid.: "Ici le trop de ressemblance / Arrête nos desseins, et nos plus doux transports."

37. Ibid.: "Et sans une métamorphose, / Ma foi, je ne voy point de remède à ce mal."

38. Benserade, "Sur l'amour d'Uranie avec Philis," in *Oeuvres*, 327–28 and passim: "Vous estes les zeros, et nous sommes les nombres qui vous faisons valoir." For this source, I am grateful to Marianne Legault, "*Iphis & Iante.*"

39. Ibid., 328.

40. Waller, "On the Friendship Betwixt Sacharissa and Amoret," in *Poems etc. Written on Several Occasions*, 41–42. In later editions the poem is retitled "On the Friendship Between Two Ladies" and is known best by that name.

41. Cheek, *Sexual Antipodes*, 2–3.

42. A portion of this text is translated in Merrick and Ragan, *Homosexuality in Early Modern France*, 119–24.

43. Busbecq, *Legationis turcicae epistolae* (1589); I use here an English translation of 1694, *The Four Epistles of A.G. Busbequius*, 181, emphasis mine.

44. Sandys, *Relation of a Journey*, 69.

45. Sharp, *The Midwives Book*, 45.

46. Marten, *A Treatise of the Venereal Disease*, 194–95.

47. *Tractatus de Hermaphroditis: or, A Treatise of Hermaphrodites*, 60.

48. Testimony of Allan Maconochie, Lord Meadowbank, serving as Lord Ordinary to the suit. Cited in Lillian Faderman, *Scotch Verdict*, 65, emphasis mine.

49. Démeunier, *L'esprit des usages*, 2:314.

50. Moreau de St.-Méry, *Voyage aux États-Unis*, 325, 307: "elles ne sont point étrangères au goût de chercher les plaisirs d'une imagination égarée dans une personne de leur propre sexe" (307); *Moreau de St. Méry's American Journey*, 286, 302.

51. Nussbaum, *Torrid Zones*, 14–17 and passim.

52. "El mundo es nuevo. Han pasado los siglos de barbarie, la ambición romana, la fiereza de los septentrionales, el entusiasmo brutal de los mahometanos." Quoted in Kitts, "Ayala and Women's Rights," 372.

53. Chapone, *The Hardships of the English Laws in Relation to Wives*, 71.

54. Mary Wortley Montagu, *Turkish Embassy Letters*, letter of 1 April 1717. The letter circulated in manuscript fair copy and was published in 1763.

55. As I note below, that this period also featured a number of women in positions of sultanic power, a situation as unusual as the one I described in chapter 2 with respect to Europe, might also have been a silent partner to this conversation.

56. Donald Quataert, *The Ottoman Empire*, 2–3.

57. Grosrichard, *The Sultan's Court*, 20.

58. Ibid., 24.

59. Peirce, *The Imperial Harem*, 17.

60. Yegenoglu, *Colonial Fantasies*, 73.

61. Walsh, *Dialogue Concerning Women*, 34–35, 103–4.

62. The choice of Twickenham may be a jibe at Lady Mary Wortley Montagu, who as I noted earlier spent several years in Turkey, whose *Turkish Embassy Letters* would be published in 1763, and who lived in Twickenham. Those letters will liken the baths to a "female coffee house" but will resoundingly reject the imputation of the sapphic; the women mingle, she insists, "without any distinction of rank by their dress, all being in the state of nature, that is, in plain English, stark naked, without any Beauty or defect conceal'd, yet there was not the least wanton smile or immodest Gesture amongst 'em" (1 April 1717).

63. Katherine Philips, Margaret Cavendish, Anne Finch, Mary Astell, and Aphra Behn, all of whom figure in chapter 4, are decidedly partisan, and all on the Stuart side; they are sometimes described as "Tory feminists."

64. See, for example, *A Letter to a Modern Dissenting Whig*, 25; Ned Ward, *Honesty in Distress* (1708); and at least two plays by Nathaniel Lee.

65. "A New Ballad: To the Tune of *Fair Rosamond*," 1. A second ballad, "Masham Display'd: To the Tune of *The Dame of Honour*," figures Masham as a Jacobite "Traitor" who "Side[s] with the *French* Pretender" and though having neither "Beauty, Birth nor Sense," "controul[s] the Nation."

66. Manley, *Secret Memoirs and Manners of Several Persons of Quality, of Both Sexes (The New Atalantis)*, 2:43.

67. Ibid., 2:57. The tone of Manley's representation of the Cabal has become a rather

polarized subject in the wake of David Robinson's "For How Can They Be Guilty," which argues, against Ros Ballaster and others, that the text is "antilesbian in intent, insistently and consistently" (190).

68. Mandeville, *Virgin Unmask'd*, 127.

69. King, *The Toast*, 1:22, 27, 67.

70. Trotter, *Agnes de Castro*, 5–6. Further references are in parentheses within the text. I thank my colleague Susan Staves for introducing me to Trotter's play.

71. Rowe, "Song," in *A New Miscellany of Original Poems*, 18–19. "The Game of Flats" may not have been Rowe's title; it does not appear at the head of the poem until 1715. A footnote appended by 1733 claims that "These *Stanzas* were made on Mrs. B———le, and a Lady her Companion, whom she calls *Captain*."

72. In perhaps the earliest instance, Sally O'Driscoll's research on eighteenth-century ephemera has shown the use of "flat sport" for sapphic behavior in a 1684 pamphlet called "The She-Wedding, or a Mad Marriage." Given Rowe's naturalizing project, it is ironic that the 1718 *Treatise of Hermaphrodites*, which quotes the poem, describes it as "finely illustrating" the "*unnatural* Pleasures of this kind" (17, emphasis mine).

73. *An Epistle from Sapho to Philaenis*, passim.

74. Barker, *A Patch-Work Screen for the Ladies*, 97, 99. Further references will appear within the text.

75. Upton, *Europe 1600–1789*, 16–17.

76. King, "'The Unaccountable Wife,'" 166. It seems plausible that Barker would be both attracted to and repelled by the possibility of such leveling. On the one hand, she was an early feminist who did not marry and who championed women's right to remain single. On the other, Barker was a Catholic and almost certainly a Jacobite who supported the deposed Stuart monarchy throughout her life and thus aligned herself with those who would maintain that "chain of being" at least at the upper echelons.

77. On Barker's Jacobitism, which included voluntary exile at St.-Germain-en-laye, see King, *Jane Barker, Exile*, esp. 12–13, and Eicke, "The Extremity of the Times," ch. 4.

78. *The Sappho-an*, 26, 45, and passim. The text has been dated to 1749 on the basis of a handwritten note on the title page of one of the few extant copies. Further references will appear in the body of the text.

79. I will discuss Carter's poetry in chapter 4. See also Lanser, "Bluestocking Sapphism" and "Tory Lesbians," for discussions of the sapphic inflections in Carter's private writings.

80. Eicke, "The Extremity of the Times," 47.

81. *The Female Rebels*, 5.

82. Ibid., 7.

83. *The Travels and Adventures of Mademoiselle de Richelieu*, 1:4. Further references will appear in the body of the text.

84. Lamb, "'Be Such a Man as I,'" 98 and *passim*.

85. Cohen, *Drama of a Nation*, 311.

86. Iarocci, *Properties of Modernity*, 8,15.

87. This is arguably also true of the decline of Golden Age theater in approximately the same period. That change has been attributed in part to the death in 1665 of the reigning monarch, Philip IV, himself a strong patron of the theater and to the ensuing

Wars of the Spanish Succession. I do not know whether these factors would also be at work in the decline of the novel, which happens somewhat earlier.

88. Resina, "The Short, Happy Life of the Novel in Spain," 302–7.

89. Ginger, *Painting and the Turn to Cultural Modernity*, 86.

90. Kitts, "Ignacio López de Ayala," 362.

91. Feijoo, *Defensa de la mujer:* "defender a todas las mujeres, viene a ser lo mismo que ofender a casi todos los hombres]." "Si las mujeres son iguales a los hombres en la aptitud para las artes, para las ciencias, para el gobierno político, y económico, ¿por qué Dios estableció el dominio, y superioridad del hombre, respecto de la mujer, en aquella sentencia del cap. 3 del Génesis *Sub viri potestate eris?* Pues es de creer, que diese el gobierno a aquel sexo, en quien reconoció mayor capacidad" (par. 148).

92. On female homoeroticism and the Fronde, see Wahl, *Invisible Relations*, ch. 5, passim.

CHAPTER 4

1. Erasmus, *All the Familiar Colloquies*, 481.

2. Hugo, *Notre Dame de Paris [The Hunchback of Notre Dame]* (1831), book 5, ch. 2, "Ceci tuera cela": "L'invention de l'imprimerie est le plus grand événement de l'histoire. C'est la révolution mère. . . . [C]'est la pensée humaine qui dépouille une forme et en revêt une autre. . . .Avant l'imprimerie, la réforme n'eût été qu'un schisme, l'imprimerie la fait révolution."

3. I have in mind such changes as urbanization and boarding schools that fostered women's (and men's) access to non-kin relations within elite social spheres. I am not suggesting that friendship between women was a new phenomenon or exclusively an elite one; Sharon Farmer's fine study of thirteenth-century Parisian working women ("Down and Out") would already disprove that claim.

4. I am not, however, suggesting collaboration or even intentionality.

5. Wahrman, *The Making of the Modern Self*, xvii.

6. Montaigne, *Essais*, ch 27; Hyatte, *The Arts of Friendship*, 87.

7. On this transformation, see Perry, *Novel Relations*.

8. Brathwait, *The English Gentleman*, 456 and passim. So fragile does Brathwait find the power of bloodline that, a full century before the social movement against wet nursing, he exhorts noblewomen to feed their own infants lest their offspring imbibe lowborn "Nurses manners" with "Nurses milke" (*The English Gentlewoman*, 161).

9. Curtis, "The Alienated Intellectuals of Early Stuart England," 328. Charles Wilson makes a similar argument about the European continent in *The Transformation of Europe*.

10. E. P. Thompson, *The Making of the English Working Class*, 11.

11. Brathwait, *The English Gentleman*, 69.

12. Ibid., 243.

13. Brathwait, *The English Gentlewoman*, 41. Brathwait also cautions women against wearing men's clothes or any "commixture" thereof (10).

14. Heilbrun, *Writing a Woman's Life*, 100.

15. Bray, *The Friend*, 11.

16. Stewart, *Close Readers*, xxiii.

17. Taylor, *Discourse of the Nature, Offices, and Measures of Friendship*, 326.

18. Ibid., 108 (emphasis in original).

19. Bray, *The Friend*, 190, 217.

20. The qualifier of equality disappears by 1762 from all subsequent dictionary entries, while the *Encyclopédie* embodies the somewhat more mobile eighteenth-century spirit when it suggests that friendship must "find equality or create it [trouver de l'égalité ou l'y mettre]." "Amitié," *Encyclopédie*, 1:361.

21. Goodrich, "Laws of Friendship," 25, 27.

22. Bacon, "Of Friendship," 162.

23. Browne, *Religio Medici*, 103–4.

24. Taylor, *Discourse*, 93–98.

25. Sautman and Sheingorn, "Introduction: Charting the Field," in *Same-Sex Love and the Middle Ages*, 20.

26. Bray, *The Friend*, 10.

27. Finch, "The Petition for an Absolute Retreat," in *Miscellany Poems*, 44.

28. Finch, "Friendship Between Ephelia and Ardelia," in *Miscellany Poems*, 252–53.

29. Finch, "The Petition for an Absolute Retreat," in *Miscellany Poems*, 41.

30. Masters, "My Love describ'd to CAMILLA," in *Poems on Several Occasions*, 140.

31. Sor Violante, *Rimas varias*, 2; "a que es conforme simpatía, / de quien lealtad hasta la muerte ostenta," quoted and translated in Gwyn Fox, *Subtle Subversions*, 165–66.

32. See DeJean, *Ancients Against Moderns: Culture Wars and the Making of a Fin de Siècle*, ch. 3.

33. Culler, "Apostrophe," 63.

34. The poems form an appendix to Eisenbichler, "'Laudomia Forteguerri Loves Margaret of Austria.'" It is worth noting that they were allegedly first published without Forteguerri's approval, not an uncommon claim in this period whether or not disingenuous.

35. Visscher, "Aan joffrouw Georgette de Montenay [To Miss Georgette de Montenay]," trans. Myra Heerspink Scholz, in *Women's Writing from the Low Countries*: "Ik wenste zulk een speelgenoot. / Maar kan 't in t'lichaam niet geschiên, miojn geest zal lijkwel bij u vliên" (234–35).

36. See Powell, "Baroque Flair." Powell is one of the scholars who has most fully studied the form that I call sapphic apostrophe, particularly in its Spanish iterations.

37. Lanyer, "The Description of Cooke-ham," in *Salve Deus Rex Judaeorum*, n.p.

38. Rohan, "Sur une dame nommée Aimée, 1617," in *Poésies d'Anne de Rohan-Soubise*, 46–47. In naming her beloved "Aimée," of course, Rohan's poem plays with the double meaning of the word as both common noun and proper name. The poem is given in both the original and English translation in *The Defiant Muse: French Feminist Poems*, 70–73.

39. Catalina Clara Ramirez de Guzmán, "A la ausencia de una amiga, hablando con ella," in Gwyn Fox, *Subtle Subversions*, 162–63.

40. Violante, *Rimas*. See the introductory discussion and selections of Sor Violante's poetry in *Tras el espejo la musa escribe*, ed. Olivares and Boyce, 39–43 and 356–58.

41. Zayas y Sotomayor, "Soneto (con estrambote)," in *Tras el espejo*, 224.

42. A few of the poems I quote here, for instance the work of "Marcia Belisarda," pseudonym for Sor Maria de Santa Isabel, were not published during her lifetime, possibly for reasons of censorship or religious interdiction, but were clearly prepared for publication and may have circulated in manuscript.

43. Questier's, "Op haer kouse-band die zij op mijn kamer had laaten leggen," in *The Defiant Muse: Dutch and Flemish Feminist Poems*, 60–61: "Wou my de hulp-Goddin van 't groot Aegyptenlant / Zoo gunstig zyn als zy wel eertyds Iphis deede / Ik liet, spyt Engelland, een Waapen voor my smeeden / En wiert een Ridder van dees nieuwe Kousebant."

44. See Lia van Gemert, "Hiding Behind Words?"

45. Rowe, *Poems*, 58; *Miscellaneous Works*, 1:72–73.

46. Behn, "Verses, designed by Mrs A. Behn to be sent to a fair Lady," in *The Works of Aphra Behn*, 1:356. Behn, "To the Fair Clarinda," in Ibid., 1:288.

47. Philips, "Orinda to Lucasia parting, October 1661," in *Collected Works*, 211.

48. Cavendish, *CCXI Sociable Letters*, 423.

49. Killigrew, *Poems*, 99.

50. Sor Juana Inés de la Cruz, *A Sor Juana Anthology*, 36: "Yo, pues, mi adorada Filis, / que tu deidad reverencio, que tu desdén idolatro / y que tu rigor venero: bien asi, como la simple / amante que, entornos ciegos, / es despojo de la lamma / por tocar el lucimiento."

51. Astell, *Letters Concerning the Love of God*, 40. The same Lady Catherine is also inscribed within the marble and alabaster monument in Westminster Abbey to Mary Kendall (1677–1710); see Traub, *Renaissance of Lesbianism*, 70–72, and Bray, *The Friend*, 228.

52. Louise-Geneviève Gillot de Sainctonge, "Pour Madame T. . . ," in *Poèmes galantes*, 177: "cette belle a bien changé mon ame"; "plus on sent d'amour moins on peut l'exprimer."

53. Sainctonge, "Épître à Madame la Marquise de C****," in *Poesies divers*, 1:273: "Que vous avez, gentille Dame, / Un entier pouvoir sur mon âme."

54. Simiane, "Madrigal," in *Portefeuille*, 80.

55. Masters, "My Love describ'd to CAMILLA," 139.

56. Philips, "Orinda to Lucasia Parting," in *Collected Works*, 212–13.

57. Smith, *Homosexual Desire in Shakespeare's England*, 105.

58. This phenomenon does not find a parallel in literature by men; homoerotic poems by men to men notwithstanding, the *dominant* apostrophic practice for male writers of the period is male to female.

59. On the conventionally assumed relationship between lyric persona and author, see Lanser, "The 'I' of the Beholder."

60. Bray, *The Friend*, 139, emphasis in original.

61. Manley, *The New Atalantis*, 2:57–58.

62. Mermin, "Women Becoming Poets," 343–44.

63. Andreadis, *Sappho in Early Modern England*, 70. A related approach argues for gender neutrality, as Gwyn Fox does when she suggests that a particular sonnet of Sor Violante with a female speaker ("Quien dice que la ausencia es homicida") masks

the addressee's identity in order to create "a social world not subject in every aspect to gender constructions, hence broadening the message of her poem beyond that of a mere love sonnet," an argument that might be more plausible if Sor Violante had not written so many poems to women. Fox, *Subtle Subversions*, 206.

64. See van Gemert, "Hiding Behind Words."

65. Hobby, "Katherine Philips: Seventeenth Century Lesbian Poet."

66. Andreadis, *Sappho in Early Modern England*, 75. Andreadis extends her research and its support for a sapphic Philips in "Reconfiguring Early Modern Friendship."

67. Paula Loscocco proposes an intertextual motive when she reads Philips's friendship poems as a radical rewriting of Donne, but this too seems too limited an explanation for the many, many poems Philips addresses to women. See her "Inventing the English Sappho."

68. Traub, *The Renaissance of Lesbianism*, 297–98.

69. Fraisse, *Les femmes et leur histoire*, 11.

70. Beauvoir, *The Second Sex*, 8. The French original: "Les femmes . . . ne disent pas 'nous' . . . elles ne se posent pas authentiquement comme Sujet. . . . Elles vivent dispersées parmi les hommes, rattachées par l'habitat, le travail, les intérêts économiques, la condition sociale à certains hommes—père ou mari—plus étroitement qu'aux autres femmes" (*Le deuxième sexe*, 21).

71. Rancière, *Disagreement*, 22, 35.

72. Žižek, *The Ticklish Subject*, 188. For a modern example of an "obscenity" in Žižek's sense, we might consider the venomous early response to the English word "Ms.," (re)born in a magazine in December 1971—and recall that *The New York Times* would not accept Ms. in lieu of Miss or Mrs. until 1986.

73. Rancière, *Disagreement*, 55, 58, 42.

74. Volckmann, "Brief an Mariana Ziegler" from *Erstlinge Unvollkommener Gedichte* (Leipzig, 1736) in *The Defiant Muse: German Feminist Poems*, ed. Cocalis, 25: "Frau! Weltberühmte Frau, der Eifer nimmt mich ein, / Auf, laß diß frevle Volck nicht sonder Straffe seyn. / Zeigt sich kein scharffer Stahl an unsern tapffern Seiten, / So laß uns diesen Schwarm mit unserm Kiel bestreiten."

75. Less contentiously but no less emphatically, Marie de Romieu's "que l'excellence de la femme surpasse celle de l'homme" (1581) insists that women are more valuable than men; *The Defiant Muse: French Feminist Poems*, ed. Stanton, 60–62.

76. Maria de Zayas, *Desengaños amorosos*," in *Novelas completas*, 669–70: "Lisis se levantó, y tomando por la mano a la hermosa doña Isabel, y a su prima doña Estefanía por la otra . . . se entraron todas tres en otra cuadra . . . [y] se fueron a un convento con mucho gusto. . . . No es trágico fin, sino el más felice que se pudo dar, pues codiciosa y deseada de muchos, no se sujetó a ninguno." On this text, see Vollendorf, "The Value of Female Friendship in Seventeenth-Century Spain."

77. Perry, *The Celebrated Mary Astell*, 141, 149.

78. Petronilla Massimi, "Unbind your angered tresses [Spieghi le chiome irate]," in *The Defiant Muse: Italian Feminist Poems*, ed. Allen, Kittel, and Jewell: "soi del nostro valor l'uomo è tiranno," 26–27.

79. See *A Letter Sent by the Maydens of London*. For a rich analysis of this text, see Ann Rosalind Jones, "Maidservants of London."

80. J. Douglas Kneale, "Romantic Aversions," 144.

81. As Pateman defines it, the "sexual contract" works in tandem with the "social contract" of civil society by establishing "men's political right over women" and the "orderly access by men to women's bodies" (*The Sexual Contract*, 2).

82. Lady Mary Lee Chudleigh, "To the Ladies," in *Poems on Several Occasions*, 45–46.

83. Louise Labé, "To Mademoiselle Clemence de Bourges of Lyon," in *Women Writers of the Renaissance and Reformation*, 149–50. Clearly, I do not credit the hypothesis that Labé was a man writing as a woman.

84. Philips, "To My Lucasia, on our Friendship," in *Collected Works*, 129.

85. Philips, "To My excellent Lucasia," in *Collected Works*, 121–22.

86. Shannon, *Sovereign Amity*, ch. 1.

87. Scudéry, *The Story of Sapho*, 143–44; *Les femmes illustres, ou Les harangues héroïques*, 441–42: "toutes ces belles choses, / Don't vostre visage est peint ; L'esclat des yeux & du teint, / Tout perdra forme & matiere; Et vous mourrez toute entiere, / Si pour vaincre la Parque, & la fatalite, / Vous n'allex par l'estude, a l'immortalite"; "Que si l'on s'esloigne du sens Literal, pour s'aprocher de mes intentions; ie seray bien glorieux, si ie puis persuader à nos Dames, ce que cette belle Lesbienne, persuadoit à son Amie: & plus encore, si ie puis persuader à toute la terre, que ce beau Sexe, est digne de nostre adoration: afin qu'on luy consacre un iour des Temples & des autels, comme ie luy consacre maintenant, L'ARC DE TRIOMPHE, QUE I'AY ESLEVÉ A SA GLOIRE."

88. John Wilmot, Earl of Rochester, "A Letter Fancy'd from Artemisia in the Town, to Cloe in the Country," in *Poems on Several Occasions*, 18. The poem charges that "whore is scarce a more reproachful name / Than poetess" (18).

89. "Cloe to Artimesa," in *A New Miscellany*, 123.

90. Margaret Cavendish, *The Convent of Pleasure*, from *Plays, Never Before Printed*, 3. Further references will appear within the text.

91. Cavendish carries out a similar blend of (less explicitly homoerotic) female affiliation and patriarchal critique in at least two other plays, *The Female Academy* and *Bell in Campo* (both 1662); all three works, as Erin Bonin's comments, "wrest female characters from patriarchal economies to envision female political agency. Likewise, Cavendish's *Sociable Letters* repeatedly posit friendship, female intimacies, and relations of similitude as utopian spaces within a society plagued by competition and ambition in a nation riven by Civil War." See Bonin, "Margaret Cavendish's Dramatic Utopias," 340.

92. Sainctonge, "Épître à Madame la Marquise de C****," *Poesies divers*, 1:272: "ravir cette liberté / Dont votre coeur est enchanté"; "fort importun maître."

93. Robyn Warhol, *Having a Good Cry*, 14–18 passim. As Warhol argues, the assumption that feelings are "expressive" rather than "performative" may well be an effect of the psychoanalytic framework that became dominant in the mid-twentieth century. If one follows a theoretical line that dates back at least to William James and is implicit in Victorian theories of acting, one can argue that feelings are produced and performative.

94. Andreadis, *Sappho in Early Modern England*, 81.

95. One might arguably compare the so-called "political lesbianism" of the 1970s,

in which a homoerotic dimension, genuinely felt, likewise furthered a collective subjectivity.

96. See Sharon Marcus, *Between Women*, ch. 1.

97. Colwill, "Epistolary Passions."

98. Susan Kirkpatrick, *Las Románticas*, 83. This particular poem is García Miranda's "A las españolas" (1851), quoted in Kirkpatrick, 84–85.

99. Excluding reprintings and catalogue listings, I count 83 instances of the phrase "female friendship" (not including "female friend") in a database covering 1700–1800, 79 of which occur between 1750 and 1799. Both novels and nonfiction works are represented, so an increase in novels is not the only explanation for these strikingly different numbers.

100. Wetenhall Wilkes, *Letter of Genteel and Moral Advice to a Young Lady*, 129.

101. Lanser, "Befriending the Body."

102. Cavendish, *The Convent of Pleasure*, 7.

103. Allestree, *The Ladies Calling*, Preface, n.p.

104. In "The Odd Women," Caroline Gonda makes a lovely coupling of the chaste and suspicious in the writings of contemporaries Sarah Scott and Charlotte Charke.

105. *Critical Review, or, Annals of Literature* 13 (March 1762), 181.

106. I have discussed in "Befriending the Body" that manipulation on the part of these women.

107. Elizabeth Montagu, Letter to Sarah Scott of 18 September 1750, Huntington MO 5719. I discuss this letter in the context of Bluestocking relationships in "Tory Lesbians."

108. The relationship between Scott and "Lady Bab" lasted until Lady Barbara's death in 1765 despite the interruption of Scott's short and disastrous marriage. Elizabeth Montagu had more than once expressed displeasure and discomfort at what was in effect, by Scott's own articulation, a same-sex marriage. One of Elizabeth Montagu's own intimacies was with Elizabeth Carter; see my "Bluestocking Sapphism" and "Tory Lesbians."

109. Carter, *Poems on Several Occasions*, 12, 39. Further references will appear within the text.

110. Feijoo, *Defensa de las damas*, section 120 (363–64): "la *Sapho de su siglo*, pues igualó a aquella celebradísima Griega en el primor de las composiciones, y la excedió mucho en la pureza de costumbres, . . . pero incomparable en la discreción."

111. Guest, *Small Change*, 17.

112. *Critical Review*, 181.

113. Scott, *Millenium Hall*, 93, 117. On the (sapphic) eroticization of pain, see Binhammer, "The 'Singular Propensity.'"

114. Scott, *Millenium Hall*, 127, 66–67.

115. See Theo Van der Meer, "Tribades on Trial." See also, for a much earlier example, Farmer, "Down and Out."

116. Rousseau, *Emile, or On Education*, 357–58, 363: *Emile, ou de l'Éducation*, 446–47, 454: "la femme est fait spécialement pour plaire à l'homme"; "la femme est faite pour plaire et pour être subjuguée"; "elle doit se rendre agréable à l'homme au lieu de le provoquer"; "Ce n'est pas ici la loi de l'amour, j'en conviens; mais c'est celle de la

nature"; "plus elles voudront leur ressembler, moins elles les gouverneront, et c'est alors qu'ils seront vraiment les maîtres."

117. Roulston, Narrating Marriage, 77–78.

118. Rousseau, *Du contrat social*, book 3, sec. 12: "Par ce qui s'est fait considérons ce qui se peut faire; je ne parlerai pas des anciennes républiques de la Grece, mais la République romaine étoit, ce me semble, un grand Etat, & la ville de Rome un grande ville. Le dernier Cens donna dans Rome quatre cent mille Citoyens portans armes, & le dernier dénombrement de l'Empire plus de quatre millions de Citoyens sans compter les sujets, les étrangers, les femmes, les enfans, les esclaves" (203).

119. Macaulay, in *The Aberdeen Magazine, Literary Chronicle, and Review*, 23 September 1790, 583.

120. Fichte, *The Science of Rights* [*Grundlage des Naturrechts*], 440–42, emphasis mine.

121. Bray, *The Friend*, 219. George Haggerty's *Men In Love* complicates Bray's arguments as well.

122. Deken, "Vriendschapszucht" in *The Defiant Muse: Dutch and Flemish Feminist Poems*, ed. Meijer et al., 72–73:

Wat valt het leeven van trouwhartige Vriendinnen,
    Als zy gescheiden zyn niet bitter, hard en straf!
    Ik min haar als myzelf, ja 'k min haar al zo teêr:
Dan ach! Naauw zie ik haar, of moet haar weêr begeeven!
Laat my toch, 't gaa hoe 't gaa, met mijn MARIA leeven!
    Gun my dees bede, ô Vriend der Vrienden! 'k wensch niet meer.

123. See Lanser, "Bluestocking Sapphism."

124. Anna Williams, "The Nunnery," *Miscellanies in Prose and Verse*, 107–11.

125. Pratt, *Shenstone-Green*, 52–55. On this work, see Perry, "Bluestockings in Utopia."

126. Ibid.

127. Baldwin, "Anna Louisa Karsch as Sappho."

128. Karsch, "An die Frau von Reichmann," *Auslesener Gedichte*, 2:87–88; "An Phillis. Eine Einladung zu den Ruinen bey Potsdam," quoted in Steidele, *"Als wenn Du mein Geliebter wärest,"* 113.

129. Luise Gottsched, quoted in Susanne Kord, "Eternal Love or Sentimental Discourse," 236–41.

130. Sollers, *Logiques*, 268.

CHAPTER 5

1. Robert, *Origins of the Novel*, 19.

2. Tocqueville, *Souvenirs*, 78: "Dans une emeute comme dans un roman, ce qu'il y a de plus difficile à inventer, c'est la fin."

3. Moretti, "Introduction" to *The Novel*, 2:x.

4. Bakhtin, *Dialogic Imagination*, 8.

5. Lukács, *Theory of the Novel*, 88, 56.

6. Pavel, "The Novel in Search of Itself," in *The Novel*, 2:3. While Pavel sees the couple as a *longue durée* feature of the novel, Joan DeJean suggests in *Ancients Against Moderns* (99 and ch. 3, passim) that the importance of the couple, over against the hero, is itself a sign of modernity—and to the "ancients" therefore a sign of the corruption of both society and literature.

7. Moretti, *The Way of the World*, 16; Resina, "Short, Happy Life of the Novel in Spain," 300.

8. Armstrong, *Desire and Domestic Fiction*, 9.

9. Laqueur, *Making Sex*, 149.

10. Perry, *Novel Relations*, 2–3. In the French context, a novel like Prévost's *L'histoire du chevalier des Grieux et de Manon Lescaut* (1731), for all its broader tragic entanglements, builds its plot upon the importance of choosing the "right" partner.

My emphasis in this chapter on English and French novels is not a fallback to my greatest expertise. As is widely acknowledged, the "rise of the novel" is heavily a French and English project between the late seventeenth and the late eighteenth century; the influential Spanish picaresque had waned by 1650, and the novel did not flourish in other European languages before 1770. For quantitative data, see Moretti, *Graphs, Maps, Trees*.

11. Doody, *The True Story of the Novel*, 294.

12. Jameson, *The Political Unconscious*, 19.

13. Miller, "Emphasis Added."

14. Armstrong, *Desire and Domestic Fiction*, 14.

15. Johnson, "Anthropomorphism in Lyric and Law." Johnson's polar opposite to the "lyric subject"—well figured in the slave who garners more sympathy than political legitimacy in the eighteenth century—is the corporation, which in modern times has sometimes been allowed legal rights while never figured as a lyric subject. I take up the question of women's rights and the novel through Johnson's formulation in "The Novel Body Politic."

16. See Bannet, *The Domestic Revolution*.

17. Moretti, *The Way of the World*, 8.

18. McKeon, *The Secret History of Domesticity*.

19. See Moore, *Dangerous Intimacies*; Haggerty, *Unnatural Affections* and *Queer Gothic*; Roulston, *Narrating Marriage*; Everard, *Ziel en zinnen*; Steidele, *"Als wenn Du mein Geliebter wärest."* I do not intend this chapter to arrogate all relevant novels to one paradigm; novels will appear in chapters 6 and 7 as well, insofar as they support different kinds of arguments from those I make here.

20. Aretino, *Dialogues*, 341–42; *Il ragionamenti*, 275: "la vidi spogliare ignuda . . . perchè egli la contemplò in ogni parte. . . . Un collo Iddio! Un petto balia! E due poccie da far corrompere I vergini, et da sfratare I martiri; io mi smarrii nel vedere il corpo con la sua gioia per elico in mezzo, e mi perdei ne la vaghezza di quella cosa, bontà de la quale si fanno tante pazie, tante nimicizie, tante spese, et tante parole. . . . Io ti giuro per lo mio mobile, e lo do a sacco, al fuoco, e ai ladri, e ai birri, se non mi posi nel vederlo la mano a la cotale, menandomela non altrimenti che si menino I cotali da

chi non ha dove intignergli." Denise Walen's *Constructions of Female Homoeroticism* (10–11) introduced me to this passage.

21. Aretino, *Il ragionamenti*, 342.

22. Bakhtin, *Dialogic Imagination*, 123.

23. Ibid., 95.

24. Ibid., 332. Bakhtin's translator, Caryl Emerson, explains in an email exchange that the Russian original does not imply the generic masculine of the English; the possessive pronoun modifies the noun "person" and thus means "his or her" or "one's."

25. As I observed in chapter 2, Moderata Fonte's *Il merito delle donne* is unusual in using exclusively female voices, and Judith Deitch has shown that a few other early works also create female interlocutors (see "Dialoguewise"). Still, as Michael Prince notes in *Philosophical Dialogue in the British Enlightenment*, "women rarely participate in any of the major philosophical dialogues written during the eighteenth century" (204). As befits a transgressive practice, the few exceptions tend to use female dialogue for transgressive purposes, either in protofeminist discourses about the status of women or in strategic deployments of sexuality that can arguably trace their roots to Lucian's *Dialogues of the Courtesans* of the second century C.E., to my knowledge the only classical work that relies almost exclusively on female voice.

26. The *Académie des dames* was originally published in Latin as *Aloisiae Sigeae Toletanae Satyra sotadica de Arcanis Amoris et Veneris* (1660). The identity of the author of *Vénus*, the "Abbé du Prat," has not been established but is thought to be either Jean Barrin or François de Chavigny de la Bretonnière.

27. Additional, probably apocryphal dialogues appear in some editions of *Vénus dans le clôitre*.

28. Bakhtin, *Dialogic Imagination*, 250.

29. Ibid.

30. *L'école des filles*, 98, 177–78.

31. Ibid., 165 (section 76): "en cette posture où la femme est dessus et l'homme dessous, il y a une ressemblance de cette métamorphose par la mutation des devoirs qui est réciproque; au moyen de quoi l'homme se revêt entièrement des passions de la femme, et cette posture lui figure qu'il a changé de sexe, et la femme réciproquement s'imagine d'être devenue homme parfait dans la situation qu'elle lui fait garder"; "si vous les voyiez de loin accouplés comme ils sont, vous les prendriez l'un pour l'autre."

32. Bernard Mandeville, *The Virgin Unmask'd*, 1.

33. David Robinson (*Closeted Writing*) faults these novels for not, in effect, validating an authentic "lesbian" orientation. I have in mind here something less ambitious in terms of sexual identity but perhaps more ambitious in terms of novel form.

34. *Académie des dames*, 257: "il n'y rien de juste ou d'injuste de soi-meme, rien de bon ou de mauvais dans les moeurs, l'usage seul qualifie toutes choses." For a rich and nuanced discussion of the *Académie* and its Latin predecessor, see Wahl, *Invisible Relations*, ch. 6.

35. Mouráo, "The Representation of Female Desire," 593.

36. See Hunt, *The Invention of Pornography*.

37. Miller, *Heroine's Text*, 146 and passim. I would not agree with Philip E. Sim-

mons, however, that these voices are simply "jocks in drag," a "men's locker room" ventriloquizing as a women's ("John Cleland's Memoirs," 53). Nor can we assume that men were the only readers of erotica. If we recall that Samuel Pepys, no shy violet, read and then burned *L'école des filles* (1655), we can understand why the traces of women's consumption of erotica might be virtually nonexistent.

38. Robert, *Origins of the Novel*, 3.

39. *La vida de Lazarillo de Tormes*, 2; Resina, "The Short, Happy Life of the Novel in Spain," 293.

40. The picaresque has persisted, of course, into the present, often in ways that resist not only the domestic(ated) novel's intricate plotting but, at its most edgy, the values of accommodation to which the conventional novel adheres; see, for example, *Vanity Fair*, *The Adventures of Huckleberry Finn*, *The Good Soldier Švejk*, *La familia de Pascual Duarte*, *Catcher in the Rye*, *The Adventures of Augie March*, and, as an early second-wave lesbian intervention, *Rubyfruit Jungle*.

41. Burney's *The Wanderer* (1814) provides a counter-example in appropriating the unmarked case for a female character.

42. The essay from which I revise and expand an earlier discussion of the "sapphic picaresque" also had the objective of challenging the absence of attention to female homoeroticism in Michael McKeon's "Historicizing Patriarchy." Apparently relying solely on the arguments of Randolph Trumbach, McKeon claims in a footnote that Afor most of the eighteenth century it was still understood that women who had sexual relations with other women also desired men, so that their feminine gender status was not thereby endangered" (320n55)." On the basis of this well disproved argument, McKeon implies that modern patriarchy has already Aemerged" by the time the sapphic became culturally significant. For my rejoinder, see "Sapphic Picaresque."

43. I am grateful to Castle's important book for introducing this story. "The Apparition of Mrs Veal" has been attributed by some scholars to Defoe. George Starr argues to the contrary in "Why Defoe Probably Did Not Write *The Apparition of Mrs. Veal*."

44. "An Epistle From Signora F———a to a Lady," n.p.

45. Haywood, *The City Jilt*, 60.

46. Haywood, *The Rash Resolve*, 126. For a fuller discussion of this and other Haywood novels with lesbian implications, see Catherine Ingrassia, "Eliza Haywood, Sapphic Desire."

47. See the first epigraph to this chapter.

48. *The Travels and Adventures of Mademoiselle de Richelieu*, 1:1. The novel claims to be a translation from the French; no French antecedent has been discovered.

49. Ibid., 1:2 and 2:230.

50. Haywood, *The British Recluse*, 9, 137.

51. Bianchi, *Breve storia della vita di Catterina Vizzani Romana*, 9.

52. Villedieu, *Henriette-Sylvie de Molière*, 87: "à qui, si je ne me trompe, ma bonne mine apprenait à aimer un homme."

53. Bianchi and Cleland, *True History*, 2; Bianchi, *Breve storia*, 3: "per varie e rimote contrade sia andato vagando per vedere di giugnere in fine al possedimento della disiata cosa."

54. "Epistle From Signora F———a to a Lady," n.p.

55. Manley, *The New Atalantis*, 2:46.

56. Rimmon-Kenan, "Place, Space, and Michal Govrin's *Snapshots*."

57. Haywood, *The British Recluse*, 138.

58. Bianchi, *Breve storia*, 3; Cleland's version turns "great disasters" into the more melodramatic "Fatigues, Dangers, and Distress" (2).

59. Villedieu, *Henriette-Sylvie de Molière*, 262: "je me trouve en état de mener une vie tranquille et assez aisée, dans quelque condition que je bveuille choisir."

60. Fielding, *The Female Husband*, 51. Further references will appear in the body of the text.

61. *Mademoiselle de Richelieu*, 2:245.

62. *Life and Imaginations of Sally Paul*, 158.

63. Ibid., 159, 154.

64. Scott, *Journey Through Every Stage*, 160.

65. *The Life and Imaginations of Sally Paul*, 155, 156, 140.

66. McKeon, "Historicizing Patriarchy," 307.

67. Johnson, "Anthropomorphism in Lyric and Law." As I noted above, Johnson's "lyric person" is the person with whom we can sympathize, the person with interiority; the "legal person" is the person recognized by law. Thus a slave can be a lyric but is not a legal person; conversely, in the modern United States, a corporation can be a legal person but never a lyric one.

68. Charke, *A Narrative of the Life of Mrs. Charlotte Charke*, 107.

69. Cleland, *Catherine Vizzani*, 15.

70. Cleland, *Catherine Vizzani*, 44; Bianchi, *Catterina Vizzani*, 24: "in Lei era molto ordinaria ed era da riporsi tra le piccole anzi che o grande, o mezzana dir si potesse."

71. Findlen, "Anatomy of a Lesbian," 223.

72. Cleland, *Catharine Vizzani*, 58.

73. Findlen, "Anatomy of a Lesbian," 221.

74. Gladfelder, *Fanny Hill in Bombay*, 88.

75. Cleland, *Memoirs of a Woman of Pleasure*, 39, 129.

76. See Beynon, "'Traffic in More Precious Commodities.'"

77. We might also add the incorporation of sapphic figures in order to render them grotesque within the emergent parallel economies of nations and families. Thus the arguably sapphic Mrs. Jewkes abets Mr. B's attempted rape of Pamela; thus too, as Felicity Nussbaum notes, at least one satire, *Pamela Censured* (1741), implicates Pamela herself as a lesbian. See Nussbaum, *Torrid Zones*, 145.

78. *La religieuse* began in 1760 as a set of letters meant to be a hoax upon a friend. The fictional correspondence was printed in the *Correspondance littéraire* in 1770 as was a revised version of the novel in 1780; the novel itself was published in book form posthumously, in 1796.

79. Richardson, *The History of Charles Grandison*, 1:43.

80. Ibid., 1:43 and 1:58.

81. Ibid., 1:42.

82. I discuss the shift in representing the sapphic subject from markers *in* the body to markers *on* the body, in "'Queer to Queer.'"

83. Sedgwick, "Privilege of Unknowing."

84. Haywood, *The Masqueraders*, 13. Further references will appear within the text. I thank Kathryn King for this reference.

85. Certainly in the eighteenth century, but arguably also throughout its history, male-male homoerotic dialogue simply does not take form in the novel in the same way as does female confidence. One could argue, of course, that the dialogue form enacted between two or more male interlocutors already lies at the heart of the "Western tradition" given its primacy as Plato's great structuring technique and its widespread subsequent use. In the eighteenth-century novel before Goethe, though, it is rare for a male narrator to address a male narratee to recount erotic desires or actions, though one might consider Clarissa a love object between Lovelace and Belford.

86. Marie-Jeanne Riccoboni, *Lettres de Milady Juliette Catesby*, 172–73: "Si à la place de cette amie si chère à votre coeur, vous voulez en acceptez une nouvelle, Milady d'Ossery est prête à répondre à vos tendre félicitations. . . . Plus de Milady Catesby; c'est ma femme, mon amie, ma maitresse."

87. Ibid., 173: "On vous attend avec impatience ici: point de fêtes, de bals sans ma chère Henriette; je dirois point de plaisirs, si la personne qui suit ma plume des yeux n'étoit déjà un peu jalouse de ma tendre amitié." In a fuller analysis of this novel in *Fictions of Authority*, I discuss the ways in which Ossery's own narration undermines itself even before Juliette regains the pen.

88. On the notion of "tendre amitié," see Wahl, *Invisible Relations*, 98ff. This evocation, "douce et tendre amie," is likewise used by Deken and Wolff's Sara Burgerhart—and in the French—as she writes to her own confidante.

89. Richardson, *Clarissa*, 1402–3.

90. Rousseau, *Julie, or the New Heloise*, 602; *La nouvelle Héloïse*, 559: "je vois les deux amies sans mouvement et se tenant embrassés, l'une évanouie et l'autre expirante. . . . J'appris qu'il avait fallu la [Claire] porter dans sa chambre, et même l'y renfermer, car elle rentrait à chaque instant dans celle de Julie, se jetait sur son corps, le réchauffait du sien, s'efforçait de le ranimer, le pressait, s'y collait avec une espèce de rage, l'appelait à grands cris de mille noms passionnés, et nourrissait son désespoir de tous ces efforts inutiles."

91. *Julie or the New Heloise*, 612; *La nouvelle Héloïse*, 567–68: "J'entends murmurer une voix plaintive! . . . Claire! Ô ma Claire! où es-tu? Que fais-tu loin de ton amie? . . . Son cercueil ne la contient pas tout entière . . . il attend le reste de sa proie . . . il ne l'attendra pas longtemps" (ellipses in original).

92. Richardson, *Clarissa*, 1403.

93. *Millenium Hall* also creates intimacies that precede marriage, most notably that between Mrs. Morgan and Miss Mancel; one sign of the impending failure of Mrs. Morgan's marriage is her husband's rejection of the female friend.

94. Without that sapphic intensity, we also see versions of this plot of rescue in Isabelle de Charrière's *Trois femmes* (1795) and Mary Wollstonecraft's *The Wrongs of Woman* (1798) as well as in three novels, Bernardin de Saint-Pierre's *Paul et Virginie* (1788), Elisabeth Post's *Het Land* (1788), and Therese Huber's *Die Ehelosen* (1829), that I will discuss in chapter 7.

95. Fenwick, *Secresy*, 91, 358.

96. Brown, *Ormond*, 241; Roulston, *Narrating Marriage*, 193.

97. Fischer, *Die Honigmonathe*, Letter 1, 8: "Du meine treue Einzige! Ich drücke Dich in Gedanken an mein Herz, und bedecke Dein liebes zorniges Gesicht mit tausend Küssen. O mitten unter Deinem Schelten fühle ich wie sehr Du mich liebst. Mein lieber Schuitzengel!"

98. Ibid., Letter 21: "Eine grosse Leidenschaft herrscht dennoch in dieser grossen Seele. Est ist die Liebe zu ihrer Freundin"; "sie ist die Hofnung meines Lebens."

99. Ibid., Letter 2, 3: "was sprichst Du von zerstörten Hoffnungen?—. . . Glaubst Du, die Natur würde sich nicht rächen?—Hat sie zwey Weiber geschaffen sich alles zu werden, und ihre unwandelbaren Gesetze zu verspotten?"

100. Ibid., 2, 4: "Wer verspottet nun die Gesetze der Natur? Wer wird dafür bussen?—Zwey Weiber können sich nicht alles seyn? Schlimm genug, dass die Geschöpfe welche den Weibern dieses sogenannte Alles seyn sollen, dieses Alles so elend repräsentiren."

101. Steidele, *"Als wenn Du mein Geliebste wärest,"* 200.

102. Maria Edgeworth, *Belinda*, 43–49, passim.

103. Ibid., 231, 233, 312. The chapter in which this conversation appears (ch. 17) is titled "Rights of Woman" in obvious critique of Wollstonecraft and her French Revolutionary colleagues.

104. DeJean, *Fictions of Sappho*, 161.

105. Staël, *Delphine*, 2:433–34: "lois presque opposées . . . femmes doivent se soumettre."

106. See Castle, "Sister-Sister," *London Review of Books* (3 August 1995).

107. Jane Austen, "Love and Freindship," in *The Oxford Illustrated Jane Austen*, 6:83–84.

108. See Castle, "Sister-Sister," and Korba, "'Improper and Dangerous Distinctions.'"

CHAPTER 6

1. [Pidansat de Mairobert], *Confession d'une jeune fille*, 209: "échappée dès votre tendre jeunesse aux séductions des hommes, goûtez le bonheur de vous trouver réunie au sein de vos pareilles."

2. Restif de la Bretonne, "La duchesse ou la femme-sylphide," in *Les contemporaines*, 45. "Tel a-été le fénomène que la Nation a-eu sous les yeus dans notre siècle: Une Femme audessus de toutes les entraves."

3. *Correspondance littéraire, philosophique et critique*, 11:159: "Il existe, dit-on, une société connue sous le nom de *la Loge de Lesbos*, mais dont les assemblées sont plus mystérieuses que ne l'ont jamais été celles des Franc-Maçons, ou l'on s'initie dans tous les secrets dont Juvenal fait une description si franche et si naïve dans la sixième satire. . . . Il faudrait être Juvenal pour oser en dire davantage."

4. Honoré-Gabriel Riquetti, comte de Mirabeau, *Erotika Biblion*, 120: "prérogatives les plus honorables, crédit immense, pouvoir sans bornes."

5. *Choix de mémoires secrets*, 261: "on n'a jamais affiché ces vices avec autant d'éclat & de scandale qu'aujourd'hui"; "nos plus jolies femmes y donnent-elles, s'en font-elles une gloire, un trophée!"

6. Maréchal, *Almanach des honnêtes femmes pour l'année 1790*, n.p.

7. For a fuller discussion of German definitions of the lesbian, see Steidele, *"Als wenn Du mein Geliebter Wärest,"* 46–47.

8. *Genuine Memoirs of the Celebrated Miss Maria Brown* (1766), 115 and 120; Dalrymple, *Travels through Spain and Portugal*, 152; Jack Cavendish, *A Sapphick Epistle* (London, 1778); Manuel, *Anecdotes Recorded by the Police of Paris* (1794), 27; W. G. Browne, *Travels in Africa, Egypt, and Syria* (1799), 386; *Letters to the Ladies, on the Preservation of Health and Beauty*, 67.

9. Quoted in Nussbaum, *Torrid Zones*, 145.

10. On the *précieuses*, see Wahl, *Invisible Relations*, ch. 5, and Stanton, "The Fiction of *Préciosité*."

11. See the story of Raucourt and Contat, for example, in *Choix des mémoires secrets*, 2:257–58.

12. *Oracle and Daily Advertiser*, 21 January 1799, 4.

13. Donoghue, *Passions Between Women*, 242. "Mrs. Y――――" is the actress Mary Ann Yates.

14. Donoghue, "'Random Shafts of Malice?'" 140–41. See also the much reprinted *Female Jockey Club* attributed to Charles Pigott, 199 and 203.

15. Letter to the London *Morning Post*, 5 December 1776. The brief letter is worth printing in full both for its geographical assumptions and for its fascination with the nomenclature for a practice the writer also disavows: "Mr. Editor, As I am fond of *neologisms*, or *neological* words, I find with pleasure our language enriched with the term, *Tribadarian*, in the Morning Post, but not our metropolis with *Tribadism*. Every country, however, particularly hot climates, produces such unnatural women. No modern language had before a word to express that *Sapphic* passion, being imputed to *Sappho*, except the *French*. *Tribade* is from the *Greek*;—I recollect no Latin word;—I generally called them *Tribadists*. I saw several notorious for it upon the continent, during my long stay of many years in different nations and courts of Europe, since my departure from the University of Oxford." The letter is signed simply "T." Despite the writer's claim, I have found no previous mention of "Tribadarian" in an issue of the *Morning Post*.

16. *Choix des mémoires secrets* (1784), 264; in translation: "Our heroes, our cultivated persons / Form a thousand companies / salons, clubs, academies."

17. Knigge, *Über den Umgang mit Menschen*, translated as *Practical Philosophy of Social Life*, 2:255–60.

18. *The Gray's-Inn Journal No. 59* for 1 December 1753, in *The Works of Arthur Murphy, Esq.* London: T. Cadell, 1786, 6:61–62.

19. Rousseau, *Emile, or On Education*, 358; *Emile, ou de l'éducation*, 446: "une femme parfaite et un homme parfait ne doivent pas plus se ressembler d'esprit que de visage."

20. Cavendish, *Sapphick Epistle*, passim.

21. Notably, in the late eighteenth century the word *pareil(le)* carries class content; the (ironically, post-Revolutionary) *Dictionnaire de l'Académie française* of 1798, unlike the previous version of 1762, defines *pareille* as referring to people of the same

social status: *pareils* are "people of your status, your birth, your character [Les gens de votre état, de votre naissance, de votre caractère]."

22. Thicknesse, *Sketches of the Lives and Writings of the Ladies of France*, 3:206–7: "mon état présent me paroit le plus doux que le ciel put m'accorder dans sa bonté. Indépendante, libre, vivant depuis ving cinq ans avec une amie, don't l'esprit, l'égalité d'humeur, et le caractère aimable répandent un continuel agrément sur notre société je gôute un tranquille repos. Nous ne connoissons ni les querelles, ni l'ennui, le mot *non*, est banni d'entre nous. Les mêmes principes nous guident et rendent naturellement nos volontés semblables. Ainsi une éternelle concorde regne dans notre petit ménage." Like most late-century encomiums to female same-sex relations, this one originates in a private letter from Riccoboni to Philip Thicknesse.

23. Desan, "Constitutional Amazons," 17.

24. The *Observateur anglais* was later reprinted as the *Espion anglais*, though with the same subtitle.

25. *Anandria: Confesions de Señorita Safo*, xi, ix.

26. *Confession d'une jeune fille*, 208. Where French translation is not needed, further references will appear within the text.

27. Ibid., 227: "point de ces contradictions entre les sentimens & les facultés: l'ame & le corps marchent ensemble."

28. Ibid., 218: "une grande famille où il n'y a d'autre hiérarchie que celle établie par la nature même pour sa conservation, & nécessaire à son régime."

29. For example, Raucourt notes that there are no "anandryne" societies among Jews or Muslims: in the case of Jews, because of religious injunctions to "grow and multiply," to which she adds that "the Jews became such a nasty people that god was obliged to renounce them [les juifs devinrent uin si vilain peuple, que dieu fut obligé de le renier]"; and in the case of Muslims, because their "seraglios" are already like a "qualified tribady [tribaderie mitigée]" (*Confession*, 211–12).

30. Ibid., 196: "Une tribade . . . [est] convaincue de l'excellence de son sexe, trouve dans lui la vraie volupté, la volupté pure, s'y voue toute entiere & renonce à l'autre sexe aussi perfide que séduisant."

31. Ibid., 219: "c'est une éleve de la secte anandryne, voilà ce que c'est que de sacrifier à *Vesta*!"

32. Ibid., 219: "C'est ainsi que vous en attirerez d'autres, que vous ferez germer dans le coeur de vos pareilles qui l'admireront, le desir, en l'imitant, de jouir de son sort."

33. Ibid.: "je me croyais la plus heureuse de femmes; lorsqu'une aventure bizarre me fit connaître la félicité suprême et me plongea bientôt après dans un abime de maux."

34. Ibid.

35. It is possible, of course, that this vision did *not* seem utopian to its author or to its readers, and that the leveling represented in the "Apologie" is meant to signal aristocratic decadence, but that postion requires something of a stretch.

36. *La curieuse impertinente*, 1:101–3: "Je le dois, car j'ai éprouvé avec elles plus de tendresse, plus de transports, plus de plaisir, que je n'en ai jamais éprouvé dans le bras d'un homme; les hommes ne savent pas aimer; toujours remplis d'affaires, d'objets étrangers & de vaines spéculations, ils sont incapables de ces attentions que le coeur

exige & que les femmes seules sont en état d'avoir. Avec quelle assiduité, avec quelle tendresse ma petite amie me servoit! avec quelle inquiétude ne s'informoit-elle pas de ma santé tous les matins! quel plaisir ne trouvoit-elle pas à m'instruire de tout ce qu'elle savoit."

37. Ibid., 2:1: "peut-elle être criminelle dans des femmes retranchées du commerce du monde? le coeur doit toujours être occupé, soit d'un objet soit d'un autre, & lorsqu'il est séparé de celui de ses affections, sans aucune espérance [sic] d'y être à jamais réuni, il se tourne naturellement vers ce qui est de plus beau dans la petite sphere où il est renfermé."

38. Chevalières ervantes, 2:29: "esclaves blanches, exposeés au marché & sans cesse manchandeés par les hommes."

39. Ibid., 2:47–51: "nous ne courons point après les prosélytes."

40. Beachy, "Masonic Apologetic Writings," 91.

41. *Apologie des Franc-Maçons*, 76–77. "Vous êtes . . . une assemblée de gens de toutes sorts d'états, religions, âges, nations, professions &c. Un mélange aussi extraor-dinaire est contraire aux lois de séparation que Dieu & la nature ont établies entre les hommes, & il ne peut subsister que par une indifférence criminelle sur toutes les reli-gions. Votre société est d'autant plus dangereuse qu'elle s'étend par toute la terre."

42. Beachy, "Masonic Apologetic Writings," 93.

43. Burke, "Freemasonry, Friendship and Noblewomen," and Burke and Jacob, "French Freemasonry, Women, and Feminist Scholarship."

44. *L'adoption ou la Maçonnerie des femmes*, 9: "il faut que toutes les femmes qui se présentent soient saines, sans grossesse, ni mois."

45. Beachy, "Masonic Apologetic Writings," 99.

46. Burke and Jacob, "French Freemasonry," 527.

47. Burke, "Freemasonry, Friendship, and Noblewomen" 285.

48. Quoted in ibid., 291.

49. Jacob, *Origins of Freemasonry*, 123.

50. Goodman, *Republic of Letters*, 258.

51. Burke and Jacob, "French Freemasonry," 545–56.

52. See Burke, "Freemasonry, Friendship and Noblewomen," the latter part of which is devoted specifically to Lamballe and her loyalty to the queen—which, Burke argues, stemmed from her Masonic ideals.

53. de Baecque, *Glory and Terror*, 82–83.

54. Restif de la Bretonne, "La duchesse," 34.

55. Ibid., 14: "Nous ne sommes pas égaux, monsieur; . . . si vous avez vos droits, j'ai les miens. . . . Non, monsieur, je ne serai pas la victime soumise de vos caprices: La Femme est la maîtresse de ses faveurs, et une Femme comme moi l'est doublement."

56. Ibid., 45: "Tel a-été le fénomène que la Nation a-eu sous les yeus dans notre siècle: Une Femme audessus de toutes les entraves, même les plus-utiles, vicieuse non-seulement aus yeus du Puriste, mais de l'Honnête-homme le plus-indulgent, et qui néanmoins avait les vertus les plus-brillantes et les plus-citoyennes, la reine des vertus, la bienfaisance! Quant aux qualités, elle les possédait toutes au degré le plus éminent. Qui la-donc-perdue? Qui la-rendue scandaleuse, dangereuse meme à beaucoup de Per-sonnes? Sa condition, seule; la manière dont on éleve les Enfans des Grands; manière

pernicieuse pour la Société, criminelle, punissable, et si-justement prohibée dans l'immortel *Traité de l'Education* de *J.-J.R* [Jean-Jacques Rousseau]."

57. See Colwill, "Pass as a Woman"; Thomas, *La reine scélérate*; Hunt, *Family Romance of the French Revolution*; and Fleischmann, *Les Maîtresses*.

58. *Les imitateurs de Charles IX*, 110. "Eh! que nous importe, en effet, la destruction de quelques milliers d'hommes? Paris regorge d'habitans; purgeons-en le royaume et assurons notre félicité."

59. *Le cadran des plaisirs de la cour*, 81: "'Les hommes, dit-elle, j'en fais comme d'une orange, quand j'ai sucé le jus, je jette l'écorce loin de moi.'"

60. *Confession générale de son altesse sérénissime, mgr. le comte d'Artois*, 11, 3, 17, 18.

61. *Confession et repentir de Mme de P**** cited in Fleischmann, *Madame de Polignac et la cour galante de Marie-Antoinette*, 130.

62. *Mémoires secrets pour servir à l'histoire de la République des lettres en France* (1776), cited in Fleischmann, *Les maitresses de Marie-Antoinette*, 26: "des conseils dictés par une politique vraiment infernale."

63. Gorani, *Les prédictions*, 120–21: "Si cette femme n'etait que libertine & pédante, elle ne serait que méprisable, & je n'en parlerais pas; mais elle prodigue à son amant, à ses tribades, à ses favoris, le sang de vos peuples, Sire, qu'elle se fait un plaisir de ruiner, comme faisait sa soeur Antoinette en France; mais cette femme vous déteste; elle ne s'intéresse qu'à faire retomber votre royaume sous la domination Autrichienne; c'est pour cela qu'elle a détruit, tant qu'elle a pu, ses enfans mâles, & qu'elle ne conserve que ses filles; &, si vous ignorez ces vérités, Sire, vous êtes le seul dans Naples." In keeping with the argument I make at the end of this chapter about the disappearance of "tribade," it is interesting that this passage about Maria Carolina is reprinted in several nineteenth-century sources, verbatim *except* for the omission of the word "tribade."

64. Jefferson goes so far as to say in his autobiography that "had there been no queen, there would have been no revolution. No force would have been provoked nor exercised" (*Writings of Thomas Jefferson*, 92).

65. *La liberté ou Mlle Raucour à toute la secte anandrine*, 14: "j'aime les hommes, & les femmes me predent au cul." English translation in Merrick and Ragan, 204–12.

66. Ibid., 27: "elle en a avalé les principes avec le foutre."

67. Ibid., 29: "nous sommes moins avilies, moins méprisables qu=elles; Nous foutons, nous branlons, quelquefois même, puis qu=il faut l=avouer, nous gamahuchons; mais c=est pour gagner notre vie, & qu=importe, apres tout, de qu=elle maniere on la gagne? Les uns se procurent leur subsistance a la sueur de leurs fronts, nous vivons de celle de nos culs."

68. Hunt, *Family Romance of the French Revolution*; see also Landes, *Women and the Public Sphere*.

69. Desan, "Constitutional Amazons," 21, 31.

70. Palmer, *Twelve Who Ruled*, 6, preface.

71. Wollstonecraft, *Mary, a Fiction*, 51, 110, 35–36, 87.

72. Wollstonecraft, *Vindication of the Rights of Woman*, 110. Further references will appear within the text.

73. Binhammer, "Thinking Gender with Sexuality," 677, 683. See also Binhammer, "The Sex Panic of the 1790s."

74. *The Cherub*, 20–21.

75. Moreau de St.-Méry, *Moreau de St. Méry's American Journey*, 289, 286.

76. See Theo Van der Meer, "Tribades on Trial."

77. Colwill, "Pass as a Woman," 71.

78. See Desan, *The Family on Trial* and Hesse, *The Other Enlightenment*.

79. McMillan, *France and Women*, 42, 44.

80. Maréchal, *Project d'une loi*, i.

81. Fraisse, *Reason's Muse*, 2.

82. *Zedlers Universal-Lexicon*, 45:302: "TRIBADES, heissen solche Weibsbilder, welche ein so grosses und langes Schaamzunglein haben, dass es fast einer männlichen Ruthe gleichet, und damit bin andern ihres geschlechts die Stelle einer Mannsperson vertreten können."

83. Prévost, *Manuel lexique ou dictionnaire portatif* (1755): "nom qu'on donne aux Femmes lascives, qui cherchent a se procurer, entre'elles, plaisirs qu'elles ne peuvent recevoir que d'autre sexe."

84. *Dictionnaire de l'Academie*, 1762; see also *Dictionnaire royale*, 1:610.

85. *Encyclopédie*, 16:617: "femme qui a de la passion pour une autre femme, une espèce de dépravation particulière aussi inexplicable que celle qui enflamme un homme pour un autre homme."

86. "*Tribaden*: Anandrinen, bei den Griechen, eine eigene Sekte von wollüstigen Weibern, die sich mit ihrem eigenen Geschlechte vermischte, sich selbst schändete."

87. *Chambaud's Dictionary*, also 1787, uses the same definition of "a woman loving her own sex."

88. In discussing the 1795 prosecution of "tribades" in Amsterdam, Van der Meer also suggests that "while sodomites both in judicial and theological discourse were becoming a separate category, tribades seem to have been perceived as women who misbehaved in general." See "Tribades on Trial," 438.

89. "The Present State of Morals and Society, in France." In *The Scourge, or, Literary, Theatrical, and Miscellaneous Magazine* 9 (Feburary 1815): 125.

CHAPTER 7

1. Mereau, "An einen Baum am Spalier," from *Gedichte* (1:15), in *Bitter Healing*, ed. Blackwell and Zantop, 378–79: "Armer Baum! An deiner kalten Mauer / fest begunden, stehst du traurig da, / . . . / und die bilderreiche Phantasie / stellt mir ihrer flüchtigen Magie / eine menschliche Gestalt schnell vor mich hin, /die, auf ewig von dem freien Sinn / der Natur entfernt, ein fremder Drang /auch wie dich in steife Formen zwang."

2. Thrale, *Thraliana*, 2:740 (1 April 1789) and 2:949 (9 December 1795).

3. "Extraordinary Female Affection," *St. James Chronicle*, 20 July 1790, also published in the *General Evening Post* and the *London Chronicle*.

4. "The Present State of Morals and Society, in France," 125.

5. Byron, letter to Elizabeth Pigot (5 July 1807), in *Byron: A Self-Portrait*, 30.

6. Sha, *Perverse Romanticism*, 17.

7. Bloom, Afterword to *Frankenstein*, 215.

8. Rousseau, *Confessions*, 1:1: "Je sens mon cœur et je connais les hommes. Je ne suis fait comme aucun de ceux que j'ai vus; j'ose croire n'être fait comme aucun de ceux qui existent. Si je ne vaux pas mieux, au moins je suis autre."

9. I part ways here with Faramerz Dabhoiwala, who claims for the eighteenth century a full-scale sexual revolution benefiting men and women of all sexual persuasions. In the end, though, Dhaboiwala too admits that "it was primarily the heterosexual libido of white, propertied men that was celebrated"; see *The Origins of Sex*, 343.

10. Richardson, "Romanticism and the Colonization of the Feminine," passim.

11. Waller, *The Male Malady*, 3.

12. Curran, "Of Gene Pools," n.p.

13. These data come from Spaas, "*Paul et Virginie*: The Shipwreck of an Idyll," 317.

14. Bernardin de Saint-Pierre, *Paul et Virginie*, preface, p. vi: "Je me suis proposé aussi d'y mettre en évidence plusieurs grandes vérités, entre autres celle-ci: que notre bonheur consiste à vivre suivant la nature et la vertu." Translation mine.

15. *Paul and Virginia*, 22; *Paul et Virginie*, 19: "l'une se rappelant que ses maux étaient venus d'avoir négligé l'hymen, et l'autre d'en avoir subi les lois; l'une, de s'être élevée au-dessus de sa condition, et l'autre d'en être descendue: mais elles se consolaient en pensant qu'un jour leurs enfants, plus heureux, jouiraient à la fois, loin des cruels préjugés de l'Europe, des plaisirs de l'amour et du bonheur de l'égalité." Further references to the English translation by Helen Maria Williams will appear within the text; endnotes will be given for longer quotations from the French.

16. Ibid., 9–10: "Ah! Dieu veut finir mes peines, puisqu'il vous inspire plus de bonté envers moi, qui vous suis étrangère , que jamais je n'en ai trouvé dans mes parens."

17. Ibid., 17–18: "Elles-mêmes, unies parles mêmes besoins, ayant éprouvé des maux presque semblables, se donnant les doux noms d'amie, de compagne et de soeur n'avaient qu'une volonté, qu'un intérêt, qu'une table. Tout entre elles était commun."

18. Ibid., 18: "Seulement si d'anciens feux plus vifs que ceux de l'amitié se réveillaient dans leur âme, une religion pure, aidée par des moeurs chastes, les dirigeait vers une autre vie, comme la flamme qui s'envole vers le ciel lorsqu'elle n'a plus d'aliment sur la terre."

19. Ibid., 18–19: "Elles prenaient plaisir à les mettre ensemble dans le même bain, et à les coucher dans le même berceau. Souvent elles les changeaient de lait. 'Mon amie, disait Mme de la Tour, chacune de nous aura deux enfants, et chacun de nos enfants aura deux mères.' Comme deux bourgeons qui restent sur deux arbres de la même espèce, dont la tempête a brisé toutes les branches, viennent à produire des fruits plus doux si chacun d'eux, détaché du tronc maternel, est greffé sur le tronc voisin; ainsi ces deux petits enfants, privés de tous leurs parents, se remplissaient de sentiments plus tendres que ceux de fils et de fille, de frère et de soeur, quand ils venaient à être changés de mamelles par les deux amies qui leur avaient donné le jour."

20. Schroeder, "Natural Kinds," 4, 8–9.

21. Everard, *Ziel en zinnen*, 46.

22. Post, *Het Land*, 180.

23. Ibid.: "Het graf van mijne Emilia moet ook het mijne zijn; één zark moet ons

beiden dekken, terwijl de sombere treuerwilg, dien de natuur leerde weenen, op onze sluimerende asch zijne ruischende bladeren hangen."

24. The compound "Lommerlust" is almost untranslatable: it evokes both shade or foliage and delight or desire.

25. Sha, *Perverse Romanticism*, 12.

26. Kairoff, *Anna Seward*, 114.

27. Seward, *Llangollen Vale*, 6. Further references will appear in parentheses in the body of the text.

28. See my "Befriending the Body" for a discussion of Butler and Ponsonby's "compensatory" class politics, and Anne Lister's likewise.

29. Butler will live until 1829 and Ponsonby until 1832.

30. I have in mind "Sonnet IV. To Honora Sneyd," "The "Epistle to Miss Honora Sneyd, May 1772: Written in a Summer Evening, from the Grave of a Suicide," "Ingratitude," "Sonnet X. To Honora Sneyd. April 1773"; and "Honora: An Elegy," "To Time Past, Written Dec. 1772," none of which were published before the 1790s, perhaps for reasons of the declined popularity of sapphic apostrophe that I discussed in chapter 4.

31. William Wordsworth, *Complete Poetical Works*, 640. The sonnet was first published in *Miscellaneous Sonnets* (1827) as part of a five-volume edition of Wordsworth's poems.

32. Ibid.

33. Dorothy Wordsworth, "Irregular Verses," in Susan M. Levin, *Dorothy Wordsworth and Romanticism*, 201–4, lines 15–21. Further references to line numbers will appear in the text.

34. Dorothy Wordsworth, "A Holiday at Gwerndovennant: Irregular Verses," in Levin, *Dorothy Wordsworth*, 191–95, lines 90–92.

35. Haggerty, "Love and Loss," esp. 387, 401–2.

36. I analyze this poem in more detail in "Put to the Blush."

37. Visually as well as aurally distinct, this "irregularity" seems to me to be a powerful poetic statement in itself, a truth the speaker "ne'er strove to decorate" and thus refuses to reduce to the more compact and lighter tetrameter that is the poem's basic metric form. The poem's few lines of hexameter also stand out for their common theme: the brightness of youth, the joys one remembers, the beloved's "rising sigh" for what could not be.

38. Ann Batten Cristall's use of "irregular" in the subtitle for both her 1795 volume *Poetical Sketches in Irregular Verse* and for a very specific (male-female) love poem, "Thelmon and Carmel: An Irregular Poem," also links sexual content to irregular prosody.

39. Shelley, *Rosalind and Helen*, "Advertisement." Further references will appear as line numbers within the text.

40. Donovan, "Rosalind and Helen," 269.

41. In a thorough though not exhaustive search, I have found final couplets only in "Scorn Not the Sonnet," where Wordsworth is engaged in obvious play with the form, and in "October 1803," which ends with the same word—"time"—that closes the sonnet to Butler and Ponsonby.

42. Huber, *Die Ehelosen*, 1:233: "ihre erste Jugend entflohen war, de Zerstorung sie rettungslos erfasst hatte, war sie noch das liebreizendste Wesen, das je mein Auge erblickt hat. Schlank wie ein Lilienstengel, ein so vollkommener Knochenbau, dass ihre Magerkeit sie keines ihrer schoenen Umrisse beraubt hat."

43. Ibid.: "ihr Vertrauen als Freundin viel inniger sei als ihre Hingabe gegen ihn."

44. Coleridge, *Christabel*, lines 70, 246.

45. Ibid, "Preface."

46. See, for example, O'Donnell, "The 'Invention' of a Meter," and Russett, "Meter, Identity, Voice.

47. As biographers have reported, Dorothy Wordsworth wrote in her journal on 4 October 1800, after a visit in which Coleridge apparently read the poem aloud, the subjectless sentence, "Exceedingly delighted with the second part of 'Christabel.'" She records "increasing pleasure" on October 5 when Coleridge apparently read out the poem once more. Yet on the third day, the journal states without elaboration: "Determined not to print 'Christabel' with the LB." Dorothy Wordsworth, *Journals*, ed. William Knight, 24–25. I explore the possible reasons for and ramifications of this decision more fully in "Put to the Blush."

48. Eilenberg, *Strange Power of Speech*, 98–99.

49. William Wordsworth, "Michael," in *Complete Poetical Works*, 238–244, lines 154, 158. Further citations are identified by line numbers in the body of the text.

50. Elfenbein, *Romantic Genius*, 177; Conder, writing in the *Eclectic Review*, reprinted in *Coleridge: The Critical Heritage*, 210.

51. Eilenberg reports the former in *Strange Power of Speech*, 104; Nethercot reports the latter in *The Road to Tryermaine*, 32.

52. Watts, *Alaric Watts: A Narrative*, 1:239. I owe my knowledge of this reference to Elfenbein's *Romantic Genius*.

53. Spence, quoted in Donne, *Variorum*, 2:962.

54. On these two plays, see Steidele, *"Als wenn Du mein Geliebter wärest,"* 135–50.

55. Magalon and Barginet, "La mort de Sapho," in *Souvenirs poétiques de deux prisonniers*, 226: "Grèce, sois toujours libre, et que de tes guerriers / La Discorde jamais ne voile les lauriers . . . / Salut ! dans le passé votre Sapho s'élance. / Lyre, sois sur mon cœur ! La mort, c'est l'espérance . . . / Adieu, mon cher Phaon, je te pardonne . . . Allons!"

56. Lamartine, *Nouvelles méditations poètiques*, 40: "Sapho: élégie antique": "Compagnes de Sapho, portez-lui ces adieux ! / Dites-lui . . . qu'en mourant je le nommais encore ! / Elle dit, Et le soir, quittant le bord des flots, / Vous revîntes sans elle, ô vierges de Lesbos!"

CODA

1. Latour, *We Have Never Been Modern*, 10, 140.

2. Pateman, *The Sexual Contract*.

3. Perry, *Novel Relations*, 195.

4. Jameson, *The Political Unconscious*, 19.

5. Foster, *The Coquette*, 24. Elizabeth Carter, for example, writes in a letter to Catherine Talbot (1:56–57) that "people when they marry are dead and buried to all former attachments."

6. Vicinus, *Intimate Friends*, 229–30.

7. Ibid., 227.

8. Hesse, *The Other Enlightenment*, xv.

9. Amer, *Crossing Borders*, 44–45.

10. Melon, *Essai politique sur le commerce*, 709. Original in the book's first footnote.

11. Latour, *We Have Never Been Modern*, 12.

ACKNOWLEDGMENTS

In the course of its long and wide travels, this book has amassed almost as many debts as it has accrued endnotes. Some of the debts are *in* the notes: a project of this temporal and geographic scope would never have been feasible without the pioneering work of Harriette Andreadis, Marie-Jo Bonnet, Terry Castle, Emma Donoghue, Lia van Gemert, Myriam Everard, Adrienne Martín, and Angela Steidele, along with several of the scholars I thank below because my gratitude to them is personal as well as textual.

This project got started in the late 1990s while I was a faculty member at the University of Maryland, where my colleagues and graduate students created a flourishing space for intellectual pursuits and made me smarter for their presence. For deepening my eighteenth-century knowledge, I thank especially Vincent Carretta, Liza Child, Jane Donawerth, Leigh Anna Eicke, Sharon Groves, Renata Lana, Paula McDowell, and especially my fast friend, co-teacher, and co-editor Neil Fraistat, who taught me how to think like a Romanticist without expecting me to become one. From 1989 through 2001, I was fortunate to lead a Folger Institute Colloquium on Women in the Eighteenth Century in which faculty and PhD students from up and down the Atlantic Coast explored both work in progress and the progress of the field. It was in that colloquium that my understanding of gender and sexuality in the eighteenth century matured, and I thank the Colloquium and its many members, now spread across the country, for their individual and collective wisdom. The culminating gift of the 1990s was a Folger Institute Fellowship for the 1998–99 academic year that immersed me in early modern texts and the company of those who study them. The unfettered time, gracious surroundings, extraordinary holdings, unparalleled staff support, and teatime conversations would have been bliss enough, but the camaraderie of the Fellows group that we still call the Folger Five—Patricia Fortini Brown, Ann Rosalind Jones, Jessie Ann Owens, Peter Stallybrass, and myself—was very heaven. Sojourns in Paris were likewise paradisiacal during those years of intensive research; I thank my cherished friends and intellectual mentors Jack Undank and Alan Wilde for the pleasure of living with them at 15 quai de Bourbon while I spent my daytimes in the Bibliothèque de l'Arsenal, and I thank them still more for three decades of exuberant attachment.

Crucial across the full span of this project has been the welcoming academic culture of the American Society for Eighteenth-Century Studies and especially its Women's and Lesbian-Gay Caucuses. The affirming but rigorous reception of new work that I've found at ASECS is unparalleled, and most of my best ideas about the history of sexuality were born in papers delivered at ASECS annual meetings or honed in conversations both literal and textual with Paula Backscheider, Eve Tavor Bannet, John Beynon, Katherine Binhammer, Toni Bowers, Fiona Brideoake, Lisa Freeman, Caroline Gonda, Catharine Ingrassia, Paul Kelleher, Katherine Kittredge, Jeff Merrick, Rebecca Messbarger, Chris Mounsey, Sally O'Driscoll, David Robinson, Chris Roulston, and the late Hans Turley. I owe a special debt to Kathy King for deep knowledge and deep camaraderie, and to Kristina Straub both for longtime friendship and for the gift of her innovative scholarship on sexuality and class.

For the fellowship year of 2004–5 that turned my history of sexuality into the sexuality of history, I thank the Radcliffe Institute for Advanced Study at Harvard. The timing of that award coincided perfectly with my needs, and my perch on the top floor of 38 Concord Avenue remains my ideal office. For that year, which gave me both mind-stretching conversation and all manner of academic support, I thank especially Drew Faust and Judy Vichniac, along with my fellow fellows, especially Kathy Davis, Jenny Mansbridge, and, for the seeds of a differently transformative relationship, Sari Nusseibeh. I've had great research assistance straight through this project, especially from Minyang Jiang, Melissa Leigh-Gore, Chris Mayo, Jessica Partynski, and Bendta Schroeder. For valuable assistance with challenging texts, I am grateful to Barbara Geremia, Erika Paoletti, Anna Roemer, and another pioneer in lesbian studies, Sherry Velasco. Martha Vicinus, eminent leader in lesbian studies, gave me early and lasting encouragement along with the model of her pathbreaking work at the intersection of history & lit, and shared primary sources at a time when nothing was on line. At the University of Chicago Press, Doug Mitchell's e-mails have been as delightful as his editorial acumen and enthusiasm for the project have been invaluable; Tim McGovern and

Renaldo Migaldi have provided uncommonly patient, perspicacious, and professional oversight; and Richard Allen has been the most thoughtful and attentive copy editor I could have imagined, not only tracking my bibliographic lapses but lending his keen ear to my prose and his scholarly expertise to the tenor of my arguments.

At Brandeis, I am honored to dwell among colleagues of deep learning, wide interests, and passionate investments. I have benefited especially from the encyclopedic knowledge of Susan Staves, the theoretical rigor of Tom King, and the capacious intellect of Mary Campbell. The superb poet Olga Broumas has been an abiding presence for me as well as a source of Greek inscription. Faith Smith has read generously and stretched my understanding. For help with a range of notes and queries, I thank my Brandeis colleagues Dian Fox, Ann Olga Koloski-Ostrow, Jim Mandrell, Michael Randall, and Martine Voiret. For support both intellectual and personal, I thank Robin Feuer Miller, humanist par excellence, whose esteem and friendship mean more than I can say. Bernadette Brooten, whose *Love Between Women* is a model of rigor and innovation, has been a patient sounding-board, an incisive reader, a source of personal and intellectual sustenance. Jane Kamensky's formidable intelligence and ready wit, along with her zest for both scholarly and culinary adventure, have fostered a collaboration in teaching and research that remains the greatest intellectual pleasure of my Brandeis years. My colleagues on the Women's and Gender Studies Program faculty have made the demands of university engagement seem worthwhile even when those demands slowed down this book.

Close friends who are also scholars, whether nearby in Cambridge or nearby on the net, have been crucial to this long journey. Ruth Perry's generosity eased the transition from D.C. to Massachusetts, and she continues to offer expert knowledge, no-nonsense wisdom, sustaining friendship, and the gifts of laughter and of song. Lynn Festa gave my introductory pages a penetrating reading when I needed it; every conference when I can spend time with her is worth attending. Stuart Sherman has been a friend for all seasons, an exuberant compatriot and confidant whose dazzling prose remains both pleasure and aspiration; his keen attention to my sentences has improved this book as much as his support has sustained its author. Angelika Bammer, my close friend since graduate school, has been a companion through this project as through so much else, especially in our summer convergences on Kezar Lake, where she has read drafts, helped me work through dilemmas, and brought perspectives—and perspective—I didn't have. Evelyn Torton Beck, my enduring friend-and-family of four decades, just happened to appear when I needed both a reader and a Germanist at an eleventh hour; her appreciation for the work, given her own inaugural contributions to lesbian studies, has been a special gift.

For engagement over the *longue durée*, for their own extraordinary contributions to the field, and especially for their penetrating readings of the full manuscript, I thank George Haggerty and Valerie Traub. Their signal contributions to sexuality studies have shaped and inspired my work and provided the intellectual ballast that centered it. More importantly, each has been *the* galvanizing presence in their respective spheres of inquiry. As both the foremost scholar and the most generative mentor in eighteenth-century sexuality studies, George Haggerty has created the scaffolding on which the field rests. He wears his learning lightly and shares it liberally, and our conversations over two decades are also embedded in this book. Valerie Traub's work has not only shaped early modern lesbian studies but created theoretical frameworks for sexual history *tout court*; her rigor has set a high bar for my own work, and collaborating in workshops has sealed both friendship and esteem. As much through the examples of their own work in queer studies as through their responses to mine, George and Valerie have been critical in moving this project from where it began to what is has become.

The book would not have come to completion without Jo Radner, my partner for almost thirty years and my legal spouse for a decade. The rich threads of our intellectual and affective life are woven into the deepest fabric of this work. I say about our marriage what Gertrude Stein said of Paris: it's not just what it gives—though that is abundant—but what it does not take away. Her faith in this project has kept me at it when my energy has flagged; and her material support has made the long process possible. She has missed out on more summer pleasures and weekend outings, read more drafts, listened to more kvetches, and made more meals than anyone should have had to provide. She is the only person who deserves to be even happier than I am that this work has left my desktop for the printed page. I expect that my children by birth and by marriage will likewise be as grateful that this book is behind me as I am grateful for their patience and their presence in my life. It is a joy to be surrounded by adult children with the talents, integrity, and thoughtfulness, in both senses, of our blended crowd. Steve, Heather, Tom, Holly, Josh, Anna, Chris, Jack, and Emily: thank you for *being*, and for being ours. A lifetime of thanks to my sister Barb, sage in counsel and an anchor in tough times.

Since I began this book, our family has grown literally by a generation as Jo and I have welcomed grandchildren, that greatest blessing of older age. I reserve my deepest nonacademic gratitude—indeed my awe—for the precious lives of Kylie, Abbey, Mia, Cole, Gus, and Phoebe. I hope we have bequeathed them a world that will cherish their delightful differences; they are already children who will shape a future better than the one that we have given them.

Finally, I dedicate this book to Michael Ragussis, my colleague at Georgetown from my arrival there in 1980 and that rare best friend who was also best critic: the first and last reader of virtually every book and essay that left my desk, as I was of his work, for thirty years. When Michael knew he had terminal cancer, I wrote faster so that he could see every chapter in some form, and we pored together over those drafty pages. He had enough faith in the outcome to be moved when I told him I would dedicate the book to him, and after his death, his penciled comments guided me. I am fortunate to have excellent readers and beloved friends, but there is only one Michael. His memory has been a blessing that got me through this book and that will stay with me in every new adventure.

As is typical especially with projects of long provenance, several chapters of this book had their genesis in earlier papers and essays. My core claim and bits from chapters 2 and 3 are brought together in *Comparatively Queer*, while material from chapter 4 appears in *Structures and Subjectivities* and *Eighteenth-Century Studies*. Threads of chapter 5 are explored, with a different slant, respectively in *Textual Practice*, engaging work on sexual difference, and in *Postclassical Narratology*, engaging the history of form. A short piece related to chapter 6 appeared in the *Journal of Homosexuality*, and a piece of chapter 7 appears in *Romantic Praxis*. Most of these essays predate the 180 degree turn of my project and thus operate more fully within a "history of sexuality" than as manifestations of a "sexuality of history." Because they are doing a different kind of work from the work this book proposes, some of those essays read individual texts more closely or rather differently and might usefully supplement their related chapters.

PRIMARY SOURCES

L'adoption ou la Maçonnerie des femmes, en trois grades. [Chez le Silencer: A la Fidé-lité,] 1775. Rpt. Nimes: Editions Lacour-Ollé, 2009.

Allen, Beverly, Muriel Kittel, and Keala Jane Jewell, eds. *The Defiant Muse: Italian Feminist Poems from the Middle Ages to the Present.* New York: Feminist Press, 1986.

Allestree, Richard. *The Ladies Calling.* Oxford: At the Theater, 1673.

Alzieu, Pierre, Robert Jammes, and Yvan Lissorgues, eds. *Poesía Erótico Del Siglo De Oro.* Barcelona: Crítica, 2000.

A True Relation of the Apparition of one Mrs. Veal, the next day after her death: to one Mrs. Bargrave at Canterbury. The 8th of September, 1705. London: B. Bragg, 1706.

Aretino, Pietro. *Dialogues.* Translated by Raymond Rosenthal. Toronto: University of Toronto Press, 2005.

———. *Il ragionamenti.* 1534. Rome: Savelli, 1979.

Argens, Jean-Baptiste, marquis de. *Thérèse Philosophe, ou, Mémoires pour servir à l'histoire du P. Dirrag et de Mlle Eradice.* 1748. Arles: Actes Sud, 1992.

Apologie des Franc-Maçons. Paris, 1779.

Astell, Mary. *Letters Concerning the Love of God.* London: Samuel Manship and Richard Wilkin, 1694.

Austen, Jane. *The Oxford Illustrated Jane Austen.* Edited by R. W. Chapman. 6 vols. Oxford: Oxford University Press, 1954.

Aylmer, John. *An Harborowe for Faithfull and Trewe Subjectes, Against the late blowne blaste, concerninge the government of women.* London: John Day, 1559.

Bacon, Francis. *Essays or counsels, civill and morall, of Francis L. Verulam Viscount St. Alban.* London: John Haviland, 1625.

Barker, Jane. *A Patch-Work Screen for the Ladies; or, Love and Virtue Recommended.* London: E. Curll and T. Payne, 1723.

Behn, Aphra. *The Works of Aphra Behn.* Edited by Janet Todd. 7 vols. Columbus: Ohio State University Press, 1992.

Benserade, Isaac de. *Iphis et Iante: Comedie*. Paris: Anthoine de Sommaville, 1637. Rpt. Vijon: Editions Lampasque, 2000.

———. *Les oeuvres de Monsieur Benserade, première partie*. Paris: Charles de Sercy, 1697.

Bianchi, Giovanni. *Breve storia della vita di Catterina Vizzani Romana, che per ott' anni vesti abito da uomo in qualità di servidore la quale dopo vari casi essendo in fine stata ucci—sa fu trovata pulcella nella sezzione del suo cadavero*. Venice: Simone Occhi, 1744.

Bianchi, Giovanni, and John Cleland. *The True History and Adventures of Catharine Vizzani, a Young Gentlewoman a Native of Rome, who for many Years past in the Habit of a Man; was killed for an Amour with a young Lady; and found on Dissection, a true Virgin*. London: W. Reeve and C. Sympson, 1755. First published as *Historical and Physical Dissertation on the Case of Catharine Vizzani*. London: W. Meyer, 1751.

Blackwell, Jeannine, and Susanne Zantop, eds. *Bitter Healing: German Women Writers from 1700 to 1830: An Anthology*. Lincoln: University of Nebraska Press, 1990.

Bodin, Jean. *De la démonomanie des sorciers*. Paris: Jacques Du Puy, 1580.

Les bordels de lesbos, ou le génie de Sapho. St. Petersburg, 1790.

Borris, Kenneth. *Same-Sex Desire in the English Renaissance: A Sourcebook of Texts 1470–1650*. New York: Routledge, 2003.

Brantôme, Pierre de Bourdeille, seigneur de. 1665. *Recueil des dames, poésies et tombeaux*. Paris: Gallimard, 1991.

Brathwait, Richard. *The English Gentleman: Containing Sundry Excellent Rules or Exquisite Observations, Tending to Direction of Every Gentleman, of Selecter Ranke and Qualitie; How to Demeane or Accommodate Himselfe in the Manage of Publike or Private Affaires*. London: John Haviland, 1630.

———. *The English Gentlewoman, Drawne out to the Full Body: Expressing, What Habilliments Doe Best Attire Her, What Ornaments Doe Best Adorne Her, What Complements Doe Best Accomplish Her*. London: B. Alsop and T. Fawcet, 1631.

Brown, Charles Brockden. *Ormond; or, The Secret Witness*. 1799. Edited by Mary Chapman. Peterborough, Ont.: Broadview Press, 1999.

Browne, Thomas. *Religio Medici*. London: Andrew Crooke, 1642.

Browne, William George. *Travels in Africa, Egypt, and Syria, from the year 1792 to 1798*. London: T. Cadell, 1799.

Burney, Fanny. *Evelina, or the History of a Young Lady's Entrance into the World*. London: T. Lowndes, 1778.

———. *The Wanderer*. London: Longman, Hurst, Reese, Orme, and Brown, 1814.

Busbecq, Ogier Ghislain. *Legationis turcicae epistolae quattuor*. Paris: Bey, 1589.

———. *The four epistles of A.G. Busbequius concerning his embassy into Turkey being remarks upon the religion, customs, riches, strength and government of that people*. London: J. Taylor and J. Wyat, 1694.

Butler, Eleanor, Sarah Ponsonby, and Caroline Tighe Hamilton. *The Hamwood Papers of the Ladies of Llangollen and Caroline Hamilton*. Edited by Mrs. G. H. Bell. London: Macmillan, 1930.

Byron, George Gordon, Lord. *Byron: A Self-Portrait: Letters and Diaries 1798 to 1824.* Edited by Peter Quennell. Cambridge: Cambridge University Press, 1990.

Le cadran des plaisirs de la cour, ou les aventures du petit page Chérubin, pour servir de suite à la vie de Marie-Antoinette, ci-devant Reine de France. Suivi de la confession de Mademoiselle Sapho. Paris: Chez les marchands de nouveautés. n.d.

Carlyle, Thomas. *The French Revolution.* London: J. Fraser, 1837.

Caro, Annibale. *Commento Di Ser Agretso Da Ficarvolo Sopra La Prima Ficata Del Padre Siceo.* Rome: Antonio Blado, 1538?

Carter, Elizabeth. *Poems on Several Occasions.* London: John Rivington, 1762.

Castle, Terry, ed. *The Literature of Lesbianism: A Historical Anthology from Ariosto to Stonewall.* New York: Columbia University Press, 2003.

Castoriadis, Cornelius. *L'institution imaginaire de la société.* Paris: Seuil, 1975.

Cavendish, Jack. *A Sapphick Epistle, from Jack Cavendish to the Honourable and most beautiful Mrs. D***.* London: M. Smith, [1778].

Cavendish, Margaret. *CCXI Sociable Letters.* London: William Wilson, 1664.

———. *The Convent of Pleasure.* In *Plays Never before Printed.* London: A. Maxwell, 1668.

Chapone, Sarah. *The Hardship of the English Laws in Relation to Wives.* London: 1735.

Charke, Charlotte. *A Narrative of the Life of Mrs. Charlotte Charke, (Youngest Daughter of Colley Cibber, Esq.)* London: W. Reeve, 1755.

The Cherub: Or, Guardian of Female Innocence. Exposing the Arts of Boarding Schools, Hired Fortune Tellers, Corrupt Milliners, [and] Apparent Ladies of Fashion. London: W. Locke, 1792.

Les chevalières errantes, ou les deux sosies femelles. 3 vols. Paris: Maradan, 1789.

Chorier, Nicolas. *L'académie des dames, ou la philosophie dans le boudoir du grand siècle.* 1680. Arles: Philippe Picquier, 1999.

Chudleigh, Mary. *Poems on Several Occasions.* London: Bernard Lintot, 1703.

Cleland, John. *Memoirs of a Woman of Pleasure.* London: 1748.

"Cloe to Artimesa." In *A New Miscellany.* London: A. Hammond, 1720.

Cocalis, Susan L., ed. *The Defiant Muse: German Feminist Poems from the Middle Ages to the Present: A Bilingual Anthology.* New York: Feminist Press, 1986.

Coleridge, Samuel Taylor. *Christabel; Kubla Khan, a Vision; The Pains of Sleep.* London: John Murray, 1816.

Confession et repentir de Mme de P*** ou la nouvelle Madeline convertie. Paris, 1789.

Confession générale de son altesse sérénissime, mgr. le comte d'Artois. Paris: Chez le sécrétaire des commandements de Mgr. l'Archevêque de Paris, le 23 juillet 1789.

Cristall, Ann Batten. *Poetical Sketches in Irregular Verse.* London: J. Johnson, 1795.

Critical Review, or, Annals of Literature 13 (London, 1762).

Crouch, Humphrey. *Loves Court of Conscience Written Upon Two Severall Occasions, with New Lessons for Lovers.* London: Richard Harper, 1637.

Cubillo de Aragon, Álvaro. *Añasco el de Talavera: Comedia famosa.* Granada: n.p., n.d.

———. *Añasco el de Talavera: Comedia famosa de Álvaro Cubillo.* Edited by Elena E. Marcello. In "Las comedias de costumbres de Álvaro Cubillo de Aragón. Edición crítica y estudio." Diss.: Universidad de Castilla-La Mancha, 2002.

La curieuse impertinente, traduite de l'anglois. N.p.: n.p., 1789.

Dalrymple, William. *Travels through Spain and Portugal, in 1774; with a short account of the Spanish expedition against Algiers, in 1775*. London: J. Almon, 1777.

Defoe, Daniel. *The Fortunate Mistress: or, A History of the Life and Vast Variety of Fortunes of Mademoiselle de Beleau*. London: T. Warner, 1724.

Deken, Aagje, and Elizabeth Bekker Wolff. *Historie van Mejuffrouw Sara Burgerhart*. 's Gravenhage: 1786.

Démeunier, Jean-Nicolas. *L'esprit des usages et des coutumes des différents peuples, ou observations tirées des voyageurs & des historiens*. Paris: Pissot, 1776.

Dictionnaire de l'Académie française. Editions of 1762, 1798.

Dictionnaire royale francais-anglais et anglais-français. Edited by A. Boyer. Lyons: Jean-Marie Bruyset, 1780.

Diderot, Denis. *La religieuse*. Paris, 1796.

Donne, John. *The Variorum Edition of the Poetry of John Donne*. Edited by Gary Stringer et al. 8 vols. Bloomington: Indiana University Press, 1995–2005.

Donoghue, Emma, ed. *Poems Between Women: Four Centuries of Love, Romantic Friendship, and Desire*. New York: Columbia University Press, 1997.

Du Laurens, André. *Toutes les oeuvres de Me André Du Laurens*. Paris, 1621.

Edgeworth, Maria. *Belinda*. London: J. Johnson, 1801.

Encyclopédie, ou dictionnaire raisonné des sciences, des arts et des métiers. Paris, 1765.

An Epistle from Sappho to Philaenis. London: W. Trott, 1728.

An Epistle from Signora F———a to a Lady. "Venice" [London], 1727.

Erasmus, Desiderius. *All the Familiar Colloquies*. 1518. London, 1725.

Erauso, Catalina de (attrib). *Historia de la Monja Alférez escrita por ella misma*. 1829. Edited by Jesús Munárriz. Madrid: Ediciones Hiperión, 1986.

———. *The Lieutenant Nun: Memoirs of a Basque Transvestite in the New World*. Edited by Michele Stepto and Gabriel Stepto. Boston: Beacon Press, 1996.

Estienne, Henri. *L'introduction au traité de la conformité des merveilles anciennes avec les modernes: Ou, traité préparatif à l'apologie pour Hérodote*. Geneva: Estienne, 1566.

Feijoo y Montenegro, Benito Jerónomo. *Teatro crítico universal*. Madrid: Ibarra, 1778.

The Female Rebels: Being Some Remarkable Incidents of the Lives, Characters, and Families of the Titular Duke and Dutchess of Perth, the Lord and Lady Ogilvie, and of Miss Florence McDonald. Edinburgh; rpt. London: T. Gulliver, 1747.

Fenwick, Eliza. *Secresy; or, The Ruin of the Rock*. 1795. Peterborough, Ont.: Broadview Press, 1994.

Ferrand, Jacques. *Traicté de l'essence et guérison de l'amour, ou de la mélancholie érotique*. Toulouse: Colomier, 1610.

Fichte, Johann. *Grundlage des Naturrechts nach Principien der Wissenschaftslehre*. Jena and Leipzig: Gabler, 1796.

———. *The Science of Rights*. Translated by A. E. Kroeger. London: Trübner,1889.

Fielding, Henry. *The Female Husband: Or, the Surprising History of Mrs. Mary, Alias Mr. George Hamilton*. London: M. Cooper, 1746.

———. *The Jacobite's Journal*. London: W. Strahan, 1747–48.

Finch, Anne. *Miscellany Poems on Several Occasions*. London: J. B. and B. Tooke, 1713.

Firenzuola, Agnolo. *Dialogo delle bellezze delle donne*. Florence, 1548.

———. *On the Beauty of Women*. Translated by Konrad Eisenbichler and Jacqueline Murray. Philadelphia: University of Pennsylvania Press, 1992.

Fischer, Caroline Auguste. *Die Honigmonathe. Von dem Verfasser von Gustavs Verirrungen.* Leipzig, 1802. Electronic edition: E-Book-Sammlung Zeno.org.

Flores, Angel, and Kate Flores, eds. *The Defiant Muse: Hispanic Feminist Poems from the Middle Ages to the Present.* New York: Feminist Press, 1986.

Fonte, Moderata. *Il merito delle donne: Ove chiaramente si scuopre quanto siano elle degne, e più perfette de gli uomini.* Venice: Domenico Imberti, 1600.

———. *The Worth of Women: Wherein Is Clearly Revealed Their Nobility and Their Superiority to Men.* Translated by Virginia Cox. Chicago: University of Chicago Press, 1997.

Foster, Hannah. *The Coquette; or, The History of Eliza Wharton.* Boston: Ebenezer Larkin, 1797.

Franco, Niccolò. *Le pistole vulgari.* Venice: Antonio Gardane, 1538.

Genuine Memoirs of the Celebrated Miss Maria Brown. Exhibiting the Life of a Courtezan, in the Most Fashionable Scenes of Dissipation. 2 vols. London: I. Allcock, 1766.

Goethe, Johann Wolfgang von. *Die Leiden des jungen Werthers.* 1774. Stuttgart: Reclam, 1986.

———. *Die Wahlverwandtschaften.* Tübingen: Cotta, 1809.

Goddard, William. *A Satirycall Dialogue or a Sharplye-invectiue Conference, betweene Allexander the Great, and That Truelye Woman-hater Diogynes.* London: Dordecht, 1616.

Gorani, Jean. *Les prédictions de Jean Gorani, citoyen français, sur la révolution de France.* London: W. Thompson, 1797.

Gournay, Marie le Jars de. "The Equality of Men and Women" (1644). Translated by Richard Hillman and Colette Quesnel. In *Apology for the Woman Writing and Other Works*, 69–96. Chicago: University of Chicago Press, 2002.

Hakluyt, Richard. *Principall nauigations, voiages and discoueries of the English nation: made by sea or ouer land, to the remote and farthest distant quarters of the earth at any time within the compasse of these 1500. yeeres.* London: George Bishop and Ralph Newberie, 1589.

Haywood, Eliza. *The British Recluse: Or, the Secret History of Cleomira, Supps'd Dead.* London: D. Brown, 1722.

———. *The City Jilt; or, The Alderman turn'd Beau: A Secret History.* London: J. Roberts, 1726.

———. *The Masqueraders or, Fatal Curiosity.* 1724. In *Secret Histories, Novels, and Poems*, vol. 4. London: A. Bettesworth, 1732.

———. *The Rash Resolve; or, The Untimely Discovery.* London, 1724.

Huber, Therese. *Die Ehelosen.* Leipzig: Brockhaus, 1829.

Hugo, Victor. *Notre Dame de Paris* [The Hunchback of Notre Dame]. Paris, 1831.

Les Imitateurs de Charles IX. Initially entitled *La destruction de l'aristocratisme, drame en cinq actes en prose, destiné à être représenté sur le théâtre de la Liberté.* Chantilly, 1789.

Jacob, Giles. *Tractatus de Hermaphroditus; or, a Treatise of Hermaphrodites.* London: E. Curll, 1718.

Jonson, Ben. *The Complete Poems*. Edited by George Parfitt. London: Penguin, 1975.

———. "The Forest." In Robert Chester, *Love's Martyr, or Rosalins Complaint*. London: E. B., 1601.

———. *Volpone or The Foxe*. London: Thomas Thorpe, 1607.

Juana Inés de la Cruz, Sor. *A Sor Juana Anthology*, edited by Alan S. Trueblood. Cambridge, Mass.: Harvard University Press, 1998.

Jefferson, Thomas. *Writings*. Edited by Merrill D. Peterson. New York: Viking Press, 1984.

Karsch, Anna Louisa. *Auserlesene Gedichte*. Berlin: Winter, 1764.

———. *Neue Gedichte*. Leipzig: Jakob Hinz, 1772.

Kersteman, F. L. *De Bredasche Heldinne*. 1751. Edited by R. M. Dekker, G. J. Joohannes, and L. C. van de Pol. Hilversum: Verloren, 1988.

Killigrew, Anne. *Poems*. London: Samuel Lowndes, 1686.

King, William. *The Toast, an Epic Poem in Four Books. Written in Latin by Fredrick Scheffer, Done into English by Peregrine O Donald, Esq*. Dublin, 1732.

Knigge, Adolf Freiherr. *Über den Umgang mit Menschen* [1788.] Translated as *Practical Philosophy of Social Life; or the Art of Conversing with Men*. London: T. Cadell, 1794.

Labé, Louise. "To Mademoiselle Clemence de Bourges of Lyon." In *Women Writers of the Renaissance and Reformation*, edited by Katherina M. Wilson. Athens: University of Georgia Press, 1987.

Lamartine, Alphonse de. *Nouvelles méditations poètiques*. 3d ed. Paris: Urbain canel/ Audin, 1824.

Lanyer, Aemelia. *Salve Deus Rex Judaeorum*. London: Richard Bonian, 1611.

La Roche, Sophie von. *Geschichte des Fräuleins von Sternheim, von einer Freundin derselben aus Originalpapieren*. Leipzig: Weidmanns Erben und Reich, 1771.

The Laughing Philosopher. Dublin: James Williams, 1777.

Leo Africanus, Joannes [Al-Hassan Ibn-Muhammad al-Fazi]. *Della descrittione dell'Africa*. 1550. *Geographical Historie of Africa*. Translated by John Pory. London: Bishop, 1600.

A Letter Sent by the Maydens of London, to the vertuous Matrones & Mistresses of the same, in the defense of their lawfull Libertie. London: Thomas Hacket, 1567.

Letters to the Ladies, on the Preservation of Health and Beauty. By a physician. London: Robinson and Roberts, 1770.

L'Estoile, Pierre de. *Registre-Journal du règne de Henri III*. Edited by Madeleine Lazard and Gilbert Schrenck. Geneva: Droz, 1997.

La liberté ou Mlle Raucour à toute la secte anandrine assemblée au foyer de la comédie française [A LècheCon: Et se trouve dans les coulisses de tous les théâtres, même chez Audinot], 1791.

The Life and Imaginations of Sally Paul. London: S. Hooper, 1760.

Lister, Anne. *I Know My Own Heart: The Diaries of Anne Lister, 1791–1840*. Edited by Helena Whitbread. London: Virago, 1988.

———. *No Priest but Love: Excerpts from the Diaries of Anne Lister*. Edited by by Helena Whitbread. New York: New York University Press, 1993.

Lodge, Thomas. *Rosalynde: Euphues Golden Legacie*. London: Thomas Orwin for T. G. and John Busbie, 1590.

Lucian. *The Works of Lucian, Translated from the Greek, by Several Eminent Hands*. Translated by Tho. Brown. 4 vols. Vol. 3, London: Sam Briscoe, 1710.

Lyly, John. *Gallathea: As it was playde before the Queenes Maiestie at Greene-wiche, on Newyeeres day at night*. London: John Charlwoode for the Widdow Broome, 1592.

Magalon, Joseph-Dominique, and Alexandre Barginet. *Souvenirs poétiques de deux prisonniers*. Paris: Editions Masson fils aîné, 1823.

Mairobert, Mathieu Pidansat de. *Anandría: Confesión de la Señorita Safo*. Translated and edited by Joaquin Lopez Barbadillo. Madrid: Akal, 1978.

———. *Confession d'une jeune fille*. [1778]. In *L'Espion anglais, ou correspondance secrète entre Milord All'eye et Milord All'ear*. Vol. 10. London: John Adamson, 1784.

Mandeville, Bernard. *The Virgin Unmask'd: Or, Female Dialogues Betwixt an Elderly Maiden Lady, and Her Niece*. London: J. Morphew, 1709.

Manley, Delarivier. *Secret Memoirs and Manners of Several Persons of Quality, of both Sexes. From the New Atalantis, an Island in the Mediterranean*. London: John Morphew, 1709.

Manuel, Louis-Pierre. *Anecdotes recorded by the police of Paris, of all the affairs of gallantry which have occurred in that metropolis for several years past. With biographical sketches of the Parisian women of pleasure*. London: J. Dawson, 1794.

Maréchal, Sylvain. *Almanach des honnêtes femmes pour l'année 1790: avec une gravure satyrique originale du temps, sur la duchesse de Polignac*. Paris: Duchesne et fils, 1789.

———. *Projet d'une loi portant défense d'apprendre à lire aux femmes*. Paris: Masse, 1801.

Marinella, Lucrezia. *The Nobility and Excellence of Women, and the Defects and Vices of Men*. 1600. Translated by Anne Dunhill. Chicago: University of Chicago Press, 1999.

———. *La nobiltà et eccellenza delle donne co' diffetti et mancamenti de gli huomini*. Venice: Giovan Battista Ciotti, 1592.

Marten, John. *A Treatise of the Venereal Disease*. London: Printed for the author and N. Crouch, 1711.

Masters, Mary. *Familiar Letters and Poems on Several Occasions*. London: D. Henry and R. Cave, 1755.

Meijer, Maaike, with Erica Eijsker, Ankie Peypers, and Yopie Prins, eds. *The Defiant Muse: Dutch and Flemish Feminist Poems from the Middle Ages to the Present: A Bilingual Anthology*. New York: Feminist Press, 1998.

Mereau, Sophie. *Gedichte*. Berlin: Unger, 1800.

Melon, Jean-François. *Essai politique sur le commerce*. In *Économistes financiers du 18e siècle*, vol. 1, Collection des principaux économistes. Osnabrück: Otto Zeller, 1966.

Millot, Michel. *L'école des filles, ou la philosophie des dames*. Paris: Piot, 1655.

Mirabeau, Honoré-Gabriel Riquetti, comte de. *Erotika Biblion*. 1783. Paris: Vatar-Jouannet, 1801.

Montagu, Mary Wortley. *The Turkish Embassy Letters*. Edited by Lord Wharncliffe and
    W. Moy Thomas. London: Henry G. Bohn, 1861.

Montaigne, Michel de. *Essais*. Edited by Albert Thibaudet. Bruges: Bibliothèque de la
    Pléiade, 1937.

———. *Journal de voyage en Italie, par la Suisse & l'Allemagne en 1580 & 1581*. Paris:
    Lejay, 1774.

Moreau de St.-Méry, Médéric. *Moreau de St. Méry's American Journey*. Translated by
    Kenneth Roberts and Anna Roberts. New York: Doubleday, 1947.

———. *Voyage aux États-Unis de l'Amérique, 1793–1798*. Edited by Stuart L. Mims.
    New Haven: Yale University Press, 1913.

Moreto y Cabaña, Agustín. *El desdén, con el desdén*. 1654. Valencia: Jose Ferrér de
    Orga, 1813.

Murphy, Arthur. *The Works of Arthur Murphy, Esq*. In seven volumes. London:
    T. Cadell, 1786.

A New Ballad. To the tune of Fair Rosamond. London, 1708.

Niccholes, Alexander. *A Discourse of Marriage and Wiving and of the Greatest Mystery
    Therein Contained: How to Choose a Good Wife from a Bad*. London: N[icholas]
    O[kes] for Leonard Becket, 1615.

Nicolay, Nicholas de. *Les quatre premiers livres des navigations et pérégrinations
    orientales. Avec les figures au naturel tant d'hommes que de femmes selon la
    diversité des nations, & de leur port, maintien & habitz*. Lyon: G. Roville,
    1568.

Olivares, Julian, and Elizabeth S. Boyce, eds. *Tras el espejo la musa escribe: Lírica
    femenina de los Siglos de Oro*. Madrid: Siglo Veintiuno, 1993.

Paré, Ambroise. *Deux Livres de Chirurgie*. Paris, 1573.

Parsons, James. *A Mechanical and Critical Enquiry into the Nature of Hermaphrodites*.
    London: J. Walthoe, 1741.

The Passionate Pilgrime by W. Shakespeare. London: W. Iaggard, 1599.

Peréz de Montalbán, Juan. *La monja Alférez*. Newark, DE: Juande la Cuesta, 2007.

Philips, Katherine. *Collected Works*. Edited by Patrick Thomas. Stump Cross, Essex:
    Stump Cross Books, 1990.

———. *Poems by the Incomparable Mrs. K. P.* London: Marriott, 1664.

Pigott, Charles. *The Female Jockey Club, or a Sketch of the Manners of the Age*. Lon-
    don: D. I. Eaton, 1794.

Pizan, Christine de. *La cité des dames*. Translated and edited by Thérèse Moreau and
    Éric Hicks. Paris: Stock, 1986.

———. *Trésor de la cite des dames*. Paris: Iehan André, 1504.

Post, Elisabeth. *Het Land: in Brieven*. Amsterdam: Johannes Allart, 1788.

Poulain de la Barre, François. *De l'égalité des deux sexes*. Paris: Jean du Puis, 1673.

Pratt, Samuel Jackson. *Shenstone Green, or, The New Paradise Lost*. London: R. Bald-
    win, 1779.

Restif de la Bretonne, Nicolas Edme. *Les contemporaines ou aventures des plus jolies
    femmes de l'âge présent*. 1780–83. Paris: Alphonse Lemerre, 1876.

Riccoboni, Marie-Jeanne. *Lettres de Milady Juliette Catesby à Milady Henriette Cam-
    pley, son amie*. Paris: Desjonquères, 1759.

Richardson, Samuel. *Clarissa, or the History of a Young Lady.* 1747–48. Harmonds-worth: Penguin, 1985.

———. *The History of Sir Charles Grandison.* 6 vols. London, 1753–54.

Rohan, Anne de. *Poésies d'Anne de Rohan-Soubise, et lettres d'Eléonore de Rohan-Montbazon.* Edited by Edouard de Bartlélemy. Paris: Aubry, 1862.

Rojas, Fernando de. *Tragicomedia de Calisto y Melibea.* 1499. Barcelona: L'Avenç, 1902.

Ronsard, Pierre. *Oeuvres Complètes,* edited by Gustave Cohen. 2 vols. Paris: Biblio-thèque de la Pléiade, 1950.

Rousseau, Jean-Jacques. *Les Confessions.* Geneva: n.p., 1782.

———. *Du contrat social ou principes du droit politique.* Amsterdam: M. M. Rey, 1762.

———. *Emile, or On Education.* Translated by Alan Bloom. New York: Basic Books, 1979.

———. *Emile, ou de l'éducation.* 1762. Paris: Garnier Frères, 1961.

———. *Julie, ou la nouvelle Héloïse.* 1761. Edited by Michel Launay. Paris: Garnier-Flammarion, 1967.

Rowe, Elizabeth Singer. *Miscellaneous Works in Prose and Verse.* London: R. Hett, 1739.

———. *Poems on Several Occasions, Written by Philomela.* London: John Dunton, 1696.

Rowe, Nicholas. *Poems on Several Occasions.* London, 1714.

Sade, marquis de. *Philosophie dans le boudoir.* "Londres," 1795.

———. *La nouvelle Justine, suivie de l'histoire de Juliette, sa soeur.* Paris: [En Hol-lande], 1797.

Sainctonge, Louise-Geneviève Gillot de. *Poesies divers.* Dijon: Antoine de Fay, 1714.

———. *Poèmes galantes.* N.p., 1696.

Saint-Pierre, Jacques-Bernardin Henri de. *Paul et Virginie.* Paris: À l'imprimerie de Monsieur, 1789.

Saint-Pierre, Jacques-Bernardin Henri de, and Helen Maria Williams. *Paul and Virginia, translated from the French.* London: Verner and Hood, 1796.

The Sappho-an: An Heroic Poem, of Three Cantos. London: Charles Brasier, [1749].

Satan's Harvest Home; or, The Present State of Whorecraft, Adultery, Fornication, Procuring, Pimping, Sodomy, And the Game at Flatts. London, 1749.

Schaden, Adolphe von. *Die moderne Sappho: Ein musikalisch-dramatisches Durchein-ander ohne Sinn und ohne Verstand.* Leipzig, 1819.

Scott, Sarah. *A Journey Through Every Stage of Life.* London, 1754.

———. *Millenium Hall.* Edited by Gary Kelley. Peterborough, Ont.: Broadview, 1995.

Scudéry, Madeleine de. *Les femmes illustres, ou Les harangues héroïques.* Paris: An-toine de Sommaville & Augustin Courbé, 1642.

———. *The Story of Sapho.* Translated by Karen Newman. Chicago: University of Chi-cago Press, 2003.

Serna, Melchor de la. "El sueño de la viuda." In *Cancionero de poesías varias: Manu-scrito 2803 de la Biblioteca Real de Madrid.* Edited by José J. Labrador Herraiz and Ralph A. DiFranco. Madrid: Editorial Patrimonio Nacional, 1989.

Seward, Anna. *Llangollen Vale, With Other Poems.* London: G. Sael, 1796.

Sharp, Jane. *The Midwives Book, or, The Whole Art of Midwifry Discovered.* London: Simon Miller, 1671.

Shelley, Percy Bysshe. *Rosalind and Helen: A Modern Eclogue.* London: C. and J. Ollier, 1819.

Sheridan, Frances. *Memoirs of Miss Sidney Bidulph*. London: R. Dosley, 1761.

Simiane, Pauline. *Portefeuille de Madame ***. Paris: Christophe Ballard, 1715.

Staël, Germaine de. *Delphine*. 1802. 2 vols. Paris: Éditions des femmes, 1981.

Stanton, Domna C., ed. *The Defiant Muse: French Feminist Poems from the Middle Ages to the Present*. New York: Feminist Press, 1986.

Swetnam, Joseph. *The Araignment of Leuud, Idle, Froward, and Vnconstant Women or the Vanitie of Them, Choose You Whether: With a Commendation of Wise, Vertuous and Honest Women: Pleasant for Married Men, Profitable for Young Men, and Hurtfull to None*. London: George Purslowe, 1615.

Tahureau, Jean. *Les dialogues de Jacques Tahureau*. Paris: Gabriel Buon, 1568.

Taylor, Jeremy. *A Discourse of the Nature, Offices, and Measures of Friendship: With Rules of Conducting It / Written in Answer to a Letter from the Most Ingenious and Vertuous M.K.P. By J.T.* London: R. Royston, 1657.

Thevet, André. *Les vrais pourtraits et vies d'hommes illustres*. Paris: I. Keruert et Guillaume Chaudiere, 1584.

Thicknesse, Ann. *Sketches of the Lives and Writings of the Ladies of France*. London: Dodsley and W. Brown, 1781.

Thrale, Hester. *Thraliana: The Diary of Mrs. Hester Lynch Thrale 1776–1809*. 2 vols. Edited by Katharine C. Balderston. Oxford, 1942.

Tilney, Edmund. *The Flower of Friendship: A Renaissance Dialogue Contesting Marriage*. 1568. Edited by Valerie Wayne. Ithaca: Cornell University Press, 1962.

Tocqueville, Alexis de. *Souvenirs*. Paris: Calmann Levy, 1893.

Torche, Antoine de. *La toilette galante de l'amour*. Paris: E. Loyson, 1670.

Torquemada, Antonio de. *Jardin de flores curiosas, en que se tratan algunas materias de humanidad, philosophia, theologia y geographia, con otras curiosas y apacibles*. 1570. Anveres: Juan Corderio, 1575.

———. *The Spanish Mandeuile of Miracles. Or the Garden of Curious Flowers Vvherin Are Handled Sundry Points of Humanity, Philosophy, Diuinitie, and Geography, Beautified with Many Strange and Pleasant Histories*. Translated by Sir Lewis Lewkenor. London: James Roberts for Edmund Matts, 1600.

The Travels and Adventures of Mademoiselle de Richelieu. London: M. Cooper, 1744.

Trotter, Catharine. *Agnes de Castro, A Tragedy. As it is Acted at the Theatre Royal, by His Majesty's Servants. Written by a Young Lady*. London: H. Rhodes, R. Parker, and S. Briscoe, 1696.

Tyard, Pontus de. *Oeuvres poétiques*. Paris: Galiot du Pré, 1573.

Van Gemert, Lia, ed. *Women's Writing from the Low Countries, 1200–1875: A Bilingual Anthology*. Translated by Myra Heerspink Scholz, Brenda Mudde, and Paul Vincent. Amsterdam: Amsterdam University Press, 2010.

Vega, Lope de. *Fuente ovejuna: comedia famosa*. Madrid/Barcelona: Calpe, 1919.

———. *Three Major Plays*. Translated and edited by Gwynne Edwards. New York: Oxford University Press, 1999.

Vélez de Guevara, Luis. *La Serrana de la Vera*. 1613. Edited by William R. Manson and C. George Peale. Newark, Del.: Juan de la Cuesta/Hispanic Monographs, 2002.

La vida de Lazarillo de Tormes, y de sus fortunas y adversdades. 1554. Edited by Asima F. X. Saad Maura. Miami: Stockcero, 2007.

Villedieu, Madame de. *Mémoires de la vie de Henriette-Sylvie de Moliere*. Liège: Balthazar van Boech, 1676.

Violante do Céu, Sor. *Rimas varias de la madre soror Violante del cielo*. Rouen: de Maurry, 1646.

Volckmann, Anna Helena. *Erstlinge Unvollkommener Gedichte*. Leipzig, 1736.

Waller, Edmund. *Poems &c*. London: Humphrey Moseley, 1645.

Walsh, William. *A Dialogue Concerning Women, Being a Defence of the Sex Written to Eugenia*. London: R. Bentley and J. Tonson, 1691.

Wanley, Nathaniel. *The Wonders of the Little World, or, a General History of Man in Six Books: Wherein by Many Thousands of Examples Is Shewed What Man Hath Been from the First Ages of the World to These Times*. London: T. Basset et al., 1673.

Watts, Alaric Alfred. *Alaric Watts: A Narrative of His Life*. London: Richard Bentley & Son, 1884.

The Whores Rhetorick, Calculated to the Meridian of London; and Conformed to the Rules of Art. In Two Dialogues. London: George Shell, 1683. Rpt. Delmar, N.Y.: Scholars' Facsimiles and Reprints, 1979.

Wilkes, Wetenhall. *Letter of Genteel and Moral Advice to a Young Lady*. London, 1753.

Williams, Anna. *Miscellanies in Prose and Verse*. London: T. Davies, 1766.

Wilmot, John, Earl of Rochester. *Poems on Several Occasions*. London, 1701.

Wollstonecraft, Mary. *Mary, a Fiction*. London: J. Johnson, 1788.

———. *A Vindication of the Rights of Woman*. 1792. Edited by Carol H. Poston. New York: Norton, 1988.

———. *The Wrongs of Woman; or, Maria*. In *Posthumous Works of the Author of A Vindication of the Rights of Woman: in Four Volumes*. London: J. Johnson and G. Robinson, 1798.

Wordsworth, William. *The Complete Poetical Works of Wordsworth: Cambridge Edition*. Boston and New York: Houghton Mifflin, 1904.

Zayas y Sotomayor, Maria de. *Novelas completas*. 1637. Edited by Maria Martinexz del Portal. Barcelona: Editorial Bruguera, 1973.

Zedler, Johann. *Grosses vollstandiges Universallexicon aller Wissenschafften und Künste*. 64 vols. Halle: Zedler, 1732–50.

Zwinger, Theodor. *Theatrum vitae humanae*. Basel: Oporinum, Ambrosium et Aurelium Frobenios, 1565.

SECONDARY SOURCES

Abelove, Henry. "The Queering of Lesbian/Gay History." *Radical History Review* 62 (1995): 45–57.

———. "Some Speculations on the History of Sexual Intercourse during the Long Eighteenth Century in England." *Genders* 6 (1989): 125–30.

Ambrosini, Federica. "Toward a Social History of Women in Venice From the Renaissance to the Enlightenment." In *Venice Reconsidered: The History and Civiliza-*

tion of an Italian City-State, 1297–1797, edited by John Jeffries Martin and Dennis Romano, 420–53. Baltimore: Johns Hopkins University Press, 2000.

Amer, Sahar. *Crossing Borders: Love Between Women in Medieval French and Arabic Literatures*. Philadelphia: University of Pennsylvania Press, 2008.

———. "Lesbian Sex and the Military: From the Medieval Arabic Tradition to French Literature." In *Same Sex Love and Desire among Women in the Middle Ages*, edited by Francesca Canadé Sautman and Pamela Sheingorn, 101–22. London: Palgrave, 2001.

Andreadis, Harriette. "Reconfiguring Early Modern Friendship: Katherine Philips and Homoerotic Desire." *SEL* 46, no. 3 (Summer 2006): 523–42

———. "The Sapphic-Platonics of Katherine Philips, 1632–1664." *Signs: A Journal of Women in Culture and Society* 15, no. 1 (1989): 34–60.

———. *Sappho in Early Modern England: Female Same-Sex Literary Erotics, 1550–1714*. Chicago: University of Chicago Press, 2001.

Aravamudan, Srinivas. *Enlightenment Orientalism: Resisting the Rise of the Novel*. Chicago: University of Chicago Press, 2012.

Armstrong, Nancy. *Desire and Domestic Fiction: A Political History of the Novel*. New York: Oxford University Press, 1987.

Babcock, Barbara. Introduction to *The Reversible World: Symbolic Inversion in Art and Society*, edited by Barbara Babcock, 13–36. Ithaca: Cornell University Press, 1978.

Baecque, Antoine de. *Glory and Terror: Seven Deaths of the French Revolution*. Translated by Charlotte Mandell. London: Routledge, 2001.

Bakhtin, M. M. *The Dialogic Imagination: Four Essays*. Translated by Caryl Emerson and Michael Holquist. Edited by Michael Holquist. Austin: University of Texas Press, 1981.

Baldwin, Claire. "Anna Louisa Karsch as Sappho." *Women in German Yearbook* 20 (2004): 62–97.

Bannet, Eve Tavor. *The Domestic Revolution: Enlightenment Feminisms and the Novel*. Baltimore: Johns Hopkins University Press, 2000.

Barbeito Carneiro, María Isabel. "Feminist Attitudes and Expression in Golden Age Spain: From Teresa De Jesús to María De Guevara." In *Recovering Spain's Feminist Tradition*, edited by Lisa Vollendorf, 48–68. New York: Modern Language Association, 2001.

Barzun, Jacques. *From Dawn to Decadence: 500 Years of Western Cultural Life 1500 to the Present*. New York: HarperCollins, 2000.

Bates, Catherine. *Masculinity, Gender and Identity in the English Renaissance Lyric*. Cambridge: Cambridge University Press, 2007.

Beachy, Robert. "Masonic Apologetic Writings." In *Gender and Fraternal Orders in Europe, 1300–2000*, ed. Máire Fedelma Cross, 91–101. Basingstoke: Palgrave Macmillan, 2010.

Beauvoir, Simone de. *Le deuxième sexe*. Paris: Gallimard, 1949; rpt. 1976.

———. *The Second Sex*. Translated by Constance Borde and Sheila Malovany-Chevallier. New York: Vintage, 2011.

Bender, John. *Imagining the Penitentiary: Fiction and the Architecture of Mind in Eighteenth-Century England*. Chicago: University of Chicago Press, 1987.

Benkov, Edith. "The Erased Lesbian: Sodomy and the Legal Tradition in Medieval Europe." In *Same Sex Love and Desire among Women in the Middle Ages*, edited by Francesca Canadé Sautman and Pamela Sheingorn, 101–22. London: Palgrave, 2001.

Bennett, Judith. "Confronting Continuity." *Journal of Women's History* 9, no. 3 (1997): 73–94.

———. "'Lesbian-Like' and the Social History of Lesbianisms." *Journal of the History of Sexuality*, no. 1–2 (January/April 2000): 1–24.

———. "Remembering Elizabeth Ethingham and Agnes Oxenbridge." In *The Lesbian Premodern*, edited by Noreen Giffney, Michelle M. Sauer, and Diane Watt, 131–43. New York: Palgrave Macmillan, 2011.

Berlant, Lauren, and Michael Warner. "Sex in Public." *Critical Inquiry* 24 (1998): 547–66.

Beynon, John. "'Traffic in More Precious Commodities': Sapphic Erotics and Economics in *Memoirs of a Woman of Pleasure*." In *Launching Fanny Hill: Essays on the Novel and Its Influences*, ed. Patsy Fowler and Alan Jackson, 3–26. New York: AMS Press, 2003.

Binhammer, Katherine. "The Sex Panic of the 1790s." *Journal of the History of Sexuality* 6, no. 3 (1996): 409–34.

———. "The 'Singular Propensity' of Sensibility's Extremities: Female Same-Sex Desire and the Eroticization of Pain in Late-Eighteenth-Century British Culture." *GLQ* 4 (2003): 471–98.

———. "Thinking Gender with Sexuality in 1790s' Feminist Thought." *Feminist Studies* 28, no. 3 (2002): 667–90.

Black, Christopher F. "Society." In *The Sixteenth Century*, edited by Euan Cameron, 89–115. The Short Oxford History of Europe. Oxford: Oxford University Press, 2006.

Blank, Paula. "Comparing Sappho to Philaenis: John Donne's 'Homopoetics.'" *PMLA* 110, no. 3 (May 1995): 358–68.

Bloom, Harold. Afterword. *Frankenstein*, by Mary Shelley. New York: Bantam, 1957.

Bock, Gisela. *Women in European History*. Oxford: Blackwell Publishers, Inc., 2002.

Bonin, Erin Lang. "Margaret Cavendish's Dramatic Utopias and the Politics of Gender." *SEL* 40, no. 2 (2000): 339–54.

Bonnet, Marie-Jo. *Un choix sans équivoque: recherches historiques sur les relations amoureuses entre les femmes Xvie–Xxe siècle*. Paris: Denoël 1981.

Braudel, Fernand. *The Wheels of Commerce*, vol. 2 of *Civilization and Capitalism, 15th–18th Century*. Translated by Sian Reynolds. New York: Harper and Row, 1982.

Braunschneider, Theresa. "The Macroclitoride, the Tribade, and the Woman: Configuring Gender and Sexuality in English Anatomical Discourse." *Textual Practice* 13, no.3 (1999): 509–32.

Bray, Alan. *The Friend*. Chicago: University of Chicago Press, 2003.

Brideoake, Fiona. "'Extraordinary Female Affection': The Ladies of Llangollen and the Endurance of Queer Community." *Romanticism on the Net* (2004–2005): 36–37.

Brooten, Bernadette. *Love between Women: Early Christian Responses to Female Homoeroticism*. Chicago: University of Chicago Press, 1996.

Brown, Irene Q. "Domesticity, Feminism, and Friendship: Female Aristocratic Culture and Marriage in England, 1660–1760." *Journal of Family History* 17 (1982): 406–24.

Buckley, Veronica. *Christina, Queen of Sweden: The Restless Life of a European Eccentric*. New York: HarperCollins, 2004.

Burke, Janet M. "Freemasonry, Friendship and Noblewomen: The Role of the Secret Society in Bringing Enlightenment Thought to Pre-Revolutionary Women Elites." *History of European Ideas* 10, no. 3 (1989): 283–93.

Burke, Janet M., and Margaret C. Jacob. "French Freemasonry, Women, and Feminist Scholarship." *Journal of Modern History* 68 (1996): 513–49.

Butler, Judith. "Imitation and Gender Insubordination." In *Inside/Out: Lesbian Theories, Gay Theories*, edited by Diana Fuss, 13–31. New York: Routledge, 1991.

Calvino, Italo. *If On a Winter's Night a Traveler*. New York: Harcourt Brace, 1981.

Cameron, Euan, ed. *The Sixteenth Century*. The Oxford Short History of Europe. Oxford: Oxford University Press, 2006.

Campbell, Mary Baine. *Wonder & Science: Imagining Worlds in Early Modern Europe*. Ithaca: Cornell University Press, 1999.

Castle, Terry. *The Apparitional Lesbian: Female Homosexuality and Modern Culture*. New York: Columbia University Press, 1993.

———. "Sister-Sister." *London Review of Books* 17, no. 15 (3 August 1995): 3–6.

Cheek, Pamela. *Sexual Antipodes: Enlightenment Globalization and the Placing of Sex*. Stanford: Stanford University Press, 2003.

Clark, Peter, ed. *The European Crisis of the 1590s*. London: George Allen & Unwin, 1985.

Cohen, Walter. *Drama of a Nation: Public Theater in Renaissance England and Spain*. Ithaca: Cornell University Press, 1985.

Colwill, Elizabeth. "Epistolary Passions: Friendship and the Literary Public of Constance de Salm, 1767–1845." *Journal of Women's History* 12, no. 3 (Autumn 2000): 39–68.

———. "Pass as a Woman, Act Like a Man: Marie-Antoinette as Tribade in the Pornography of the French Revolution." In *Homosexuality in Early Modern France*, ed. Jeffrey Merrick and Bryant T. Ragan Jr., 54–79. New York: Oxford University Press, 1996.

Conder, Josiah. *Coleridge: The Critical Heritage*, ed. J. R. de Jackson. London: Routledge, 1970.

Cox, Virginia. "The Single Self: Feminist Thought and the Marriage Market in Early Modern Venice." *Renaissance Quarterly* 48 (1995): 513–81.

Craft-Fairchild, Catherine. "Sexual and Textual Indeterminacy: Eighteenth-Century English Representations of Sapphism." *Journal of the History of Sexuality* 15, no. 3 (Sept 2006): 408–31.

Crompton, Louis. "The Myth of Lesbian Impunity: Capital Laws from 1270 to 1791." *Journal of Homosexuality* 11 (1980): 11–25.

Culler, Jonathan. "Apostrophe." *Diacritics* 7, no. 4 (Winter 1977): 59–69.

———. *Structuralist Poetics*. London: Routledge, 1975.

Curran, Stuart. "Dynamics of Female Friendship in the Later Eighteenth Century." *Nineteenth-Century Contexts* 23 (2001): 221–39.

———. "Of Gene Pools, Genetic Mapping, Recessive Chromosomes, and Freaks of Nature," *Romantic Circles*, www.rc.umd.edu/reference/misc/confarchive/nassr96/curran.html.

Curtis, Mark H. "The Alienated Intellectuals of Early Stuart England." *Past and Present* 23 (1962): 25–43.

Dabhoiwala, Faramerz. *The Origins of Sex: A History of the First Sexual Revolution.* Oxford: Oxford University Press, 2012.

Darnton, Robert. "An Early Information Society: News and the Media in Eighteenth-Century Paris." *The American Historical Review* 105, no. 1 (Feb 2000): 1–35.

Daston, Lorraine, and Katharine Park. "The Hermaphrodite and the Orders of Nature." *GLQ* 1 (1995): 419–38.

Davis, Natalie Zemon. *Society and Culture in Early Modern France: Eight Essays.* Stanford: Stanford University Press, 1975.

———. "Women on Top: Symbolic Sexual Inversion and Political Disorder in Early Modern Europe." In *The Reversible World: Symbolic Inversion in Art and Society,* edited by Barbara Babcock, 147–90. Ithaca: Cornell University Press, 1978.

DeJean, Joan. *Ancients Against Moderns: Culture Wars and the Making of a Fin de Siècle.* Chicago: University of Chicago Press, 1997.

——— *Fictions of Sappho, 1546–1937.* Chicago: University of Chicago Press, 1989.

Dekker, Rudolf M. *Humour in the Dutch Culture of the Golden Age.* 1997 in Dutch. Basingstoke and New York: Palgrave, 2001.

———. "Sexuality, Elites, and Court Life in the Late Seventeenth Century: The Diaries of Constantijn Huygens, Jr." *Eighteenth-Century Life* 23 (1999): 94–109.

Dekker, Rudolf M., and Lotte C. van de Pol. *The Tradition of Female Transvestism in Early Modern Europe.* New York: St. Martin's Press, 1989.

Deich, Judith. "Dialoguewise: Discovering Alterity in Elizabethan Dialogues." In *Other Voices, Other Views: Expanding Canon in English Renaissance Studies,* edited by Helen Ostovich, Mary V. Silcox, and Graham Roebuck, 46–73. Newark: University of Delaware Press, 1999.

Desan, Suzanne. "Constitutional Amazons: Jacobin Women's Clubs in the French Revolution." In *Re-creating Authority in Revolutionary France,* ed. B. T. Ragan Jr. and E. A. Williams, 11–35. New Brunswick: Rutgers University Press, 1992.

———. *The Family on Trial in Revolutionary France.* Berkeley and Los Angeles: University of California Press, 2004.

DiGangi, Mario. *The Homoerotics of Early Modern Drama.* Cambridge: Cambridge University Press, 1997.

Dinshaw, Carolyn. *Getting Medieval: Sexualities and Communities, Pre- and Postmodern.* Durham: Duke University Press, 1999.

Doan, Laura. *Disturbing Practices: History, Sexuality, and Women's Experience of Modern War.* Chicago: University of Chicago Press, 2013.

———. "Lesbian Studies after *The Lesbian Postmodern*: Toward a New Genealogy." *Journal of Lesbian Studies* 11, nos. 1–2 (2007): 21–35.

Donato, Clorinda. "Public and Private Negotiations of Gender in Eighteen-Century England and Italy: Lady Wortley Montagu and the Case of Catterina Vizzani." *British Journal for Eighteenth-Century Studies* 29 (2006): 169–89.

Donoghue, Emma. "Doing Lesbian History, Then and Now." *Historical Reflections/Réflexions Historiques* 33, no. 1 (2007): 15–22.

————. *Passions between Women: British Lesbian Culture, 1668–1801*. London: Scarlet Press, 1993.

————. "'Random Shifts of Malice?' The Outings of Anne Damer." In *Sapphism in the Long Eighteenth Century*, edited by John C. Beynon and Caroline Gonda, 127–45. London: Ashgate, 2010.

Donovan, John. "'Rosalind and Helen': Pastoral, Exile, Memory." *Romanticism* 4 (1998): 241–73.

Doody, Margaret Anne. *The True Story of the Novel*. Brunswick, N.J.: Rutgers University Press, 1996.

Duberman, Martin Bauml, Martin Vicinus, and George Chauncey, Jr., eds. *Hidden from History: Reclaiming the Gay and Lesbian Past*. New York: NAL Books, 1989.

Dugaw, Dianne. *Warrior Women and Popular Balladry, 1650–1850*. Chicago: University of Chicago Press, 1989.

Dugaw, Dianne, and Amanda Powell. "Sapphic Self-Fashioning in the Baroque Era: Women's Petrarchan Parody in English and Spanish." *Studies in Eighteenth Century Culture* 35 (2006): 127–60.

Duque, Pedro J. "Lope De Vega y Shakespeare." In *Lope De Vega y los origines del teatro Español*, edited by Manuel Criado de Val, 851–69. Madrid, 1981.

Eicke, Leigh Anna. "The Extremity of the Times: Women and Jacobitism in British Literary Culture." Ph.Diss., University of Maryland, 2002.

Eisenbichler, Konrad. "'Laudomia Forteguerri Loves Margaret of Austria.'" In *Same Sex Love and Desire among Women in the Middle Ages*, edited by Francesca Canadé and Pamela Sheingorn Sautman, 277–304. London: Palgrave, 2001.

Elfenbein, Andrew. "Lesbian Aestheticism on the Eighteenth-Century Stage." *Eighteenth-Century Life* 25 (Winter 2001): 1–16.

————. *Romantic Genius: The Prehistory of a Homosexual Role*. New York: Columbia University Press, 1999.

Evans, Richard. *In Defense of History*. New York: Norton, 1999.

Everard, Myriam. *Ziel en zinnen: Over liefde en lust tussen vrouwen in de tweede helft van de achttiende eeuw*. Groningen: Historische Uitgeverij, 1994.

Faderman, Lillian. *Scotch Verdict: Miss Pirie and Miss Woods v. Dame Cumming Gordon*. New York: Columbia University Press, 1994.

————. *Surpassing the Love of Men: Romantic Friendship and Love between Women from the Renaissance to the Present*. New York: William Morrow, 1981.

Farmer, Sharon. "Down and Out and Female in Thirteenth-Century Paris." *American Historical Review* 103 (1998): 345–72.

Farnsworth, Jane. "Voicing Female Desire in 'Poem xlix.'" *Studies in English Literature* 36 (1996): 57–72.

Ferguson, Harvie. *Modernity and Subjectivity: Body, Soul, Spirit*. Charlottesville: The University Press of Virginia, 2000.

Findlen, Paula. "Anatomy of a Lesbian: Medicine, Pornography, and Culture in Eighteenth-Century Italy." In *Italy's Eighteenth Century: Gender and Culture in the Age of the Grand Tour*, edited by Paula Findlen, Wendy Roworth, and Catherine Sama, 216–50, 418–30. Stanford: Stanford University Press, 2008.

Fleischmann, Hector. *Les maitresses de Marie-Antoinette.* Paris: Editions des biblio-
philes, n.d.

———. *Madame de Polignac et la cour galante de Marie-Antoinette.* Paris: Bibliothèque
des curieux, 1910.

Fletcher, Anthony. *Gender, Sex and Subordination in England, 1500–1800.* New Haven:
Yale University Press, 1995.

Foucault, Michel. *Les anormaux: cours au Collège de France* (1974–1975). Paris:
Gallimard–Le Seuil, 1999.

———. *The Archaeology of Knowledge.* Translated by A. M. Sheridan Smith. New York:
Pantheon Books, 1972.

———. *The History of Sexuality, Volume I.* Translated by Robert Hurley. New York:
Pantheon, 1978.

———. *The Order of Things: An Archaeology of the Human Sciences.* New York: Random House, 1970.

Fourquet, François. *L'idéal historique.* Paris: CERFI, 1974.

Fox, Gwyn. *Subtle Subversions: Reading Golden Age Sonnets by Iberian Women.*
Washington, D.C.: Catholic University of America Press, 2008.

Fradenburg, Louise, and Carla Freccero, eds. *Premodern Sexualities.* London and New
York: Routledge, 1996.

Fraisse, Geneviève. *Les femmes et leur histoire.* Paris: Gallimard, 1998.

———. *La muse de la raison: la démocratie exclusive et la différence des sexes.*
Aix-en-Provence: Alinéa, 1989; *Reason's Muse: Sexual Difference and the Birth of
Democracy.* Translated by Jane Marie Todd. Chicago: University of Chicago Press,
1994.

Frieda, Leonie. *Catherine de Medici.* London: Weidenfeld and Nicolson, 2003.

Garber, Marjorie. "Foreword: The Marvel of Peru." In *Lieutenant Nun: Memoirs of a
Basque Transvestite in the New World by Catalina De Erauso,* edited by Michele
Stepto and Gabriel Stepto, vii–xxiv. Boston: Beacon Press, 1996.

———. *Vested Interests: Cross-Dressing and Cultural Anxiety.* New York and London:
Routledge, 1992.

Giddens, Anthony. *The Consequences of Modernity.* Stanford: Stanford University
Press, 1990.

Giffney, Noreen, Michelle M. Sauer, and Diane Watt. *The Lesbian Premodern.* New
York: Palgrave Macmillan, 2011.

Gigante, Denise. "Zeitgeist." *European Romantic Review* 18, no. 2 (April 2007): 265–72.

Gilbert, Ruth. *Early Modern Hermaphrodites: Sex and Other Stories.* Basingstoke,
Hampshire: Palgrave, 2002.

Ginger, Andrew. *Painting and the Turn to Cultural Modernity in Spain: The Time
of Eugenio Lucas Velásquez, 1850–1870.* Cranbury, N.J.: Associated University
Presses, 2007.

Gladfelder, Hal. *Fanny Hill in Bombay: The Making and Unmaking of John Cleland.*
Baltimore: Johns Hopkins University Press, 2012.

Goldberg, Jonathan. "Margaret Cavendish, Scribe." *GLQ* 10, no. 3 (2004): 433–52.

———, ed. *Queering the Renaissance.* Durham: Duke University Press, 1994.

Goldberg, Jonathan, and Madhavi Menon. "Queering History." *PMLA* 120, no. 5 (Oct. 2005): 1608–17.

Gonda, Caroline. "Lesbian Narrative in The Travels and Adventures of Mademoiselle de Richelieu." *British Journal for Eighteenth-Century Studies* 29 (2006): 191–200.

———. "The Odd Women: Charlotte Charke, Sarah Scott, and the Metamorphoses of Sex." In *Lesbian Dames: Sapphism in the Long Eighteenth Century*, edited by John C. Beynon and Caroline Gonda, 111–26. London: Ashgate, 2010.

Goodman, Dena. *The Republic of Letters*. Ithaca: Cornell University Press, 1994.

Goodrich, Peter. "Laws of Friendship." *Law and Literature* 15, no. 1 (2003): 23–52.

Graille, Patrick. *Les hermaphrodites au XVIIe et XVIIIe siècles*. Paris: Les Belles Lettres, 2001.

Greenblatt, Stephen. *Shakespearean Negotiations*. Berkeley and Los Angeles: University of California Press, 1988.

Griffiths, Richard. "'Les trois sortes d'aimer': Impersonation and Sexual Fantasy in French Renaissance Love Poetry." *Journal of the Institute of Romance Studies* 3 (1994–95): 111–27.

Grosrichard, Alain. *The Sultan's Court: European Fantasies of the East*. Translated by Liz Heron. London: Verso, 1998.

Grise, C. Annette. "Depicting Lesbian Desire: Contexts for John Donne's "Sapho to Philaenis."" *Mosaic* 29 (1996): 41–57.

Guest, Harriet. *Small Change: Women, Learning, Patriotism, 1750–1810*. Chicago: University of Chicago Press, 2000.

Guillén, Claudio. *The Challenge of Comparative Literature*. Translated by Cola Franzen. Cambridge, Mass.: Harvard University Press, 1993.

Habermas, Jürgen. *The Structural Transformation of the Public Sphere: An Inquiry into a Category of Bourgeois Society*. Translated by Thomas Burger with Frederick Lawrence. Cambridge, Mass.: MIT Press, 1989.

Haggerty, George. "Love and Loss: An Elegy." *GLQ* 10 (2004): 385–405.

———. *Men in Love: Masculinity and Sexuality in the Eighteenth Century*. New York: Columbia University Press, 1999.

———. *Queer Gothic*. Champaign: University of Illinois Press, 2006.

———. *Unnatural Affections: Women and Fiction in the Later 18th Century*. Bloomington: Indiana University Press, 1998.

Halperin, David M. "Forgetting Foucault: Acts, Identities, and the History of Sexuality." *Representations*, no. 63 (1998): 93–120.

———. *How to Do the History of Homosexuality*. Chicago: University of Chicago Press, 2002.

Harris, Joseph. "Disruptive Desires: Lesbian Sexuality in Isaac De Benserade's *Iphis et Iante* (1634)." *Seventeenth Century French Studies* 24 (2002): 151–63.

———. *Hidden Agendas: Cross-Dressing in 17th-Century France*. Biblio 17, vol. 156, Tubingen: Gunter Narr, 2005.

Harvey, Karen. *Reading Sex in the Eighteenth Century: Bodies and Gender in English Erotic Culture*. Cambridge: Cambridge University Press, 2004.

Heilbrun, Carolyn G. *Writing a Woman's Life*. New York: Ballantine, 1988.

Hesse, Carla. *The Other Enlightenment: How French Women Became Modern.* Princeton: Princeton University Press, 2001.

Hill, Christopher. Introduction to *Crisis in Europe,1560–1660: Essays from Past and Present,* edited by Trevor Aston, 1–4. London: Routledge and Kegan Paul, 1965.

Hitchcock, Tim. *English Sexualities, 1700–1800.* New York: St. Martin's Press, 1997.

Hobby, Elaine. "Katherine Philips: Seventeenth Century Lesbian Poet." In *What Lesbians Do in Books,* edited by Elaine Hobby and Chris White, 183–204. London: Women's Press, 1991.

Holstun, James. "'Will You Rent Our Ancient Love Asunder?': Lesbian Elegy in Donne, Marvell, and Milton." *ELH* 54, no. 4 (1987): 835–67.

Honegger, Claudia. *Die Ordnung der Geschlechter: Die Wissenschaften vom Menschen und das Weib 1750–1850.* Munich: Deutscher Taschenbuch Verlag, 1991.

Hotchkiss, Valerie R. *Clothes Make the Man: Female Cross Dressing in Medieval Europe.* New York and London: Garland, 1996.

Hull, Isabel V. *Sexuality, State, and Civil Society in Germany, 1700–1815.* Ithaca: Cornell University Press, 1996.

Hull, Suzanne W. *Chaste Silent & Obedient: English Books for Women, 1475–1640.* San Marino, Calif.: Huntington Library, 1982.

Hume, Robert D. *Reconstructing Contexts: The Aims and Principles of Archaeo-Historicism.* Oxford: Oxford University Press, 1999.

Hunt, Alan. *Governance of the Consuming Passions: A History of Sumptuary Law.* Basingstoke and London: Macmillan, 1996.

Hunt, Lynn. *The Family Romance of the French Revolution.* Berkeley and Los Angeles: University of California Press, 1992.

———, ed. *The Invention of Pornography: Obscenity and the Origins of Modernity, 1500–1800.* New York: Zone Books, 1993.

Hunt, Margaret. "The Sapphic Strain: English Lesbians in the Long Eighteenth Century." In *Singlewomen in the European Past, 1250–1800,* edited by Judith Bennett, and Amy Froide, 270–96. Philadelphia: University of Pennsylvania Press, 1999.

Hutson, Lorna. "The Body of the Friend and the Woman Writer: Katherine Philip's Absence from Alan Bray's *The Friend* (2003)." *Women's Writing* 14 (2007): 196–214.

———. *The Usurer's Daughter: Male Friendship and Fictions of Women in Sixteenth-Century England.* London: Routledge, 1994.

Hyatte, Reginald. *The Arts of Friendship: The Idealization of Friendship in Medieval and Early Renaissance Literature.* Leiden/New York/Köln: E. J. Brill, 1994.

Iarocci, Michael. *Properties of Modernity: Romantic Spain, Modern Europe, and the Legacies of Empire.* Nashville: Vanderbilt University Press, 2006.

Ingrassia, Catherine. "Eliza Haywood, Sapphic Desire, and the Practice of Reading." In *Lewd and Notorious: Female Transgression in the Eighteenth Century,* edited by Katharine Kittredge, 210–32. Ann Arbor: University of Michigan Press, 2003.

Israel, Jonathan I. *The Dutch Republic: Its Rise, Greatness, and Fall, 1477–1806.* Oxford: Clarendon Press, 1995.

———. *Radical Enlightenment: Philosophy and the Making of Modernity, 1650–1750.* Oxford: Oxford University Press, 2001.

Jacob, Margaret. *Origins of Freemasonry*. Philadelphia: University of Pennsylvania Press, 2006.

Jameson, Fredric. *The Political Unconscious: Narrative as a Socially Symbolic Act*. Ithaca: Cornell University Press, 1981.

Jankowski, Theodora. *Pure Resistance: Queer Virginity in Early Modern English Drama*. Philadelphia: University of Pennsylvania Press, 2000.

Jeffreys, Sheila. "The Queer Disappearance of Lesbians: Sexuality in the Academy." *Women's Studies International Forum* 17, no. 5 (1994): 459–72.

Johnson, Barbara. "Anthropomorphism in Lyric and Law." *Yale Journal of Law and the Humanities* 10 (1998): 549–74.

Jones, Ann Rosalind. "Maidservants of London: Sisterhoods of Kinship and Labor." In *Maids and Mistresses, Cousins and Queens: Women's Alliances in Early Modern England*, edited by Susan Frye and Karen Robertson, 21–32. New York: Oxford University Press, 1999.

Jordan, Constance. *Renaissance Feminism: Literary Texts and Political Models*. Ithaca: Cornell University Press, 1990.

Kairoff, Claudia. *Anna Seward and the End of the Eighteenth Century*. Baltimore: Johns Hopkins University Press, 2012.

King, Kathryn R. *Jane Barker, Exile: A Literary Career, 1675–1725*. Oxford: Clarendon, 2000.

———. "'The Unaccountable Wife' and Other Tales of Female Desire in Jane Barker's *A Patchwork Screen for the Ladies*." *Eighteenth Century: Theory and Interpretation* 35, no. 2 (Summer 1994): 155–72.

King, Thomas A. *The Gendering of Men, 1600–1750*, vol. 1: *The English Phallus*. Madison: University of Wisconsin Press, 2004.

Kirkpatrick, Susan. *Las Románticas: Women Writers and Subjectivity in Spain, 1835–1850*. Berkeley and Los Angeles: University of California Press, 1989.

Kitts, Sally-Ann. *The Debate on the Nature, Role and Influence of Women in Eighteenth-Century Spain*. Lewiston: Edwin Mellen Press, 1995.

———. "Ignacio López de Ayala and the Paradoxical Nature of Women's Rights Discourse in Eighteenth-Century Spain." *Dieciocho: Hispanic Enlightenment* 33, no. 2 (Fall 2010): 361–82.

———. "Mary Wollstonecraft's *A Vindication of the Rights of Woman*: A Judicious Response from Eighteenth-Century Spain." *The Modern Language Review* 89, no. 2 (Apr 1994): 351–59.

Klawitter, George. *The Enigmatic Narrator: The Voicing of Same-Sex Love in the Poetry of John Donne*. New York: Peter Lang, 1994.

Klosowska, Anna. "Erotica and Women in Early Modern France: Madeleine de l'Aubespine's Queer Poems." *Journal of the History of Sexuality* 17, no. 2 (May 2008): 190–215.

———. *Queer Love in the Middle Ages*. New York and Basingstoke: Palgrave Macmillan, 2005.

Kneale, J. Douglas. "Romantic Aversions: Apostrophe Reconsidered." *ELH* 58 (1991): 141–65.

Knox, Ronald A. *Enthusiasm: A Chapter in the History of Religion.* Oxford: Oxford University Press, 1950.

Konnert, Mark. *Early Modern Europe: The Age of Religious War, 1559–1715.* Peterborough, Ont.: Broadview Press, 2006.

Korba, Susan M. "'Improper and Dangerous Distinctions': Female Relationships and Erotic Domination in *Emma.*" *Studies in the Novel* 29, no. 2 (1997): 139–63.

Kord, Susanne. "Eternal Love or Sentimental Discourse? Gender Dissonance and Women's Passionate Friendships." In *Outing Goethe and His Age,* edited by Alice A. Kuzniar, 228–52. Stanford: Stanford University Press, 1996.

Krimmer, Elisabeth. *In the Company of Men: Cross-dressed Women around 1800.* Detroit: Wayne State University Press, 2004.

Kuhn, Thomas S. *The Structure of Scientific Revolutions.* Chicago: University of Chicago Press, 1955.

Kunzle, David. "World Upside Down: The Iconography of a European Broadsheet Type." In *The Reversible World: Symbolic Inversion in Art and Society,* edited by Barbara Babcock, 39–94. Ithaca: Cornell University Press, 1978.

Lamb, Susan. "'Be Such a Man as I': Mademoiselle Makes the Tour of Europe in Men's Clothes." *Studies in Eighteenth-Century Culture* 27 (1998): 75–102.

Landes, Joan. *Women and the Public Sphere in the Age of the French Revolution.* Ithaca: Cornell University Press, 1988.

———. *Visualizing the Nation: Gender, Representation, and Revolution in Eighteenth-Century France.* Ithaca: Cornell University Press, 2001.

Lanser, Susan S. "Befriending the Body: Female Intimacies as Class Acts." *Eighteenth Century Studies* 32, no. 2 (1998–99): 179–98.

———. "Bluestocking Sapphism and the Economies of Desire." *Huntington Library Quarterly* 65, nos. 1–2 (2003): 257–75.

———. *Fictions of Authority: Women Writers and Narrative Voice.* Ithaca: Cornell University Press, 1992.

———. "The 'I' of the Beholder." In *The Blackwell Companion to Narrative Theory,* edited by James Phelan and Peter Rabinowitz, 206–19. Oxford: Blackwell, 2005.

———. "Mapping Sapphic Modernity." In *Comparatively Queer: Crossing Time, Crossing Cultures,* ed. Jarrod Hayes, Margaret Higonnet, and William Spurlin, 69–89. London: Palgrave Macmillan, 2010.

———. "The Novel Body Politic." In *The Eighteenth Century Novel: Companion to Literature and Culture,* edited by Paula Backsheider and Catherine Ingrassia, 481–503. Oxford: Blackwell, 2005.

———. "Of Closed Doors and Open Hatches: Heternormative Plots in Eighteenth-Century (Women's) Studies." *ECTI: Eighteenth Century: Theory and Interpretation* 53 (2012): 273–90.

———. "The Political Economy of Same-Sex Desire." In *Structures and Subjectivities: Attending to Early Modern Women,* edited by Joan Hartman and Adele Seeff, 157–75. Newark, Del.: University of Delaware Press, 2007.

———. "Put to the Blush: Romantic Irregularities and Sapphic Tropes." *Romantic Praxis* (January 2006), www.rc.umd.edu/praxis.

———. "'Queer to Queer': The Sapphic Body as Transgressive Text." In *Lewd and Notorious: Female Transgression in the 18th Century*, edited by Katharine Kittredge, 21–46. Ann Arbor: University of Michigan Press, 2003.

———. "Sapphic Picaresque, Sexual Difference, and the Challenges of Homoadventuring." *Textual Practice* 15, no. 2 (2001): 1–18.

———. "Tory Lesbians: Economies of Intimacy and the Status of Desire." In *Lesbian Dames: Sapphism in the Long Eighteenth Century*, edited by John C. Beynon and Caroline Gonda, 173–89. Farnham and Burlington: Ashgate, 2010.

Lapp, John C. "Pontus De Tyard and the *Querelle Des Femmes*." *Modern Language Notes* 64 (1949): 331–33.

Laqueur, Thomas. *Making Sex: Body and Gender from the Greeks to Freud*. Cambridge, Mass.: Harvard University Press, 1992.

Latour, Bruno. *We Have Never Been Modern*. Translated by Catherine Porter. Cambridge, Mass.: Harvard University Press, 1993.

Legault, Marianne. "*Iphis & Iante*: Traumatisme de l'incomplétude lesbienne au Grand Siècle." *Dalhousie French Studies* 81 (2007): 83–93.

Levin, Susan M. *Dorothy Wordsworth and Romanticism*. New Brunswick: Rutgers University Press, 1987.

Liddington, Jill, ed. *Female Fortune: Land, Gender, and Authority: The Anne Lister Diaries and Other Writings*. London: Rivers Oram Press, 1998.

Loscocco, Paula. "Inventing the English Sappho: Katherine Philips's Donnean Poetry." *Journal of English and Germanic Philology* (2003): 59–87.

Loselle, Andrea. "Introduction." *Substance* 118 (2009): 3–4.

Lukács, Georg. *Theory of the Novel*. Cambridge, Mass.: MIT Press, 1974.

Lupo, Paola. *Lo specchio incrinato: Storia e immagine dell'omosessualità femminile*. Venice: Marsilio, 1998.

MacCulloch, Diarmaid. *The Reformation*. New York and London: Viking, 2004.

Marcus, Sharon. *Between Women: Friendship, Desire, and Marriage in Victorian England*. Princeton: Princeton University Press, 2007.

Martín, Adrienne L. *An Erotic Philology of Golden Age Spain*. Nashville: Vanderbilt University Press, 2008.

———. "The Mediation of Lesbian Eros in Golden Age Verse." In *Lesbianism and Homosexuality in Early Modern Spain*, edited by María-José Delgado, and Alain Saint-Saëns. 343–62. New Orleans: University Press of the South, 2000.

Martin, Biddy. "Extraordinary Homosexuals and the Fear of Being Ordinary." *Differences* 6, no. 2–3 (1994): 100–25.

McKendrick, Melveena. *Women and Society in the Spanish Drama of the Golden Age*. Cambridge: Cambridge University Press, 1974.

McKeon, Michael. "Historicizing Patriarchy: The Emergence of Gender Difference in England." *Eighteenth-Century Studies* 28 (1995): 295–322.

———. *The Origins of the English Novel*. Baltimore: Johns Hopkins University Press, 1987.

———. *The Secret History of Domesticity*. Baltimore: Johns Hopkins University Press, 2005.

———. "The Seventeenth- and Eighteenth-Century Sexuality Hypothesis." *Signs* 37 (2012): 791–801.

———. Forum. *PMLA* 128, no. 2 (March 2013): 474–76.

McMillan, James F. *France and Women, 1789–1914: Gender, Society and Politics*. London and New York: Routledge, 2000.

Meakin, H. L. *John Donne's Articulations of the Feminine*. Oxford: Clarendon, 1998.

Meijer, Maaike. "Pious and Learned Female Bosom Friends in Holland in the Eighteenth Century." In *Among Men, among Women: Sociological and Historical Recognition of Homosocial Arrangements: Papers of the Gay Studies and Women's Studies Conference*, edited by M. Duyvis et al., 404–19. Amsterdam: University of Amsterdam, 1983.

Mermin, Dorothy. "Women Becoming Poets: Katherine Philips, Aphra Behn, Anne Finch." *ELH* 57 (1990): 335–55.

Merrick, Jeffrey, and Bryant T. Ragan Jr., eds. *Homosexuality in Early Modern France*. New York and Oxford: Oxford University Press, 2001.

Miller, Nancy. *The Heroine's Text: Readings in French and English Novel, 1722–1782*. New York: Columbia University Press, 1980.

———. "Emphasis Added: Plots and Plausibilities in Women's Fiction." *PMLA* 96 (1981): 36–48.

Moore, Lisa L. *Dangerous Intimacies: Toward a Sapphic History of the British Novel*. Durham, N.C.: Duke University Press, 1997.

Moretti, Franco, ed. *The Novel*. 2 vols. Princeton: Princeton University Press, 2006.

———. "The Slaughterhouse of Literature." *Modern Language Quarterly* 61 (2000): 207–27.

———. *The Way of the World: The Bildungsroman in European Culture*. New York: Verso, 2000.

Mourão, Manuela. "The Representation of Female Desire in Early Modern Pornographic Texts, 1660–1745." *Signs: Journal of Women in Culture and Society* 24, no. 3 (1999): 573–602.

Mousnier, Roland. *Les Xvie et Xviie siècles: les progrès de la civilisation européenne et le déclin de l'orient (1492–1715)*. Paris: Presses universitaires de France, 1954.

Mueller, Janel. "Lesbian Erotics: The Utopian Trope of Donne's 'Sapho to Philaenis.'" In *Homosexuality in Renaissance and Enlightenment England: Literary Representations in Historical Context*, edited by Claude J. Summers, 103–34. New York: Haworth Press, 1992.

Nauert, Charles G. "The Mind." In *The Short Oxford History of Europe: The Sixteenth Century*, edited by Euan Cameron. Oxford: Oxford University Press, 2006.

Nethercot, Arthur. *The Road to Tryermaine: A Study of the History, Background, and Purposes of Coleridge's "Christabel."* Chicago: University of Chicago Press, 1939.

Nussbaum, Felicity. *Torrid Zones: Maternity, Sexuality, and Empire in Eighteenth-Century English Narratives*. Baltimore and London: Johns Hopkins University Press, 1995.

O'Donnell, Brennan. "The 'Invention' of a Meter: 'Christabel' Meter as Fact and Fiction." *JEGP* 100, no. 4 (October 2001): 511–36.

Palmer, R. R. *Twelve Who Ruled*. 1941. Princeton: Princeton University Press, 1969.

Parker, Patricia. "Gender Ideology, Gender Change: The Case of Marie Germain." *Critical Inquiry* 19 (1993): 337–64.

Parker, Todd. *Sexing the Text: The Rhetoric of Sexual Difference in British Literature, 1700–1750*. Albany: SUNY Press, 2000.

Pateman, Carole. *The Sexual Contract*. Stanford: Stanford University Press, 1988.

Pavel, Thomas. "The Novel in Search of Itself: A Historical Morphology." In *The Novel*, edited by Franco Moretti, 2:1–31. Princeton: Princeton University Press, 2006.

Peirce, Leslie. *The Imperial Harem: Women and Sovereignty in the Ottoman Empire*. Oxford: Oxford University Press, 1993.

Perry, Ruth. "Bluestockings in Utopia." In *History, Gender, and Eighteenth-Century Literature*, edited by Beth Fowkes, 263–73. Athens: University of Georgia Press, 1994.

———. *The Celebrated Mary Astell: An Early English Feminist*. Chicago: University of Chicago Press, 1986.

———. *Novel Relations: The Transformation of Kinship in English Literature and Culture, 1748–1818*. Cambridge: Cambridge University Press, 2004.

Powell, Amanda. "Baroque Flair: Seventeenth-century European Sapphic Poetry." *Humanist Studies & The Digital Age* 1, no. 1 (2011): 151–65.

Prescott, Anne Lake. "Male Lesbian Voices: Ronsard, Tyard and Donne Play Sappho." In *Reading the Renaissance: Ideas and Idioms from Shakespeare to Milton*, edited by Marc Berley, 109–29. Pittsburgh: Duquesne University Press, 2003.

Price, J. L. *Culture and Society in the Dutch Republic During the 17th Century*. London: B. T. Batsford, 1974.

Price, Paola Malpezzi. *Moderata Fonte: Women and Life in Sixteenth-Century Venice*. Cranbury, N.J.: Associated University Presses, 2003.

Prince, Michael. *Philosophical Dialogue in the British Enlightenment: Theology, Aesthetics, and the Novel*. Cambridge: Cambridge University Press, 1996.

Puff, Helmut. *Sodomy in Reformation Germany and Switzerland, 1400–1600*. Chicago: University of Chicago Press, 2003.

———. "Toward a Philology of the Premodern Lesbian." In *The Lesbian Premodern*, edited by Noreen Giffney, Michelle M. Sauer, and Diane Watt, 145–60. New York: Palgrave Macmillan, 2011.

Quataert, Donald. *The Ottoman Empire, 1700–1922*. 2d ed. Cambridge: Cambridge University Press, 2005.

Rancière, Jacques. *Disagreement: Politics and Philosophy*. [*La mésentente*, 1995.] Translated by Julie Rose. Minneapolis: University of Minnesota Press, 1999.

Resina, Joan Ramon. "The Short, Happy Life of the Novel in Spain." In *The Novel*, edited by Franco Moretti, 1:291–312. Princeton: Princeton University Press, 2006.

Richardson, Alan. "Romanticism and the Colonization of the Feminine," in *Romanticism and Feminism*, ed. Anne K. Mellor, 13–25. Bloomington: Indiana University Press, 1988.

Rimmon-Kenan, Shlomith. "Place, Space, and Michal Govrin's *Snapshots*." *Narrative* 17 (2009): 220–34.

Rizzo, Betty. *Companions without Vows: Relationships among Eighteenth-Century British Women*. Athens: University of Georgia Press, 1994.

Robert, Marthe. *Origins of the Novel*. [*Roman des origines et origines de roman*, 1972.] Translated by Sacha Rabinovich. Bloomington: Indiana University Press, 1980.

Robinson, David Michael. "The Abominable Madame de Murat." In *Homosexuality in French History and Culture*, edited by Jeffrey Merrick and Michael Sibalis, 53–67. New York and London: Haworth Press, 2001.

———. *Closeted Writing and Lesbian and Gay Literature: Classical, Early Modern, Eighteenth-Century*. Aldershot, Hampshire: Ashgate, 2006.

———. "For How Can They Be Guilty: Lesbian and Bisexual Women in Manley's *New Atalantis*." *Nineteenth-Century Contexts* 23 (2001): 187–220.

———. "Pleasant Conversation in the Seraglio: Lesbianism, Platonic Love, and Cavendish's *Blazing World*." *The Eighteenth Century* 44, nos. 2–3 (2003): 133–66.

Robson, Ruthann. "Lesbianism in Anglo-European Legal History." *Wisconsin Women's Law Journal* 5 (1990): 1–42.

Roulston, Chris. *Narrating Marriage in Eighteenth-Century England and France*. Burlington and Surrey: Ashgate, 2010.

Russett, Margaret. "Meter, Identity, Voice: Untranslating *Christabel*." *SEL* 43, no. 4 (Autumn 2003): 773–97.

Sanchez, Melissa E. *Erotic Subjects: The Sexuality of Politics in Early Modern English Literature*. Oxford and New York: Oxford University Press, 2011.

———. "'Use Me But as Your Spaniel': Feminism, Queer Theory, and Early Modern Sexualities." *PMLA* 127, no. 3 (2012): 493–511.

Sanfeliú, Luz. *Juego de damas: Aproximación histórica al homoerotismo femenino*. Málaga: Universidad de Málaga, 1996.

Sautman, Francesca Canadé. "'Just Like a Woman': Queer History, Womanizing the Body, and the Boys in Arnaud's Band." In *Queering the Middle Ages*, edited by Glenn and Steven F. Kruger Burger, 160–89. Minneapolis: University of Minnesota Press, 2001.

Sautman, Francesca Canadé, and Pamela Sheingorn, eds. *Same Sex Love and Desire among Women in the Middle Ages*. London: Palgrave, 2001.

Schleiner, Winfried. "Linguistic 'Xeno-homophobia' in Sixteenth-Century France: The Case of Henri Estienne." *Sixteenth Century Journal* 34 (2003): 747–60.

Schmale, Wolfgang. "Europa: die weibliche Form." *L'homme: Zeitschrift für feministische Geschichtswissenschaft* 11 (2000): 211–33.

Schroeder, Bendta. "Natural Kinds: Botany, Aesthetics, and the Taxonomy of Families in British Literature, 1760–1807." Ph.D. diss., Brandeis University, 2010.

Schwarz, Kathryn. *Tough Love: Amazon Encounters in the English Renaissance*. Durham: Duke University Press, 2000.

Scott, Joan. "Gender: A Useful Category of Historical Analysis" *American Historical Review* 91 (1986): 1052–75.

Sedgwick, Eve Kosofsky. *Epistemology of the Closet*. Berkeley and Los Angeles: University of California Press, 1990.

———. "Privilege of Unknowing." *Genders* 1 (1988): 102–24.

Sha, Richard. *Perverse Romanticism: Aesthetics and Sexuality in Britain 1750–1832.*
   Baltimore: Johns Hopkins University Press, 2009.

——. "Romanticism and the Sciences of Perversion." *Wordsworth Circle* 36, no. 2
   (Spring 2005): 43–46.

Shannon, Laurie. "Nature's Bias: Renaissance Homonormativity and Elizabethan
   Comic Likeness." *Modern Philology* 98, no. 2 (2000): 183–210.

——. *Sovereign Amity: Figures of Friendship in Shakespearean Contexts.* Chicago:
   University of Chicago Press, 2002.

Simons, Patricia. "Lesbian (In)Visibility in Italian Renaissance Culture: Diana and
   Other Cases of *Donna Con Donna.*" *Journal of Homosexuality* 27, nos. 1/2 (1994):
   81–122.

Simmons, Philip E. "John Cleland's Memoirs of a Woman of Pleasure: Literary Voyeur-
   ism and the Techniques of Novelistic Transgression." *Eighteenth-Century Fiction*
   3, no. 1 (Oct 1990): 43–64.

Smarr, Janet Levarie. *Joining the Conversation: Dialogues by Renaissance Women.* Ann
   Arbor: University of Michigan Press, 2005.

Smith, Bruce. *Homosexual Desire in Shakespeare's England.* Chicago: University of
   Chicago Press, 1991.

Sollers, Philippe. *Logiques.* Paris: Seuil, 1968.

Spaas, Lieve. "*Paul et Virginie*: The Shipwreck of an Idyll." *Eighteenth Century Fiction*
   13 (2001): 315–24.

Spurlin, William J., Jarrod Hayes, and Margaret R. Higonnet, eds. *Comparatively Queer:
   Interrogating Identities across Time and Cultures.* London: Palgrave Macmillan,
   2010.

Stallybrass, Peter. "Patriarchal Territories: The Body Enclosed." In *Rewriting the
   Renaissance: The Discourse of Sexual Difference in Early Modern Europe*, edited
   by Margaret Fertuson, Maureen Quilligan, and Nancy J. Vickers, 123–142. Chicago:
   University of Chicago Press, 1986.

Stanley, Liz. "Epistemological Issues in Researching Lesbian History: The Case of Romantic Friendship." In *Working Out: New Directions for Women's Studies*, edited
   by Hilary Hinds, Ann Phoenix, and Jackie Stacey, 161–72. London and Washington:
   Falmer Press, 1992.

Stanton, Domna C. "The Fiction of Préciosité and the Fear of Women." *Yale French
   Studies*, No. 62 (1981): 107–34.

Starr, George. "Why Defoe Probably Did Not Write *The Apparition of Mrs. Veal.*"
   Eighteenth-Century Fiction 15 (2003): 421–39.

Steidele, Angela. *"Als wenn Du mein Geliebter wärest": Liebe und Begehren zwischen
   Frauen in der deutschsprachigen Literatur, 1750–1850.* Stuttgart: Metzler, 2003.

Steinberg, Sylvie. *La confusion des sexes: le travestissement de la Renaissance à la
   Révolution.* Paris: Fayard, 2001.

Stephens, Dorothy. "Into Other Arms: Armoret's Evasion." In *Queering the Renaissance*, edited by Jonathan Goldberg, 190–217. Durham, N.C.: Duke University
   Press, 1994..

Stewart, Alan. *Close Readers: Humanism and Sodomy in Early Modern England.*
   Princeton: Princeton University Press, 1997.

Straub, Kristina. *Sexual Suspects: Eighteenth-Century Players and Sexual Ideology.* Princeton: Princeton University Press, 1992.

Taylor, Charles. *Modern Social Imaginaries.* Durham, N.C.: Duke University Press, 2004.

Thomas, Chantal. *La reine scélérate: Marie-Antoinette dans les pamphlets.* Paris: Seuil, 1989.

Thomas, Keith. "Women and the Civil War Sects." In *Crisis in Europe 1560–1660,* edited by Trevor Aston, 332–57. London: Routledge and Kegan Paul, 1965.

Thompson, E. P. *The Making of the English Working Class.* New York: Vintage, 1996.

Traub, Valerie. *Desire and Anxiety: Circulations of Sexuality in Shakespearean Drama.* London and New York: Routledge, 1992.

———. "The (In)Significance of 'Lesbian' Desire in Early Modern England." In *Queering the Renaissance,* edited by Jonathan Goldberg, 62–83. Durham: Duke University Press, 1994.

———. "The New Unhistoricism in Queer Studies." *PMLA* 128, no. 1 (January 2013): 21–39.

———. "The Present Future of Lesbian Historiography." In *Blackwell Companion to Lesbian, Gay, Bisexual, Transgender, and Queer Studies,* edited by George Haggerty and Molly McGarry, 124–45. Oxford and Malden: Blackwell, 2007.

———. *The Renaissance of Lesbianism in Early Modern England.* Cambridge: Cambridge University Press, 2002.

———. "The Rewards of Lesbian History." *Feminist Studies* 25, no. 2 (Summer 1999): 363–94.

Trevor-Roper, H. R. "The General Crisis of the Seventeenth Century." In *Crisis in Europe, 1560–1660: Essays from Past and Present,* edited by Trevor Aston, 63–102. London: Routledge and Kegan Paul, 1965.

Trumbach, Randolph. "London's Sapphists: From Three Sexes to Four Genders in the Making of Modern Culture." In *Third Sex, Third Gender: Beyond Sexual Dimorphism in Culture and History,* edited by Gilbert Herdt, 111–36. New York: Zone Books, 1994.

Turchi, Peter. *Maps of the Imagination: The Writer as Cartographer.* San Antonio: Trinity University Press, 2004.

Upton, Anthony F. *Europe, 1600–1789.* New York: Bloomsbury USA, 2001.

Valentine, David. "The Categories Themselves." *GLQ* 10, no. 2 (2004): 215–20.

Valverde, Mariana. "Governing out of Habit." *Studies in Law, Politics, and Society* 18 (1998): 217–42.

van der Meer, Theo. "Tribades on Trial: Female Same-Sex Offenders in Late Eighteenth-Century Amsterdam." *Journal of the History of Sexuality* 1, no. 3 (1991): 424–45.

van Gemert, Lia. "Hiding Behind Words? Lesbianism in Seventeenth-Century Dutch Poetry." *Thyramis* 2 (1995): 11–44.

Velasco, Sherry. "Interracial Lesbian Erotics in Early Modern Spain: Catalina De Erauso and Elena/O De Céspedes." In *Tortilleras: Hispanic and U.S. Latina Lesbian Expression,* edited by Lourdes Torres and Inmaculada Pertusa, 211–27. Philadelphia: Temple University Press, 2003.

———. *Lesbians in Early Modern Spain.* Nashville: Vanderbilt University Press, 2011.

———. *The Lieutenant Nun: Transgenderism, Lesbian Desire, and Catalina De Erauso.* Austin: University of Texas Press, 2000.

Vicinus, Martha. *Intimate Friends: Women Who Loved Women, 1778–1928.* Chicago: University of Chicago Press, 2004.

———. "Lesbian History: All Theory and No Facts or All Facts and No Theory?" *Radical History Review* 60 (1994): 57–75.

———. "Sexuality and Power: A Review of Current Work in the History of Sexuality." *Feminist Studies* 8, no. 1 (1982): 131–56.

Vickery, Amanda. *The Gentleman's Daughter: Women's Lives in Georgian England.* New Haven: Yale University Press, 1998.

Vollendorf, Lisa. "The Value of Female Friendship in Seventeenth-Century Spain." *Texas Studies in Literature and Language* 47, no. 4 (Winter 2005): 425–45.

Wahl, Elizabeth. *Invisible Relations: Representations of Female Intimacy in the Age of Enlightenment.* Stanford: Stanford University Press, 1999.

Wahrman, Dror. *The Making of the Modern Self: Identity and Culture in Eighteenth-Century England.* New Haven: Yale University Press, 2004.

Walen, Denise A. *Constructions of Female Homoeroticism in Early Modern Drama.* New York and Basingstoke: Palgrave Macmillan, 2005.

Waller, Margaret. *The Male Malady: Fictions of Impotence in the French Romantic Novel.* New Brunswick: Rutgers University Press, 1993.

Watson, Nicola J. *Revolution and the Form of the British Novel, 1790–1825.* Oxford: Oxford University Press, 1994.

Watt, Diane. "Why Men Still Aren't Enough." *GLQ* 26, no. 3 (2010): 451–64.

Warhol, Robyn. *Having a Good Cry: Effeminate Feelings and Pop-Culture Forms.* Columbus: Ohio State University Press, 2003.

Whitaker, Shirley B. *The Dramatic Works of Álvaro Cubillo de Aragón.* North Carolina Studies in the Romance Languages and Literatures. Chapel Hill: University of North Carolina Department of Romance Languages, 1975.

Wiegman, Robyn. "The Desire for Gender." In *Blackwell Companion to Lesbian, Gay, Bisexual, Transgender, and Queer Studies,* edited by George Haggerty, and Molly McGarry, 217–36. Malden, Mass., and Oxford: Blackwell, 2007.

Williams, Raymond. *Writing in Society.* London: Verso, [1983] 1993.

Wilson, Charles. *The Transformation of Europe 1558–1648.* Berkeley and Los Angeles: University of California Press, 1976.

Woodward, Carolyn. "'My Heart So Wrapt': Lesbian Disruptions in Eighteenth-Century British Fiction." *Signs: A Journal of Women in Culture and Society* 18 (1993): 838–65.

Yegenoglu, Meyda. *Colonial Fantasies: Toward a Feminist Reading of Orientalism* Cambridge: Cambridge University Press, 1998.

Žižek, Slavoj. *The Ticklish Subject: The Absent Centre of Political Ontology.* London: Verso, 1999.